SHAPED BY WAR AND TRADE

PRINCETON STUDIES IN AMERICAN POLITICS:
HISTORICAL, INTERNATIONAL, AND COMPARATIVE PERSPECTIVES

SERIES EDITORS
Ira Katznelson, Martin Shefter, Theda Skocpol

A list of titles in this series appears at the back of the book

SHAPED BY WAR AND TRADE

INTERNATIONAL INFLUENCES ON AMERICAN POLITICAL DEVELOPMENT

Ira Katznelson and Martin Shefter, Editors

PRINCETON UNIVERSITY PRESS   PRINCETON AND OXFORD

Library of Congress Cataloging-in-Publication Data

Shaped by war and trade : international influences on American political
    development / editors Ira Katznelson and Martin Shefter.
        p. cm. — (Princeton studies in American politics)
    Includes bibliographical references and index.
    ISBN 0-691-05703-6 (alk. paper) — ISBN 0-691-05704-4 (pbk. : alk. paper)
    1. United States—Politics and government.   2. United States—
    Foreign relations—History.   3. United States—Foreign economic
relations—History.   I. Katznelson, Ira.   II. Shefter, Martin,
1943–   III. Series.
JK31 .S48 2002
320.973—dc21   2001036335

British Library Cataloging-in-Publication Data is available

This book has been composed in Electra

Printed on acid-free paper. ∞

www.pup.princeton.edu

Printed in the United States of America

10 9 8 7 6 5 4 3 2 1

10 9 8 7 6 5 4 3 2 1
(Pbk.)

Political development is shaped by war and trade.

— Peter Gourevitch, "The Second Image Reversed"

Contents

Acknowledgments

THE LINEAGE OF this book can be traced to a programmatic statement by Eric Foner, Martin Shefter, Theda Skocpol, Stephen Skowronek, and David Vogel. In a memorandum entitled "The International System and the Development of American Institutions," they urged scholars to study the relationship between America's changing location in the international economy and state system and the development of its political institutions. In response to this call, the editors of the Princeton Studies in American Politics (Ira Katznelson, Martin Shefter, and Theda Skocpol) convened a group of scholars working in the fields of American political development and international relations to discuss a volume devoted to their interaction. Funds for an exploratory meeting in Cambridge, Massachusetts, were generously provided by the Committee on States and Social Structures of the Russell Sage Foundation.

The participants in that session — the contributors to this volume as well as Joanne Gowa, Jon Ikenberry, and David Vogel — wrote memoranda, exchanged ideas, and blocked out plans for the book. Draft papers were mercilessly discussed at a second session, which met at Harvard's Center for International Affairs. Substantially revised versions of these papers became the chapters of *Shaped by War and Trade*.

As editors, we are grateful for the unusually collegial process that made this volume possible. Special thanks go to key figures at Princeton University Press: Walter Lippincott, who encouraged us from the start; Malcolm Litchfield, who oversaw an enormously helpful review process; and Chuck Myers, who superintended the final stages of moving our ideas into book form. We are also indebted to two anonymous reviewers, whose uncommon care and tough-minded suggestions greatly improved this book.

Contributors

Bayliss Camp is a Ph.D. candidate in Sociology at Harvard University.

Aaron L. Friedberg is Professor of Politics and International Affairs at Princeton University. He is the author of *The Weary Titan: Britain and the Experience of Relative Decline, 1895–1905*, and *In the Shadow of the Garrison State: America's Anti-Statism and Its Cold War Grand Strategy*.

Judith Goldstein is Professor of Political Science at Stanford University. She is the author of *Ideas, Interests, and American Trade Policy*; and the co-editor of *Ideas and Foreign Policy: Beliefs, Institutions, and Political Change* (with Robert Keohane), and *Legalization and World Politics* (with Miles Kahler, Robert Keohane, and Anne-Marie Slaughter).

Peter A. Gourevitch is Professor at and Founding Dean (1986–96) of the Graduate School of International Relations and Pacific Studies, University of California at San Diego. He is the author of *Politics in Hard Times: Comparative Responses to International Economic Crises*, and *Paris and the Provinces*. He co-edited *Unions and Economic Crises: Britain, West Germany, and Sweden*. He served as co-editor of the journal *International Organization* from 1996 to 2001.

Andrew Karch is a Ph.D. candidate in Government at Harvard University.

Ira Katznelson is Ruggles Professor of Political Science and History at Columbia University. His books include *Black Men, White Cities*; *City Trenches*; *Schooling for All* (with Margaret Weir); *Marxism and the City*; *Liberalism's Crooked Circle*; and *Working-Class Formation* (edited with Aristide Zolberg). He is a Fellow of the American Academy of Arts and Sciences and served as President of the Social Science History Association in 1998.

Robert O. Keohane is James B. Duke Professor of Political Science, Duke University. He is the author of *After Hegemony: Cooperation and Discord in the World Political Economy*, and *International Institutions and State Power: Essays in International Relations Theory*; and the co-author of *Power and Interdependence: World Politics in Transition* (with Joseph S. Nye Jr.), and *Designing Social Inquiry: Scientific Inference in Qualitative Research* (with Gary King and Sidney Verba). Between 1974 and 1980 he was editor of the journal *International Organization*. He is a Fellow of the American Academy of Arts and Sciences. Keohane was President of the International Studies Association, 1988–89, and of the American Political Science Association, 1999–2000.

Ziad Munson is a Ph.D. candidate in Sociology at Harvard University.

Ronald Rogowski is Professor of Political Science, University of California at Los Angeles. He is the author of *Commerce and Coalitions*, and *Rational Legitimacy*. A Fellow of the American Academy of Arts and Sciences, Rogowski was Vice President of the American Political Science Association in 1994.

Martin Shefter is Professor of Government at Cornell University. He is the author of *Political Crisis/Fiscal Crisis: The Collapse and Revival of New York City*; *Politics by Other Means: The Declining Importance of Elections in America* (with Benjamin Ginsberg); and *Political Parties and the State: The American Historical Experience*. He edited *Capital of the American Century: The National and International Influence of New York City*. Shefter served as President of the History and Politics section of the American Political Science Association in 1996–97.

Theda Skocpol is Victor S. Thomas Professor of Government and Sociology at Harvard University and Director of its Center for American Political Studies. Her books include *States and Social Revolutions: A Comparative Analysis of France, Russia, and China*; *Bringing the State Back In* (with Peter Evans and Dietrich Rueschemeyer); *Protecting Soldiers and Mothers: The Political Origins of Social Policy in the United States*; and *Civic Engagement in American Democracy* (with Morris Fiorina). Skocpol is a member of the American Academy of Arts and Sciences; was President of the Social Science History Association in 1996; and will be President of the American Political Science Association in 2003.

Bartholomew H. Sparrow is Associate Professor of Government at the University of Texas at Austin. He is the author of *From the Outside In: World War II and the American State*, and *Uncertain Guardians: The News Media as a Political Institution*. He is co-editor of *Politics, Discourse, and American Society: New Agendas*.

Aristide R. Zolberg is University-in-Exile Professor of Political Science in the Graduate Faculty of the New School University. His most recent books are *Working-Class Formation*, co-edited with Ira Katznelson, and *Escape from Violence*, co-authored with Astri Suhrke and Sergio Aguayo.

Part I

INTRODUCTION

One

Rewriting the Epic of America

IRA KATZNELSON

"Is the traditional distinction between international relations and domestic politics dead?" Peter Gourevitch inquired at the start of his seminal 1978 article, "The Second Image Reversed." His diagnosis — "perhaps" — was motivated by the observation that while "we all understand that international politics and domestic structures affect each other," the terms of trade across the domestic and international relations divide had been uneven: "reasoning from international system to domestic structure" had been downplayed. Gourevitch's review of the literature demonstrated that long-standing efforts by international relations scholars to trace the domestic roots of foreign policy to the interplay of group interests, class dynamics, or national goals[1] had not been matched by scholarship analyzing how domestic "structure itself derives from the exigencies of the international system."[2]

Gourevitch counseled scholars to turn their attention to the international system as a cause as well as a consequence of domestic politics. He also cautioned that this reversal of the causal arrow must recognize that international forces exert pressures rather than determine outcomes. "The international system, be it in an economic or politico-military form, is underdetermining. The environment may exert strong pulls but short of actual occupation, some leeway in the response to that environment remains."[3]

A decade later, Robert Putnam turned to two-level games to transcend the question as to "whether domestic politics really determine international relations, or the reverse." Contrary to Gourevitch, he judged that there is "a theoretical sophistication on the international-to-domestic causal connection far greater than is characteristic of comparable studies on the domestic-to-international half of the loop."[4] He cited the important scholarship by Gourevitch, as well as James Alt, Peter Evans, and Peter Katzenstein, that had appeared since the publication of "The Second Image Reversed."[5]

Today, the pendulum seems to have shifted once again. Momentum has moved to the large and growing body of work by scholars of international relations that has broken with the model of the state as a unitary rational actor to ask when and how domestic factors account for the choices states make in foreign policy. Arguably, this is where the cutting edge of IR scholarship presently is located. Several students of international relations have been investigating the domestic roots of international geopolitical and economic affairs, seeking to open up the category of "state" by examining the cacophony of national politics.[6] IR scholars working on subjects as diverse as crisis bargaining, the sources and outcomes of wars, the democratic peace thesis, and trade policy have been exploring how the international behavior of states is influenced by their domestic institutions, decisions, and policies.[7]

Notwithstanding the significant implications of these theory-driven research programs in the subfields of comparative politics and international relations for comprehending distinctive features in American political development, high walls continue to separate studies by Americanists of the U.S. politics at home from their studies of "foreign" affairs.[8] Outside of IR, the rare exceptions tend to be found in comparative studies that include the United States as one of their cases.[9] Conspicuously absent are investigations by Americanists either of international sources of domestic politics or the mutual constitution of international relations and domestic affairs. Thus, more than two decades since Gourevitch called for a new research perspective stressing the former, the degree and character of influence exercised by international factors on American political development remains remarkably unprobed, and too tight a restriction of attention to domestic factors continues to produce conclusions biased by an artificially limited universe of variables.

I

Convinced that this division between American politics and international relations is terribly constraining, the contributors to this exploratory volume emphasize the impact international factors have on domestic politics, suggest analytical strategies that borrow from work underway elsewhere, and display examples of scholarship that overcomes traditional barriers and divisions. Though estimable, Putnam's goal to move immediately and directly to two-level models that encompass influence flowing in both directions seems premature, given the rudimentary state of current knowledge and research. Though some subjects, like the analysis of international bargaining, require simultaneous and interactive treatment, the present situation in the main warrants greater modesty.

Thus, as a heuristic exercise, *Shaped by War and Trade* primarily appraises the ways and extent to which international forces shape domestic outcomes. Seeking to complement the growing body of scholarship on the domestic sources of geopolitics and international economic policies, we focus on how American political development has been influenced by the country's position in the global military and economic orders. The volume brings together scholars working in international relations, comparative politics, and American political development who wish not simply to confirm the importance of neglected subjects but also to demonstrate some productive directions that might be taken to move beyond the image of a world consisting of self-contained states. This book, thus, is more than an effort to collect between a set of covers essays that attempt to understand international influences on American political history. We aim to show how work linking American politics to the international economy and state system can be fruitful when guided by a set of broadly common theoretical and substantive concerns.

More particularly, we are searching for terms of partnership with students of war and trade who have been paying attention to politics inside the United States because they seek to address two questions: why a country adopts policies a realist would regard as less than optimal, and how a country's institutions, parties, coalitions, ideology, and other key features of its political life shape its choices in the international arena.[10]

Briefly consider three recent examples of this genre.[11] Seeking to comprehend why some wealthy countries become great powers while others do not, Fareed Zakaria's *From Wealth to Power* examines the lag in America's propensity to throw its weight around as an assertive international actor. From the end of the Civil War to 1896, the United States abstained from activity that realists would have expected it to undertake and for which it possessed ample material resources. Zakaria's analysis is state-centered and institutional. America's "national power," he argues, "lay dormant beneath a weak state, one that was decentralized, diffuse, and divided." The international ambitions both of presidents and secretaries of state, he argues, were foiled by the combination of a tiny national bureaucracy, a state structure fragmented by federalism, and the power of Congress to deny the executive branch sufficient funding to pursue its goals. Only with the modernization of the American state and the birth of the modern presidency at century's end could foreign policy activism develop effectively.[12]

Helen Milner takes up many of Zakaria's themes but seeks to elevate them to the level of systematic, portable theory. Starting from the position "that domestic politics and international relations are inextricably interrelated," her *Interests, Institutions, and Information* is grounded in the various bureaucratic, marxist, psychological, game-theoretic, and liberal (democratic peace) traditions that "have tried to explain state actions in foreign policy as a result of internal variables." Its main contribution is the development of a strategic causal theory assessing the influence of domestic on international affairs. Milner focuses on bargaining in specific institutional settings by actors with distinctive preferences and divergent information. Linking the domestic and international domains in her story are elite actors (individuals, groups, legislators) who participate in both settings (that is, in both games) concurrently. The probability that states will coordinate, as well as the terms of their coordination, varies in time and place, she argues, depending on the play of this two-tiered game and on the effects of such factors as the balance of capacities between legislatures and executives and the distribution of imperfect information. Her "central argument is that co-operation among nations is affected less by fears of other countries' relative gains or cheating than it is by the *domestic distributional consequences* of cooperative endeavors."[13] Both to test and to show the power of the model, Milner develops a number of cases within which the United States played a central role in the making of the postwar world, including Bretton Woods and the International Trade Organization, the never ratified Anglo-American Oil Agreement of 1944, and the 1992 North American Free Trade Agreement, ratified only after much controversy in 1993.

John Owen studies ten diplomatic crises spanning an even longer period, from the Jay Treaty of 1794 to the Spanish-American War of 1898, in order to identify the domestic mechanisms that reduce the chance that liberal states will make war on one another and increase the likelihood that they will take up arms against illiberal adversaries. *Liberal Peace, Liberal War* uses fine-grained case studies of the interplay of elite and public opinion, Congress, and the presidency in order to move beyond treatments of states as unitary, rational actors. The centerpiece of this effort is his serious treatment of liberalism as a body of ideas, as a worldview, and as a set of institutions. Owen underscores the significance, both within and outside the American state, of the ways in which liberal elites characterize other states. The international behavior of the United States in the nineteenth century, he argues, may be inexplicable in purely realist terms, but is much more intelligible when one takes account of the interplay of actors, institutions, and ideas on the domestic scene.

These studies embody the trend of boundary crossing we wish to emulate, although we will be moving mainly in the other causal direction. They operationalize state-society linkages institutionally. Milner is attracted by the deductive reasoning, explicit models, and systematic analysis of rational choice institutionalism. Zakaria is drawn to historical institutionalism, persuaded that relations among variables are transformed by their particular configuration in time and space. Owen focuses on distinctive American institutions and ideologies as complements to rational-actor and historical-institutionalist analysis. This volume is principally, though not exclusively, oriented to the second and third of these programs, the ones most closely identified with the main themes of American Political Development (APD) as a field. The essays collected here probe how the international situation of the United States has molded the character of the American state and the ideas and institutions underpinning its liberalism. These essays echo Gourevitch's plea to transpose the causal direction of inquiry in order to better understand the issues APD has pressed to the fore. Like Zakaria,

Milner, and Owen, the scholars who contributed to this volume treat the state not as a unitary macrostructure that is simply either weak or strong[14] but as a multidimensional conceptual variable.

II

The neglect of international factors is pronounced in the subfield of APD. Even outstanding works that deal with such manifestly international subjects as the role of tariffs in American industrialization[15] overlook these concerns.[16] More than a small irony is at work. In a programmatic essay that played a large role in the emergence of APD, Theda Skocpol urged her colleagues to produce "solidly grounded and analytically sharp understandings of the causal regularities that underlie the histories of states, social structures, and transnational relations in the modern world."[17] The first part of her agenda helped push forward the then still-nascent work of APD by promoting studies that overcame the conventional separation of American from comparative politics. By contrast, her call for attention to the international dimension, like Gourevitch's proposal a half-dozen years earlier, has gone largely unheeded.

Students of statemaking in Europe, building on the landmark scholarship of Max Weber and Otto Hintze, have been attentive to the constitutive impact of the global economy and of international geopolitics in shaping domestic politics and institutions. Charles Tilly's work explaining the emergence and character of states in early modern Europe, for example, has stressed how the preparation for and conduct of war affects the development of regime types, tax systems, fiscal policy, armed forces, patterns of bargaining between groups and classes, the mix of repression and rights, and the configuration of political institutions. Hendryk Spruyt has drawn attention to the ways trade patterns transformed the probabilities of success for such competing forms of rule in Renaissance Europe as city states and trading leagues. Thomas Ertman has accounted for variations in state infrastructures and political regimes in early modern Europe by the way geomilitary competition entwined with the organization of local government.[18] The macroanalytical tradition in historical sociology also has focused on the impact of other cross-border processes, including the flows of people and ideas.[19] By contrast, APD scholars have been attuned almost exclusively to internal processes and developments, such as electoral realignments, sectionalism, the changing balance within the federal system, and the extension of welfare state activity.

Thus, despite its resonant and relevant intellectual lineage, APD has continued to pay nearly exclusive attention to domestic institutions and policies. Its most influential journal, *Studies in American Political Development*, now approaching nearly two full decades of publication, has published hardly any articles exploring the influence of international factors on domestic processes and behavior. With the exception of one article on immigration policy, a second on the ideas composing Charles Beard's approach to foreign policy, and a third on the role of the Council on Foreign Relations, *Studies* has assayed American political development in a wholly internalist manner.[20] Moreover, none of this subfield's landmark books, including Stephen Skowronek's *Building a New American State*, Richard Bensel's *Yankee Leviathan*, and Theda Skocpol's *Protecting Soldiers and Mothers*, has made international subjects integral to its analysis, even though each prominently discusses the military, the preeminent hinge institution between domestic politics and international relations.[21] Unlike IR's recent theory-oriented efforts to understand these linkages,[22] APD largely remains bereft of such guides. The loss to intellectual vibrancy has been considerable. We have missed many opportunities to see how propositions that sprang from the increasingly robust alliance between international relations and comparative politics hold up when tested against the history of American politics or to use an American focus to bring together studies of international strategy and political economy.

III

These ambitions are not new. The range of such issues and the promise of such a venture were charted, if not attended to, quite some time ago. In 1931, the noted amateur historian, James Truslow Adams, published a widely read book, *The Epic of America*.[23] The following year, the presidential address to the American Historical Association by Berkeley historian Herbert Bolton advocated "a broader treatment of American history, to supplement the purely nationalistic presentation to which we are accustomed." Calling his own address "The Epic of Greater America," Bolton strongly advocated a research program to situate the United States, and the Americas more generally, in global perspective. He argued that the price of scholarly provincialism had been high: "the study of thirteen English colonies and the United States in isolation has obscured many of the larger factors in their development."[24]

As a remedy, he proposed shifts in scale and content. Familiar aspects of American history, he submitted, should be rethought and conceptualized as international subjects. Treating, for example, Britain's settlement of thirty (not just thirteen) colonies in North America, from Guiana to Hudson Bay, within the larger context of the geopolitical and economic rivalries among Europe's leading powers, and taking slavery in the United States into account as part of a worldwide pattern, Bolton sought to show how the myopia inherent in the traditional country-centered approach to history might be overcome by conceiving "domestic" variables as conjointly domestic and international. Research conducted on this broadened basis and from this reoriented perspective, he believed, would encourage new comparisons and make it possible to enlarge the character of causal accounts by historians and social scientists.[25]

Bolton's lecture is more than a period piece. Confining his examples mainly to the pre–Civil War experiences of settlement and expansion, he stressed the international jostling for territory in the New World among Spain, Portugal, Holland, France, England, Sweden, and Denmark, thus casting the contest for North America in far broader terms than the conventional way dates and locations are treated. Bolton underscored the interpenetration of sovereignty, space, boundaries, administration, empire, center-periphery relations, trade, production, war, demography, and culture. Further, he invited attention to fresh comparisons between the westward movements of Mexico, Canada, and the United States in North America and Brazil's drive to the Andes. He highlighted contingent ties joining language, identity, nation, and state. He urged that the American Revolution be understood as having lasted nearly a half-century, arguing that in a wider context it is clear that American sovereignty was not secured until the 1820s, after a long period of menace to the north, west, and south. He recalled how the white-Indian story was always simultaneously a tale of relations with foreign states, since Indian country was the outpost of four different empires. He made conflict between the United States and Canada and on the Spanish and Mexican borderlands central to the antebellum period's key "domestic" stories of statebuilding and economic development. He restored the themes of coercion and strong stateness to the making of the early American republic. And he showed how European capital and immigration, interacting with boundless natural resources and commercialization, contributed toward shaping what more recently has been called the market revolution.[26]

Alas, Bolton's bracing call to overcome the artificiality of the line separating domestic and international subjects mainly fell on deaf ears. The costs in unrealized prospects for studies in American political development continue to be paid. He rightly had observed that we cannot write credible American history without a supranational dimension any more than we can write credible European history without one. Here, too, frontiers and processes have had shifting boundaries, and the internal and external operations of power have been shaped, limited, and determined by mutual interaction. From the initial moments of European settlement to the post–Cold War epoch, America's story has been shaped by its location and participation in an array of global relations and processes, including the country's origins at the nexus of competing empires, its early struggles to secure and extend sovereignty against multiple adversaries, recurrent wars (hot and cold), cross-national elements of its expansion westward, cross-border movements of capital and labor (both free and slave), the significance of trade (not least as a source of government revenue), and the geopolitical and economic global leadership roles the United States has assumed in this century, especially since the Second World War.

IV

Might the epic of America be rewritten in the spirit of Bolton by incorporating war and trade as key generative features of American political development? With respect to which hallmark issues studied by APD would attention to an international dimension be significant, and how should the character and extent of such international effects be studied and understood? Obviously, efforts to specify the key elements of the domestic explanandum and the international explanans as a contribution to APD must be central aspects of this enterprise. What do international explanations of domestic affairs consist of? How important are international, as compared to more confined, factors in explanations of outcomes in the American experience? What are the mechanisms that link international relations, broadly conceived, to domestic institutional and political affairs? How, exactly, do these causes shape these results? These questions cannot be answered if we do not know what an international explanation is. What, in short, does it mean to say that international influences fashion American political development?[27] How, in sum, do systematic considerations of international influences — especially war and trade — mold and constrain American political development?

Let's return to Gourevitch's foundational paper. He observed that apart from invasion and occupation, the aspects of the international system that most affect domestic politics and policy are "the distribution of power among states, or the international state system; and the distribution of economic activity and wealth, or the international economy." It is the task of analysis, he counseled, to explore the magnitude of influence exerted by these aspects of international affairs on domestic politics. Quickly noting that the phrase "'Impact on domestic politics' could include a variety of effects: specific events, specific decisions, a policy, regime type, and coalition pattern," he decided to focus, for reasons of parsimony, on the latter two.[28] He asked, specifically, how choices between regime types — such as constitutional versus authoritarian, liberal versus totalitarian, and presidential versus parliamentary — are shaped by war and trade and how these external influences help determine the character and social base of political coalitions. By reviewing extant literatures, he demonstrated that others had begun to ask these questions, and that they could be answered in quite satisfactory ways.

Much as Gourevitch proposes, the essays in this volume explore the impact that war and trade have had on the political regime and on political coalitions in the United States. Regimes and coalitions, however, take distinctive shapes in this liberal and democratic setting. APD scholars long have emphasized how the question of "regime" in the United States is best apprehended as a set of puzzles about the contours and particularities of the country's liberal state. Since the founding, the main American regime issues have been concerned less with the existence of a liberal constitutional regime than with its scope and character. Likewise, the subject of political coalitions is closely tied to distinctively American situations, characterized, among other factors, by federalism, the separation of powers, and a profound history of sectionalism, especially North/South. It is not enough, in short, to identify regimes and coalitions as broad spheres of dependent variables; they need to be specified more precisely as objects of analysis.

A good starting point for these efforts is J. P. Nettl's approach to the modern state developed in his 1968 article "The State as a Conceptual Variable," where he sought to offer "a means of integrating the concept of state into the current primacy of social science concerns and analytical methods." This volume's attempt to assign a central role to transnational factors and processes in the development of the country's distinctive regime can be pushed forward, we believe, by revisiting Nettl's article and, especially, by attending to his analytical agenda's unrealized or neglected dimensions. His conceptual "brushstroke configuration" of the state proved more influential than might have been expected, given the degree of silence he then addressed.[29] But Nettl's main analytical move, the effort to parse the state into four distinctive dimensions, each of which he proposed to treat as a separate variable before probing their interrelationships, was not heeded by scholars, who conflated these dimensions into a single continuum, along which states were ranked from weak to strong based on measures of autonomy and capacity. This way of reading Nettl (and it is the dominant one) contributes little to our understanding of the distinguishing features of the American regime, except to show that it is relatively weak and permeable to societal influences. By contrast, this book suggests returning to the full multidimensional complexity of Nettl's theoretical scheme as a means of specifying a regime-focused object of analysis.[30] As we soon will discover, one dividend this approach yields is an ability to transcend simplistic depictions of the American national state as extremely weak.

"The State as a Conceptual Variable" made two provocative moves. Explicitly distinguishing its approach from prebehavioral treatments of the state in the late nineteenth and early twentieth centuries, Nettl proposed institutional and behavioral measures for degrees of "stateness." He hoped thereby to consolidate the gains political science had achieved in dealing with concepts as variables. In this way, he guarded against any return to metaphysical treatments of the state in the Hegelian tradition, and he made it possible to treat stateness as a concatenation of processes, sites, and outcomes, each of which possesses qualities of variation and contingency. Any given state at any specific historical moment thus is conceptualized configurationally. Nettl identified the central analytical dimensions of the state that interrelate contingently and distinctively in space and time. While resisting any general theory of state formation, he also refused to decompose the state into numerous variables treated in isolation from one another.

To overcome both "the all too general notion of state" and the tendency to slice and dice political analysis into distinctive variables as if they were unrelated to each other, Nettl arranged the concept of state into a limited number of distinct, but not hermetically sealed, domains of stateness, each ranging from weak to strong. Their combined features and relationships of these domains characterize particular historical states.

Nettl proposed four such dimensions. In the first, he treats the state as a "summating concept." This aspect of stateness connotes "the institutionalization of power," incorporating the state's claim to sovereignty over people and territory and its superordination over less inclusive and less coercive associations. Nettl notes that this understanding of the "state" is akin to other abstract and inclusive concepts, such as "nation" and "society." Notwithstanding the generality of the concept, the integrative abilities and sovereignty of states, he insists, vary in particular historical settings and always are shaped and contested within them.

A second component of stateness — its "inside" component — is institutional. The state is associated with a public sector characterized by a complex ensemble of authorities, organizations, and rules distinguishable from "private" domains. The state produces regulations and develops policies that transact with the economy, civil society, and other states. This aspect of the state varies in terms of its organizational complexity, its autonomy, and the scope of its regulative capacity. Nettl notes that the "autonomy of the state vis-à-vis other associations or collectivities becomes an empirical question for each individual case," and it is from here that there are potential "inroads on external autonomy involved in international systems and pressures for political unification."[31]

The state also is a cultural construct. This "cultural disposition to allot recognition to the conceptual existence of a state" is a reflection of historical traditions signaling the "existence, primacy, autonomy, and sovereignty of a state"; intellectual traditions based on the role that the prevailing political ideas and theory assign to the state; and cultural and cognitive processes that provide the mechanisms by which individuals incorporate, generalize, and ascribe a role and status to the state. Stateness, from this perspective, is not only macrostructural or institutional; it possesses, crucially, a set of microfoundations.[32]

Finally, there is the state's "outside" face. The modern sovereign state, Nettl avers, is the "basic, irreducible unit" of international relations. Within the global arena, the state is akin "to the individual person in society." Even where a state is otherwise weak, in this dimension its autonomy usually is unquestioned. Here, Nettl took up the banner of realism, locating the state as a unitary, rational, strategic actor in a global system of states. "In this international context the concept of the state," he noted, "in addition to being a unit also generates the almost exclusive and acceptable locus of resource mobilization," because in this sphere the state is considered to be acting *for* society. In this treatment, Nettl comes close to asserting an invariant structural truism. While doing so, however, he draws attention to the hinge role played by the state as "the gatekeeper between intrasocial and extrasocial flows of action." In the international arena, states may vary in their degree of strength according to their place and integration in the global system of power, parallel to the variations in "stateness" along the other dimensions he identifies.[33]

One way to treat the international dimension as causal is to work from a neorealist model and project the likely impact of the place of the state within the global system on its domestic regime and political coalitions. Another way of doing this is to broaden the notion of international determinants to include a wider array of factors than Nettl's realism easily can accommodate. Each essay in this volume makes one or the other of these choices, either deducing the likely impact of international factors from lean, largely rationalist models of international geopolitics and political economy or assessing international factors more thickly, with more taste for variation and historical particularity. But all the essays treat outcomes to stateness in the manner of Nettl's multidimensional approach to sovereignty, institutions, and political culture.

In other words, Nettl invites us to approach the state as a complex construct. He provides guidelines for establishing analytic equivalence between instances in spite of substantial variation, introduces a normative dimension into positive theory, and refuses to choose between domestic and international approaches to stateness. Moreover, his distinctions and categories, and the relations among them, can help us construct a complex dependent variable. Within Nettl's summating dimension, we can distinguish the degree of effective domestic control over land and population; overarching constitutional arrangements; membership rules governing citizenship, immigration, and political participation; and the competitive place of the state vis-à-vis the macrostructures and integrating ideas offered by the economy and civil society. For institutions, we can bear in mind their formal qualities, including federalism, separation of powers, and rights-based rules of the game; informal and semiformal instantiations, such as sectionalism, parties, opinion, interest groups, and coalitions; and policy content with respect to regulation and redistribution. For the culture of stateness, we can take up a wide variety of ideas, symbols, and representations. And for international participation, we can distinguish between aspects of participation in the global economy and in geopolitical engagement, dealing with them in our inquiries as independent variables. Indeed, by treating each of Nettl's sites of stateness as variables, it becomes possible to begin to ask with some precision how international influences have affected and molded outcomes at his other three levels of stateness.

Brought to Bolton's unrealized agenda, Nettl's matrix thus can help make the international dimension a constitutive part of analyses of American political development. It redresses the division of labor that leads scholars of international relations to focus mainly on Nettl's dimensions of sovereignty and international power and students of American political development to analyze his more institutional and cultural domains. A marriage between Bolton and Nettl, as it were, can enrich our historical and empirical understandings of the American state, permitting us to transcend simple portraits of a nineteenth-century state of great modesty only partially strengthened by episodes of twentieth-century statebuilding, most notably in the Progressive Era and the New Deal. Conceiving the state as a configuration of Nettl's dimensions can improve understandings of American institutions by placing them in a comparative and historical frame.

Nettl's model also helps us to make sense of two other entwined themes that have been at the substantive core of the APD field from the start: the status of the United States as a liberal regime and the related subject of American exceptionalism. For both, the pivotal text has been Louis Hartz's vexing *The Liberal Tradition in America*, which claims that the most important underlying force in American history has been its unchallenged political liberalism. This, Hartz argues, is explained by the absence of feudalism on American soil.[34] Lacking an adversary, the contractual, individualist, and constitutional liberalism fashioned by John Locke gained free sway in the United States and was able to snuff out pre- or antiliberal impulses of diverse kinds. Hartz argued that all significant features of the American regime are contained within the boundaries of this exceptional history and situation.

Hartz's non-narrative version of American exceptionalism has been robustly criticized for refusing to credit the significance of multiple ideologies or changes to the regime. Hartz's contention about "the moral unanimity" of American liberal society certainly overstates the uncontested quality of America's "nationalist articulation of Locke,"[35] and fails sufficiently to recognize the depth of conflict over the deep illiberalism of race.[36] Despite flaws, there remains a great deal of power to Hartz's analysis, especially if we follow David Greenstone and regard liberalism as a "boundary condition" embodying norms of speech and action in American politics. A boundary condition, Greenstone observes, is "a set of relatively permanent features of a particular context that affect causal relationships within it" even as it remains subject to dispute.[37] As just such a boundary condition, liberalism's grammar of rules — its bundle of institutions and norms — was never settled once and for all. Liberalism has been consistently dominant in America, but not unchanging or unchallenged.

Hartz's account of the ascendancy of liberalism in the United States includes a comparative dimension (the United States versus Europe) and a strong causal dimension (a country without a feudal past lacked the fissures of class generated by struggles against feudalism). But, like the larger APD tradition, *The Liberal Tradition in America* contains no international dimension. Nor is there room for periodization in an account that downplays the moments when debate about liberalism's rules has been most vigorous. Once we introduce conflicts over liberalism's grammar at key moments of indeterminacy into the story of American political development, we can see that there is not a genuine contradiction between the claim that the United States is the West's most durably liberal regime and the view from the inside that stresses conflict in constitutional jurisprudence, the politics of social movements, electoral mobilizations, and recurring discord about language and culture. None of these sites of conflict, instability, and crisis ever is detachable from international contexts and causes in time and in space. Thus, only by fully restoring American political history to its international context can we come to know what is distinctive about it.

V

This volume's inquiry into how war and trade shaped American sovereignty, domestic institutions, and the political culture of stateness necessarily is open and exploratory, given the current state of knowledge and research. There is no single approach or answer to the puzzle of the importance of international affairs. But despite the particular and often preliminary character of the chapters below, there are recurring broad moves at work, at times in the same paper. The essays consider international influences in two main ways: as specific pressures and restraints that help to constitute particular historical situations and as relatively constant causes operating in broadly similar ways across time because of systemic pressures immanent in the logic of geopolitics and the global political economy.

The first approach treats international causes as shaping outcomes at specific historical junctures but recognizes that the resulting pattern may be reproduced subsequently without the continuing presence of the formative

causes. Approached this way, the subject of international influences inter-
sects key issues in periodization. At relatively indeterminate moments,
whether caused by "shocks" like depression and war or by endogenous processes, new configurations of sovereignty, institutions, and political culture
may be fashioned.

The second approach is composed of probabilistic understandings about
how a given cause is likely to shape outcomes, irrespective of the particular
moment or event. Thus, some authors approach the task of assaying the
effects of international engagement by starting with a set of expectations
about how armed conflict (and preparation for it) and cross-border commerce might influence outcomes in each of Nettl's domestic domains, without anticipating that these factors would be equally influential in each dimension. It would be reasonable, for example, to hypothesize that
sovereignty would be heightened by military pressure but undermined by
trade; that participation in international relations would be advanced by
military pressure and often by trade; that institutions of executive power
would be enhanced by war and corporatism by trade; that the regulative and
redistributive activities of the state would expand under the impact both of
trade and military pressure; and, that a sense of stateness would become
more pronounced as military pressures increase but would diminish with
the interdependence of trade. Each of these propositions is underpinned by
immense literatures, but few have been investigated systematically for their
effects on American political development.

Aristide Zolberg closes the introductory section of *Shaped by War and
Trade*, while opening the book's substantive treatment of international influences on American political development by providing a synoptic and comparative view of "International Engagement and American Democracy." At
the heart of his chapter lies a reformulation of Tocqueville's assertion that
American distinctiveness lies in the absence of neighbors: "the singularity of
the United States arose from that fact that it did not yet exist as an actor
during the global wars of the early modern era, which shaped the structure
of the major European states, and that it participated only marginally in the
global war of 1792–1815, which further stimulated the development of state
structures among the European belligerents. This allows for a developmental pattern that diverged sharply from the European norm."

Zolberg develops this insight by surveying more than two centuries of
U.S. engagement in global geopolitics and in the process accomplishes two
vital tasks. First, he reminds us that international influences are not independent of specific circumstances. Second, he demonstrates that the manner in which factors hold sway is the result not only of such "objective"
features as the location of the country in geopolitical space but also of decisions taken within its domestic institutions about how to act and maneuver
in such space.

The book then divides into three main sections. The first reviews America in the antebellum period, presenting two views which probe the impact of international pressures on domestic statebuilding in a period usually stylized too simply as one in which the American state was weak. Robert Keohane's "International Commitments and American Political Institutions in the Nineteenth Century" argues that it is necessary to do more than contrast the relative capacities of the antebellum and postbellum American national state as a foreign policy actor. Surveying five treaty commitments undertaken by the United States before the Civil War and one following it, he seeks to explain how "the American state was dynamically responsive to pressures to increase its capacity to fulfill commitments" and cautions that to stereotype "it as a 'weak state' for the entire antebellum period obscures the dynamics of statebuilding." In carrying out this project, he also seeks to remedy what he believes to be the weakest part of Nettl's analysis, its treatment of the international dimension of stateness.

My own essay, "Flexible Capacity: The Military and Early American Statebuilding," is the second in the section and complements Keohane's by reevaluating the distinctive status of public authority before the Civil War and by underscoring how a liberal regime with a federal system came to terms with security requirements by building a military peculiar to and characteristic of the United States, an "expansible" one, in John Calhoun's term, geared to flexibly expand during times of stress and war and rapidly contract in peacetime. Read together, these two chapters recast not only Nettl but Hartz, because they emphasize the ways that the country's distinctive political order responded to the particular security challenges that it faced.

The second section of the book, "War and Trade," is oriented less to a single period than to institutionalist accounts of international-domestic linkages in specific domains. Martin Shefter's "War, Trade, and U.S. Party Politics" distinguishes among changes in the party system caused by three major international forces. He notes that mass immigration has influenced the balance of power and the structure of cleavages in the party system but devotes the bulk of his chapter to an analysis of how international economics and geopolitics have had a differential impact on different segments of the electorate, thus "generating cleavages that the nation's parties have represented"; and how the reshaping of domestic institutions during times of international stress has changed interactions between the state and the party system.

In "Patriotic Partnerships," Theda Skocpol, Ziad Munson, Andrew Karch, and Bayliss Camp take note of the dramatic impact large-scale wars have had on the landscape of organized voluntarism in the United States. Focusing on organizations with large memberships, they map the ways the Civil War and World War I proved highly favorable to civic development and to the growth of associational partnerships with government. Their analysis proceeds to explain why wars had such a vitalizing effect and why specific wars produced different results with respect to the pattern of organizational formation. Wars, they observe, affect voluntary organization by their patterns of mobilization, the manner in which the line between friends and enemies is defined and redefined, and by the character and impact of victory and defeat. By incorporating war so directly into a treatment of civicness — long thought to be a distinctive hallmark of America's liberal regime — these authors demonstrate, by contrast, the limits of exclusively internalist treatments of social capital.

Ronald Rogowski and Judith Goldstein turn to trade. Both pose a similar puzzle: Why has American trade policy been less protectionist than might have been expected, given both the distribution of preferences and power of, in the House of Representatives, an institution based on small districts likely to amplify parochial interests? Rather than being content with the stipulation that open trade regimes are in the interest of the United States, these two authors work their way through the problem of resistance to this putatively national interest. Rogowski's "Trade and Representation" argues both deductively and empirically that domestic political outcomes with respect to international trade are greatly influenced by the geographic concentration of particular kinds of economic activity. The more key activities cluster, he argues, fewer districts will dominate and the less likely are the restrictive efforts of these districts to prevail. By contrast, when economic concentration diminishes — and this is the direction in which the country's economy has been tending since the 1920s — protectionist pressures tend to increase.

This analysis lends urgency to Judith Goldstein's institutionalist account. Drawing on formal theory concerned with the problem of reneging, her chapter, "International Forces and Domestic Politics: Trade Policy and Institution Building in the United States," argues that politicians favoring liberal trade can deploy international solutions to constrain domestic institutions, in order, in turn, to bind their potentially protectionist constituencies. This chapter identifies two mechanisms of international influence: (1) international engagement changes group preferences, and (2) "international politics alters the 'tool kit' of options available to leaders for making policy."

The third section investigates American stateness from the Second World War through the Cold War to the post–Cold War period. Aaron Friedberg's "American Antistatism and the Founding of the Cold War State" seeks to understand how America's historical preference for a lack of engagement in international politics collided with hot and cold warfare in the 1940s and 1950s to produce "pressures for the construction of a powerful central state." Surveying policy with respect to manpower, armaments, and strategy, among other subjects, he argues that key outcomes stressing private-public partnerships and flexibility can only be understood in the context of strong international pressures engaging antistate cultural preferences, themselves the products of past international situations.

Bartholomew Sparrow's "Limited Wars and the Attenuation of the State" pushes further along these lines. He traces "the apparent paradox of the enhancement of state capacity . . . coincident with a weakening of the attachment that Americans have to their government" by examining limited war, taxation, and political communications and builds a complex model of international influence on postwar America, as favoring both the extension of state capacity and resistance to it. Further, he proposes a modification of Nettl's approach to stateness by downplaying state autonomy and underscoring the importance of social ties and governmental legitimacy.

Peter Gourevitch's "Reinventing the American State: Political Dynamics in the Post–Cold War Era" highlights an underattended feature of his 1978 essay. As he notes, international factors will affect national behavior in a liberal democracy when they shape the preferences of domestic actors, who, apart from cases of extreme duress, must decide whether, and how, to respond to international pressures. Arguing much as Shefter does in his chapter on parties, Gourevitch stresses that international forces appear in domestic politics by generating cleavages and influencing the development of the national state's institutions. What is most striking in these respects, he maintains, is that the configuration of institutions, policies, and preferences that at midcentury had produced the New Deal/Cold War policy system have now broken "into component pieces, each floating autonomously, like electrons in a chemical soup . . . available for new forms of linkage and attachment into new compounds."

Shaped by War and Trade concludes with Martin Shefter's survey of its arguments concerning how international factors have been constitutive of the political regime in the United States. Like the volume as a whole, his "International Influences on American Political Development" uses historical evidence and analysis to take up Herbert Bolton's call to rewrite the epic of America.

Notes

1. Examples he cited include Richard H. Snyder, H. W. Bruck, and Burtin Sapin, *Foreign Policy Decision-Making* (New York: Free Press, 1962); Gabriel Kolko, *The Politics of War* (New York: Random House, 1968); and Stephen D. Krasner, *Defending the National Interest: Raw Materials Investments and U.S. Foreign Policy* (Princeton: Princeton University Press, 1978).

2. Peter Gourevitch, "The Second Image Reversed: The International Sources of Domestic Politics," *International Organization* 32 (Autumn 1978): 881, 882. His

"perhaps" was more optimistic than Gabriel Almond's assertion earlier in the decade that "Political Science has tended to neglect serious empirical study of the interrelations between national politics and international politics." Gabriel A. Almond, "National Politics and International Politics," in *The Search for World Order: Studies by Students and Colleagues of Quincy Wright*, ed. Albert Lepawsky, Edward H. Bucharig, and Harold D. Lasswell (New York: Appleton-Crofts, 1971). In a later review, Almond took note of the growing body of work crossing this divide. Gabriel A. Almond, "Review Article: The International-National Connection," *British Journal of Political Science* 19 (April 1989). An important tandem effort to Gourevitch's was Peter J. Katzenstein, ed., *Between Power and Plenty: Foreign Economic Policies of Advanced Industrial States* (Madison: University of Wisconsin Press, 1978), which stressed comparative historical analysis of international-domestic linkages. For an earlier statement announcing the end of the separation of domestic politics and international relations, see Emile Lederer, "Domestic Policy and Foreign Relations," in *War in Our Time*, ed. Hans Speier and Alfred Kahler (New York: Norton, 1939).

3. Gourevitch, "Second Image," 900.

4. Robert D. Putnam, "Diplomacy and Domestic Politics: The Logic of Two-Level Games," *International Organization* 42 (Summer 1988): 427, 433. A slightly earlier call for an interdependent research program looking at links between the two level game of international and domestic politics is Stephan Haggard and Beth A. Simmons, "Theories of International Regimes," *International Organization* 41 (Summer 1987).

5. James E. Alt, "Crude Politics: Oil and the Political Economy of Unemployment in Britain and Norway, 1970–1985," *British Journal of Political Science* 17 (April 1987), 149–99; Peter B. Evans, *Dependent Development: The Alliance of Multinational, State, and Local Capital in Brazil* (Princeton: Princeton University Press, 1979); Peter J. Katzenstein, *Small States in World Markets: Industrial Policy in Europe* (Ithaca: Cornell University Press, 1985); and Peter Gourevitch, *Politics in Hard Times: Comparative Responses to International Economic Crises* (Ithaca: Cornell University Press, 1986). On the other side of the coin, for the same period one might record as key examples, Aristide Zolberg, "Origins of the Modern World System: A Missing Link," *World Politics* 33 (January 1981); Aristide Zolberg, "Beyond the Nation-State: Comparative Politics in Global Perspective," in *Beyond Progress and Development*, ed. J. Berting, W. Blockmans, and U. Rosenthal (Rotterdam: Erasmus Universiteit, 1986); and Ronald Rogowski, *Commerce and Coalitions* (Princeton: Princeton University Press, 1989).

6. See James D. Fearon, "Domestic Politics, Foreign Policy, and Theories of International Relations," *Annual Review of Political Science* 1 (1998): 289–313.

7. See, for example, Susan Peterson, *Crisis Bargaining and the State: The Domestic Politics of International Conflict* (Ann Arbor: University of Michigan Press, 1996); Richard N. Rosecrance and Arthur A. Stein, *The Domestic Bases of Grand Strategy* (Ithaca: Cornell University Press, 1993); Bruce Bueno de Mesquita and David Lalman, *War and Reason: Domestic and International Imperatives* (New Haven: Yale University Press, 1992); Bruce Russett, *Grasping the Democratic Peace* (Princeton: Princeton University Press, 1992); Jack Snyder, *Myths of Empire: Domestic Politics and International Ambition* (Ithaca: Cornell University Press, 1991); Helen V. Milner, *Resisting Protectionism* (Princeton: Princeton University Press, 1998); and

Sharyn O'Halloran, *Politics, Process, and American Trade Policy* (Ann Arbor: University of Michigan Press, 1994). While stressing the domestic sources of international processes and decisions, these works stop short of the claim that all politics ultimately are domestic in nature. The latter position is characteristic of the British sociological institutionalist theorists of IR surveyed in John Kurt Jacobsen, "Are All Politics Domestic? Perspectives on the Integration of Comparative Politics and International Relations Theories," *Comparative Politics* 29 (October 1996).

8. Although some international relations specialists have been crossing the IR-American political development divide in the direction charted by Gourevitch, Americanists have failed to make the reciprocal move. For examples, see Robert O. Keohane, "Associationist American Development, 1776–1860: Economic Growth and Political Disintegration," in *The Antinomies of Interdependence*, ed. John Ruggie (New York: Columbia University Press, 1983); and Robert O. Keohane and Helen V. Milner, eds., *Internationalization and Domestic Politics* (Cambridge: Cambridge University Press, 1996).

9. A significant instance is Margaret Levi, *Consent, Dissent, and Patriotism* (New York: Cambridge University Press, 1997).

10. For this distinction, see Fearon, "Domestic Politics."

11. Fareed Zakaria, *From Wealth to Power: The Unusual Origins of America's World Role* (Princeton: Princeton University Press, 1998); Helen Milner, *Interests, Institutions, and Information: Domestic Politics and International Relations* (Princeton: Princeton University Press, 1997); John W. Owen IV, *Liberal Peace, Liberal War: American Politics and International Security* (Ithaca: Cornell University Press, 1997).

12. Zakaria, *Wealth*, 11.

13. Milner, *Interests*, 3, 9.

14. This, though, is a tendency in Zakaria's work.

15. Richard Bensel, *The Political Economy of American Industrialization, 1877–1900* (New York: Cambridge University Press, 2000).

16. There are exceptions, to be sure, to this general rule. On the impact of war, for example, see Bartholomew H. Sparrow, *From the Outside In: World War II and the American State* (Princeton: Princeton University Press, 1996); and Daniel Kryder, *Divided Arsenal: Race and the American State during World War II* (New York: Cambridge University Press, 2000).

17. Theda Skocpol, "Bringing the State Back In: Strategies of Analysis in Current Research," in *Bringing the State Back In*, ed. Peter Evans, Dietrich Rueschemeyer, and Theda Skocpol (New York: Cambridge University Press, 1985), 28.

18. Charles Tilly, *Coercion, Capital, and European States, AD 990–1990* (Oxford: Basil Blackwell, 1990); Hendrik Spruyt, *The Sovereign State and its Competitors* (Princeton: Princeton University Press, 1994); Thomas Ertman, *Birth of the Leviathan: Building States and Regimes in Medieval and Early Modern Europe* (Cambridge: Cambridge University Press, 1997). Also see Brian M. Downing, *The Military Revolution and Political Change: Origins of Democracy and Autocracy in Early Modern Europe* (Princeton: Princeton University Press, 1992).

19. Aristide R. Zolberg, "International Migration Policies in a Changing World System," in *Human Migration: Patterns and Policies*, ed. William H. McNeill and Ruth S. Adams (Bloomington: University of Indiana Press, 1978); Dietrich Ruesche-

meyer and Theda Skocpol, eds., *States, Social Knowledge, and the Origins of Modern Social Policies* (Princeton: Princeton University Press, 1996).

20. Peter H. Schuck, "The Politics of Rapid Legal Change: Immigration Policy in the 1980s," *Studies in American Political Development* 6 (Spring 1992): 37–92; Clyde W. Barrow, "The Diversionary Thesis and the Dialectic of Imperialism," *Studies in American Political Development* 11 (Fall 1997): 248–91; and Inderjeet Parmar, "'Mobilizing America for Internationalist Foreign Policy,'" *Studies in American Political Development* 13 (Fall 1999): 337–73.

21. Stephen Skowronek, *Building a New American State: The Expansion of National Administrative Capacities, 1877–1920* (Cambridge: Cambridge University Press, 1982); Richard Bensel, *Yankee Leviathan: The Origins of State Authority in America, 1859–1877* (Cambridge: Cambridge University Press, 1990); and Theda Skocpol, *Protecting Soldiers and Mothers: The Political Origins of Social Policy in the United States* (Cambridge: Harvard University Press, 1992).

22. A useful overview of the field with respect to these matters can be found in the special issue "*International Organization* at Fifty: Exploration and Contestation in the Study of World Politics," *International Organization* 52 (Autumn 1998). For an attempt to integrate across subfields using rational choice theory, see that issue's article by Helen Milner, "Rationalizing Politics: The Emerging Synthesis of International, American, and Comparative Politics," 759–86.

23. James Truslow Adams, *The Epic of America* (Boston: Little Brown, 1931).

24. Herbert E. Bolton, "The Epic of Greater America," *American Historical Review* 38 (April 1933): 448.

25. Bolton, "Epic," 454.

26. Charles Sellers, *The Market Revolution: Jacksonian America, 1815–1846* (New York: Oxford University Press, 1991); Melvyn Stokes and Stephen Conway, eds., *The Market Revolution in America: Social, Political, and Religious Expressions, 1800–1860* (Charlottesville: University of Virginia Press, 1996).

27. Here, deliberately, I am repeating Fearon's language almost verbatim, with only an inversion of the words "international" and "domestic"

> What exactly is a domestic-political explanation of foreign policy? What things have to be present for us to call an explanation of some foreign policy choice a domestic-political explanation? The question turns out to be surprisingly tricky, but it deserves an answer. Consider the two linked research questions that animate much of this literature. First, how important is domestic politics, relative to systemic or structural factors, in the explanation of states' foreign policies? And second, how, exactly, does domestic politics shape foreign policy? Neither question can be answered if we don't know what a domestic-political explanation is. (Fearon, "Domestic Politics," 291)

28. Gourevitch, "Second Image," 882–83.

29. J. P. Nettl, "The State as a Conceptual Variable," *World Politics* 20 (July 1968). Much influential work in comparative history, sociology, and political science has stood on his shoulders. Examples include the SSRC volumes on *The Formation of National States in Western Europe* and *Bringing the State Back In*, as well as leading state-centered scholarship in American political development, including Skowronek, *State*; Bensel, *Leviathan*; and Skocpol, *Protecting*.

30. Nettl's elusive and opaque exposition and his explicit decision to put the international aspects of his formulation to the side make it challenging to draw on his work. Still, more than three decades later, his suggestive article provides a useful guide to linking institutional and behavioral scholarship on the state.

31. Nettl, "State," 565.

32. Ibid., 566.

33. Ibid., .563–64.

34. Louis Hartz, *The Liberal Tradition in America* (New York: Harcourt, Brace, & World, 1955).

35. Hartz, *Liberal Tradition*, 10–11.

36. See Rogers M. Smith, "Beyond Tocqueville, Myrdal, and Hartz: The Multiple Traditions in America," *American Political Science Review* 87 (September 1993); and Rogers M. Smith, *Civic Ideals: Conflicting Visions of Citizenship in U.S. History* (New Haven: Yale University Press), 1997.

37. J. David Greenstone, *The Lincoln Persuasion: Remaking American Liberalism* (Princeton: Princeton University Press, 1993), 42, 45.

Two

International Engagement and American Democracy: A Comparative Perspective

ARISTIDE R. ZOLBERG

Introduction

Lastingly inspired by Tocqueville's insightful comparison of the American regime with its European counterparts, explanations of the precocious emergence of liberal democracy in the United States are overwhelmingly "internalist," focusing on the contributions of culture, social structure, and economic conditions to the shaping of political regime.[1] Much less noted, however, is that Tocqueville begins his systematic summary enumeration of the factors that contribute to liberal democracy with an element of America's "particular and accidental situation" that, in contrast with all the others, pertains to the *international* sphere:

> The Americans do not have any neighbors, and consequently no great wars, no financial crisis, and neither ravages nor conquest to fear; they need neither heavy taxes, nor a numerous army, nor great generals; and they have almost nothing to fear from a scourge more terrifying for republics than all those together, military glory.[2]

No conquest to fear, no great generals, no military glory? Even Tocqueville's French readers might have been aware that this was egregiously inaccurate: only a decade and a half before his visit, the fledgling American capital was destroyed by a British expeditionary force, and in 1828 the Americans chose as their president Andrew Jackson, a "great general" of that very war, who was in the course of elaborating a populist regime committed to a boldly expansionist policy at the expense of its Indian and Spanish neighbors. As with his statements regarding equality of conditions, Tocqueville blithely sweeps aside historical details that might stand in the way of a brilliant generalization. It has been suggested that he mistakenly took as face value American professions that the new republic rejected war as an instrument of policy thereby contributing to the creation of the "American war myth."[3] In the light of Tocqueville's overall skeptical persona, it is more likely that he went along knowingly, to support arguments that fit his general theory regarding structural differences between regime types and his ambivalent assessment of dawning democracy. However, for the time being I shall set aside the issue of what Tocqueville believed, in order to elucidate his theoretical argument.

As always, Tocqueville's proposition is implicitly comparative, and although he speaks of "Europe," he has in mind, first and foremost, France. As he would subsequently elaborate in his other masterwork, *The Ancien Régime and the Revolution*, Tocqueville viewed the French state as a dangerous monstrosity, bred in the cockpit of warring European monarchs and emerging from its recent revolutionary struggles at home and abroad with an even greater capacity for destroying society. Because they were ineluctably trapped within an international system of states of their own making, France and the other European countries faced simultaneously the temptations of engaging in conquest and the need to protect themselves against other predators much like themselves. Whether designed as an offensive machine or a defensive one, the state steadily expanded and became more centralized. In contrast, the United States was isolated and, as of 1830, relatively safe; hence, its governing institutions were not afflicted by acromegaly.

This reasoning was hardly original. Indeed, the effect of war on politics and society was a central concern to Enlightenment thinkers generally, as indicated, for example, by Rousseau's 1758 pronouncement, made in the course of a critique of the abbé de Saint-Pierre's *Project for Perpetual Peace*: "It is not necessary to have thought long about the means of perfecting any government to perceive the difficulties and obstacles that arise less from its constitution than from its foreign policy—to the extent that we are forced to give over to our defense most of the attention that should be devoted to enforcing the law and to think more about being in a state of readiness to resist others than about perfecting the government itself."[4] Rousseau was Tocqueville's most abhorred "dreamer," but this insight was based on his practical experience of the relationship between domestic and international politics as secretary to the French ambassador to Venice during the War of the Austrian Succession, and there are indications that he planned to write a sequel to the *Social Contract* that would focus on international relations.[5] That Tocqueville shared this view of war is hardly surprising, given France's history; but of special relevance here is that the American Founders did so as well, and that it profoundly affected their political choices.

International Situation, Strategic Stance, and Regime

It is surely no happenstance that the weighty role of war in state—and regime—formation was rediscovered by American sociologists and political scientists in the 1970s, at a time when the United States was involved in the most divisive external conflict in its history, the reverberations of which occasioned widespread upheavals and an institutional crisis at the highest level of government.[6] Incorporation of the strategic factor into the main body of social theory was facilitated also by the precisely contemporaneous revival of the work of Otto Hintze, who attempted to integrate Ranke's assertion of the "primacy of external policy" into Weber's theoretical framework.[7] The notion that the European state was forged in battle, and that war fostered the expansion of state activity in all spheres of social action, accounting for the growth of both "infrastructural" and "despotic" power, is now widely accepted by social scientists.[8] Together with the contemporaneous emergence of "dependency" and its derivative world-systems analysis as critiques of modernization theory, and some attempts to link international political economy and comparative politics, this idea has helped to give the macro-analytic social sciences generally a more "externalist" orientation.[9]

However, initially Hintze's theoretical subtleties got lost in translation. Beyond arguing that the imperatives of war transformed feudal Europe into a congeries of more extensive and more centralized states, Hintze also emphasized that the concomitant need for increased revenue fostered the institutionalization of representative "estates" (*ständestaat*) and thereby the beginnings of constitutional rule (*rechtstaat*). In other writings, he suggested that variation in strategic situations — for the same state over time or between states — might foster different patterns of international activity, and thereby different regime forms.[10] The idea of treating a state's situation in relation to the external world as a sort of variable leading to differentiation was part of the intellectual heritage of nineteenth-century social theorists. Notably, Herbert Spencer incorporated into his framework the classical distinction between Athens and Sparta, the one a "commercial" state and the other a "military" state, respectively disposed toward liberalism (coupled with imperialism and slavery) and despotism — and used it to explain the contrast between the developmental paths of England and the Netherlands, on the one hand, and France, on the other.[11]

This initial seminal but rough-hewn proposition equating "war" with "absolutism" is now being steadily refined. For example, recent research suggests that there is a considerable difference between the impact of "global" and more limited "interstate" wars, with only the former having a permanent "ratcheting" effect on state growth.[12] In a similar vein, historically extensive involvement in land war tended to produce the more extreme versions of absolutism: more demanding states that engaged in extensive extraction of fiscal and human resources sought greater centralization at the expense of local autonomy, and — Hintze to the contrary notwithstanding — developed executive dominance at the expense of representative institutions.[13] Moreover, states vary considerably in their approach to harnessing the capacity to meet these objectives.[14] This variation can itself be accounted for largely by a combination of cultural and structural factors shaped by previous experiences — in short, it is "path-dependent." However, greater allowance needs to be made for "agency" as well: although at any given time states face different strategic challenges and opportunities, the givens of the situation usually leave some room for a choice of objectives — as indicated, for example, by the huge volume of historical literature devoted to the questions of whether World War I and the Cold War were necessary.

In short, one might think of the situational strategic variable as a continuum on which states might be located at any given time ("time" being shorthand for a particular configuration of the international strategic system under specific technological conditions), but this variable must be considered in tandem with another one, ranging from "disengagement" to "engagement," which captures a state's perception of and response to a given situation. Thus, the situation identified as "isolation" — from powerful and threatening states with the technological and organizational capacity to inflict harm — located at the negative end of the first continuum, might easily be coupled with a stance of "strategic disengagement," located at the negative end of the second. It should be noted that "disengagement" is not to be equated with "pacifism," in the sense of an absolute rejection of the use of force as an instrument of policy. Although the negative values of the two variables have received much less theoretical attention than the positive ones, one might surmise that a combination of the two negatives would be conducive to a low degree of state centralization and a balance of state-society relationships weighted toward society — in short, that it would allow for the formation of a minimally predatory state.

In the early modern period, however, by virtue of the predatory character of the actors constituting the European system of states, no state approximated the ideal-typical "isolation" situation; and since those that adopted a "disengagement" stance or simply failed to develop the capacity for mustering adequate strategic power were steadily eliminated, the survivors clustered around the "statist" pole.

In this perspective, Britain constitutes an intermediate case, whose ambiguous standing can be seen in its categorization as the ideal-typical "weak state" from a French perspective but as a "strong state" from an American one.[15] The example of Britain also demonstrates why "a state's relation to its neighbors" is a much more heuristic concept than a mere consideration of geographical givens. As the battle of Agincourt reminds us, during its protracted formative period as a state England was *not* an island; it only became one when sixteenth-century rulers decided to relinquish their predecessors' territorial ambitions on the Continent. This enabled the crown to forego the development of a standing army, and the absence of an army in turn constituted the critical condition in a sequence that reduced the likelihood of an absolutist outcome later on, when later rulers sought to emulate their Continental betters. However, Britain remained very much engaged in the European system of states, and participated in every one of the global wars that erupted from the late fifteenth century onward.[16] Confronted with Spanish, and subsequently French, strategic might on sea as well as land, the British state achieved a high degree of executive control and centralization. The crown's adamant commitment to the creation of a united kingdom out of the ethnically diverse countries that shared the North Sea's two islands is attributable in large part to perennial strategic concerns. Britain's engagement in the global war of 1688–1713 had a "ratcheting" effect, reflected in a doubling of state expenditures as a proportion of GNP, and this process was reenacted in more acute form a century later.[17]

For a "disengaged state" to emerge on the Continent we must await the emergence of the post–Congress of Vienna Concert of Europe, a configuration of the international system that provided limited room for "neutral" states. The survival of the latter was assured not solely by their own defensive capacity but also by the commitment of powerful neighbors whose interests this served. Two states benefited from such arrangements in the middle third of the nineteenth century, Switzerland and Belgium, and it is noteworthy that both deviated from the standard centralized state pattern, albeit in somewhat different ways. Although both were surrounded by powerful and threatening neighbors, both shunned large standing armies, and both emerged as "consociational democracies." But after its midcentury civil war, Switzerland reconstructed itself as a very loose confederation of formally equal cantons, while independent Belgium (1830–) retained the Napoleonic system it inherited from the period of French annexation (1795–1814). Nevertheless, the much greater weight of municipal politics in Belgium as compared to France indicated a considerable degree of *de facto* deconcentration of power, thereby providing support for the hypothesis that disengagement functioned as a distinct variable.[18] It is also noteworthy that its "disengagement" at the European level did not prevent Belgium from emerging as an imperial power in Africa — although unlike France, England, and the Netherlands, it did not engage in extensive military campaigns to achieve this result. Belgium also demonstrates that "relations to neighbors" is a more relevant factor than geographical location, as its situation was drastically altered when Germany violated its neutrality in 1914.

The Tocqueville Hypothesis Restated

This context helps us to understand how Tocqueville came to perceive the "absence of neighbors" as a singular feature of the American situation. His point is obviously not to be taken literally, since at the time of writing

Britain controlled what are now the Canadian provinces of Quebec (which Tocqueville visited) and Ontario; the Spanish Empire ruled territories to the south and west; and much of the continent was inhabited by Indians, whom the United States was in the course of systematically dispossessing by the force of arms, as Tocqueville himself pointed out in the final chapter of volume 1. Moreover, by the time the United States emerged as a state, the Atlantic Ocean was no longer an unbridgeable strategic divide: throughout the eighteenth century North America was an arena for both direct and indirect confrontations among the leading world powers, whose navies were capable of ferrying large expeditionary forces to fight transatlantic wars. The conflict known in Europe as "the War of the Austrian Succession" and in America as the "French and Indian Wars" resulted in the expulsion of France from North America. America's subsequent seven-year-long war of national liberation unfolded amidst mounting global tensions that erupted not long afterward into a quarter-century-long world war between the two superpowers, in the course of which the United States itself was invaded and its new capital destroyed. Disputes with Britain flared up perennially throughout the 1830s and 1840s, and during that same period the harnessing of strategic might was a sine qua non for the pursuit of U.S. policy regarding Texas.

Thus, with respect to both variables sketched out in the previous section, half a century after independence the United States was located at some distance from the negative pole. Actual and potential strategic necessity was in fact successfully invoked in the wake of American independence as justification for constructing a much stronger national government than one might expect on the basis of strict isolation and disengagement, in sharp contrast with what was provided for under the Articles of Confederation.

Given these qualifications, Tocqueville's seminal observation might be reformulated as follows:

> The singularity of the United States arose from the fact that it did not yet exist as an actor during the global wars of the early modern era, which shaped the structure of the major European states, and that it participated only marginally in the global war of 1792–1815, which further stimulated the development of state structures among the European belligerents. This allowed for a developmental pattern that diverged sharply from the European norm, perhaps even a regime that constituted something other than a "state" in the contemporaneous European usage.[19]

Although Tocqueville presents America's strategic disengagement as a *providential cause*, this was no mere geopolitical given, but rather the result of a *policy choice* facilitated by the country's geopolitical situation. However, unlike the small European neutrals fostered by the Concert of Europe, by virtue of its continental size and economic promise the United States had the potential for ascending to the status of a great power, as Tocqueville anticipated. This was in fact realized at the dawn of the twentieth century. The United States emerged as a major actor when the next global war erupted, and, after the collapse of what Polanyi termed "nineteenth century civilization," undertook to reconstruct and lead the international system.[20] Escaping the dictates of "path dependency," within a few decades the disengaged country without any neighbors propelled itself to global hegemony.

Historically, the global leadership role had been assumed by countries structually prepared for the task by virtue of their state-centered political institutions. But since the United States deviated sharply from these precedents, the demands of its new role could be expected to induce considerable institutional stress, centering on tensions between the executive and the representative components of its system. Compounding the process was the fact that whereas previous great powers achieved that status before the age of liberal democracy, and by and large managed to insulate their externally oriented decision-making apparatus from the pressures of accountability, the United States rose to global leadership well after such accountability was institutionalized. We should therefore expect to observe recurrent crises over the exercise of *raison d'état* in the sphere of strategic and foreign policy throughout the twentieth century.

The Founding Baseline

Although the revolutionary generation was determined to remain at arm's length from European conflicts and profoundly mistrusted military institutions, this is not to say that they abhorred the use of force as an instrument of national policy. Indeed, when neutrality and embargoes on trade failed, they paradoxically resorted to war itself to achieve their "disengagement" objective.[21] Although the American outlook during this early period was hardly homogeneous, it was shaped by contemporary experiences and might be characterized as a "limited-war mentality," guided by "the tenets of the traditional European *jus ad bellum*, which argued for patience and forbearance before sovereigns resorted to force of arms" — a concept which Europe itself appeared to be in the course of relinquishing.[22]

The American regime was shaped by a double set of considerations. On the one hand, its architects adhered to the republican orthodoxy that monarchs lay at the heart of war, and hence that popular control of the war power would contribute to a pacific future. But on the other hand, the difficulties the Continental Congress encountered in asserting its authority and raising troops and the collapse of efforts to strengthen its powers in the wake of Lord Cornwallis's surrender at Yorktown figured prominently in arguments advanced on behalf of a stronger and more centralized national government with an enhanced military capability, vociferously voiced by

Washington and other experienced officers.[23] The latter considerations were fully spelled out in the very first *Federalist Papers*.[24] In no. 3, John Jay points out that a united America would be less likely to give foreign powers legitimate grounds for waging war than would a set of disparate states, and then goes on to demonstrate in no. 4 that under the proposed plan the United States would also be able to defend itself more effectively against aggressive rivals. He concludes by arguing in no. 5 that the alternative, a multiplicity of American states, would be a source of perennial conflict. Hamilton elaborates this further in nos. 6–9, invoking Montesquieu on behalf of federalism as a mechanism for "reconciling the advantages of monarchy" — that is, greater capacity to maintain external security — "with those of republicanism."[25] In no. 11 he restates the argument on behalf of a strong national government in relation to the creation of a navy, and in nos. 22–29 returns to the necessity of an "energetic" constitution to resolve what we would today term the "prisoner's dilemma" experienced by the confederated states during the war of independence with regard to the mustering of an army. Finally, if the national government is to provide for the common defense, he argues, it must have general powers of taxation (no. 30).

These conflicting considerations also pervaded the contemporaneous debate over the actual organization of the country's armed forces. At the end of the war, faced with the prevailing strong feeling that standing armies in peace time were incompatible with republicanism, Washington agreed that a *large* force was dangerous but maintained that a *small* one was indispensable to the national security and urged in particular the establishment of a permanent garrison at West Point under the control of Congress (rather than of New York). In fact, most of the men under arms were quickly disbanded, and as of the summer of 1787, Secretary of War Knox reported that there were only about 500 men in service. However, in April 1790 Congress added four more companies of infantry, bringing the total authorized strength to 1,216.[26]

Given the external situation the United States faced around the time of the founding, it might have been constructed as a Swiss-type confederation, as advocated by the anti-Federalists. The Articles of Confederation, in fact, attempted to establish just such a union. The Federalists ultimately won the day, but since republican principles prevailed, the central government remained limited. Although the growing ideological character of the European war sharpened the confrontation between Federalists and Jeffersonian Republicans in the realm of foreign policy, the two camps nevertheless shared a concern to keep the young nation out of the global war, and succeeded in doing so, against heavy odds, for twenty years. Set forth in Washington's Farewell Address, which was elaborated into a foundational myth, the basic motif of early U.S. foreign policy was prudential isolation: "The new, weak United States should take advantage of its physical distance from Europe and steer clear of the rivalries which be set that continent."[27] Isolation was desirable not only because American independence might be threatened by more powerful outsiders "but because of the possible domestic effects of too ambitious a foreign policy. . . . The American polity was founded upon a finely balanced set of institutional mechanisms. If any of those institutions — particularly the executive branch — were substantially to gain in power by comparison with the others, the founding compromises would be placed in jeopardy."[28]

Seymour Martin Lipset has suggested that, in addition, "The 'neutralism' of early American foreign policy, like that of many contemporary new states, was of extreme importance in reducing some of the internal tensions which might serve to break down a weak authority structure."[29] However, while "neutralism" may well have had that effect, this does not explain why it was adopted, since neither then nor today do political leaders always choose that which is functionally appropriate. Indeed, in the very first years after the ratification of the new Constitution, interpenetration did take place between domestic and external issues: "Despite Washington's best efforts to insulate and protect the United States from being buffeted by the conflict raging in Europe, he and his successors, down through Madison at least, were unsuccessful. Indeed, the American republic was almost inexorably drawn into the vortex of the European storm, and this mortally threatened its very existence."[30]

After the outbreak of the French Revolution, British and Irish democrats came to be viewed as disloyal "Jacobins," and in the face of severe repression, many fled to the United States, where their arrival precipitated a political crisis. From the perspective of the Republican opposition, they were hailed as victims of political persecution — that is, refugees deserving of asylum — but from that of the ruling Federalists, whose domestic conservatism was complemented by rapprochement with Britain, they were dangerous subversives. Contrary to the myth that the United States has always welcomed the oppressed, the Federalists responded by enacting the notorious Alien and Sedition Acts, which barred the door to European advocates of democracy and intimidated their American friends. But enactment of these controversial laws in turn helped mobilize support on behalf of the Republicans, and their repeal constituted one of Jefferson's highest priorities after he came to power in 1800.[31]

Nevertheless, by and large disengagement did prevail. A very important consideration was the firm belief, which the American republicans shared with most Enlightenment thinkers — as witnessed by the quote from Rousseau — that standing armies constituted a permanent threat to representative institutions. Referring to the American stance during this period, Samuel Huntington has observed that "liberalism does not understand and is hostile to military institutions and the military function." It would be more accurate to suggest that it is precisely because liberalism *does* understand military institutions and the military function that it is suspicious of them.[32] The hostility of the Founders to standing armies, shared also by Tocqueville, arose from their interpretation of European experiences in the age of absolutism, and the validity of their analysis with regard to the development of representative institutions in the seventeenth and eighteenth centuries has been confirmed by recent historical studies, as noted earlier. It would be further confirmed by the development of Germany, where, in the course of consolidation (1850–70), the forces of liberalism were defeated in a fateful struggle for control over military institutions, resulting in the institutionalization of a modernized absolutism.[33]

In practice, the founders of the American state sought to deal with the problem of civil-military relations by virtually eliminating the military altogether. Besides the navy, only small forces were required, primarily to fight Indians. The solution was to divide power: "The national government if it monopolized military power would be a threat to the states; the President if he had sole control over the armed forces would be a threat to the Congress. Consequently, the Framers identified civilian control with the fragmentation of authority over the military."[34] Defense was to be founded mainly on militia forces, with control shared between the federal government and the states; and the division of power between executive and legislative was applied to the small national military establishment as well.

Huntington has further suggested that at the time of the founding, "National security was a simple given fact — the starting point of political analysis — not the end result of conscious policy. . . . American awareness of the role of power in foreign politics was dulled by the absence of external threats."[35] But the reasoned arguments regarding national security in the *Federalist Papers* suggest that the architects of the American state were anything but dull with respect to the matter in question. Rather, it was because they were very much aware of "the role of power in foreign politics" that they insisted on congressional control over military and foreign policy. Addressing himself to those who deplore that the proposed constitution fails to prohibit the creation of a standing army in time of peace, Hamilton argues in *Federalist* no. 24 that such a prohibition would be improper; although the United States is separated from Europe by an ocean, "there are various considerations that warn us against an excess of confidence or security," notably the colonial ambitions of Britain and Spain.[36] On these grounds, as well as for purposes of quelling domestic insurrection, it would be advisable to maintain a small military establishment even in time of peace. He then goes on to point out that opposition to a standing army usually focuses on the danger of reinforcing the executive, and that the constitutional proposal overcomes this by vesting control in the popularly elected legislature, with the additional guarantee of a two-year limit on appropriations for support of an army. Hamilton returns to this again in no. 26, where he explains the circumstances under which the prohibition on standing armies originated in England and stresses once again that the key issue was not the existence of an army but parliamentary control of it.

We must therefore conclude that far from being a quixotic creation, the American state reflected the views of astute practitioners of realpolitik, aware that the ambitious new republic would inevitably be embroiled in international rivalries and must therefore be endowed with the capacity of mustering external might. Aware of equally realistic objections to the domestic political consequences of acquiring such capacity, they devised an ingenious compromise.[37]

The resulting arrangements were more like those of the mighty British Empire than of Montesquieu's hypothetical republics. As Huntington correctly points out, by and large the Founders followed the English model: the president inherited the powers of the king, and was made commander in chief of the armed forces, while Congress inherited the powers of Parliament. However, the power to make war was granted *exclusively* to Congress, thus shifting the balance in favor of the legislature. The importance of this move went well beyond the United States, because in so doing, the Constitution makers "established a significant precedent in the evolution of representative government."[38]

Toward Greater Engagement

Over the next half-century, the American state bypassed "transient opportunities for self-limitation" and became firmly committed to "parochial imperialism" — hailed as "Manifest Destiny."[39] Confrontations with Indians who resisted encroachments by white settlers pointed up the advantages of an effective standing army as the enforcer of treaties exacted by the Americans and transformed what had been an object of suspicion into a popular symbol of national greatness. Concurrently, confrontations with the European powers brought about a decisive reinterpretation of the reigning strategic doctrine in accordance with the famous Roman adage *Si vis pacem, para bellum* ("If you want peace, prepare for war"). Consequently, by the time Tocqueville and Beaumont landed, the American stance had shifted decisively toward greater engagement, and in relation to the external world the American state had harnessed sufficient capacity to become an actor to be reckoned with. However, circumstances made it possible to achieve this with minimal predatory pressure, so that in relation to American society the American state still ranked well below the European norm with regard to infrastructural and despotic power. This disjunction between the internal and external faces of the state remained the hallmark of the American regime throughout the long nineteenth century.[40]

Early in the first Washington administration, the Indians of the Northwest inflicted repeated defeats on American soldiers, drawn mostly from poorly trained militias. The culminating incident, the annihilation of a detachment under the command of Arthur St. Clair, territorial governor of the Northwest, in November 1791, "gave the Federalists the opportunity to overhaul the War Department and to create the regular standing army that many of them wanted."[41] This policy shift was quickly legitimized by the victory of the reorganized professional army under General Anthony Wayne at Fallen Timbers (in present-day Ohio) in 1794, which led to the cession of much of the Ohio territory to the United States and to the evacuation by Britain of its last posts on American territory. In the same vein, in 1811 the Indian confederacy organized by Tecumseh and his brother the Prophet was smashed by a mixed force of a thousand American army troops and Kentucky frontiersmen headed by the governor of the Indiana Territory, General William Henry Harrison.

Under the treaties with the defeated Indians, the federal government took on the obligation to protect them. Although, in the mid-1820s, President Monroe duly sent federal troops to protect the Cherokee land from intrusion, they were subsequently withdrawn by Andrew Jackson, who also refused to enforce Chief Justice Marshall's ruling on behalf of the Cherokees against the state of Georgia (1828). The military thus came to be envisioned as a one-sided instrument of white imperialism; and although the republican doctrine of war emphasized constraints imposed by the traditional *jus in bello* (laws of war), these checks were deliberately ignored in dealing with "uncivilized" peoples.[42] In 1838, for example, federal forces were deployed to herd fifteen thousand Cherokee families into detention camps prior to their deportation to Oklahoma.

Despite their determination to stay out of the global war that had first erupted in 1792, the Americans declared war on Great Britain in 1812, a decision which reflected a shift in their doctrinal stance and brought about a significant regime change. The decision to wield force in support of American policy was slow in coming, and American opinion was divided and confused. Desperate for advantage during the Napoleonic wars, after the breakdown of the Peace of Amiens (1803) both the English and the French assaulted neutral merchant shipping, including American vessels, which not only transported the country's own imports and exports but also engaged in a thriving carrying trade on behalf of the belligerents. However, Secretary of the Treasury Gallatin opposed expanding the navy, because he questioned the contribution of foreign commerce to the country's development, thinking that it made more sense to promote manufacture. Bereft of adequate means of defense, in 1807 the United States enacted an embargo, whereby

American ships were prohibited from traveling to foreign ports, and foreign ships from gathering any cargo in the United States. Designed to bring the French and the English to reason, the embargo prompted instead domestic economic hardship, political discontent, and an increase in smuggling.[43]

The embargo, vociferously opposed by the Federalist camp, called for enforcement by state militias and was challenged as an abuse of congressional powers. However, in 1808 the authority of the national government was upheld by a Federalist judge in a U.S. district court in Massachusetts.[44] Nevertheless, the embargo was repealed fourteen months after its inception. This humiliating retreat by the American government in turn created a profound crisis of confidence.

Even the ruling Republican camp was sharply divided. Where all agreed, in keeping with traditional doctrine, that war posed extreme dangers for the young republic, because it would raise taxes, increase executive prerogatives, and stimulate the passion for glory and distinction, some concluded that war should therefore be shunned altogether, whereas others — notably John Quincy Adams and Henry Clay, a leader of the "War Hawks" — interpreted the conflict with Britain as a trial of American virtue, a test of the republican citizen's capacity for disinterested support of the common good, the more welcome as the Republic was sinking into decay and corruption. By 1810 this crystallized into the notion that the Republic must absorb the shock of violent conflict to prove its worth.[45] Thus, although the policy debate was prompted by a modification of external circumstances that moved the United States away from the "isolated" pole, the shift toward greater engagement was but one alternative.

Matters came to a head in 1811 when the British blockaded the port of New York and stepped up their impressment of American seamen, while reputedly backing Tecumseh's resistance to American settlement. As war fever mounted, the embargo was renewed. Even as diplomatic negotiations were beginning to bear fruit, on June 1, 1812, President Madison called upon Congress for an immediate declaration of war. On the sixteenth, London made a major concession, but two days later, unaware of this development, Congress delared war on Great Britain.

Given an American force of only seven thousand troops, with hardly any experienced officers, the decision to go to war required a rapid enhancement of capacity. Although conscription was considered, in the end it was not resorted to. In 1814, however, Congress took the unprecedented step of authorizing the enlistment of young men aged eighteen to twenty-one without permission of their parent or master, a move which, in the context of the times, must be read as an unprecedented assertion of state authority.[46] Determined not to allow the war to inferfere with his economic policy, Gallatin undertook to meet ordinary expenditures from existing taxes, while paying for the war by special loans. But when the costs of the war exceeded revenue, the Republicans refused to raise taxes, and the country's financial institutions, largely controlled by Federalists, refused to lend the administration any money. Consequently, in 1813 the government issued huge sums in Treasury certificates, a move that shortly brought it to the edge of bankruptcy.

However, the war's successful outcome saved the day and vindicated the national leadership's doctrinal shift. Gallatin praised the war for strengthening nationalist sentiment, and hence consolidating the republic, and suggested that it "has laid the foundation of permanent taxes and military establishment, which [previously] the Republicans had deemed unfavorable to the happiness and free institutions of the country."[47] This is also the judgment of later historians: the war "overcame Republican parsimony and fear of standing forces" and contributed to establish the American "war myth" that security is necessary for the continuance of peace.[48]

Moreover, although the precipitous invasion of Canada by an inadequate American force immediately after the proclamation of war and the government-approved foray into Texas by a few hundred American volunteers in aid of revolts against Spanish authority were both abysmal failures, they reflected intimations of "Manifest Destiny."[49] These were further encouraged by Andrew Jackson's victory at New Orleans in 1815, which "riveted imaginations on the southwest and aroused further interest in the Floridas, and even Texas."[50]

In the wake of the Vienna settlement, Europe and the Atlantic world settled down to a century of peace, in the course of which the dynamics of state development were largely internal, with the singular exception of Germany, as already noted. Under these circumstances, the American state's potential capacity for mustering external power remained largely untapped. Meanwhile, as Tocqueville suggested, the American economic pie grew effortlessly in comparison with Europe's, thanks to the abundance of land and natural resources, fertilized by a large flow of British venture capital in the middle third of the nineteenth century, and a supply of labor growing rapidly through very high rate of natural reproduction and a steady stream of immigrants. Hence, although the United States economy might be categorized as "backward" in the Gerschenkron sense, this backwardness did not stimulate the same type of active state intervention as in central or eastern Europe.[51] The unusual combination of economic and strategic circumstances, involving a mix of interconnected internal and external factors, goes a long way toward explaining the development of a powerful capitalist economy without a strong state, and why liberal ideas — which in Britain itself were not incompatible with a modicum of "collectivism" — gave rise, when transplanted into American soil, to an ideology of extreme laissez-faire.

Given this pattern of development, when the protracted sectional conflict escalated, the national government was bereft of statist elements that might have the will or the capacity to play a mediating role between the adversaries.[52] The one national institution that might have played such a roll was the army, headed for two decades by Winfield Scott, another "great general," who after leading American forces into central Mexico in 1847 was nominated for the presidency five years later, again belying Tocqueville's facile generalization. However, Scott urged the government to accept the separation of North and South as an accomplished fact, and the secretary of war was himself a southerner, who unhesitatingly used his national position to aid his section. By default, responsibility for maintaining the integrity of the state fell to New York senator William Henry Seward, Lincoln's designated secretary of state. He proposed to launch a war against Spain and France over Santo Domingo and Mexico as a way of reuniting the nation, but his proposal was rejected by Lincoln, and he could do nothing to prevent the absorption of regional federal services and resources into the Confederacy.[53]

In the course of the war, both the Union and the Confederacy mobilized huge bodies of manpower to fight what is generally acknowledged as the first industrialized war, and faced the concomitant challenge of funding them. As in the war of 1812, the Union government sought to avoid painful direct extraction by suspending the domestic gold standard and conferring legal-tender status on paper greenbacks. However, this move was now coupled with the creation of a national bank that superseded locally chartered banks of issue, and the bank in turn permanently placed a large part of the national debt with finance capitalists. The net effect was the creation of a dependent financial class tied to the success of the central state's extraction and its fiscal policy more generally. As against this, the Confederacy had no option but to engage in extensive direct mobilization of resources, adumbrating a twentieth-century "garrison state" approach (see below). This contrast prevailed with regard to manpower as well. To begin with, the Union had a much larger eligible population base; the South was not only smaller, but a large part of its population consisted of black slaves. Athough the Union eventually established a draft, there were many exemptions and it was possible to buy one's way out of service; in the South, mobilization was much more strict and thorough.

In the course of the war both sections became more "statist," but the South did so to a higher degree than the North. However, this transformation was wiped out with the Confederacy itself; and by way of its financial policy, the Union in effect mortgaged radical Republican efforts to transform the South, which were antithetical to the interests of finance capitalists. Although leading members of the new Republican Party, notably William Seward, argued that the wartime state apparatus should be maintained and enlisted in the service of capitalist development, the new structures were in effect dismantled. The failure of Reconstruction left the United

States as "really two nations joined together by force of arms" and effectively ended further significant central state explansion for the remainder of the nineteenth century.[54] During the Progressive Era, the administrative capacity of the national state was considerably broadened, but the resulting apparatus continued to be characterized by a double decentralization, separation of powers and federalism, and the capture of key spheres of policy making by the organized interests concerned.[55]

Ascent to Global Power

In contrast with the formative path of other great powers, the rise of the United States to that status occurred with a minimum of strategic effort, largely as a by-product of continental expansion and economic growth. At the turn of the twentieth century, however, the inward-looking liberal democracy transformed itself quite abruptly into a far-flung empire, with outright colonial possessions in the Pacific, as well as in the Caribbean, its own *mare nostrum*, where it also established a de facto protectorate over a congeries of small independent states. Concurrently, the United States also attained a clearly dominant position in relation to Mexico. Bartholomew Sparrow has suggested that this turning point entailed "strategic adjustment," a lasting change in the ends and means of military force whereby the United States extended its foreign policy beyond a traditional conservatism to foster more proactively global conditions that served its interests.[57] Within the theoretical framework guiding the present analysis, this constituted a further shift toward the engagement pole.

However, the effects of this widening grasp were hardly visible from the heartland. America's ascent created little or no domestic strain, beyond occasional misgivings on the part of "conscience" intellectuals and minority politicians. This is because its unusual modalities did not require the central government to engage in extraordinary extractive efforts. In the new Athens, the major instrument of empire was the navy, which was developed into one of the mightiest in the world. As evidenced in the Netherlands and Britain, naval power did not pose the same problems for liberal states as did land forces. In contrast with armies as constituted at that time, a navy was a capital-intensive enterprise, consisting of a small but highly skilled labor force operating very expensive equipment and did not necessitate elaborate governmental arrangements. Moreover, while armies were of little use outside of war, navies had peacetime functions as well, for they were essential to the policing of commercial sealanes. And unlike armies, they provided little threat to the governments they served.[57] The navy developed its own professional infantry, the Marines, who were designed to operate only abroad and who came to incarnate more than any other institution the myth of American empire. Consequently, *naval* imperialism is perfectly compatible with the liberal commercial state; with but minor exceptions, it might even be considered a sine qua non for its successful emergence and maintenance. Overall, the importance of ships in the American strategic position "impelled the military to forge steadier, more continuous peacetime relationships with private industry" — an early version of the "military-industrial complex," or of what Aaron Friedberg has termed the "contract state."[58]

Given the known effects of World War I on the European belligerents, it might be expected to have resulted in a significant reinforcement of the state in America as well. It did not, and the fact that it did not poses interesting theoretical questions. Part of the explanation is that the conflict was much more limited for the United States than for most European countries, because it became involved only very late in the game. But this was itself the result of a policy choice; and once the decision was made to go to war, there were further choices to be made regarding the elaboration of strategic capability.[59]

In keeping with its established traditions, the United States initially inclined toward neutrality; there was no consensus on the causes of the war or on the rights and wrongs committed by the two sides. The business community generally inclined toward neutrality, as it meant they would be able to expand their markets abroad, which they indeed quickly began to do. The political class also favored neutrality, because it feared the potentially divisive effects of the conflict on domestic politics: Americans of German ancestry constituted the second largest ethnic group in the nation, and one which had preserved a distinct identity in much of the country, with the aid of supporting institutions (churches and bilingual parochial schools, and even some public schools in the Midwest). Moreoever, Americans of Irish descent, particularly prominent in the large urban political machines along the East Coast, were also opposed to U.S. involvement on the side of Britain. The Socialist Party, which mobilized an all-time high level of electoral support in the 1912 presidential election and gained a large following within the ranks of organized labor as well — about one-third of the American Federation of Labor membership — held fast to the antiwar position of the Second International, which its European counterparts relinquished when the war got under way.

In accordance with established American doctrine, Woodrow Wilson believed neutrality was not incompatible with defensive preparedness, but he experienced severe difficulties in securing even a limited form of military conscription and getting American industry to organize itself voluntarily for war production. Moreover, despite his concern with defense, Wilson himself shared in the traditional liberal distaste for military professionalism; reportedly, he threatened to dismiss the entire Army General Staff in 1915, after reports that they were preparing a plan of action in the event of war with Germany.[60]

But neutrality was difficult to maintain. As the war wore on, Great Britain grew increasingly dependent on American supplies. Germany could not allow its enemies to be supported in this manner by a neutral and therefore waged submarine warfare against American shipping, knowing that this would in turn probably bring the United States into the war. This was a risk the German leaders were willing to take, because they believed internal divisions within the United States and the structural factors that worked against strong government leadership would make American involvement ineffective. In the event, this proved a fatal miscalculation. Albeit reelected on a platform of neutrality in 1916, in 1917 Woodrow Wilson undertook to lead the United States in a crusade to "make the world safe for democracy," an objective that reflected the strategic adjustment noted earlier: "By asserting its rights not only to protect its own interests but to change the basic international structures that had presumably placed those interests under threat in the first place, the United States was seeking a new role for itself in international affairs, a role much closer to that of the sympathetic revolutionary state it had so often tried to be in nineteenth-century international politics."[61]

To acquire the capacity to pull this off, the United States had to transform itself into a military-industrial state. In the absence of presidential authority to exercise institutional leverage from above, achievement of this objective required the creation of a national consensus in support of the undertaking, so as to provide pressure from below. Ultimately, an industrial system was created for the purpose of waging war and placed under the command of a national administration with unprecedented powers, which, by the end of the conflict, "exercised extraordinary control over American industrial life."[62]

However, in the absence of a professional governmental bureaucracy, the key institution was a cadre of volunteer managers from the upper ranks of the industrial, banking, and financial sectors. A parallel approach was applied to the sphere of propaganda, recruiting journalists, publicists, and academics. Ultimately, however, the volunteer system failed, and in 1917 centralized administrative control was established by way of the powerful War Industries Board and related agencies. Concomitantly, on the financial side, the War Revenue Act of 1917 authorized a graduated income tax and raised other taxes; in effect, most of the cost of the war was to be borne by corporations and those with large incomes. But costs skyrocketed, and most of the war ended up being charged to future generations by way of government borrowing.

By fostering an enormous expansion of the American economy, both absolutely and relative to other industrial countries, World War I had the effect of propelling the United States to the vanguard of the international economy; and as a result of the crusade launched by Woodrow Wilson, the country found itself cast in the leading political role as well. This combination replicated the position that Britain occupied a century earlier, albeit now on a more global scale. Unlike Britain, however, the United States did not assume the mantle of leadership in either sphere but instead withdrew from the fray. Most obviously, Wilson's failure to obtain support within the United States itself for membership in the League of Nations contributed to keeping the world in an unstable state for another generation, leading inexorably to another and more destructive world war.

In Europe, the war had a "ratcheting effect" on state development. Decision making was centralized, and in order to harness material and human resources, governments everywhere expanded their activities and exercised greater control over various sectors of society.[63] But in the United States this occurred only to a limited extent, with the federal income tax as the war's major institutional legacy. Afterward, "The speed with which Congress dismantled the [governmental industrial] machine at the war's end, to the point of leaving Washington office workers to find money for their passage home when federal funds were abruptly cut off, suggests that national management was basically viewed as something temporary, even dangerous."[64] It was to be "normalcy" with a vengeance, punctuated by attempts to roll back history altogether.

Like earlier leading powers, the United States sought to buttress its position and reduce the transaction costs of coalition by endowing its camp with an aura of legitimacy. The experience of previous global wars suggests that this process tends to foster an interpenetration of internal and external conflicts, with a long-term shift from the religious alignments of the sixteenth and seventeenth centuries to the ideological ones of the end of the eighteenth. In 1917 the United States undertook to make the world safe for democracy; but when events in Russia confirmed their recent experience with Mexico, the American leadership came to identify revolution, rather than traditional autocracy, as the major threat to democracy.[65] Major elements of the reactionary wave included the persecution of political radicals, the imposition on American society of the moralistic norms of traditional Protestantism (through Prohibition), and the enactment of immigration laws that sought to reestablish America's "Anglo-Saxon" character by stemming the tide from southern and eastern Europe, as well as Asia. The American Socialist movement, which maintained its antiwar stance even after 1917, was especially vulnerable to charges of unpatriotic behavior, and never recovered from the blow.

Yet withdrawal from the world was impossible, because the United States had become the world's banker, and conversely, its own economy was inexorably affected by conditions abroad. It is now widely recognized that the reluctance of the United States to take over the British leadership role in the global financial market aggravated the Great Depression, which in turn contributed to the collapse of liberal regimes in much of Europe.[66] By the time of Hoover's election in 1928, the inability to devise a solution to the economic problems caused by international debts and reparations acted as a major constraint on the ability of the new administration to deal with domestic issues. Karl Polanyi's observation that in the interwar period every single internal crisis within Europe was either triggered or exacerbated by some external economic problem is thus applicable to the United States as well, as Peter Gourevitch has demonstrated.[67]

Observing ongoing developments in Germany and Japan, Harold Lasswell suggested as early as 1937 that mid–twentieth-century war required an unprecedented degree of material, organizational, and human mobilization on the part of the belligerents, and that the resulting dynamics would bring about a new type of political regime, the "garrison state."[68] It is noteworthy that Lasswell's "developmental model" bridged the theoretical gap between the analysis of domestic and international politics institutionalized in the course of political science's development as a profession. In short, he foresaw a vast enhancement of both infrastructural and despotic power — notably, a severe restriction of civil liberties and political dissent; the rise of populist warlord-politicians; a shift of the decision-making center from business and political elites to "specialists on violence" and in the molding of minds (i.e., propaganda, by way of mass media); and the elaboration of central planning.

The political-leader-as-warlord role indeed prevailed on both sides of the conflict: World War II was fought by Hitler, Mussolini, and Hiro-Hito against Stalin, Churchill, Roosevelt, Chiang Kai-shek, and de Gaulle. Lasswell's developmental model proved largely valid for Germany, Japan, and the Soviet Union. It had only limited applicability to Great Britain and the United States; but American engagement, coming on top of the New Deal, in the course of which politics had already begun to undergo a profound nationalization, did foster a vast expansion of the national government, both in absolute size and in relation to that state and local levels. The presidency too swelled: its incumbent came to personify the country as no man had ever done before. In keeping with Lasswell's analysis, the national government also developed an unprecedented apparatus of internal propaganda designed to manufacture consent and consensus and engaged in egregious violations of civil rights in the name of national security, notably the forced relocation and incarceration of nearly the entire West Coast population of Japanese descent.

In the aftermath of World War I, private industry had withdrawn almost entirely from the military sector, so that on the eve of the new conflict, "the United States had almost no capacity for the manufacture of arms" beyond what was available in a small string of government arsenals.[69] When the time came to rearm, President Roosevelt followed the advice of Henry Stimson: "if you are going to try to go to war, or to prepare for war, in a capitalist country, you have got to let business make money out of the process or business won't work."[70] By and large, this was indeed how things worked out. It should be noted, however, that this reliance on the private sector does not completely invalidate the Lasswellian model, which is concerned mainly with *political* transformation. Indeed, as has been well documented, the Nazis adopted a very similar approach to arms production and never developed a plan. The leading instance of governmental production and full-scale planning was, of course, the Soviet Union, but this development was not attributable mainly to the advent of the "garrison state."

The National Security State and the Imperial Presidency

In the years following the second World War, as in those following the first, there were traditional forces — including political progressives as well as conservatives — that feared the consequences of America's imperial role and sought to pull back. But these were much weaker than before, and with the onset of the Cold War the conservatives rallied around the flag, as did most of the progressives. Those who did not were driven from the political scene altogether as disloyal. However, the imperial transformation did not affect the components of the political process most grounded in American society, that is, parties and interest groups. The paradoxical result was an enormously reinforced "imperial presidency" severely constrained in its actions by "interest group liberalism."[71] This combination constituted an institutional oxymoron whose contradictions provided a major theme of debates within American political science after World War II. Although the transformations induced by engagement in the Cold War fell far short of the "garrison state" anticipated by Lasswell, some of its elements are clearly recognizable in the American state of that era and highly disturbing when evaluated from the perspective of liberal norms.[72]

Because the imperial presidency was engendered by America's new global role, successive presidents were driven to assume the awesome responsibilities of "leader of the free world," regardless of party, ideological orientation, or personal inclination. From this vantage point, residual institutions that were the product of a domestically oriented political development often appeared as impediments to the fulfillment of urgent obligations. The resulting situation has been aptly summarized as follows:

> The war had given the United States such an overabundance of economic and military power that no lasting postwar settlement was possible without the active participation and support of the U.S.A. The great midcentury conflict created in Washington a governmental machine whose members grasped this fact, and were

prepared to go beyond public opinion in order to find the means through which a system of economic and political stability could be established in at least most of the world. But the public never understood the international underpinnings of its own economic miracle, and failed to be touched by the magic wand of imperial delight which would have made it enthusiastic about the establishment of the *pax Americana*.[73]

Once again, the external situation should not be considered as a determinative "given" in relation to these developments; interpretations of the postwar world by the Washington establishment and the actions that flowed from them played an important part in shaping global realities as well. Since this proposition now appears obvious and unexceptionable, it is noteworthy that it was not widely accepted at the time, and that the denial itself had awesome consequences. As George Kennan observed with respect to the Korean War, for example, "the idea that in doing things disagreeable to our interests the Russians might be reacting to features of our own behavior — was one to which the mind of official Washington would always be strangely resistant. Our adversaries, in the ingrained American way of looking at things, had always to be demonic, monstrous, incalculable, and inscrutable. It was unthinkable that we, by admitting that they sometimes reacted to what we did, should confess to a share in the responsibility for their behavior."[74]

A full elucidation of this point would require a thorough discussion of the origins of the Cold War, which remains one of the most complex historiographic puzzles of the twentieth century. For present purposes, it suffices to sketch the main components of the nascent American orientation. Ironically, the reigning outlooks of the leadership groups of the two emerging superpowers were almost the opposite of what a naive social scientist might expect on the basis of "ideology," for it was the Americans who were the more consistently "materialist" of the two. From the Soviet vantage point, recent experiences demonstrated the primacy of strategic power, determined by geopolitics; by contrast, American political leaders were persuaded, on the basis of analyses developed by the financial community, with the aid of the prestigious New York Council on Foreign Relations, the destabilization of Europe and the outbreak of World War II were largely attributable to international economic conditions.[75] Accordingly, it was imperative for the United States to take the lead in creating global planning and stabilization structures that would prevent a recurrence of depression and war. While committed to military preparedness, with the United States benefiting from a monopoly of atomic weapons and producing almost half the world's goods, "American officials keenly appreciated the leverage that U.S. economic power afforded them, and the lack of any immediate military threat to U.S. security encouraged a reliance upon economic power as the principal instrument of diplomacy."[76] An economic approach, which was in keeping with the argument set forth by Polanyi in 1944, was more compatible with conventional liberal preferences than a strategic one, and also suited the interests of the business community. The determinacy of economic conditions came to be reflected as well in the core hypotheses of postwar comparative politics and political sociology.[77] One of the major developments of the postwar period, still awaiting full analysis, was the rallying of organized labor to this orientation as well. Labor modified its domestic strategies and objectives accordingly, and thereby rendered itself dependent on the establishment and maintenance of American global hegemony.[78]

The American approach was expressed in the institutionalization of the "Bretton Woods" system and also underlay the Marshall Plan. Predicated on the notion that "Communist political penetration of war-disrupted societies posed greater danger to Western security than did Communist military aggression," the Marshall Plan was designed in part as a *substitute* for the rearmament of Western Europe and a permanent U.S. military presence there.[79] Although the formation of NATO would appear to contradict this economistic stance, it should be remembered that the major impetus for NATO came from the Europeans themselves. Some in Congress advocated a security alliance with Western Europe as early as 1947, and in that same year the Greek civil war prompted the enunciation of the Truman Doctrine; but there was hardly a consensus in Washington on the subject. The first step toward the formation of what emerged as NATO was an explicit mutual defense agreement between France and England in March 1947 (Treaty of Dunkirk), ostensibly directed against Germany, but in reality preparatory to French acceptance of a German revival as the sine qua non of an effective anti-Soviet policy.[80] NATO was in part the price the United States had to pay to France for German reconstruction and rearmament. In March 1948 the alliance was extended to include the three Benelux countries as well, and together the five then sought a guarantee from the United States. Galvanized by the Prague coup of the previous February, official Washington was now ready to acquiesce.

The coup also prompted the drafting of the famous "NSC 68," in which the recently created National Security Council called for a worldwide counteroffensive against the Soviet bloc. Although this marked the onset of a new and much more proactive orientation, the fiscal conservatism of the Truman administration foreclosed increased expenditures on military budgets, and most of America's eggs thus remained in the economic basket. The Korean War was the true watershed; interpreted as an unprovoked and sinister communist aggression, as Kennan charged, it appeared to refute the central concept of economic containment and left no choice but an urgent and bold implementation of the NSC doctrine.

This was a distinct "strategic adjustment," which constituted a fateful turning point in American political development as well. Roosevelt's undisputed authority as commander in chief in World War II "gave Americans in the postwar years an exalted conception of presidential power." Moreover, "War had accustomed those in charge of foreign policy to a complacent faith in the superior intelligence and disinterestedness of the executive branch" in contrast with Congress, which remained mired in "politics."[81] After Roosevelt's death, Congress attempted to rectify the balance, but Harry Truman, although he himself emerged from the ranks of the Senate, contributed decisively to shift the balance permanently to the presidential side through his leadership role during the Korean conflict.

The key theorist of presidential power was Dean Acheson. Both the president and his secretary of state saw the invasion of South Korea by the North Korean Army as a crucial challenge to the postwar structure promoted by Bretton Woods and the Marshall Plan. Their first resort was to the United Nations; and on June 25, after obtaining Security Council action, Truman consulted his foreign policy and defense officials and decided to commit American air and sea forces. Not until two days later did he meet with congressional leaders from both parties. He received their support, but when he announced the decision publicly, he cited the action as his authorization, not the assent of Congress. However, over the next several days, congressional concern over the *form* of the decision grew, and pressure mounted to have the president request a joint resolution approving his actions, with full assurance that he would get it. But on July 3, Dean Acheson "recommended that Truman *not* ask for a resolution but instead rely on his constitutional powers as President and Commander in Chief"; the State Department cited many instances in which presidents had sent American forces into combat on their own initiative, and Truman, "impressed by the appearance of precedent and concerned not to squander the power of his office, accepted his Secretary of State's recommendation."[82] Although initially excluded, Congress subsequently confirmed and in effect ratified the intervention by voting military appropriations and extending the draft.

"[T]he capture by the Presidency of the most vital of national decisions, the decision to go to war," has been identified by Arthur Schlesinger as the key process in the rise of the "national security state," which in turn stimulated broad transformational effects. Truman's crucial contribution establishes that the process cannot be attributed simply to one political party, to conservative ideology, or to the effects of one president's neurotic personality, as would be suggested later on with regard to Richard Nixon. Rather, it is the result of a transformation of America's role in world affairs, at a time when the nature of that world itself was drastically changing. Concurrently, the question of "loyalty" moved to the fore in political debates, spilling well beyond external policy to the very core of domestic concerns in every sphere, from labor unions to universities.[83] Although the second episode of the twentieth century's protracted global war had involved a struggle against counterrevolutionary Germany, the crusade against revolution remained a dominant theme of American foreign policy and injected issues of national security into domestic debates over the extension of democracy to the social sphere. The crusade against revolution abroad thereby provided additional legitimacy for the repression of socialism in America. Beyond the injustice to the individuals involved, the elimination of the American left from the political arena and the intimidation of "liberals" had a lasting effect on American political culture and further limited the likely scope of the American welfare state.

The process proved to be self-reinforcing: the Korean outcome established a "path dependency" that rendered the Indochina War, Watergate, and Irangate more likely. A full examination of this process in all its ramifications, which extend well beyond political institutions into the economic and cultural spheres, still remains to be carried out. Meanwhile, however, the general validity of the proposition set forth here concerning the impact of global leadership on the transformation of basic American political structures has been confirmed by ongoing developments. As Theodore Draper pointed out in the bicentennial year of the Constitution, the activities of "Reagan's Junta" were not merely an accident but a renewed manifestation of "the American problem of being a superpower and a democracy."[84]

Conclusion

America's predicament in the twentieth century is unprecedented, and one of the ironies of the age is that it arose precisely at the moment when the European states' decline to the status of minor powers freed them from the imperatives of engagement-driven statism and allowed for greater responsiveness to societal considerations. The assumption by the United States of the mantle of global strategic and economic leadership five decades ago fostered a deep tension between the dictates of national security and the operations of the liberal democratic regime. However, two sharply contending definitions of the problem have emerged. From one perspective, reflected here, assumption of the superpower role has corrupted liberal democracy by generating an obsessive concern with national security. This led to the suppression of dissent from the left, which entailed a further weakening of the already weak voice of the American working class in the postwar period, as well as to the emergence of an "imperial presidency" that tends to escape accountability. But from another perspective, it is liberal democracy that loomed as the problem, hampering the American state from meeting its vital responsibilities as the guarantor of global freedom.

The latter perspective is at the root of the neoconservative intellectual movement. Within American political science, for example, at the very time the "pluralist" school was establishing its hegemony in the 1950s, Samuel Huntington drew the conclusion that "The requisite for military security is a shift in basic American values from liberalism to conservatism."[85] This view was widely propagated after Vietnam. In the early 1980s, it approached hegemony as neoconservatives within the academy and elsewhere successfully advocated "realistic" foreign and defense policies to meet a "clear and present danger." They further insisted that their execution required a fundamental reordering of American priorities.[86]

Reversing the question, those committed to democratic liberalism must ask what international objectives are appropriate for a democracy that is cast in the role of a great power. Rousseau argued that those who are preoccupied with security and defense regard government as merely an *object* threatened by others. This passive view is compounded by the presentation of these concerns as a matter of *necessity* ("we are forced to give over to our defense. . ."). In reality, however, governments are also *subjects* in the international system, and their international activities deflect from "the attention that should be devoted to enforcing the law" and "perfecting the government itself." The very activities of states contribute to the determination of the security problems they face. It follows that the question of what foreign and defense policies are appropriate for a liberal democracy is an ineluctable one for citizens and for normative theorists. At no time since the collapse of the "century of peace" has the moment been more opportune to restore it to our agenda.

Notes

The ideas of this paper were initially developed within the framework of the Project on Global Leadership and U.S. Democracy organized at the New School for Social Research with support from the MacArthur Foundation (Spring 1989) and at a session of the Conference Group on Political Economy organized by Richard Vallely at the annual meeting of the American Political Science Association (August 1989). I have also benefited from comments by participants in earlier sessions of the workshop on International Influences on American Politics. Specific suggestions by Alberta Sparaglia, Robert Latham, Bartholomew Sparrow, and Triadafilos Triadafilopoulos have been most helpful. In the intervening period since I began work on this subject, Daniel H. Deudney covered some of the same ground from a somewhat different perspective in "The Philadelphian System: Sovereignty, Arms Control, and Balance of Power in the American States-Union, circa 1787–1861," *International Organization* 49, no. 2 (Spring 1995): 191–228. I am grateful to John Ikenberry for bringing Deudney's work to my attention.

1. The most influential interpretation is that of Louis Hartz. See his *The Founding of New Societies: Studies in the History of the United States, Latin America, South*

Africa, Canada, and Australia (New York: Harcourt, Brace & World, 1964), 69-122. See also Samuel N. Huntington, "Political Modernization: America vs. Europe," *World Politics* 18, no. 2 (1966).

2 Alexis de Tocqueville, *De la démocratie en Amérique*, (Paris: Gallimard, 1961), 1:290 (my translation).

3. Reginald C. Stuart, *War and American Thought from the Revolution to the Monroe Doctrine* (Kent, Ohio: Kent State University Press, 1982), 188.

4. Grace G. Roosevelt, *Reading Rousseau in the Nuclear Age. With full translations of Jean-Jacques Rousseau's "État de guerre" and of his "Extrait" and "Jugement" of the Abbé de Saint-Pierre's Projet de paix perpétuelle* (Philadelphia: Temple University Press, 1990), 200.

5. Roosevelt, *Reading Rousseau*, 11–12. However, there is also a considerable body of writing by Kant in the same tradition.

6. The single most important text was Tilly's "Reflections on the History of European State-Making," in Charles Tilly, ed., *The Formation of National States in Western Europe* (Princeton: Princeton University Press, 1975). Although the volume also contains a lengthy essay on the subject by Samuel Finer, this had nowhere the same impact.

7. The seminal work is "The Formation of States and Constitutional Development: A Study in History and Politics," in *The Historical Essays of Otto Hintze*, ed. Felix Gilbert (New York: Oxford University Press, 1975), 157–77.

8. See, for example, Aristide R. Zolberg, "Strategic Interactions and the Formation of Modern States: France and England," in *The State in Global Perspective*, ed. Ali Kazancigil (London: Gower/UNESCO, 1986), 72–106 (originally published in *International Social Science Journal*, 1980); Michael Mann, *The Sources of Social Power*, 2 vols. (Cambridge: Cambridge University Press, 1986, 1993); Margaret Levi, *Of Rulers and Revenue* (Berkeley: University of California Press, 1988); Karen A. Rasler and William R. Thompson, "War Making and State Making: Governmental Expenditures, Tax Revenues, and Global Wars," *American Political Science Review* 75 (1985): 491–507.

9. I have attempted a preliminary synthesis for political analysis in Aristide R. Zolberg, "Beyond the Nation-State: Comparative Politics in Global Perspective," in *Beyond Progress and Development*, ed. Jan Berting, Wim Blockmans, and U. Rosenthal (Aldershot, U.K.: Avebury/Gower, 1987), 42–69.

10. Otto Hintze, "Military Organization and the Organization of the State," in *The Historical Essays of Otto Hintze*, ed. Felix Gilbert (New York: Oxford University Press, 1975), 178–215.

11. For an elaboration of this point, see Zolberg, "Strategic Interactions." A seminal work in the classical tradition is Edward Whiting Fox, *History in Geographic Perspective: The Other France* (New York: Norton, 1971). An interesting application to international relations theory is Richard Rosecrance, *The Rise of the Trading State* (New York: Basic Books, 1986).

12. Karen A. Rasler and William R. Thompson, "War Making and State Making: Governmental Expenditures, Tax Revenues, and Global Wars," *American Political Science Review* 75 (1985): 491–507.

13. As noted, in "The Formation of States." Hintze argues that the need to secure resources for war contributed to the formation of a representative estates system.

However, it is evident that the destruction of these institutions during the absolutist period was also attributable to the needs of war. In "Military Organization" he seeks to resolve this problem by suggesting that the fiscal pressures induced by war nevertheless set the stage for the reemergence of constitutional government in a subsequent period. For a more systematic and satisfying recent account, see Brian Downing, *The Military Revolution and Political Change: Origins of Democracy and Autocracy in Early Modern Europe* (Princeton: Princeton University Press, 1992).

14. See, for example, Aaron L. Friedberg, "Why Didn't the United States Become a Garrison State?" *International Security* 16, no. 4 (Spring 1992): 109–42.

15. For a French perspective, see Bertrand Badie and Pierre Birnbaum, *The Sociology of the State* (Chicago: University of Chicago Press, 1983); for an American one, Samuel P. Huntington, *Political Order in Changing Societies* (New Haven: Yale University Press, 1968).

16. Rasler and Thompson, "War Making and State Making," 495, n. 4.

17. Ibid., 501.

18. Aristide R. Zolberg, "Belgium," in *Crises of Development in Western Europe and the United States*, ed. Raymond Grew (Princeton: Princeton University Press, 1978), 99–138.

19. Deudney (193) suggests that Tocqueville (as well as Hegel) "doubted the American Union was a state" in the contemporaneous European sense of the term, which presumed a greater degree of hierarchy. Although he seeks to resolve the categoric problem by coining the term "real-state" for the European variety, the literature on the sociology of the state offers less awkward solutions that emphasize variation in structural properties. See the seminal article by J. P. Nettl, "The State as a Conceptual Variable," *World Politics* 20, no. 4 (1968): 559–92; and Michael Mann, "The Autonomous Power of the State: Its Origins, Mechanisms and Results," *Archives Européennes de Sociologie* 25 (1984): 185–213.

20. Karl Polanyi, *The Great Transformation: The Political and Economic Origins of Our Time* (Boston: Beacon Press, 1957 [1944]).

21. For general historical background, I am relying on Bernard Bailyn, Robert Dallek, David Brion Davis, David Herbert Donald, John L. Thomas, and Gordon S. Wood, *The Great Republic: A History of the American People*, 4th ed. (Lexington, Mass.: D. C. Heath, 1992).

22. Reginald C. Stuart, *War and American Thought from the Revolution to the Monroe Doctrine* (Kent, Ohio: Kent State University Press, 1982). Although Stuart correctly asserts that by 1793, "a new age of ideological war had arrived for Europeans" (5), he neglects to indicate that adherence to *jus ad bellum* was in effect reinstated by the powers in 1815 and prevailed for another century.

23. This section is largely based on Stuart, *War and American Thought*, 33–65.

24. Alexander Hamilton, James Madison, and John Jay, *The Federalist Papers* (New York: Mentor Books, 1961 [1788]).

25. *Federalist Papers*, 73.

26. Francis Paul Prucha, *The Sword of the Republic: The United States Army on the Frontier, 1783–1846* (Toronto: Macmillan, 1969), 6.

27. Richard Ullman, "The 'Foreign World' and Ourselves," *Foreign Policy* 7, no. 2 (1976): 100; Lawrence S. Kaplan, *Entangling Alliances with None: American Foreign Policy in the Age of Jefferson* (Kent, Ohio: Kent State University Press, 1987).

28. Ullman, "'Foreign World' and Ourselves," 102.

29. Seymour Martin Lipset, *The First New Nation* (New York: Norton, 1979), 66.

30. James Roger Sharp, *American Politics in the Early Republic: The New Nation in Crisis* (New Haven: Yale University Press, 1993), 70.

31. James Morton Smith, *Freedom's Fetters: The Alien and Sedition Laws and American Civil Liberties* (Ithaca: Cornell University Press, 1956).

32. Samuel N. Huntington, *The Soldier and the State* (Cambridge: Harvard University Press, 1957), 144.

33. Hajo Holborn, *A History of Modern Germany, 1840–1945* (New York: Knopf, 1969), 139–62; Gordon A. Craig, *Germany 1866–1945* (New York: Oxford University Press, 1978).

34. Huntington, *The Soldier and the State*, 168.

35. Ibid., 145.

36. *Federalist Papers*, 160.

37. Once again, my interpretation parallels that of Deudney.

38. Huntington, *The Soldier and the State*, 178.

39. George Liska, *Career of Empire: American and Imperial Expansion over Land and Sea* (Baltimore: Johns Hopkins University Press, 1978), 338.

40. The notion of "internal" and "external" faces is from J. P. Nettl, "The State as a Conceptual Variable," *World Politics* 20, no. 4 (1968): 559–92.

41. Bailyn et al., *The Great Republic*, 321.

42. Stuart, *War and American Thought*, 141.

43. This historical account is largely based on Steven Watts, *The Republic Reborn: War and the Making of Liberal America, 1790–1820* (Baltimore: Johns Hopkins University Press, 1987). Although I am limiting myself to the theme of engagement, Watts sees the war as fostering a transition from republican traditions toward modern liberal capitalism, involving the consolidation of the market economy and society, liberal political structure and ideology, and a bourgeois culture of self-controlled individualism.

44. Richard B. Morris, ed., *Encyclopedia of American History* (New York: Harper & Row, 1976), 164.

45. This is the sense in which Watts writes of "the Republic reborn."

46. Watts, *The Republic Reborn*, 291.

47. Cited in Watts, *The Republic Reborn*, 317.

48. Reginald C. Stuart, *War and American Thought from the Revolution to the Monroe Doctrine* (Kent, Ohio: Kent State University Press, 1982), 147.

49. Stuart, *War and American Thought*, 112.

50. Ibid., 149.

51. Alexander Gerschenkron, *Economic Backwardness in Historical Perspective* (Cambridge: Harvard University Press, 1962).

52. My discussion of the Civil War is based on Richard Franklin Bensel, *Yankee Leviathan: The Origins of Central State Authority in America, 1859–1877* (Cambridge: Cambridge University Press, 1990).

53. For Seward's proposal, see Bensel, *Yankee Leviathan*, 12, n. 18.

54. Ibid., 14, 425.

55. Morton Keller, *Affairs of State* (Cambridge: Harvard University Press, 1977);

Stephen Skowronek, *Building the New American State* (Cambridge: Cambridge University Press, 1982).

56. Bartholomew H. Sparrow, "Strategic Adjustment and the American Navy: The 1890s, the Press, and the 1990s" (Paper presented at the Workshop on Strategic Adjustment, Joint Center for International and Security Studies, Monterey, Calif., February 10–11, 1995).

57. The latter point was brought to my attention by Bartholomew Sparrow.

58. Friedberg, "Garrison State," 137.

59. Barry Karl, *The Uneasy State: The United States from 1915 to 1945* (Chicago: University of Chicago Press, 1983), 34–49.

60. Harry Howe Ransom, *Can American Democracy Survive the Cold War?* (Garden City, N.J.: Doubleday, 1963), 15.

61. Karl, *The Uneasy State*, 38.

62. Ibid., 39.

63. Rasler and Thompson, "War Making and State Making."

64. Karl, *The Uneasy State*, 46.

65. Lloyd Gardner, *A Convenant with Power: America and World Order from Wilson to Reagan* (New York: Oxford University Press, 1984).

66. Charles P. Kindleberger, *The World in Depression, 1929–1939* (Berkeley: University of California Press, 1973), 291–308.

67. Polanyi, *The Great Transformation*, 228–29; Peter A. Gourevitch, *Politics in Hard Times: Comparative Responses to International Economic Crises* (Ithaca: Cornell University Press, 1986).

68. Harold D. Lasswell, "Sino-Japanese Crisis: The Garrison State versus the Civilian State," *China Quarterly* II (Fall 1937): 643–49. A more fully developed version appeared as "The Garrison State," *American Journal of Sociology* 46, no. 4 (1941): 455–68.

69. Friedberg, "Garrison State," 137.

70. Ibid., 138.

71. Arthur Schlesinger Jr., *The Imperial Presidency* (Boston: Houghton Mifflin, 1973); Theodore Lowi, *The End of Liberalism*, 2nd ed. (New York: Norton, 1979).

72. My emphasis on the political sphere proper differs considerably from Aaron Friedberg's concerns. While agreeing with his contention that what emerged in the United States in the course of the Cold War is more aptly termed a "contract state," and that this was superior to the Soviet approach, I believe that engagement in the Cold War generated significant and, in my view, undesirable and unnecessary political changes, and that these to a significant degree could be dismantled, if not reversed.

73. Bradley F. Smith, *The War's Long Shadow: The Second World War and Its Aftermath* (New York: Simon & Schuster, 1986), 166–67.

74. George F. Kennan, *Memoirs 1925–1950* (Boston: Little, Brown, 1967), 498.

75. See, for example, Friedberg, "Garrison State," 118, 119–120.

76. Robert A. Pollard, *Economic Security and the Origins of the Cold War, 1945–1950* (New York: Columbia University Press, 1985), 2.

77. The notion that economic development was a necessary and perhaps sufficient condition for democracy was set forth by Seymour Martin Lipset, notably in

"Some Social Requirements of Democracy: Economic Development and Political Legitimacy," *American Political Science Review* 53, no. 1 (1959): 69–105 (reprinted in his *Political Man: The Social Bases of Politics* (Garden City, N.Y.: Doubleday, 1963).). Another influential work was Walter W. Rostow, *The Stages of Economic Growth: A Non-Communist Manifesto* (Cambridge: Cambridge University Press, 1960).

78. I owe this point to Ira Katznelson, who is carrying on further research along these lines in his work on postwar liberalism.

79. Pollard, *Economic Security*, 223.

80. Anton W. DePorte, *Europe between the Superpowers: The Enduring Balance* (New Haven: Yale University Press, 1979), 138.

81. Schlesinger, *The Imperial Presidency*, 123.

82. Ibid., 132–33.

83. I cannot do justice to this vast subject here. For an overall view, see the appropriate chronological section in Robert Justin Goldstein, *Political Repression in Modern America, from 1870 to the Present* (Cambridge, Mass.: Shenkman, 1978). Important works on the early Cold War period include Edward Shils, *The Torment of Secrecy: The Background and Consequences of American Security Policies* (Glencoe, Ill.: Free Press, 1956); Victor S. Navasky, *Naming Names* (New York: Penguin, 1981); Ellen Schrecker, *The Age of McCarthyism: A Brief History with Documents* (Boston: St. Martin's Press, Bedford Books, 1994).

84. Theodore Draper, "The Fall of an American Junta," *New York Review of Books*, October 22, 1987, 45–58.

85. Huntington, *The Soldier and the State*, 457.

86. Norman Podhoretz, *The Present Danger* (New York: Simon & Schuster, 1980); Samuel N. Huntington, *American Politics: The Promise of Disharmony* (Cambridge: Harvard University Press, 1981).

Part II ———————————————————

AMERICA IN THE ANTEBELLUM WORLD

Three

International Commitments and American Political Institutions in the Nineteenth Century

ROBERT O. KEOHANE

IN HIS INTRODUCTION to this volume, Ira Katznelson laments that in the literature on American political development the role of international influences "remains remarkably unprobed." To a student of international relations, such inattention to international factors seems like the scholarly equivalent of Wall Street sharks leaving "money on the table" in their bargaining. Students of international relations have been acutely aware for twenty years of how Kenneth Waltz's "second image" — the role of the state and society in shaping foreign policy — could be "reversed."[1] This volume seeks to develop and deepen our understanding of the impact on American political development of the structure of world politics and international events.

The concern of this volume is with the state, and Katznelson's introduction focuses on J. P. Nettl's discussion of the state as a "conceptual variable." For a student of international and transnational relations, however, Nettl's treatment of the state in its external relations is anachronistic. Referring to sovereignty, he declares that "for almost all intents and purposes, the state acts for the society internationally and internal affairs relating to foreign affairs are a state prerogative."[2] That statement was not true for most states even when Nettl wrote it.[3] It is even less true now. Transnational relations are extensive, meaning that nonstate actors — firms, nongovernmental organizations, networks of individuals and groups — operate extensively across state borders.[4] Nettl invokes the concept of an ideal-typical sovereign state. No such state exists, and few states even approximate this ideal type.

Nettl sees the state as a "gatekeeper" between the insulated compartments of domestic and foreign affairs. It is more appropriate now — and has been for several decades — to view the state as an organization seeking to manage complex interdependence rather than serving as a "gatekeeper." The modern state seeks to affect the terms of its engagement with world markets and the economic, social, and political networks in which it is enmeshed, rather than simply to control flows through channels controlled by "gates." These channels have long since been submerged by the sheer

volume of goods, people, money and, most of all, ideas that they were originally intended to constrain. Indeed, twenty-four-hour markets and the huge
availability of information in cyberspace transcend the image of flows across
borders. Individuals have continual access to global markets and the Worldwide Web, and it is increasingly difficult to say where in physical space
those markets, and the web, exist.

Many have come to recognize this profound change in world politics.[5]
But all too often, we stereotype the past in the terms that we reject for the
present. We "invent the past" by inserting into it our construction of the
modern state: Nettl's gatekeeper, standing guard between the ordered internal life of the society and the disorder outside. The period between 1648
and 1948, or later, is seen as the "Westphalian Era" in world politics, in
which sovereignty really meant that states possessed internal supremacy and
external independence.[6]

This chapter explores whether the United States in the nineteenth century was an effective "gatekeeper," in Nettl's phrase. I undertake this exploration through a particular "lens," that of American foreign policy commitments. Frequently during its early history, and occasionally later in the
nineteenth century, the United States undertook to make treaty commitments that upset some of its own citizens. When these commitments were
challenged, political struggles ensued that help to reveal the strengths and
weaknesses of the national state — whose leaders had either made the commitments themselves or had reputational incentives to seek to fulfill them. I
explore some of these episodes as a window through which we can see the
American state, if not more clearly, at least from a new angle.

In international politics, no world government exists to enunciate binding
rules, adjudicate their application, or enforce them on recalcitrant states.
State sovereignty means that states can renege on their commitments, since
no more inclusive government exercises enforcement powers over them.
One dimension of this problem, discussed briefly in the second section of
the chapter, is deliberate breach: government's decision not to fulfill states
treaty commitments. The principal focus of this chapter, however, is *commitment incapacity*: the inability of the institutions of weak states — such as
the antebellum United States — to implement actions necessary to fulfill
treaty commitments.

During the first decades of its history, the central government of the
United States, although responsible for carrying out its foreign obligations,
was quite weak not only with respect to its potential enemies but also toward
its own population, who considered themselves citizens of their respective
states as much as citizens of the nation as a whole. The government was not
always able to obtain sufficient obedience to implement its international
obligations. That is, the institutions of the antebellum state often suffered
from commitment incapacity.

The contrast between the antebellum and postbellum American states is dramatic. By the 1880s, the United States was capable of serving as a "gate-keeper," for better or worse, between domestic and transnational society. This institutional change did not prevent the United States from reneging on its international commitments — as we shall see, it flagrantly reneged on immigration treaties with China. Nonetheless, after the Civil War the United States had the capacity to maintain its international commitments, even if it did not always choose to do so.

The difference between the antebellum and postbellum state reflected, of course, the impact of the American Civil War. This chapter treats the impact of the Civil War as exogenous to the story being told here; that is, the war had a major effect on how international commitments were treated but is not itself explained by the previous behavior of the United States toward its international commitments. Hence much of the massive difference in institutional capacity between the antebellum and postbellum eras cannot be explained by international relations.

During the antebellum period itself, the United States experienced substantial institutional change. Between the Treaty of Peace with Great Britain in 1783 and the onset of the Civil War in 1861, the United States acquired greater effective internal sovereignty, that is, the ability to control events within its own borders and on its frontiers. Gradually, the problem of commitment incapacity became less important, and incidents in which the United States could not fulfill its commitments, less dangerous and less frequent. Even though many institutional changes were exogenous, resulting from economic and demographic growth, some of them were endogenous to the commitment problem. That is, the American state sometimes responded to its inability to fulfill commitments by constructing institutions that could do so more effectively. From the formation of the Constitution onward, American nationalists sought to strengthen American political institutions in order to strengthen the state's ability to conduct foreign relations.

In the first section of the chapter, I describe five episodes before the Civil War in which institutions of the U.S. state were unable, at least for a time, to implement international commitments that the United States had undertaken. I am deliberately selecting cases of weakness, since I am engaging here in descriptive inference.[7] That is, I am describing weakness (as revealed by these episodes), not seeking to explain variation in it. My purpose is to show that U.S. institutions were sufficiently weak during this period of time that they were, on important issues, sometimes unable to ensure that international commitments were fulfilled. They faced different types of resistance: from agents of foreign powers, from the states of the Confederation and labor of the Union, and from other agencies of the national government. But in each of the cases selected, national institutions were weak.

Since I have selected cases in which national political institutions failed, to some extent at least, in implementing their desired policies, it would be unwarranted to infer that the U.S. state was weak in general. During the antebellum period the territory of the country vastly expanded, to encompass the "manifest destiny" about which John Quincy Adams so eloquently spoke. In the course of this expansion, the United States fought an undeclared war against Spain, held Great Britain to a standoff in the War of 1812, defeated a number of Indian nations, secured Oregon and Washington in an exercise of brinkmanship with Great Britain, and conquered a huge portion of Mexico, including what is now Texas and California and areas in between. Some of these activities entailed deliberate violations of treaty commitments. Aggressive expansion, not weakness, is the overall theme of American history between 1787 and 1860.

In the second section I turn to the postbellum period. The United States had fewer international commitments after 1865 than it had during the first half of the century, so there is less material to work with. However, the long-running controversies of the 1870s and 1880s over Chinese immigration provide an instructive comparison with earlier episodes. As in the Indian cases, a dominant majority sought to renege on international treaties that protected a weak minority: Indian tribes before the mid-1830s, Chinese immigrants between 1868 and 1889. In the later period, however, U.S. national institutions, especially the federal courts, were able to make their decisions stick even when opposed by powerful local and state political forces. The second section of the chapter illustrates this difference by describing political and legal actions surrounding Chinese immigration in the postbellum period.

My emphasis on "American political institutions" is deliberate. I have never been sympathetic with the concept of "state strength," and I certainly do not endorse it here. "The state" is a complex of institutions, with varying capacities and limitations. The ability to achieve purposes is not well indexed by the size of a bureaucracy or the reliance of state organizations on directives as opposed to markets. Such ability varies considerably across issue areas within a state, as well as across states.[8] Hence I avoid stereotyping the United States as a "weak state" during the entire antebellum period, and I discuss "state institutions" rather than "the state" — not least because those institutions were often in conflict with one another.

Commitment Incapacity before the Civil War

Before the Civil War, the United States faced many challenges to its ability to fulfill its commitments: from various states, from foreign emissaries, and from individuals and groups. In resisting these challenges, the federal government itself was not always united. When the challengers succeeded —

notably in relations between settlers and Indian tribes — the federal executive often adjusted its practices, or even connived at the violation of commitments. Even when the challengers failed, as did the French revolutionary emissary, Citizen Genet and the states who resisted debt repayment, the exitent and duration of their challenges indicate how precarious the authority of the federal government was, at least in the first decade after the Treaty of Peace. But ultimately, challenges not supported by the federal government did fail. I consider five sets of challenges here, beginning with those to fulfillment of the 1783 Treaty of Peace with Great Britain. I then consider attempts by French revolutionaries to use the United States as a base in their war with Britain; Federalist policies toward Indian nations before the War of 1812; Jacksonian policies toward the eastern Indians during the 1830s; and finally, raids against Canada, from United States territory, during the 1830s. In concluding the discussion of each situation, I ask three questions: (1) Which political institutions, if any, were unable to implement their decisions in timely fashion? (2) What forces blocked such implementation? and (3) Were subsequent institutional actions taken to make such implementation feasible in the future?

The Treaty of Peace and the Constitution

The Treaty of Peace with Great Britain in 1783 "was peculiar in that only one of its two signatories possessed the attributes of sovereignty. America could bind Britain, but Britain could not bind America. The American party to the treaty was Congress, and Congress had only a limited power delegated by the thirteen sovereign states. It had no obligation to bind them, and not one of them incurred a single legal obligation under the Treaty of Paris."[9]

This constitutional anomaly led to trouble immediately. Several states, particularly in the South, refused to honor the treaty's provisions for the safe return of Loyalists and payment of debts to British merchants. "If we are to pay the debts due the British merchants," someone remarked, "what have we been fighting for all this while?"[10] Congress only had the authority to "earnestly recommend" to the states to restore the estates of Loyalists who had not borne arms against the United States; it had no authority to implement article 4 of the treaty, which provided that creditors should "meet with no lawful impediment to the recovery of the full value in sterling money of all bona fide debts heretofore contracted."[11] These provisions left much room for accusations of disloyalty and treason against Loyalists, who were left with feeble means of redress.[12]

Noncompliance by the United States gave the British a justification for refusing to return several frontier forts and for discriminating severely against American trade. In 1786 John Jay, who was trying to manage American foreign relations, secretly informed Congress that violations of the treaty by various states had preceded British violations, arguing that the United States needed a strong central government to enforce compliance, which would then put the United States in a position to demand British compliance in return.[13] Congress and the weak Confederation executive tried to secure fulfillment, declaring in 1786 that the states had no right to pass acts "interpreting, explaining or construing a national treaty," but responses by the states to this admonition were quite mixed.

Alexander Hamilton, in *Federalist* paper number 22, emphasized that the new Constitution was essential if the United States was to be able to fulfill its commitments and therefore to conduct effective foreign relations: "No nation acquainted with the nature of our political association would be unwise enough to enter into stipulations with the United States, by which they conceded privileges of any importance to them, while they were apprised that the engagements on the part of the Union might at any point be violated by its members. . . . The treaties of the United States, to have any force at all, must be considered as part of the law of the land."[14] Consistent with Hamilton's argument, article 6 of the Constitution contains the "Supremacy Clause," providing that the Constitution, laws of the United States, and treaties "shall be the supreme Law of the Land, and the Judges in every State shall be bound thereby, any Thing in the Constitution or Laws of any State to the Contrary notwithstanding."

Because the Constitution was ratified, and the Supremacy Clause enforced by the federal courts, the United States was eventually able to keep its commitments, although the process took quite a while. "Not until the Constitution of 1787 was adopted, the national courts established, and the Virginia supreme court overruled by the new Supreme Court of the United States, were the British merchants to have the victory in Virginia that had come to them in other states before the end of the Confederation."[15] Only with the decision of the Supreme Court in *Ware v. Hylton* (1796) did it become established law in the United States that British debtors could receive judgments in courts throughout the country. Even then, British subjects did not always find justice in state courts. The Jay Treaty of 1794 provided for arbitration by a joint British-American arbitral tribunal. When that tribunal dissolved in acrimony, the Convention of 1802 both reasserted the treaty rights of British subjects in American courts and provided that the United States pay Britain an indemnity of six hundred thousand pounds sterling, which was then distributed by a British commission. "The federal court in Virginia heard and decided cases for the recovery of pre-Revolutionary debts until well into the nineteenth century."[16]

Despite the foot-dragging, the Constitution did enable the United States to conduct foreign affairs more effectively. In the Jay Treaty of 1794, ratified in 1795, Great Britain agreed to evacuate the frontier forts on American territory, marking what one could call the beginning of the era of effective territorial sovereignty for the United States.

In this episode, therefore, the answers to our three key questions are as follows:

1. The executive of the Confederation was unable to implement the provisions of the Treaty of Peace.
2. Its attempts to do so were thwarted by the states, particularly in the South, under pressure from debtors and others who stood to gain by reneging on the treaty's commitments.
3. Partly as a result of (1) and (2), fundamental institutional change occurred, in order to assure the supremacy of United States actions over those of the individual states. The Constitution established institutions that increased the capacity of the national government to keep its promises.

Revolutionary France and the U.S. State, 1793

When the onset of war between Great Britain and France became known in the United States in April 1793, President George Washington issued a proclamation of neutrality, although such neutrality was not meant to renounce the treaties of 1778 between the United States and France.[17] Secretary of State Thomas Jefferson assumed the responsibility of pursuing a policy of neutrality without violating commitments of the Treaty of Alliance or the Treaty of Amity and Commerce with France. Articles 17 and 22 of the Treaty of Amity and Commerce provided that French ships of war could take prizes from Britain into American ports, but not vice versa; and that "foreign privateers" could not fit out their ships in American ports. The French emissary to the United States, Edmond Charles Genêt (or Citizen Genêt, as he is usually called), took advantage of the treaty and widespread pro-French sentiment to establish himself as an alternative center of authority in the United States, mobilizing adherents to his cause. He claimed the right to establish prize courts within the United States and even set about outfitting warships and privateers in American ports. On this privilege the treaty was silent, but Jefferson and the cabinet sought to deny it, using the language of obligation and neutrality to bolster their defense of American territorial sovereignty, which Jefferson accused Citizen Genêt of violating.[18]

Despite Jefferson's clear statement of policy and his warnings, Genêt continued to agitate and incite American citizens to military action. He bragged to his Ministry of Foreign Affairs that "I excite the Canadians to free themselves from the yoke of England, I arm the Kentuckians, and I prepare by sea an expedition which will support their descent on New Orleans."[19] Indeed, he incited military action by adventurers, to capture New Orleans from Spain, and establish Louisiana as an independent state.[20]

In July of 1793 Citizen Genêt arranged for a fighting ship, the *Little*

Democrat, to put to sea from Philadelphia, in direct defiance of orders from the United States government. Emphasizing neutral duties as well as rights, Jefferson, in close consultation with the cabinet, denied Genêt's claim to the right to arm ships in American ports, arguing that the treaty provision denying enemies of France the right to outfit ships in American ports, "leaves the question as to France open, & free to be decided according to circumstances." But American neutrality meant that "since we are bound by treaty to refuse [the right to arm ships] to the one party [Britain], and are free to refuse it to that other [France], we are bound by the laws of neutrality to refuse it to that other." Documenting Genêt's repeated violations of United States sovereignty, Jefferson successfully demanded his dismissal, in a memorable and unanswerable diplomatic communication.[21]

By demonstrating in devastating fashion Genêt's violation of American sovereignty, Jefferson was eventually able to vindicate the United States promise of neutrality (subject to provisions of the treaties with France). Although Jefferson was personally favorably disposed toward France, Britain's minister to the United States, George Hammond, declared that he had "every reason to be satisfied with the conduct of the federal government."[22] Genêt's successor, Fauchet, in March 1794 revoked the military commissions bestowed by Genêt and forbade Frenchmen to violate United States neutrality.[23]

By strict construction of the treaties — reserving only those special rights to France specifically required by the treaties — Washington's cabinet managed, in 1793, to avoid war with either Britain or France, as well as to maintain America's international obligations.[24] Only after Jefferson's departure from office at the end of that year did U.S. policy veer more sharply toward Britain's side, and only then could France persuasively argue that the United States had reneged on its obligations under the treaties.[25]

Despite this impressive diplomatic success, what is most notable for our purposes is the inability of the U.S. government, in 1793, to prevent the emissary of a foreign power from raising troops, arming ships, and encouraging treasonous action — within the territorial boundaries of the United States. Genêt's activities were perhaps the greatest threat to the exercise of United States sovereignty within its territorial boundaries in the history of the republic. Had they been allowed to continue, the United States could not have kept its commitment to be neutral in the Anglo-French conflict and would almost surely have been drawn into the war, which might have led to civil war as well.

In this case the answers to our three key questions are as follows:

1. The executive of the United States was unable to prevent Genêt from raising troops and arming ships within its territories and only with great effort forced him to desist.
2. Timely implementation of executive orders was prevented by a limited capacity of the United States for intelligence, a weak army, and widespread sympathy

for the French cause within the U.S. population, including much of its leadership (indeed, especially in factions loyal to Thomas Jefferson and James Madison).

3. Institutional change was delayed by continuing internal conflict, through the War of 1812 (during which some states in New England threatened to secede). The end of the Napoleonic Wars in 1815 took the pressure off United States military and police institutions, which remained weak until the Civil War.

Early Federalist Indian Policy

Under the Articles of Confederation, the initial policy of Congress (adopted in October 1783) was to regard the Indian tribes as conquered adversaries, since most of them had fought on the British side during the conflict: the Indians were to pay reparations in the form of land cessions for their depredations during the war. Unfortunately for the architects of this policy, the Indians had not really been defeated in the West and had no intention of accepting punishment for fighting on the British side. Yet the confederal government tried to implement this policy of dictation, and southern states, such as Georgia and North Carolina, went even further with it, seeking to confiscate Indian lands. Although several treaties with Indian groups were concluded, the Indian signatories were typically either unrepresentative or acted under duress. The result was war, not peace. When moderate treaties were negotiated, as they were at Hopewell in 1785–86 with the Cherokees, Choctaws, and Chickasaws, state governments protested and sought to undermine them, and settlers violated them egregiously.[26]

At this time, the southern Indians were allied with Spain and the Northwestern Indians with Britain, which remained in control of the forts. Since neither the confederal government nor the states had the military power to subdue the Indians, by 1786 the United States faced war and chaos on its frontiers. Between 1783 and 1787, sovereignty was in abeyance: "Nowhere along the seaboard or the backcountry on either side of the Ohio River was there a clear-cut center of authority, white or red," and by 1786 "the United States attempt to treat Indian affairs as a domestic problem and the Indians themselves as unwelcome guests on their own land was a total failure. That failure was compounded by the collapse of the treaty system through which Indian relations were customarily handled."[27]

The strategy devised by federalist leaders to deal with this situation contained both internal and external components. Domestically, it was necessary for the national government to assert its control over Indian affairs. At the Constitutional Convention of 1787, James Madison adduced as an example of encroachments by the states on federal authority that some had entered into treaties with the Indians or made war against them. In the Constitution, the federal government was provided with plenary powers for dealing with Indian tribes, as Chief Justice John Marshall later noted. The Constitution, he said, "confers on Congress the powers of war and peace; of making treaties, and of regulating commerce with foreign nations, and among the several states, and with the Indian tribes. These powers comprehend all that is required for the regulation of our intercourse with the Indians. They are not limited by any restricts on their free actions; the shackles imposed on this power, in the confederation, are discarded."[28]

The United States needed to prevent the formation in the South and Northwest of powerful Indian coalitions allied with Spain and Britain, respectively, yet the policy of conquest was likely to bring such coalitions about. Hence, the new government changed tactics. The United States began once again to pursue Britain's policy of treating the Indian tribes as foreign nations rather than as members of the domestic polity. The United States abandoned the attempt at conquest in favor of a system of compensated treaty cessions, the first of which was negotiated at Fort Harmar in January 1789. This strategy was required by Indian independence and military power, but it was also consistent with domestic imperatives, since use of the treaty power—which required that the Indians be regarded as sovereign nations—was the most feasible way for the national government to regain control of Indian affairs from the southern states. As Secretary of War Knox reported in 1789: "The independent nations and tribes of Indians ought to be considered as foreign nations, not as the subjects of any particular State. Each individual State, indeed, will retain the right of pre-emption of all land within its limits, which will not be abridged, but the general sovereignty must possess the right of making all treaties, on the execution or violation of which depend peace or war."[29]

Thus, Knox proposed what Dorothy Jones has characterized as a "layering of sovereign powers." The Indians were independent foreign nations and they could not be deprived of their soil without their consent; states were to have preemption rights, but only the United States could acquire Indian territory, by treaty. This legal structure, however, fit uneasily with the crucial demographic fact of the day: the continued flow to the frontier of land-seeking white settlers, who had little respect for Indian rights. The only way to reconcile Indian sovereignty with expansion of settlements was to obtain the Indians' "consent" to cession, or, failing that, to seize land by war. Knox was trying to adapt traditional colonial policy to contemporary purposes, but without possessing the imperial British authority to restrict settlement.[30]

Until the election of Andrew Jackson to the presidency in 1828, United States policy toward Native Americans was accompanied by protestations of respect for Indians' rights to the soil and for the principle of cession only by consent. Beginning in 1790, a series of trade and intercourse acts had been enacted, to control trade with the Indians, invalidate all Indian cessions except those made through a public treaty with the United States, and punish crimes committed by whites against Indians in Indian country. These acts, according to Francis Paul Prucha, "sought to provide an answer to the charge that the treaties with the Indians, which guaranteed their rights to the territory behind the boundary lines, were not respected by the United States." The federal government sought to maintain the boundary lines and protect the Indians' rights; until the Jacksonian period, it is striking how conscientious many federal officials were about maintaining "scrupulous regard for treaty obligations." Illegal settlers were frequently removed from Indian lands. Yet the policy was ineffective. The federal authorities never had more than a handful of troops available to police an extended frontier, and the civil authorities within the states generally supported the frontiersmen, who regarded Indians as enemies to be exterminated, and traders, who pursued commerce by fair means or foul. Indeed, court action was sometimes initiated against military officers who attempted to enforce the laws, making these officers liable for substantial financial punishment.[31] Sometimes, especially after Jackson's election, top officials of the federal government deliberately encouraged or forced land cessions, despite treaty guarantees. As the Indians became militarily weaker, the incentive of the United States government to control settler and state depredations fell.

With respect to Indian policy in the early federal period, therefore the answers to our three questions are as follows:

1. Federal government officials, from U.S. attorneys up to the president himself, were often unable to implement the provisions of treaties made with the Indian tribes, despite the Supremacy Clause.
2. Resistance came from the settlers on the frontier, using decentralized, democratic institutions, over which they had preponderant influence.
3. The treaty powers conferred by the Constitution had an impact after 1789, but when federal actions were ineffective further measures to strengthen the federal government's ability to enforce Indian treaties were thwarted by popular sentiment, especially on the frontier.

The Eastern Indians and Justice Marshall's Court

In 1828 and 1829, the state of Georgia enacted laws that distributed Indian lands to several counties and declared that after June 1, 1830, Georgia law would be supreme within the Cherokee territory. The Cherokee Nation filed suit in the Supreme Court for an injunction to stop Georgia from executing its Indian laws, calling on the federal government to defend the Indians' treaty rights to self-government and possession of the soil. However, Chief Justice Marshall, in his opinion of March 18, 1831, declared that although the Cherokees had "unquestionable" rights to the land they occupied, the Court did not have jurisdiction over the case, because the Indians were "domestic dependent nations" and therefore not entitled to sue as a foreign nation.[32]

Encouraged by the substantive position on Indian rights of several justices, the Cherokees and their political and legal allies pursued another case, well suited both to a court judgment and to discrediting Jackson's policy in the eyes of the public. This time the appeal came from judgments in state courts against two missionaries, friendly to the Indians, whom Georgia had arrested for continuing to live in the Cherokee territory after December 1830, without a license from the state. In *Worcester v. Georgia,* Marshall declared Georgia's extension of its law over the Indians unconstitutional. The Cherokee Nation had not given up its sovereignty in treaties with the United States: the only limitation on its sovereignty was that it could not maintain political relations with nations other than the United States. State law must yield, because it was in conflict both with federal law, which sought to preserve the national character of the tribes, and with valid treaties between the United States and the Cherokee Nation.[33]

However, Georgia's intransigence and the weakness of federal law enforcement made it impossible in 1832 to enforce the Court's order that the state release the missionaries. President Andrew Jackson was never even called upon to enforce the decision: as he wrote to a friend, "The decision of the supreme court has fell [sic] still born, and they find that it cannot coerce Georgia to yield to its mandate."[34]

Enforcement was impossible because the political battle was being won by the forces favoring the removal of all eastern Indians to reservations beyond the Mississippi River. Andrew Jackson expressed a widespread sentiment when he declared in his message to Congress in December 1830, "What good man would prefer a country covered with forests and ranged by a few thousand savages to our extensive Republic, studded with cities, towns, and prosperous farms, embellished with all the improvements which art can devise or industry execute, occupied by more than 12,000,000 happy people, and filled with all the blessings of liberty, civilization, and religion?"

The Jackson administration regarded treaties not as moral obligations but as matters of expediency. As expressed by Governor George C. Gilmer of Georgia, "Treaties were expedients by which ignorant, intractable, and savage people were induced without bloodshed to yield up what civilized peoples had a right to possess by virtue of that command of the Creator delivered to man upon his formation — be fruitful, multiply, and replenish the earth, and subdue it."

To the House committee reporting the 1830 Indian Removal Bill, the practice of extinguishing Indian title by payments of money was "but the substitute which humanity and expediency have imposed, in place of the sword, in arriving at the actual enjoyment of property claimed by the right of discovery, and sanctioned by the natural superiority allowed to the claims of civilized communities over those of savage tribes."[35]

The Civilized Tribes were supported at first by religious groups and by Jackson's political opponents, the National Republicans of Henry Clay. Their protests relied on appeals to justice and the sanctity of treaties. For instance, Senator Theodore Frelinghuysen of New Jersey, in a Senate speech in 1830, emphasized the administration's violation of its treaty obligations:

> Every administration of this Government, from President Washington's, have, with like solemnities and stipulations, held treaties with the Cherokees; treaties, too, by almost all of which we obtained further acquisitions of their territory. Yes, sir, whenever we approached them in the language of friendship and kindness, we touched the chord that won their confidence; and now, when they have nothing left with which to satisfy our cravings, we propose to annul every treaty — to gainsay our word — and by violence and perfidy drive the Indian from his home.[36]

These protests were insufficient to block passage of a Removal Bill in 1830, but the struggle continued, with the Indian appeals to the courts as a focal point. Indeed, the Whigs took up the antiremoval cause in the presidential campaign of that year. However, they dropped the issue after Clay's defeat for the presidency and Jackson's proclamation against nullification in December 1832. Suddenly, Clay's nationalists were allied with the Jacksonians against John C. Calhoun of South Carolina, whose state both groups sought to isolate. At this point, it became important not to antagonize Georgia, and "the Cherokees and the missionaries had become an embarrassment."[37] The Cherokee Nation's treaty status was no longer politically enmeshed with the Whig interest: the missionaries accepted pardons, and the Cherokees were persuaded not to renew their struggle in the Supreme Court. Indian removal gradually became accepted policy, implemented even by the Whigs when they finally captured the presidency in 1841.[38] The result was the resettlement of the Five Civilized Tribes in Indian Territory,[39] the movement of many other tribes westward with less specific assurances of permanent tenure, and the emergence of a so-called "Permanent Indian Frontier," which was vaguely defined but remained more or less intact until after the end of the war with Mexico in 1848.

With respect to this case the answers to our three key questions are as follows:

1. The federal courts were unable to implement their decisions with respect to the Cherokees.
2. Implementation of court decisions was blocked by the Jackson administration, with the support of a majority of voters.
3. In view of strong political support for Indian removal, institutional changes to strengthen the Supreme Court's authority were not forthcoming.

The Cherokee case is not a clear case of commitment incapacity by the executive, since President Jackson's government could have fulfilled the agreements with the Cherokees, but preferred to collude with Georgia in reneging on those agreements and removing the Cherokees from their ancestral lands. However, the Cherokee case does illustrate the weakness of the federal courts, which found that their decisions fell "still born." The courts were incapable of ensuring that United States commitments to the Indian nations were fulfilled.

Raids against Canada

Throughout much of the nineteenth century many Americans desired to acquire Canada for the Union, and American armies invaded Canada during both the Revolutionary War and the War of 1812. Even after peace came in 1815 (after the signing of the Treaty of Ghent in December 1814), and the boundary was delimited, some Americans still sought to annex Canada. In 1837 a rebellion in Upper Canada attracted support from certain Americans, who used a ship called the *Caroline* to ferry weapons across the Niagara River to the rebels. On December 29, 1837, British troops crossed into American territory and burned the *Caroline*, creating outrage in the United States. President Van Buren, however, acted with restraint toward Britain and denounced American citizens who aided the rebels "in perfect disregard of their own obligations and of the obligations of the Government to foreign nations."[40] Britain and the United States agreed to arbitrate the dispute.[41]

Three years later, one Alexander McLeod went to New York State on a business trip, apparently boasted about his part in the burning of the *Caroline*, and was arrested for arson and murder. The British minister in Washington protested, calling for McLeod's release and demanding that the United States recognize that "the destruction of the steamboat 'Caroline' was a public act of persons in Her Majesty's Service, obeying the order of their superior authorities. That act, therefore, according to the 'usages of nations,' can only be the subject of discussion between the two National Governments."[42]

The new Whig administration, first of Harrison, then Tyler, was in an awkward position, since public and congressional opinion held that McLeod should be tried in court. Moreover, the case was in state rather than federal court. Secretary of State Webster accepted the British view and took the issue to the Supreme Court of the state of New York on a writ of habeas corpus, seeking McLeod's release; however, the New York Supreme Court refused. The British minister commented, with a combination of anxiety and bemusement, to Palmerston, secretary of state for foreign affairs:

> The decision of the Supreme Court of New York, as it now stands, has placed the Government of the United States in the most extraordinary and embarrassing posi-

tion in which a National government probably ever found itself. The Federal Government has formally placed upon record, has officially communicated to Her Majesty's Government, and has published to the world, its admission of the principle of international law insisted upon by Great Britain. But the same Government now finds itself overruled by an inferior power within one of its own States, and is made liable to be forced into a war with Great Britain in order to support a claim which it has begun by solemnly disavowing.[43]

War was averted, since the British remained firm but patient; the American administration sought peace; and, in a stroke of good fortune for the administration, in October 1841 a jury acquitted McLeod.[44]

This episode illustrates the dangers that the decentralization of the United States posed for its foreign relations. The United States was in violation of international law not due to the actions of the federal government but rather to those of armed bands of citizens and the officers and courts of the state of New York. Indeed, after McLeod's acquittal Webster arranged for Congress to enact a law "providing for the discharge, or the removal from state to federal courts, of anyone accused of an unlawful act proved to have been committed under the orders of a foreign sovereign."[45] Here is another example, less portentous than the enactment of the Constitution but nevertheless, relevant to our argument, of institutional change in the United States prompted by international conflict.

With respect to this incident, the answers to our three questions are as follows:

1. The executive branch of the United States was unable for some time, and at the risk of war, to fulfill treaty commitments.
2. It was blocked by the courts of the state of New York, reflecting popular sentiment.
3. Subsequent institutional changes did strengthen the role of the federal government in such situations.

Throughout the antebellum period, state governments often hindered the conduct of U.S. foreign relations, making it difficult for the United States to keep its treaty commitments. Sometimes, most notably in 1787–89, a coalition could be mobilized to enhance the institutional capacity of the national government. Often, however, popular pressure or state recalcitrance blocked efforts to maintain treaty commitments.

Commitment Capacity after the Civil War: The Chinese Immigration Cases

The U.S. state was vastly strengthened by the Civil War, as we can see by examining the protracted conflict over Chinese immigration, and how it was handled by Congress, the president, and the federal courts. The key point is not the conclusion of the story — eventual reneging by the United States — but the maintenance of treaty restraints for a substantial period of time.

The United States concluded the Burlingame Treaty in 1868, providing for free immigration and most-favored-nation (MFN) treatment for Chinese nationals. This treaty imposed obligations on U.S. cities and states, as well as on the federal government, that were perceived by many Americans as burdensome. Both the Burlingame Treaty and its successor treaty, negotiated in 1880, were soon contested in city halls and legislatures on the West Coast and in Congress. Until 1889, however, Chinese rights under the treaties were successfully protected by federal courts. Only when Congress explicity overrode the treaty of 1880 did the Supreme Court acquiesce. The history of U.S. policy toward Chinese immigration is not one of commitment in capacity but of eventual deliberate reneging on treaty obligations.

The first Chinese arrived in California in 1849, with the Gold Rush, and laws discriminating against them were enacted beginning in 1852. San Francisco and the state of California passed legislation preventing Chinese from testifying against white people in court and enacted a discriminatory capitation tax against them. Although no treaty commitments protected Chinese subjects in the United States until 1868, the California Supreme Court overturned the capitation tax (*Lin Sing v. Washburn* [1862]) on the grounds that it encroached on the federal prerogative of regulating international commerce, established in the *Passenger* cases of 1849. The court reasoned that discriminating against Chinese had the effect of discriminating against foreign commerce, an area reserved to federal jurisdiction.[46]

After the Civil War, Chinese laborers were brought to the United States in large numbers to build the transcontinental railways; and in 1868 the United States and China negotiated the Burlingame Treaty. At this time Chinese subjects in the United States also gained constitutional protection against discrimination in the Fourteenth Amendment, which guaranteed equal protection of the laws, and statutory protection in the Civil Rights Act of 1870, which provided that Chinese could testify in court and forbade discriminatory "penalties, taxes, license, and exactions of every kind."[47] Hence, after 1868 and especially after 1870, the Chinese and citizens supporting them could appeal to federal law against discriminatory statutes enacted by the city of San Francisco and the state of California. The Chinese and their supporters invoked the Burlingame Treaty and its revision (the Ansell Treaty of 1880) in their attempts to persuade the federal courts to overturn these discriminatory statutes.

Such attempts were often successful: federal courts enforced the provisions of the Burlingame Treaty on local and state legislative bodies. For example, in a case involving regulation of San Francisco laundries, *In re Quong Woo*, Supreme Court Justice Stephen Field (sitting as circuit judge) invoked the

Burlingame Treaty to show that Quong Woo, a Chinese subject, had the right, because of China's most-favored-nation (MFN) status, to operate a laundry in the United States. And in 1880, after the California legislature passed a law forbidding any corporation to employ Chinese, the U.S. circuit court held this law invalid, because it violated the Burlingame Treaty as well as the Four-teenth Amendment to the United States Constitution.[48]

In the 1880s, the federal courts in California, and particularly two judges — Ogden Hoffman of the U.S. District Court for Northern California and Lorenzo Sawyer of the U.S. Circuit Court for California — actively pro-tected the rights of Chinese. Most of the cases involved requests by Chinese persons for writs of habeas corpus after having been detained or arrested by U.S. authorities, particularly the San Francisco collector of port; between 1882 and 1891 over seven thousand such "Chinese Admiralty" cases were filed, 85–90 percent of which were apparently successful. Judges Hoffman and Sawyer did not simply accept the determination of the collector of port about the status of Chinese persons: "Despite pressure from federal officials, the press, and the public, Hoffman and Sawyer believed that their judicial duty required them to interpret the successive Chinese exclusion acts in light of the 1868 and 1880 treaties with China."[49] In *In re Chin Ah On* (1883), Hoffman held that a Chinese laborer who lived in California in 1880 but left before passage of the 1882 act was permitted to return without a certificate, on the grounds that the act had only sought to bar *new* immi-gration. And article 2 of the 1880 treaty provided that Chinese laborers in the United States when the treaty was signed could leave and return freely. Honor required that the United States keep its obligations: to deny Chin Ah Oh the right to land, Hoffman believed, "would be to attribute to the legis-lative branch of government a want of good faith and a disregard of solemn national engagements which, unless upon grounds which leave the court no alternatives, it would be indecent to impute to it." In *Chew Heong v. United States* (1884), Justice Field (as circuit judge) decided over the dissents of three others (the Supreme Court judge prevailed even when in a minority) that Chinese laborers who had left before certificates were available could be denied reentry because they did not have certificates; but on appeal this decision was reversed by the U.S. Supreme Court, which argued that in view of the importance of the sanctity of treaties, if, "by any reasonable construction," the later statute could be interpreted as consistent with a treaty, the treaty must stand.[50]

Hence, for a significant period of time, the treaties had an impact, despite strong political opposition, because of the actions of federal courts. Short of clear congressional mandates to the contrary, the federal courts helped to protect Chinese from arbitrary actions by local, state and federal officials seeking to discriminate against them. Unlike efforts by the federal courts to protect the Indians in the 1830s, these court orders were operationally effective. The ability of the federal courts to override state policy, as well as the administrative actions of agents of the national government, was now assured. The contrast with the antebellum period is quite marked.

Unfortunately for the Chinese judicial capacity to protect them was not enough. Political sentiment progressively intensified against them, and the Forty-fifth Congress (1877–79) responded to it. The Committee on Education and Labor in the House and the Committee on Foreign Relations in the Senate urged renegotiation of the Burlingame Treaty. In 1879 Congress passed the Fifteen Passenger Bill, which provided that no vessel should bring more than fifteen Chinese to the United States at a time. The mostly Democratic supporters of this measure acknowledged that it would constitute abrogation of articles 5 and 6 of the Burlingame Treaty, which guaranteed free migration and travel and residence privileges, but the chairman of the Committee on Education and Labor (Willis of Kentucky) made clear in his report his understanding that subsequent laws "control any contravening treaty." Among the opponents, Senator Hoar (R, Mass.) declared that the bill was a breach of faith and violated principle.[51]

President Hayes vetoed the measure on March 1, 1879. He did not question the legal right of the United States to abrogate a treaty but held that abrogation of articles 5 and 6 of the Burlingame Treaty would constitute a denunciation of the whole treaty, and that Congress cannot unilaterally amend a treaty. Denunciation of the treaty would be likely to lead to reciprocal Chinese action that could be harmful to American missionaries in China and to U.S. commercial interests; renegotiation would be a wiser course. Treaty denunciation, said Hayes, is constitutionally permitted but "justifiable only upon some reason both of the highest justice and the highest necessity."[52]

To avoid congressional passage of abrogation legislation over a presidential veto, President Hayes then asked Congress to authorize a special commission to negotiate a revised treaty, which would give the United States the right to limit immigration from China. The American commissioners, led by the president of the University of Michigan, James B. Angell, proposed that the United States be permitted to entirely prohibit immigration of Chinese laborers, but the Chinese did not accept this provision: article 1 of the Treaty of 1880 provided instead that "the United States may regulate, limit, or suspend such coming or residence, but may not absolutely prohibit it." Furthermore, "the limitation or suspension shall be reasonable." Article 2 reaffirmed MFN treatment for Chinese subjects going to the United States and laborers already there, and article 3 made clear the responsibility of the United States to "exert all its powers" to protect Chinese from ill treatment in the United States. The Angell Treaty was agreed to readily by the Senate and replaced the Burlingame Treaty.[53]

Taking advantage of the leeway offered by the 1880 treaty, Congress passed a measure in 1882 that would have limited Chinese immigrants to fifteen per vessel, prohibited immigration of Chinese laborers for twenty years, and imposed a passport and registration system on Chinese in America.[54] President Chester A. Arthur vetoed this act on the grounds that a twenty-year prohibition was inconsistent with article 1 of the Angell Treaty (a twenty-year prohibition of entry was equivalent, he argued, to absolute prohibition) and violated U.S. assurances given during negotiation of that treaty. Secondarily, he argued that the passport-registration system served no good purpose and violated assurances that Chinese in the United States would be given MFN treatment.[55] After Arthur's veto was sustained, a new bill was passed, which limited exclusion to ten years and abandoned the registration system.[56] In 1884 Congress tightened up the requirements for the establishment by a Chinese person of prior residency in the United States: thereafter, possession of a certificate was the only permissible evidence by which a laborer could establish the right of reentry.[57]

Under continuing pressure to restrict Chinese immigration, the United States and China negotiated during 1887–88 a new treaty that prohibited entry of Chinese laborers for twenty years, except for returning laborers with relatives or property of one thousand dollars or more in the United States. In secret session the Senate added provisions nullifying the certificates in the hands of Chinese laborers currently outside the United States. The Chinese minister, perhaps not understanding that these changes would exclude twenty thousand Chinese laborers, accepted them and sent them to Peking; and Congress passed a bill to implement its measures when finally ratified.[58]

When newspaper reports appeared indicating that China would not ratify the treaty, Congress passed the Scott Act, banning all Chinese laborers from reentry. It was approved by the president on October 1, 1888, and went into effect immediately. Returning Chinese who had been on the high seas when it was enacted were refused reentry to the United States.[59] Cleveland justified this act on the grounds that the United States had had every reason to expect China to ratify the treaty as amended and that "an emergency had arisen" as a result of its failure to do so: "I can not but regard the expressed demand on the part of China for a re-examination and renewed discussion of the topic so completely covered by mutual treaty stipulations as an indefinite postponement and practical abandonment of the objects we have in view, to which the Government of China may justly be considered as pledged."[60]

The Scott Act was a plain violation of the 1880 treaty, canceling perhaps 20,000 certificates. The issue went to the Supreme Court in 1889. The year before, the Court had prepared the ground by ruling that "A treaty is placed on the same footing, and made of like obligation, with an act of legislation. . . . When the two relate to the same subject, the courts will always endeavor to construe them so as to give effect to both, if that can be done without violating the language of either; but if the two are inconsistent, the one last in date will control the other, provided always the stipulation of the treaty on the subject is self-executing."[61]

Now, in *Chae Chan Ping v. United States* (Chinese Exclusion Cases, 1889), the Court used that precedent to rule that the Scott Act was constitutional. A Chinese national who had resided in the United States from 1875 to 1887 and had left with a certificate in hand could be denied reentry, notwithstanding the Burlingame and Angell Treaties and the legislation of 1882 and 1884. Although this act of Congress was a clear violation of the two treaties, the Supreme Court ruled that "it is not on that account invalid or to be restricted in its enforcement. The treaties were of no greater legal obligation than the act of Congress," and "in either case the last expression of the sovereign will must control." Indeed, according to the Court, "the power of exclusion of foreigners being an incident of sovereignty, . . . the interests of the country require it cannot be granted away or restrained on behalf of any one."[62]

The rest of the story is anticlimactic. In 1892 Congress debated the Geary Act, which in its original version would have prohibited all Chinese immigration, not just of laborers. The final version, as amended by the Senate Foreign Relations Committee, extended the Scott Act for ten years and provided that Chinese laborers in the United States must register and hold internal passports, under penalty of being deported. This act was a clear violation of article 2 of the 1880 treaty, which provided Chinese laborers "all the rights, privileges, immunities and exemptions which are accorded to the citizens and subjects of the most favored nation." In providing for imprisonment and subsequent deportation of Chinese found unlawfully residing in the United States, the Geary Act declared that the burden of proof would be on the Chinese person arrested, and that no bail should be allowed to Chinese in habeas corpus proceedings. Before President Harrison signed the bill, the Chinese minister protested that it was a violation of the treaty of 1880. But in 1893 the Supreme Court ruled (with three dissents) that the Geary law was constitutional.[63]

Conclusion

"Stateness" varies with respect to international and transnational relations, just as it does along other dimensions. The American state has not always been an effective gatekeeper toward the outside world. In its early history, the executive branch was often hamstrung by administrative incapacity, lack of political support, and even — for example, on the frontier — a military too weak to control recalcitrant members of civil society. The federal courts were also weak. As the Cherokee cases indicate, the courts could not count on implementation of their orders by the Executive.

A strong state roughly corresponding to Nettl's gatekeeper was constructed, in the United States, by the nationalism of the Civil War and doctrines such as those enunciated by the Supreme Court in the Chinese immigration cases. The United States was never a perfectly effective gatekeeper, but between 1889 and the 1960s analysts could be pardoned for imagining it as such. Complex interdependence and globalization have once more called this state capacity into question. In Europe now, it is quite obvious that sovereignty has been utterly transformed: individual states are subject to European law and have effectively lost the ability either to control immigration or to print money—two of the classic attributes of sovereignty. They have armies, but their military establishments are so integrated into NATO, and so dependent on logistics provided by the United States, that they can hardly be considered autonomous fighting forces. Matters have not gone nearly so far for the United States, but it has become manifest that the United States cannot prevent illegal drugs and illegal immigrants from flowing over its borders.

It is unlikely that the United States will return soon to the condition of weakness that characterized its state during its first fifty years. But new developments may be in store. In the era of the Internet, what Joseph S. Nye has called "soft power" is increasingly important.[64] States may need not only hierarchical administrative capacity, but also the ability to operate in international institutions and in transnational and transgovernmental networks. Without prejudging the nature of such developments, it is nevertheless worthwhile to note, as we enter the new Millennium, that the American state has been transformed before. The next major changes in American state capacity are likely to be more affected by global forces than the transformation of the mid-nineteenth century.

Notes

1. Peter A. Gourevitch, "The Second Image Reversed: The International Sources of Domestic Politics," *International Organization* 32 (1978): 881–912. For an attempt to apply Gourevitch's insight to the United States, see Robert O. Keohane, "Associative American Development, 1776–1860: Economic Growth and Political Disintegration," in *The Antinomies of Interdependence: National Welfare and the International Division of Labor*, ed. John Gerard Ruggie (New York: Columbia University Press, 1983), 83–84.

2. J. P. Nettl, "The State as a Conceptual Variable," *World Politics* 20 (July 1968): 564.

3. Robert O. Keohane and Joseph S. Nye, eds., *Transnational Relations and World Politics* (Cambridge: Harvard University Press, 1972).

4. There is a huge literature on this subject. For an early statement, see Robert O. Keohane and Joseph S. Nye Jr., eds., *Transnational Relations and World Politics* (Cambridge: Harvard University Press, 1972).

5. For a recently updated discussion, see Robert O. Keohane and Joseph S. Nye Jr., *Power and Interdependence: World Politics in Transition*, 3rd ed. (New York: Addison-Wesley Longman, 2001 [1977]).

6. For a classical discussion of sovereignty and the state in "international society," see Hedley Bull, *The Anarchical Society: A Study of Order in World Politics* (New York: Columbia University Press, 1977). For a recent discussion of gaps between the fiction and the reality of "Westphalian sovereignty," see Stephen D. Krasner, *Sovereignty: Organized Hypocrisy* (Princeton: Princeton University Press, 1999).

7. Gary King, Robert O. Keohane, and Sidney Verba, *Designing Social Inquiry: Scientific Inference in Qualitative Research* (Princeton: Princeton University Press, 1994), chap. 2.

8. See Helen V. Milner, *Resisting Protectionism: Global Industries and the Politics of International Trade* (Princeton: Princeton University Press, 1988), especially 274–89.

9. A. L. Burt, *The United States, Great Britain and British North America: From the Revolution to the Establishment of Peace after the War of 1812* (New York: Russell & Russell, 1961), 97.

10. Lawrence S. Kaplan, *Colonies into Nation: American Diplomacy, 1763–1801* (New York: Macmillan, 1972), 154.

11. Treaty of Peace between Great Britain and the United States, 1783, articles 4 and 5.

12. Samuel Flagg Bemis, *The Diplomacy of the American Revolution* (Bloomington: Indiana University Press, 1957 [1935]), 235. See also James H. Kettner, *The Development of American Citizenship, 1608–1870* (Chapel Hill: University of North Carolina Press, 1978), 184; Richard W. Van Alstyne, *Empire and Independence: The International History of the American Revolution* (New York: Wiley, 1965), 221. For detailed lists of complaints on both sides, see the correspondence between the British minister in the United States, George Hammond, and Secretary of State Thomas Jefferson between 1791 and 1793. *American State Papers: Foreign Relations*, 1: 188–213.

13. *American State Papers: Foreign Relations*, 1: 165.

14. Alexander Hamilton, *The Federalist*, no. 22 (1787). *The Federalist Papers*, ed. Edward Meade Earle (New York: Modern Library, 1937), 131, 137.

15. Merrill Jensen, *The New Nation: A History of the United States during the Confederation, 1781–1789* (New York: Knopf, 1950), 265–68, quotations on 281.

16. *The Papers of John Marshall*, ed. Charles F. Hobson, (Chapel Hill: University of North Carolina Press, 1987), 5: 260–63, quotation on 263.

17. Alexander DeConde, *Entangling Alliance: Politics and Diplomacy under George Washington* (Durham, N.C.: Duke University Press, 1958), 88; Samuel Flagg Bemis, *Jay's Treaty: A Study in Commerce and Diplomacy* (New York: Macmillan, 1924), 140. See also Robert W. Tucker and David C. Hendrickson, *Empire of Liberty: The Statecraft of Thomas Jefferson* (New York: Oxford University Press, 1990) and Gerald A. Combs, *The Jay Treaty: Political Battleground of the Founding Fathers* (Berkeley: University of California Press, 1970).

18. Jefferson's reply to Citizen Genêt, June 5, 1793, in *The Writings of Thomas Jefferson*, ed. Ford Leiscester Ford (New York: Putnam's, 1895), 6: 282–83. It also appears in *American State Papers: Foreign Relations*, 1: 150.

19. Genêt to Ministry of Foreign Affairs, June 19, 1793, in Dumas Malone, *Jefferson and the Ordeal of Liberty* (Boston: Little, Brown, 1962), 104.

20. Malone, *Jefferson*, 104–9.

21. Jefferson to the U.S. Minister to France, Gouverneur Morris, August 16, 1793, in *Writings of Thomas Jefferson*, 6: 380. This message was read paragraph by paragraph to the cabinet; see Malone, *Jefferson*, 126. According to Samuel Flagg Bemis, Hamilton took the lead within the cabinet in arguing that the treaty did not provide implicit privileges to France to sell their prizes in America through consular courts or to fit out privateers in American waters. Bemis, "Thomas Jefferson," in *The American Secretaries of State and Their Diplomacy*, ed. Bemis (New York: Knopf, 1927), 2: 80. Genêt, a young man at the time, never actually returned to France; fearing persecution, he took up residence in the United States for the rest of his long life.

22. Tucker and Hendrickson, *Empire of Liberty*, 55. Malone shows that although Jefferson's private views remained quite Francophile, his actions as secretary of state were disciplined in his defense of American neutrality. John Quincy Adams later remarked that "Mr. Jefferson's papers on that controversy present the most perfect model of diplomatic discussion and expostulation of modern times," and British foreign secretary George Canning declared in 1823 that "if I wished for a guide in a system of neutrality, I should take that laid down by America in the days of the presidency of Washington and the secretaryship of Jefferson, in 1793." Malone, *Jefferson*, 128, 80. Malone also argues that Jefferson was never overruled in the cabinet in 1793; his frustrations came from the tensions between his private views and the obligations of office, rather than from political defeats in the cabinet. When he left office, he was not disillusioned with the drift of policy: "In the realm of foreign affairs Washington saw eye to eye with his Secretary of State at the end of the latter's service" (Ibid., 149).

23. Ibid., 108.

24. Jefferson's demand for Genêt's dismissal had partisan as well as national motivations. Genêt had threatened to appeal to the public against President Washington, which Jefferson knew would lead to a reaction against his own faction. Writing to Madison in early August 1793, he remarked, "He will sink the republican interest if they do not abandon him." Ibid., 121.

25. Some historians dissent from this favorable evaluation. Lawrence S. Kaplan declares that "the Jeffersonians deluded themselves in believing they could have both neutrality and the alliance," since France would object to any such arrangement that did not defend freedom of the seas. Kaplan, *Entangling Alliances with None* (Kent, Ohio: Kent State University Press, 1987), 90. But for over eight months in 1793, Jefferson managed to reconcile neutrality and the alliance, forcing the ignominious recall of Citizen Genêt for his egregious behavior, which gave the United States more cause than France to complain of treaty violations. It was *British* spoliations in late 1793, not French interference in American politics, that brought the next crisis. Tucker and Hendrickson (*Empire of Liberty*) give Jefferson very little credit for the cleverness of his policy, viewing him principally as a reformer and moralist and comparing his diplomacy unfavorably with that of Hamilton.

26. Reginald Horsman, *Expansion and American Indian Policy, 1783–1812* (East Lansing: Michigan State University Press, 1967), 3–31. In 1789 Secretary of War Knox criticized the "disgraceful violations" of the Hopewell Treaty with the Cherokees. Ibid., 52, 56.

27. Dorothy V. Jones, *License for Empire: Colonialism by Treaty in Early America* (Chicago: University of Chicago, 1982), 155–56.

28. *Worcester v. Georgia*, 6 Pet. 515 (1832), cited in Francis Paul Prucha, *American Indian Policy in the Formative Years*, (Cambridge: Harvard University Press, 1962), 43–44.

29. Report, "Relating to the Southern Indians," July 6–7, 1989, in *American State Papers, Indian Affairs*, 1:13, cited in Jones, *License*, 166. See also Horsman, *Expansion*, 57.

30. On layered sovereignty, see Jones, *License*, 168. See Horsman, *Expansion*, for Knox's criticism of the policy of conquest (71) and the provisions of the Treaty of Greenville (102).

31. Prucha, *American Indian Policy*, 48, 83–84; Horsman, *Expansion*, 158–60. The quotation about scrupulous regard for treaty obligations is from Prucha, *American Indian Policy*, 157, referring to U.S. policy immediately after the War of 1812.

32. Joseph Burke, "The Cherokee Cases: A Study in Law, Politics and Morality," *Stanford Law Review* 21 (February 1969): 500–31, especially 513–15.

33. Burke, *Cherokee Cases*, 523.

34. Robert V. Rimini, *Andrew Jackson and the Course of American Freedom, 1822–1832* (New York: Harper & Row, 1981).

35. Both quotes are from Prucha, *American Indian Policy*, 242.

36. Francis Paul Prucha, ed., *Documents of United States Indian Policy* (Lincoln: University of Nebraska Press, 1990), 71.

37. Burke, *Cherokee Cases*, 530.

38. *Cherokee Nation v. Georgia*, 5 Pet. (1831); *Worcester v. Georgia* 6 Pet. (1832); excerpted in Prucha, *Documents*, 58–62. For a good discussion, see Ronald N. Satz, *American Indian Policy in the Jacksonian Era* (Lincoln: University of Nebraska Press, 1975), 39–63.

39. The so-called "Five Civilized Tribes" were the Cherokees, Chickasaws, Choctaws, Creeks, and Seminoles.

40. Proclamation by President Martin Van Buren, November 21, 1838, 25th Cong., 3rd sess., 1838–39, H. Doc. 1.

41. Great Britain apologized in 1842 for its violation of United States neutrality. Hugh L. Keenleyside, *Canada and the United States* (New York: Knopf, 1952), 91.

42. Diplomatic Note of the British Minister (Fox) to the United States, December 13, 1840, Public Record Office, Foreign Office, North American File, ("Papers Relating to the Arrest of Mr. McLeod, 1840–41").

43. Fox to Palmerston, July 28, 1841, Public Record Office, Foreign Office, North American File, 414 ("Papers Relating to the Arrest of Mr. McLeod, 1840–41").

44. During the trial, Governor Seward of New York "confidentially informed the Secretary of State that McLeod (despite his boasts) was known to have a good alibi, and that in the remote contingency of a conviction he would be pardoned." Samuel Flagg Bemis, *A Diplomatic History of the United States* (New York: Holt, 1942), 260–61.

45. Ibid.

46. Charles J. McClain and Laurene Wu McClain, "The Chinese Contribution to the Development of American Law," in *Entry Denied: Exclusion and the Chinese Community in America, 1882–1943*, ed. Sucheng Chan (Philadephia: Temple University Press, 1991), 7–8.

47. Ibid., 8 (citing section 16 of this act).

48. Ibid., 16; Mary Roberts Coolidge, *Chinese Immigration* (New York: Holt, 1909), 124–25. Other cases — for instance, *Ho Ah Kow v. Nunan* (1876) and *Yick Wo v. Hopkins* (1886) — invoked the Fourteenth Amendment to protect Chinese against discrimination.

49. Christian G. Fritz, "Due Process, Treaty Rights, and Chinese Exclusion, 1882–1891," in Chan, *Entry Denied*, 29, 46–49; Lucy E. Salyer, "Laws Harsh as Tigers: Enforcement of the Chinese Exclusion Laws, 1891–1924," in Chan, *Entry Denied*, 58.

50. *Chew Heong v. United States*, 112 U.S. 436, 5 Sup. Ct. 255, 26 L.Ed. 770 (1884), cited in *South African Airways v. Dole*, 817 F. 2d 119 (D.C. Cir. 1987), 125–26. Fritz, "Due Process," 35, citing Justice Hoffman's opinion, 18 F. 506 (D. Cal, 1883).

51. Mary Roberts Coolidge, *Chinese Immigration* (New York: Holt, 1909), 133–36; *Congressional Record*, House, January 28, 1879, 793.

52. *Congressional Record*, House, March 1, 1879, 2276.

53. James B. Angell, "The Diplomatic Relations between the United States and China," *Journal of Social Science* 17 (May 1883): 24–36; Coolidge, *Chinese Immigration*, 152–61.

54. For the text, see *Congressional Record*, House, 1882, 2227.

55. *Congressional Record*, Senate, April 4, 1882, 2551–52; see also statement opposed to measure by Senator Platt (R, Conn.), including explanation of negotiations by commissioners to China, *Congressional Record*, Senate, March 8, 1882, 1702–5.

56. President Arthur signed this measure into law on May 6, 1882. See Coolidge, *Chinese Immigration*, 178; George F. Howe, *Chester A. Arthur: A Quarter Century of Machine Politics* (New York: Dodd, Mead, 1934), 168; Tien-lu Li, *Congressional Policy of Chinese Immigration* (New York: Arno Press, 1978 [1916]).

57. Fritz, "Due Process," 40; Coolidge, *Chinese Immigration*, 185.

58. Coolidge, *Chinese Immigration*, 195; Li, *Congressional Policy*, 58.

59. Fritz, "Due Process," 48; Coolidge, *Chinese Immigration*, 194–200.

60. *Foreign Relations of the United States 1888*, 1: 358.

61. *Whitney v. Robertson*, 124 U.S. 190, 194 (1888). Quoted in Louis Henkin, *Foreign Affairs and the Constitution* (Mineola, N.Y.: Foundation Press, 1972), 163.

62. *The Chinese Exclusion Case*, 130 US 581; quotations at 600, 609.

63. *Foreign Relations of the United States 1892*, 107–8; Tsui to Blaine, May 5, 1892, *Foreign Relations of the United States 1892*, 149; Coolidge, *Chinese Immigration*, 223.

64. Joseph S. Nye Jr., *Bound to Lead: The Changing Nature of American Power* (New York: Basic Books, 1990).

Four

Flexible Capacity: The Military and Early American Statebuilding

IRA KATZNELSON

> It may surprise Americans, who traditionally have
> regarded themselves as a peaceable and unmilitary
> people, to learn that the range of warfare in their
> national experience has been quite wide, and the
> incidence quite frequent.
> —*American Military History*, Army Historical
>   Series.

IN MODERN sovereign states, the military is the most important buckle fastening international to domestic affairs. As effects and causes of international relations, as key symbols and guardians of national sovereignty, and as crucial links joining a state's international role to civil society and the economy, armies and navies are basic instruments of political development.

Not surprisingly, the military plays an important role in some of the best historical-institutionalist scholarship on the United States. Reform of the army is one of three cases in Stephen Skowronek's *Building a New American State*. The military is viewed as an agent of sectional control in Richard Bensel's *Yankee Leviathan*. Pensions for Civil War veterans are shown as shaping a protomodern welfare state in Theda Skocpol's *Protecting Soldiers and Mothers*. Bartholomew Sparrow's *From Outside In* chronicles the massive importance of military mobilization for state formation during the Second World War. Focusing on the same conflict, Daniel Kryder's *Divided Arsenal* probes the role of the military in both reinforcing and changing the Jim Crow stereotype.[1] Each of these scholars treats the military as a key institution.

Such studies tend to target particular times and situations. Each takes the military into account as an aspect of particular historical processes and puzzles, but none inserts the history and organization of America's armed forces into a more systematic and more general understanding of the role the military itself has played over a long period of time in shaping the country's political history. And none considers the armed forces as a hinge institution transmitting international influences to American political development. In consequence, students of APD still lack adequate accounts of the place of the military in statebuilding.

There is, of course, a significant literature in comparative politics and historical sociology, including recent major work by Brian Downing and Charles Tilly, that focuses on just these themes, primarily in Europe.[2] This body of scholarship has concentrated on mobilization and extraction under the impact of a given state's place and ambitions in the international system, focusing both on the formation of a world of modern states before West-phalia and on the project of statebuilding after a modern international order of states was fashioned in the seventeenth century. The United States, how-ever, remains largely unintegrated into this literature, in part, I surmise, because its military experience is not easily assimilated into the concepts and categories this body of work uses to measure state capacity.

There also is a massive, and burgeoning, body of scholarship on Ameri-can military history written for audiences interested in war generally, in specific wars, or in the institutional history and deployment of the armed forces of the United States.[3] Alas, this specialized knowledge delineates very few ties between its subjects and the larger American context in which the military has been embedded.

The very isolation and incompleteness of these intellectual conversations suggests a considerable opportunity. Thanks to Skowronek, Bensel, Skocpol, Sparrow, and Kryder, among others, we possess a generous preliminary set of ideas about how to incorporate the military as a constitutive element of American statebuilding; thanks to the Europeanists, we have a rich set of hypotheses which could be tested on the American data; and thanks to the hard work of military historians, we possess ample materials with which to launch more systematic work.

This paper on the military and statebuilding in the United States before the Civil War raises historical and conceptual issues pointing toward the integration of the military and war (essentially nonliberal forces and closely tied to international relations) into the story (essentially liberal and domes-tic) of American political development. I am keen, in particular, to under-stand how a focus on international influences via the lens of military might help us reconsider the distinctive status of public authority in America, question the quite common portrait of the antebellum state as an under-developed and insubstantial entity lacking strength or endowments, and, more broadly, indicate how the early American military experience chal-lenges prevalent ideas about war and states in the comparative-historical literature on Western state formation. Above all, I want to probe how the world's most liberal state engaged with the predatory arena of international and military affairs.

This essay pivots on an evocative but elusive paragraph that opens Stephen Skowronek's account of "The Early American State" and on key features of John Brewer's treatment of the English state between 1688 and 1873.[4] Characterizing the early American state as a "great anomaly," Skowronek wrote:

> An analysis of American state building around the turn of the century requires a closer look at the early American state. This state was not a directive force in social affairs, nor was it an ideal reified in American culture. To Tocqueville, Hegel, and Marx, it appeared as pure instrumentality, an innocuous reflection of the society it served. Yet, this organization of coercive power was no less indispensable for its unobtrusive character. The early American state maintained an integrated legal order on a continental scale; it fought wars, expropriated Indians, secured new territories, carried on relations with other states, and aided economic development. Despite the absence of a sense of the state, the state was essential to social order and social development in nineteenth-century America.[5]

He then added: "The early American state can be described much as one would describe any other state." Listing organizational orientations and capacities, procedural routines, and intellectual talents as the dimensions for such an assessment, he famously went on to argue that lawyers and professional politicians directed the "courts and parties [that] formed the bulwark of the early American state."[6] This was the secret, he maintained, for its paradox of being capable but evanescent.

Focusing on the military reveals, to the contrary, that the early American state cannot be described "much as one would describe any other." The regime's particularities as a liberal state based on popular sovereignty, consent, and representation demand an approach to state formation that makes constitutive these distinctly liberal features of the polity. Attention to the country's English parentage is particularly instructive for this reason. Important scholarship on the English state and empire directs attention to questions that might elude us if we were to simply compare the United States to the nations of continental Europe.

The founding of the United States was not simply a rupture with the past. Marked by powerful continuities with the colonial era, the United States was the product of a very British revolution.[7] In key respects, both regimes were liberal. The basis of legitimation had shifted in Britain over the course of the seventeenth and eighteenth centuries from an absolute and divine monarchical right to rule to the notion of a sovereign people bearing rights and enforcing standards of conduct on the monarch via representation in parliament.[8] Under these changing conditions, the settler empire in North America was ruled more by consent than by imposition. The American periphery was joined to the British center in a delicately balanced equilibrium, and after the Revolution, as a country with growing continental ambitions, the United States faced a comparable challenge.[9]

From this perspective, the English state bequeathed a liberal legacy to the American. In England, the state slowly had devolved into a representative, though not democratic, constitutional monarchy. As a result of doctrinal developments, institutional change, and public pressures, stateness no longer was the preserve of small elites who could determine outcomes by closed internal bargaining. Instruments of representation (elections, opinion, political parties, quasi-autonomous legislative decision making) became centerpieces of governance. Colonial America was characterized by a more radical version of this political order. Slavery aside (and, arguably, because of slavery), its society was marked by a flatter hierarchy, fewer rigidities, wider property holding, a more democratic public sphere, and faster demographic, territorial, and economic expansion than the mother country. All these differences, of course, were accentuated by a revolution that jettisoned monarchical rule and by a constitution that created a national state defined by federalism and the separation of powers.[10]

The English state in the century before American independence shows how a putatively "weak" state in fact can be very capable. England did not develop a "strong" state by continental measures, yet it became the globe's preeminent power, notwithstanding the loss of its American colonies. To make this achievement possible, a distinct form of statebuilding had to occur, one that led to enhanced fiscal stability and capacity, augmented borrowing capabilities, and an effective military.

This dualism of stateness and political liberalism is suggestive for students of American political development. Assessing this hybrid, Brewer argued that the two were linked causally. Strong resistance, in the name of liberty, to a hyperstrong state on an unlimited absolutist model proved central to England's institutional transformations. "The war against the state helped to shape the changing contours of government: limited its scope, restricted its ambit, and through parliamentary scrutiny, rendered its institutions both more public and accountable." This success paradoxically produced a more effective state. "Public scrutiny reduced peculation, parliamentary consent lent greater legitimacy to government action. Limited in scope, the state's powers were nevertheless exercised with telling effect."[11]

Based on this combination of restriction and effectiveness, Brewer convincingly concluded that the antinomy of weak and strong states is highly misleading. "Too often," he observed, "strength is equated with size. But a large state apparatus is no necessary indication of a government's ability to perform such tasks as the collection of revenue or the maintenance of public order."[12] Under some circumstances, quite the opposite can be the case, he stresses, because big bureaucracies can become top-heavy, inefficiently filled with patronage workers who do little.[13]

The traditional statist literature, his work reminds us, has failed to distinguish between what a state is entitled to do and what it actually can accom-

plish. Building on Michael Mann's distinction between despotic and infrastructural power, he underscored how the former may be less effective than
the latter: better to govern with fingers than thumbs.[14] A liberal state possesses advantages in solving problems of coordination and building extensive
capacities, because it is more likely to be accepted as legitimate and better
able to harness the pluralism of civil society by hitching "stateness" to competing political coalitions. Thus, liberal states can enter the world arena
assertively and confidently. Reciprocally, as open and engaged states, they
are also susceptible to international influences.

Hence, I consider the United States in its first six decades of independence as an assertive, expansive, and permeable liberal state. At the core of
this evaluation lie convictions about the *institutional* character of liberalism.
Though liberalism was first fashioned to place limits on what sovereign
states could do, it presumed their existence; liberalism was statist from the
start. Like all states, liberal ones rest on a bedrock of coercion. Like all
states, liberal states rely on organized force to protect (and sometimes enlarge) their borders and police their populations. Unlike other states, however, they compose mixed regimes. Their central innovation is representation (which literally means to present again, thus making to "present an
absent"),[15] geared both to tame the executive and bring civil society inside
an uncommonly permeable polity.[16] Consequently, liberalism is more than
a doctrine. It is an institutional design combining indivisible sovereignty and
force with representation and rights. More than a set of ideas, political liberalism defines the character of policy contests and provides representative
means to resolve them. By taking decisions based on the preferences of their
members, representative bodies shape and limit the exercise of sovereignty
and decide key policy questions concerned with how the state will be linked
to society, to the economy, and to an international arena composed of a
system of interstate relations, but not independently or autonomously of the
pressures exerted by war and trade.

Reconsidering Administrative Capacity and
   Central State Authority

Issues of force and inclusion (of people and territory) underpin each of
these zones of transaction. For this reason, the military provides a privileged
vantage from which to probe the character, ambitions, and limits of the
United States as a liberal state. A major obstacle to this research program is
the powerful view equating political liberalism and state weakness. Both the
American military and the state within which it was embedded have been
underestimated badly, widely portrayed as weak, amateur, decentralized,
negligible. The decades before the Civil War commonly are understood to

be the premodern period of American statebuilding, the era before "national administrative capacities" or "central state authority" — to note the key phrases in Skowronek's and Bensel's subtitles — had developed and the United States had not yet achieved the full ensemble of institutions and capacities thought to be hallmarks of modern states. A fresh look at early American statebuilding through the prism of military spending, deployment, and activity, especially in the period after the country's sovereignty and independence from Europe were, after much uncertainty, secured in the War of 1812, but before its unity was reconfirmed in the Civil War, calls into question the conceptual apparatus and familiar empirical claims made about antebellum state formation.[17] More particularly, the pattern of American statebuilding calls into question the portrait, so closely identified with the scholarship of Skowronek, of "early America as a state of courts and parties" and the utilization of centralization as the main indicator for state strength, as in the work of Bensel.[18]

Skowronek's *Building a New American State* effectively launched American political development as a subfield and revived interest in public administration by inserting administrative developments and an assessment of state capacity into an exciting emergent literature on statebuilding in comparative political sociology and political science. Building on work by Tilly, Skocpol, and other comparative historical social scientists, as well as by such learned students of American bureaucracy as Woodrow Wilson and Leonard White,[19] Skowronek restored a focus on the state to American political studies. His starting point was 1877, after the substantive reunification of the country on racist terms. His focus was the expansion of national public authority and ability, especially in the military, the civil service, and the apparatus of economic regulation. The prior decades he treated as constituting a prehistory to modern statebuilding, a time when, as an organizational entity, the state lacked a concentration of authority at the center, centralization of authority within the national government, a specialization of tasks, or "the penetration of institutional controls from the governmental center throughout the territory." The United States, he claims, had renounced these abilities at its founding. This portrait, implicitly drawing on Weber's standard for modern bureaucracies, explicitly measured America's liberal state against a model drawn from France or Prussia, of concentrated sovereignty and capacity as key aspects of modern stateness.[20] On such a standard, antebellum America falls short; after all, its procedural routines and its key intellectuals and elites were lodged in the court system and in the political parties, not in the executive side of the state.[21]

This also is the tack Skowronek took in characterizing the military before post-Reconstruction reforms. From this perspective, the antebellum military is weak, like the state as a whole. Listen as he contrasts the demobilization of the Union army, from some one million armed soldiers in 1865 to a mere twenty-seven thousand by 1874, to French and German mobilization during this same period: "When the Germans marched into Paris in 1870, America was firmly committed to a thorough demilitarization. Once again, international main currents in institutional development ran directly counter to the main currents in American political development. As the Prussian revolution in military organization swept Europe, the American army was being swept back into obscurity as an Indian patrol." Note both the foil and the deprecation, made possible only by forgetting the state building tasks successfully concluded by the antebellum military. Reform, from Skowronek's perspective, did not build on this legacy but contradicted it as a result of functional necessity. "There was, however," he observed, "no going back. It soon became apparent that industrial America could not afford the military innocence of the bucolic age."[22]

In effect, he embraced the perspective of Emory Upton, the late nineteenth century's leading military reformer, theoretician, and professor at West Point, who argued in 1875, on his return from Europe, that America's armed forces did not measure up to the advanced, professional, centralized Prussian model.[23] By application of this standard for effectiveness and efficiency, the United States was a laggard. Its "tiny band of regulars," Skowronek insists, were fed at the trough "of pork barrel contracts and development projects its Washington staff could distribute to congressional constituencies." Its militia structure, moreover, was composed merely of "voluntary social clubs organized by various ethnic and status groups, subsidized by the federal government, and fused with state and local party politics through ties of patronage."[24] In brief, the military, appraised by Upton's criteria, simply was an aspect of the party-dominated politics of distribution. This, we soon shall see, is a very partial portrait at best. Bucolic the United States may have been, in the sense of "agrarian"; bucolic as in "peaceful," hardly.

Likewise, it is the "European" standard of a strong, centralized state, capable of autonomous action vis-à-vis the economy and civil society as well as in the international system, that Bensel applies in *Yankee Leviathan*, where he argues, contra Skowronek, that the key period of "the origins of central state authority" came during, not after, the period of the Civil War and Reconstruction. Bensel made advances on which it is important to build: he deployed a more systematic categorization of the dimensions of public rule, leaving more room for variation, and focused more on sectionalism, Congress, and policymaking. But he too treated the pre–Civil War state, including its military, as falling short of modern standards of public administration.[25] Before the war, America's "extremely weak ante-bellum state" was merely "nascent"; it lacked "a 'statist' sensibility, an identity and interest apart from any class or partisan interest."[26]

Historians, likewise, when they think about the statebuilding dimension at all, tend to take for granted the underdeveloped qualities of the U.S. State before the Civil War. The best recent synthesis of the antebellum period, is called, emblematically, *The Market Revolution*[27] yet it makes only episodic and unsystematic references to the American state and public policy, almost as if these questions were beside the point or political developments were driven by an inexorable and inclusive project of economic modernization.

Why quarrel? We know that no market revolution is possible without a statist framework to provide stability and security through protection, regulation, and law. Markets never free-float.[28] We know, too, that the core elements of "stateness" include a claim to indivisible sovereignty over people and territory; an ensemble of institutions — understood both as rules and as organizations — differentiated from the persons who rule, the populations over which they rule, and the other main macrostructures of civil society and the economy; and a normative dimension claiming that this or that kind of regime is good and just. Further, sovereign states deploy their claims, institutional abilities, and normative assertions to police, penetrate, and regulate society and the economy and to defend or extend the territories and populations they control against the asseverations of other putative sovereigns.

By these markers, the early American state hardly can be dismissed as "weak," insignificant, or merely incipient. Its normative orientation, set in global context, was profoundly revolutionary: liberal, republican, and democratic (albeit only for a slice of the populace). Its success in claiming, protecting, and extending sovereignty was unprecedented in scope. It defined a new kind of citizenship. It invented a federal system; convened effective representation via Congress; brought into being a system of mass political parties at a time of limited communications; managed uncommon problems of center and periphery created by the scale of the country; established a physical and legal framework for economic development, rapid urbanization, and population growth; and coordinated vastly different sectional civilizations and political economies.

To be sure, viewed from a comparative perspective, the central bureaucracy of the United States was small and limited. In 1840, the country employed approxiately twenty-thousand civilians, fourteen thousand of whom worked for the post office. There were only one thousand federal employees in Washington, a town Morton Keller describes as "slovenly, indolent, half-finished . . . the physical embodiment of the American distaste for centralized government."[29] Yet the behavior and achievements of America's state belie the conventional story of restriction. The United States may have had a state of limited size and centralization, but this state was flexible, effective, and efficient. Inventing novel forms, it secured the major goals of statebuilders with an advantageous ratio of achievement to cost. In this light, the accounts given, among others, by Skowronek and Bensel are not so much wrong as insufficient. The American state was integrated and governed, not just by courts and parties, but by various sanctioned armed forces (as well as key complementary instruments of publicly organized communication and commerce, especially the far-flung network of post offices, turnpikes, and canals).[30] Nor did the United States enter the world of international relations only in the twentieth century; it was embedded in the international scene from the beginning, and it possessed a military adapted to promote the country's territorial extension, trade, and security. Like the state itself, it was a military not quite like any other.

Consider Alabama. Not one of the original thirteen states, its growing white settlement on the western edge of the cotton frontier justified admission to the Union in 1819. Early in 1812, Tecumseh, a Shawnee who led the Indians of the Northwest, retreated to Canada with some thirty-five hundred of his men to fight alongside the British, who commissioned him as a brigadier general. That year, he traveled south, inspiring the Creeks in the Alabama territory to attack Americans on the Florida border.[31] In March and April 1814, Andrew Jackson, then a general in the state militia of neighboring Tennessee, decisively defeated the Creek at the Battle of Horseshoe Bend, fighting which entailed the willful killing of women and children, as well as male combatants. The Creek conveyed most of their lands to the United States, opening some twenty million acres for settlement, and moved further into Alabama's interior, where their relations with white settlers continued to be punctuated by episodes of violence. Alongside the Cherokee, Chicksaw, Choctaw, and Seminole, the Creek came to number among the "Five Civilized Tribes" of the South, which had largely given up a nomadic life for agricultural settlement. In 1830, frustrated at the slow pace of Indian removal westward from Florida, Georgia, Mississippi, Tennessee, and Alabama, Congress passed the Removal Act, which funded the negotiation of treaties of expulsion. During Jackson's presidency, virtually all the region's Indians were expelled to the new Indian Territory created in what later became Oklahoma by the Indian Intercourse Act of 1834. Alabama's Creeks were moved forcibly in 1836. By 1840, eighty thousand Indians had been relocated.[32]

This history of war between sovereign countries and of conflict between settlers and natives and the deployment of force under federal auspices was inscribed in the land's contours.[33] From the second decade of the century to the onset of the Civil War, fifty-seven forts were established in Alabama. Some were temporary. Fort Crawford in Escambia County, for example, a square with two blockhouses at diagonal corners, located a mile from today's town of Brewton, was built in 1817 across a stream on a rising hill to protect white settlers from pillaging Indians. One hundred regulars of the seventh U.S. Infantry garrisoned the fort in 1818. Once the local Indian population had been moved on, the fort was maintained at full strength only until 1819 and was abandoned two years later. Some garrisons were tiny. Early in 1818, during an Indian uprising, a stockade had been erected on the old Federal Road, fifteen miles west of Greenville in Butler County, around the home of Captain James Suffold. Now the site of Pine Flat it was named Fort Bibb in honor of the territorial governor, William Wyatt Bibb and provided a temporary safe haven for the very small number of local settlers in times of strife. Some, like Fort Clairborne, built in 1813, during the Creek War, on the Alabama River in Monroe County, were supply bases; others, like Fort Ingersoll of Russell County, Fort Coffee in Bullock County, and Fort Eufala in Barbour County, constructed in 1836 to enforce the evacuation of the Creek, were integral to situational strategies. Others, like Fort Jackson — a name it acquired only after the War of 1812 — twelve miles north of Montgomery had a longer lineage: from it Andrew Jackson, after his victory over the Creek at Horseshoe Bend, had fought his campaign against the British and the Spanish, culminating in the Battle of New Orleans. Fort aux Alibamos, later Fort Toulouse, was originally built in 1717 by the French, in the heart of the Creek Confederacy and at the invitation of the Creek, to protect trade routes and check the influence of the British. It was turned over to Britain in 1763 at the end of the French and Indian War and fell into disuse by 1776 , only the moats and cannon still remaining by the time Jackson rebuilt it in 1813. The fort's full reconstruction was completed by the militia from the Carolinas during the later stages of the War of 1812. At the close of the war, the fort was garrisoned by regular army regiments. Jackson Town, a small settlement, was built in its shadow, only to be abandoned, along with the fort, by the end of 1817, in favor of the settlement downriver, the new town of Montgomery.

Thus we see that the military in Alabama, including both its national and state components, was small, flexible, and capable of achieving the greatest task of statebuilders: defining, expanding, and securing boundaries. In this respect, it represented a distinctive, but quite typical, microcosm of the military in the United States more generally, and it demonstrated a truism of statebuilding: organized coercion and protection are at the core of modern sovereignty.

This was no less true of the United States in its early decades than of Europe. Leaving to one side the vexing meaning of membership in state militias (while noting that in 1816 more than 748,000 American men were enrolled in militias, which ranged from ethnic — mainly Irish — associations and social clubs to well-drilled fighting forces, and in 1827 over 1,150,000, at times when the total population of the country numbered just 8,659,000 and 11,909,000, respectively),[34] expenditures on the military dwarfed all other outlays in the country's national budget, accounting for at least 72 per cent of the total each year and sometimes and up to 94 per cent of federal spending each year but one between 1808 and 1848. From 1848 through

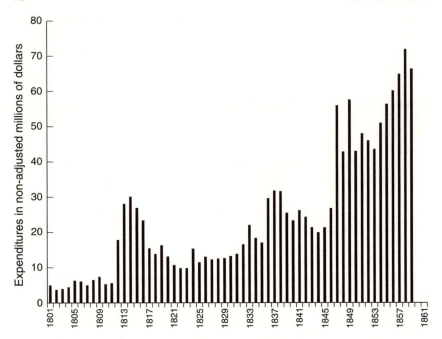

FIG. 4.1. Total U.S. Expenditures, 1800–1860. Note that for 1843 the federal government reported expenditures only for January 1–June 30. To compensate, the reported number is doubled. Source: *The American Almanac and Repository of Useful Knowledge* (various years); *Reports of the Secretary of the Treasury of the United States* (various years).

the outbreak of the Civil War in 1861, as the national government took on enhanced responsibilities for internal improvements and civilian federal expenditures increased dramatically, the military maintained about half the total share of federal spending (see figures 4.1–4.3). These monies, of course, were not limited to land-based forces. As a great trading country, the United States developed an effective navy to guard its sea lanes and secure its shipping. From 1798 to 1848, naval spending either outpaced or approximately equaled all civilian federal spending combined.[35]

The country's military, in short, developed considerable capacity in the antebellum era, serving a state without fixed territory, settled neighbors, or, most of the time, large nearby land armies. To the west, it faced indigenous peoples and uncertain borderlands; to the south, a mix of slave societies, Mexico (whose capital it came to occupy), and the Americas; to the north, a Tory offshoot; and to the east, a vast European ocean vital to American commerce. Each of these relations was fraught with danger and opportunity; each required military decision and force; each demanded effective

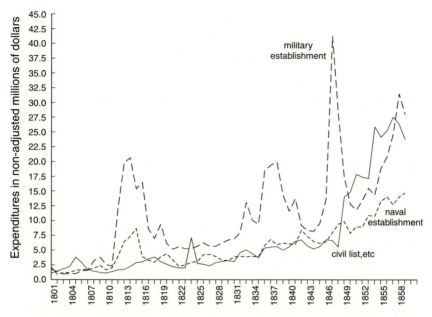

FIG. 4.2. Military, Naval, and Civil Expenditures, 1800–1860. Note that for 1843 the federal government reported expenditures only for January 1–June 30. To compensate, the reported number is doubled. Source: *The American Almanac and Repository of Useful Knowledge* (various years); *Reports of the Secretary of the Treasury of the United States* (various years).

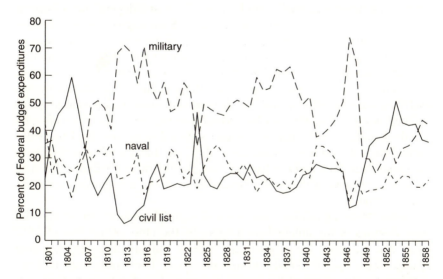

FIG. 4.3. Military, Naval, and Civil Expenditures as Percentage of Federal Budget, 1800–1860. Source: *The American Almanac and Repository of Useful Knowledge* (various years); *Reports of the Secretary of the Treasury of the United States* (various years).

ties between the state and the economy and civil society; each had vast
implications for the contours of state the country would adopt. Further, the
United States was the only Western country to internalize a slave regime;
thus it possessed a distinctive racial civilization partially integrated into a
liberal political and market capitalist order. This set of relations, too, not
least in cotton-rich and slaveholding Alabama, was mediated by the military.

America's Military: Challenges of Liberalism and Security, Center and Periphery[36]

Once the Treaty of Paris was signed in September 1783, George Washington, facing mutinies, quickly demobilized the military, keeping only some
six hundred troops in arms. When Congress charged a committee, chaired
by Alexander Hamilton, to study the contours of a postwar army under the
Articles of Confederation, Washington recommended a multitiered system:
(1) a capable navy to protect commerce; (2) state militia service for all men
between eighteen and fifty; (3) a volunteer militia under national control;
and (4) a regular army "to awe the Indians, protect our Trade, prevent the
encroachment of our Neighbors of Canada and the Floridas, and guard us
at least from surprises; also for security of our magazines." He thought these
goals could be accomplished with a small force of some 2,630 officers and
men, composing one artillery and four infantry regiments. Though Hamilton's committee endorsed a similar plan, the post-independence Congress
failed to agree on this or alternative designs. Sectional rivalry, institutional
jealousy from the states, and widespread fear of the tyrannical capacities of
standing armies blocked adoption. Yet even under the articles, the nucleus
of a small but flexible national frontier force was created. At the close of its
session in June 1784, Congress disbanded the established infantry regiments
and the extant battalion of artillery (leaving only some eighty men to guard
military stores at Fort Pitt and West Point) but created a new force of seven
hundred soldiers, really the first regular national army, recruited by assessment from state militias. Its task was to deal with Indians allied with Britain
in upstate New York and the Upper Ohio (the British had failed to evacuate
their frontier posts, as they had promised in the treaty recognizing American
independence).

Though delayed, Washington's broad design did come to characterize the
basic features of the antebellum military by the close of the War of 1812
(with the exception of a volunteer federal militia). The key enabling
changes were constitutional and administrative. The Convention in 1787
significantly strengthened the fiscal, commercial, and military potential of
the national state by providing the regime with a capacity independent of
the constituent states to raise taxes; by creating an executive branch capable

of acting without regular reference to the states; by naming the president the commander in chief, charged with deploying peacetime military force and shaping wartime military operations; by making the civil and military administration of the armed forces accountable to the president; by designating the power to raise armies, create a navy, and declare war to be central government prerogatives; and by giving the federal government the capacity to place troops from state militias under the command of the United States "to execute the Laws of the Union, suppress Insurrections and repel Invasions." In practice, however, only a puny national military was fashioned, one well short of Washington's, and especially Hamilton's, preferences. Four months into Washington's first term, Congress created the Department of War but not a navy, and the army itself, still numbering only eight hundred, was primarily stationed in forts along the Ohio River. This tiny force had virtually no field organization or supply infrastructure. Only with the large-scale mobilization of troops for the War of 1812 did military administration alter very significantly.

Yet well before the outbreak of war, elements of Washington's and Hamilton's design had taken hold, in response to four challenges, both domestic and international, that the new republic had to confront. The first was internal disorder, beginning with civil unrest in Massachusetts in 1786. Under conditions of commercial depression, agrarian crowds began to harass lawyers, disturb court proceedings, and endanger the federal government's arsenal in Springfield. Congress, having resisted Washington's plan, was sufficiently concerned to call on the region's states to muster a force of some thirteen hundred soldiers. Before the force was deployed, an attack on the arsenal, led by Daniel Shays, was resisted successfully by militiamen. Nonetheless, Shay's rebellion prodded the first postwar reinforcement of the federal military and helped goad the Constitutional Convention to enhance the military powers of the new central government. In 1794, the Whiskey Rebellion in western Pennsylvania was suppressed by the deployment of a large militia force by President Washington under the authority of the basic militia law of 1792, which had specified the enrollment in state militias of "every able-bodied white male citizen" aged eighteen to forty-five. Military control of domestic disorder became a recurrent theme of the antebellum era, in such incidents as the tax rebellion led by John Fries in 1799; the Burr Conspiracy and embargo troubles before the War of 1812; the slave rebellions, the nullification crisis, and the Chesapeake and Ohio Canal Riots in the early 1830s; and the Dorr Rebellion of 1842; and in governmental responses, including enforcement of the fugitive slave laws, and military intervention to pacify Kansas in the 1850s.[37]

The second goad to development of a capable military was the problem of security at the fringes of the country. Supported and armed by the British, the Indians of the Northwest fiercely opposed white incursion. Their resistance proved powerful (in the Kentucky Territory alone more than fifteen hundred settlers were either captured or killed during the Confederacy). A militia force drawn from Kentucky, Pennsylvania, and Virginia was deployed against the Miami Indians in tandem with a small regular army contingent but failed utterly in its effort to dislodge them. A second expedition of 1,400 troops, half federal regulars and half militia, were decimated by a brilliant attack that killed 637 and left 263 wounded. The western tribes only succumbed in 1795, ceding their Ohio lands by treaty. They did so only after military defeats inflicted by a much larger expeditionary force of some 3,000 under federal command that had proceeded systematically, stopping to build effective forts along the line of its march.[38] For the next fifteen years, Tecumseh and his brother, the Prophet, coordinated a tribal confederacy in the Northwest to confront white settlement. In 1811, William Henry Harrison, governor of the Indian Territory, arranged a partnership of some 650 local militia with 350 regular troops placed under his command by the secretary of war and mounted a decisive strike against the confederacy, successfully fighting a bloody battle (39 American battle deaths, 151 injuries, and 29 subsequent deaths, with roughly equal Indian losses) at Tippecanoe Creek. Indian fighting, of course, remained a central military task throughout the nineteenth century.

The third set of military challenges the new nation faced was related to the wars after the French Revolution in Europe. Prior to the negotiation of the Jay Treaty in 1794, Britain had seized more than three hundred American merchant ships. Then the French began capturing American vessels and incarcerating their crews, opening a period of "quasi-war" that peaked in 1798 and 1799. These developments sparked America's decision to create an effective naval fleet under the aegis of a separate Navy Department, harbor defenses, and a marine corps (as an adjunct to the navy at sea and to the army on land). Further, the army was reorganized to complement its Indian fighting with border defense capabilities. It did so by substituting a traditional regimental organization for the legion type of design suitable for frontier forays, by shifting infantry companies to significant forts at the country's borders, especially to the north, and by placing garrisons at major seaports. In 1803, a second round of conflict between the French and British led both powers to attack American commerce. The United States first responded by withdrawing its shipping from the Atlantic and then by prohibiting foreign trade.[39] In 1812, Congress declared war on the British (the Senate failing by only two votes to declare war on France as well). To prepare for war, the country ratcheted up its military capacity. In January 1812, five months before the start of the War of 1812, Congress supplemented a relatively modest military expansion during Jefferson's presidency and the early part of Madison's by adding thirteen regiments of some 26,000 men to the federal army, which brought the authorized strength of the army to 35,600 (only 5,000 of whom had been recruited and trained by June), and by empowering the mobilization of 50,000 militia members into the federal service. In addition to this great expansion of the army, Congress modernized the system of supply by creating a Quartermaster's Department within the military to replace a civilian agent system, enlarging the Corps of Engineers, reorganizing West Point, and developing an Ordnance Department responsible for the quality of weaponry and ammunition.

The fourth military challenge the United States faced was the more specific threat to American sovereignty posed by the War of 1812. This menace was concretized in Britain's conquest and sacking of Washington, D.C., including the White House and the Capitol, after its troops had been freed up by the defeat of Napoleon at Waterloo. During its ultimately successful war with the world's leading power, the United States not only put nearly 40,000 federal regulars under arms but mobilized some 450,000 members of state militias, of whom half served at the front. The federal troops proved more reliable. In the aftermath of the war, the army was further professionalized in the officer corps and reorganized to improve communications and command. Incompetents were laid off, and a peacetime strength of 10,000 regulars, still very modest by European standards in the age of Napoleonic warfare, was authorized, a level roughly maintained for the first half-decade of peace. More important, when 4,000 of these troops were demobilized in 1820, John Calhoun, who had become Secretary of War in December 1817, pioneered the concept of the "expansible military": in normal periods, small and deployed in garrisons on the frontier, yet capable of rapid growth if the United States were to become involved in an international war. This adaptable military would disperse into individual companies at many isolated, often temporary, forts. But at times of such large-scale conflict as the major Indian wars or the Mexican War, the companies were consolidated into brigades and divisions. Overarching both types of tactical deployment was a decentralized administrative structure. Geographical departments were grouped into large territorial divisions (at the outbreak of the Civil War there were six: East, West, Texas, New Mexico, Utah, and Pacific), whose commanders reported directly to the secretary of war and to the commanding general in Washington.

From the conclusion of the War of 1812 to the Civil War, in short, the military served as an instrument to control domestic insurgency, secure the frontier, protect shipping lanes, and provide a framework for the coexistence of free and slave civilizations. American soldiers and sailors enforced the compromises of 1820 and 1850, pushed westward (often ahead of settlers) to survey and build roads, guard post offices, and exile Indians, shielded sea lanes at a time of a massive expansion in trade, and successfully fought a major war with Mexico, thus dramatically extending the country's reach. (During the occupation of Mexico City, the Treaty of Guadaloupe Hidalgo

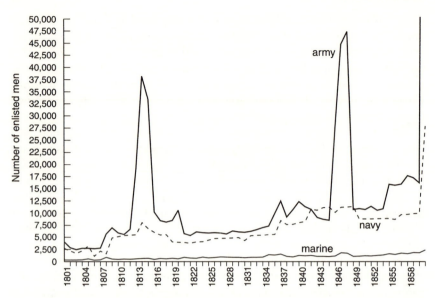

FIG. 4.4. Uniformed Personnel, U.S. Army, Navy, Marine Corps, 1801–1861.
Source: *Historical Statistics of the United States: Colonial Times to 1970.*

was negotiated, which recognized the Rio Grande as the border for Texas
and ceded what became the states of California, Arizona, New Mexico,
Utah, and Nevada, as well as portions of Wyoming and Colorado, to the
United States). At the onset of the Mexican War, the army consisted of
fewer than 9,000 troops, but these numbers more than quintupled during its
course.[40]

From the founding until the early 1850s, troop levels in the army and
navy combined usually hovered between 10,000 and 20,000 men under
arms. This steady-state military was capable of dealing with domestic distur-
bances, fighting Indians, and maintaining open sea lanes. Twice in the antebellum period, the size of the army increased fivefold in a very short period:
at the outset of the War of 1812 and of the Mexican War. This mobilization
to fight wars against traditional states with regular armies was both rapid and
effective, but so was the swift demobilization which followed these confla-
grations. There was virtually no "ratchet effect" (see figure 4.4).

The country's lean, very mobile, "expansible" military produced a remarkable, and relatively low-cost, extension to the country's sovereign capacity and international reach. But it was more than war between countries that
"made" the modern American state.[41] In addition, western development and
its associated projects of territorial government, its land agencies, land offices, and military garrisons, its post office and route expansion, drove a
salient between Mexico and Canada. There was a tight fit between the

military and westward settlement activity. If we treat revenue generated by federal land sales as a reasonable measure of settlement activity, it is not surprising that moments of major increase coincide with the most vigorous periods of Indian removal (see figures 4.5 and 4.6).

The braiding of military activity and westward settlement served, in Richard White's phrase, "as the kindergarten of the American state."[42] This evocative expression, however, captures only part of the accomplishment and character of the epoch's expansion. By the time of the Civil War, the United States had become a transcontinental republic and had begun the project of connecting and integrating the coasts by rail. When President James K. Polk presented to Congress the Treaty of Guadaloupe Hidalgo ending the Mexican War, he observed that the territories ceded by Mexico, "New Mexico and Upper California . . . constitute of themselves a country large enough for a great empire";[43] and so it was, composed half of states, half of territories. At peace with Britain, the only naval power capable of challenging it on the seas, the United States also became a great oceanic power, trading from the ports of New York, Philadelphia, Baltimore, Savannah, New Orleans, and Boston, and also from the ports on the Mississippi and the Pacific Coast. With a U.S. naval 'squadron patrolling the Pacific since 1822, the "Pacific frontage of the United States" came to be linked by the 1850s "in some cases quite routinely, with Mazatlan, Callao, and Valparaiso, with New Baranof (Sitka) and Kamchatka, Canton, Tahiti, Australia, and New Zealand, and pivotal to all these, the Hawaiian Islands." A commercial treaty was signed with China in 1844 and a decade later Commander Matthew Perry's calibrated show of force helped open diplomatic and trade relations with previously closed Japan.[44]

This striking tale of accomplishment, to which military development was integral, is, in part, the story of how the new republic — highly conscious of itself as a revolutionary government based on popular sovereignty and consent between equal (white male) citizens — grappled with the problem of institutionalized coercion. In this setting, Tilly's treatment of states as, by definition, repositories of coercion cannot simply be taken as a truism; as Peter Manicas has stressed in his interesting book *War and Democracy*, in the United States ideological purpose had a radically new role to play in military affairs. Unlike the ancient republics, "[where] no one who had to fight a war was excluded from the [direct] decision to go to war," American citizens were bound by the decisions of representative institutions; but unlike the subjects of absolutist regimes, they had to be mobilized ideologically by political leaders and parties for war and military projects, or else these would not be realized. In grappling with issues of coercion, the United States had to define and redefine what it meant by citizenship; how it saw relations among the constituent states; how it viewed the balance between its northern and southern civilizations; how it treated the boundary

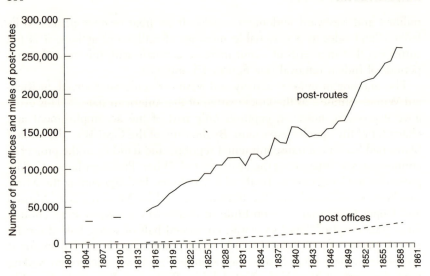

FIG. 4.5. Post Offices and Postal Route Mileage in States and Territories, 1800–1860. Source: *The American Almanac and Repository of Useful Knowledge* (various years).

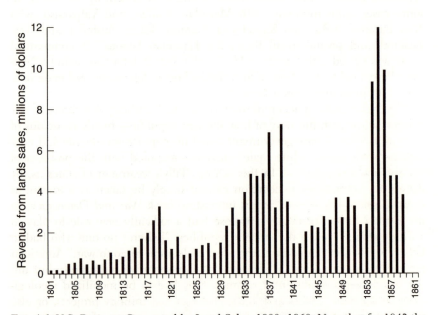

FIG. 4.6. U.S. Revenue Generated by Land Sales, 1800–1860. Note that for 1843 the federal government reported expenditures only for January 1–June 30. To compensate, the reported number is doubled. Source: *The American Almanac and Repository of Useful Knowledge* (various years).

between the savage and the civilized; and how it placed itself in the wider Europe-centered international system.[45]

Before the Civil War there was a profound irony at work. By the positioning of its troops, the United States defined US boundaries; literally, it was a state whose shape and limits were marked by military garrisons.[46] Compared to the European countries with which it had the most dealings, the number of its men under arms was small and its expenditures relatively slight. Nonetheless, it was the military that crucially defined the key contours of America's regime in space and in ambition and served, against the European grain, as an instrument to extend the heterogeneity of the population. The American people came to be shaped not only by diverse voluntary flows from Europe and involuntary diverse flows from Africa but by the French in Louisiana, Hispanics in the Southwest, Mormons in their enclave, over one hundred native nations, and a vast array of peoples in California, and defined a national project that did not require a singular people or nationality.

The military was an instrument and a marker for this multifaceted regime. America's army was organized in a manner that was at once centralized, by authority in Washington, yet decentralized, both by territorial organization of the regular forces and by the flexible instrument of state militias. In crises large and small, the bounds of state and national forces proved permeable, as their relations came to be characterized by multiple forms of collaboration and risk taking. So, too, did the line dividing public and private coercion: men over eighteen were expected to be armed (in accord with the Constitution's Second Amendment) and come to their militia service with their own rifles and guns; settlers as well as soldiers policed roads and riverways.[47] Likewise, the line of demarcation between Indian affairs and foreign policy was blurred, as there was a mutual constitution of these domains throughout the antebellum period. At some locations, the territory of the country to be patrolled by the army was fixed and clear; in others, deeply ambiguous and often entwined with other sovereignties and quasi-sovereignties.[48] The nation's small military was constantly in motion, its forts often fixed only for short periods, its navy always on the move, searching for pressure points and keen to deter interference with the country's considerable commercial and geopolitical ambitions.

This military not only solved its own multidimensional challenges but also provided answers to the country's great normative question of how to make sovereignty and popular rule compatible. It also helped to solve the practical problem of how to rule over a great variety of people and a vast expanse of territory without compromising the country's unity or sovereignty.

As Manicas acutely observes, America democratized war by simultaneously widening the scope of military inclusion far beyond the trained and disciplined personnel who served in continental Europe and by linking

public consent, given through representative liberal assemblies (state legislatures and Congress) to military tasks. Citizens and their representatives had
to sanction missions for troops and agree to appropriate tax schedules and
fiscal obligations. As a result, ideology — liberal, democratic, imperial, racist,
republican — became critical to mobilization and risk taking. A minority of
citizens (white males) were located inside the polity as voters, hence governed but not ruled, each juridically equal to the other. In this context,
novel solutions had to be found to the problem of maintaining military
subordination to civilian authority and liberal institutions without sacrificing
military discipline and effectiveness, as well as to the problem of authorizing
internal diversity between cultures, regions, classes, religons, even civilizations, inside American boundaries while sustaining a genuine union, integrated by common military institutions and authority. Further, the military
defined the contours of peoplehood. Groups excluded from actual or virtual
(as in the indirect representation of women through assumptions of patri-
archal responsibility) military service, most notably slaves but also, in most
places, free blacks, did not command the full status of citizens. America's
flexible military, in short, did more than extend and protect state sovereignty; it made, and reflected, that sovereignty, a type of soverignty compatible with a racially bounded, culturally heterogeneous, and class-strained liberal democracy.[49]

As Jack Greene notes, when discussing what he calls the "constitutional
development in the extended polities of the British Empire and the United
States," the post-Revolutionary American regime faced virtually the same
conundrum with respect to sovereignty and governance that the British Empire had failed to resolve in its long period of rule in North America: the
problem of how to balance the center and the periphery. In both cases,
political authorities had to contend with far-flung and diverse populations,
civil societies, and economies and thus had to develop formulas of governance that could balance the unity and authority of the center with appropriate decentralization. In defining the central issues of early American statebuilding this way, Greene forces a revision of the standard accounts of
statehood, which conflate centralization with capacity. The problem of integrating a state with the territory and reach of an empire was especially
formidable in the United States, because of the dissimilarity between the
colonies and states, the pervasive distrust of centralized power, the insecure
sense of national identity as compared to local and regional singularity, a
history of separate state capacities, and the absence of successful models. In
the face of these challenges, America's military and its projects of protecting
borders, extending territory, and guarding commerce tapped and reinforced
those aspects of America's ideological kitbag and culture which were shared
by whites across their regional and civilizational divide: a common opposition to "savages" of color and to the European powers, a widespread fear of

disorder, and a de facto knowledge of federalism and decentralization gained under British rule.[50] The one problem the expansible military could not solve, of course, was that of slavery and its implications. Rather, before the Civil War, it was overwhelmed by sectional conflict — but not without first providing models, albeit on a comparatively modest scale, for the swift mobilization of men under arms prepared for combat. Indeed, the very features of flexibility, mobilization, and the imbrication of public and private capacity which had produced America's uncommon antebellum military also generated capacity for the globe's first total war.

Studying Liberal Stateness

By way of a conclusion, it might be useful to distinguish my reevaluation of the antebellum state from a recent important effort to reconsider "the theme of political declension" running through the view that the national state was "a midget institution in a giant land."[51] Surveying the best new scholarship by his fellow historians while seeking to draw more attention to the effects of national state institutions and policies, Richard John persuasively argues that the early republic has been "often misunderstood."

> It has, for example, become customary for scholars to contend that the central government sank into relative insignificance following the defeat of the Federalists in the election of 1800; that the polity between 1800 and 1828 is adequately charactrized as a 'state of courts and parties'; and that the rise of the Jacksonian party in the election of 1828 was a product of more fundamental changes originating in the wider society outside of the political realm. Each of these assertions is challenged by the recent scholarship this essay surveys.[52]

John pushes back against the view that sees American statebuilding as negligible before the Civil War. The literature he surveys stresses Federalist and Jacksonian efforts to create military and civilian bureaucracies, expand territory, produce goods on a mass scale for military purposes, and put in place a vast network of post offices and roads. Through institutional innovation and public policy, and by providing security for the internal mobility of white citizens, John argues, a strong early American state "bound together in a national community millions of Americans, most of whom would never meet in person."[53]

Why differ? John treats "governmental institutions as agents of change" by choosing to "dwell less on institutional origins than on institutional effects."[54] There are important gains to be had here, not least putting to rest simpleminded antinomies contrasting state and society: American society, John shows, was shaped by state policies, bureaus, and regulations. But we also lose something through this orientation. A decision to focus on effects rather than origins cuts off considerations of stateness both from international influences, including war and trade, and from the dynamics of political representation, political liberalism's central regime feature.

A second decision John takes is to accept, in effect, the criteria for state strength found in the literature on European state formation, that is, to focus on centralized administrative capacity. His disputes with scholars who regard the early American state as insignificant are more empirical than conceptual. John simply tells a different story, while using the same instruments to identify state capacity. In consequence, he makes it difficult to get at the heart of the matter, the distinctive character of the country's liberal state. John concludes his review essay with a call for more research: "Among topics worth exploring are public finance, taxation, and the administrative workings of state, city, and local government."[55] The military, surprisingly, is conspicuously absent.[56]

A revised research program beckons, one that places the military at the center of accounts of the American liberal state. It would begin, first, with an understanding that state and empire in antebellum America were guided primarily by how Congress used the military. Congress represented the states, managed sectionalism, appropriated funds, fashioned laws, and served as the locus for party politics and the rule setter for civil society rather more than the bureaucracies studied by Leonard White for the antebellum period or by Skowronek and Bensel for the post–Civil War epoch.

Second, ties between putatively domestic and international politics would be understood not merely as an interesting new subject of inquiry but as centrally constitutive of the American regime itself, given its swath of territory, its penchant for expansion, and its special security and trading challenges. Studies of American statebuilding have suffered grievously by ignoring the international dimension.

Third, it would appreciate how Tocqueville's discussion of slavery and Indian affairs, usually saluted as brilliant but off-center, suggests pivotal driving motivations that complement the usual geopolitical and global economic pressures—shaping the small, flexible, effective American state and its military.[57] In addition to the protection of its security and commerce, the early American state had two main purposes: the management of a sectionally heterogeneous polity and the extension of its sovereignty and normative reach. If war and trade helped to make the American state, as Tilly and Spruyt, among others, argue that they helped to make European states, they did so within this particular context. Through its military, American liberalism and illiberalism were entwined, as in a braid.

Fourth, this new research program would acknowledge that the United States, by creating a liberal state of light mobilization but effective sovereignty and protection for commerce, became the archetype for a new, post-absolutist pattern of state formation. The kind of state pioneered in the antebellum period, and later remade more than once under divergent conditions, continues to confer on American statebuilding its exemplary qualities. These, arguably, are becoming increasingly important as regimes throughout the world are confronted with challenges of diversity, membership, and layered sovereignty akin to those the United States faced in its early decades.

Notes

My thoughts for this paper began to take shape at the New School. There, Aristide Zolberg first got me interested in this subject and more generally in learning to cross the international–domestic divide; Robert Latham deepened my sense of the important link between the history of militarism and liberal regimes; Charles Tilly, now my colleague at Columbia, kept pushing for an engagement between the Europe-oriented literature on state formation and new work in American political development; and Richard Bensel showed how it might be done. At Columbia, I owe keen thanks to John Lapinski, now at Yale, whose research assistance underpins the fiscal aspects of the discussion below, and to Helen Milner and Robert Shapiro for their thoughtful comments on an earlier draft. Likewise, I am in debt to Margaret Levi for her encouraging critical reading and to the discussion led off by Charles Stewart III at the MIT Conference on American Politics in May 2000.

1. Stephen Skowronek, *Building a New American State: The Expansion of National Administrative Capacities, 1877–1920* (New York: Cambridge University Press, 1982); Richard Franklin Bensel, *Yankee Leviathan: The Origins of Central State Authority in America, 1859–1877* (New York: Cambridge University Press, 1990); Theda Skocpol, *Protecting Soldiers and Mothers: The Political Origins of Social Policy in the United States* (Cambridge: Harvard University Press, 1992); Bartholomew Sparrow, *From Outside In: World War II and the American State* (Princeton: Princeton University Press, 1996); Daniel Kryder, *Divided Arsenal: Race and the American State during World War II (New York: Cambridge University Press, 2000).*

2. Brian M. Downing, *The Military Revolution and Political Change: Origins of Democracy and Autocracy in Early Modern Europe* (Princeton: Princeton University Press, 1992); Charles Tilly, *Coercion, Capital, and European States,* AD 990–1990 (Oxford: Blackwell, 1990).

3. See note 37 for significant examples.

4. Skowronek, *Building*; John Brewer, *The Sinews of Power: War, Money, and the English State, 1688–1783* (New York: Knopf, 1988).

5. Skowronek, *Building*, 19.

6. Ibid., 19, 29, 31–34.

7. Jack P. Greene, "The American Revolution," *American Historical Review* 105 (February 2000): 93.

8. Edmund Morgan, *Inventing the People: The Rise of Popular Sovereignty in England and America* (New York: Norton, 1988).

9. Jack P. Greene, *Peripheries and Center: Constitutional Development in the Ex-*

tended Polities of the British Empire and the United States, 1607–1788 (Athens: University of Georgia Press, 1986).

10. For thorough overviews, see Gordon S. Wood, *The Creation of the American Republic, 1776–1787* (Chapel Hill: University of North Carolina Press, 1969); and Stanley Elkins and Eric McKitrick, *The Age of Federalism: The Early American Republic, 1788–1800* (New York: Oxford University Press, 1993).

11. Brewer, *Sinews*, xix, ix.

12. Ibid., xix.

13. One crucial element that Brewer, Morgan, and Greene do not consider adequately is the role of race, slavery, and region in the British Empire and the United States. These "liberal" states were also (either at home or abroad) slave states, as deeply illiberal as they come. The status of this dualism poses an important question: How can the combination of liberalism and racialized limits to citizenship best be understood? Are these distinct or entwined traditions? A focus on the military can help us think about this issue, because race and the color line were so central to the country's ideological notions of "manifest destiny" and to its debates about the extension of territories and their admission as states to the Union. For discussions, see Rogers Smith, *Civic Ideals: Conflicting Visions of Citizenship in U.S. History* (New Haven: Yale University Press, 1997); Louis Hartz, *The Liberal Tradition in America: An Interpretation of American Political Thought since the Revolution* (New York: Harcourt, Brace & World, 1955); Reginald Horsman, *Race and Manifest Destiny: The Origins of American Racial Anglo-Saxonism* (Cambridge: Harvard University Press, 1981); Thomas R. Hietela, *Manifest Destiny: Anxious Aggrandizement in Late Jacksonian America* (Ithaca: Cornell University Press, 1985); and Michael F. Holt, *The Rise and Fall of the American Whig Party: Jacksonian Politics and the Onset of the Civil War* (New York: Oxford University Press, 1999).

14. Michael Mann, *The Sources of Social Power*, vol. 1, *A History of Power from the Beginning to* A.D. *1760* (New York: Cambridge University Press, 1986).

15. Wim Blockmans, "Representation (since the Thirteenth Century)," in *The New Cambridge Medieval History*, vol. 7, *c. 1415–c. 1500*, ed. Christopher Allmand (Cambridge: Cambridge University Press), 32.

16. Harvey Mansfield, Jr., *Taming the Prince: The Ambivalence of Modern Executive Power* (New York: Free Press, 1989).

17. In a provocative paper revisionist for its time, Herbert Bolton seeking "to supplement the purely nationalistic presentation to which we are accustomed," dated the American Revolution as spanning the period from 1776 to 1816, when the separation from Europe was finally established, and insisted that the Revolution be placed in the larger geopolitical setting of European history and warmaking. Herbert E. Bolton, "The Epic of Greater America," *American Historical Review* 38 (April 1933).

18. Skowronek, *Building*, 24. To be sure, he notes that "The early American state maintained an integrated legal order on a continental scale; it fought wars, expropriated Indians, secured new territories, carried on relations with other states, and aided economic development" but goes on to downplay its executive or administrative abilities and to virtually ignore its military history.

19. J. P. Nettl, "The State as a Conceptual Variable," *World Politics*, 20 (July 1968); Charles Tilly, "Reflections on the History of European State-Making," and

"Western State-Making and Theories of Political Transformation," in *The Formation of National States in Western Europe,* ed. Charles Tilly (Princeton: Princeton University Press, 1975); Theda Skocpol, *States and Social Revolutions.* New York: Cambridge University Press, 1979; Theda Skocpol, "Bringing the State Back In: Strategies of Analysis in Current Research," and Peter B. Evans, Dietrich Rueschemeyer, and Theda Skocpol, "On the Road toward a More Adequate Understanding of the State," both in *Bringing the State Bakc In,* ed. Peter B. Evans, Dietrich Rueschemeyer, and Theda Skocpol (Cambridge: Cambridge University Press, 1985); Woodrow Wilson, "The Study of Administration," *Political Science Quarterly* 2 (June 1887); Leonard White, *The Federalists: A Study in Administrative History* (New York: Macmillan, 1948); Leonard White, *The Jeffersonians: A Study in Administrative History, 1801–1829* (New York: Macmillan, 1951); and Leonard White, *The Jacksonians: A Study in Administrative History, 1829–1861* (New York: Macmillan, 1954).

20. Skowronek draws here on J. Rogers Hollingsworth, "The United States," in *Crises of Political Development in Europe and the United States,* ed. Raymond Grew, in the last volume of the SSRC Committee on Comparative Politics series Studies in Political Development (Princeton: Princeton University Press, 1978). My quarrel, of course, is not with comparison but with the particular standard of comparison applied.

21. About Congress, Skowronek is largely and inexplicably silent. I thank John Lapinski for this observation.

22. Skowronek, *Building.* 87.

23. Upton's key texts were *Armies of Asia and Europe* (New York: Appleton, 1878); and *The Military Policy of the United States* (Washington, D.C.: Government Printing Office, 1904).

24. Skowronek, *Building,* 89–92, 86.

25. In this, both Bensel and Skowronek were elaborating on the portrait of the weak, minimal state found in Hartz, *Liberal Tradition,* and Samuel P. Huntington, *Political Order in Changing Societies* (New Haven: Yale University Press, 1968).

26. Bensel, *Yankee Leviathan,* 2–3.

27. Charles Sellers, *The Market Revolution: Jacksonian America, 1815–1846* (New York: Oxford University Press, 1991).

28. The classic statement of this position is by Karl Polanyi, *The Great Transformation: The Political and Economic Origins of Our Time* (New York Rinehart, 1944).

29. The estimates are cited in Joel H. Silbey, *The American Political Nation, 1838–1893* (Stanford: Stanford University Press, 1991), 181. He also quotes Morton Keller, *Affairs of State: Public Life in Late Nineteenth Century America* (Cambridge: Harvard University Press, 1977), 98–99. See also the excellent study by James Sterling Young, *The Washington Community: 1800–1828* (New York: Harcourt, Brace, & World, 1966).

30. See Richard R. John, *Spreading the News: The American Postal System from Franklin to Morse* (Cambridge: Harvard University Press, 1995); L. Ray Gunn, *The Decline of Authority: Public Economic Policy and Political Development in New York, 1800–1860* (Ithaca: Cornell University Press, 1988); Louis Bernard Schmidt, "Internal Commerce and the Development of the American Economy before 1860," *Journal of Political Economy* 47 (December 1939); Diane Lindstrom, "American Economic Growth before 1840: New Evidence and New Directions," *Journal of Economic His-*

tory 39 (March 1979); and Stephen D. Minicucci, "Finding the cement of Interest: Internal Improvements and American Nation-Building, 1790–1860," Ph.D. diss. Massachusetts Institute of Technology, 1998).

31. The United States had concluded a treaty with the Creek Confederacy in 1790, essentially an agreement not to attack each other. For a history of Indian-white relations in the Northwest, see Richard White, *The Middle Ground: Indians, Empires, and Republics in the Great Lakes Region, 1650–1815* (Cambridge: Cambridge University Press, 1991).

32. For a treatment of this history, see Francis Paul Prucha, *The Sword of the Republic: The United States Army on the Frontier, 1783–1846* (New York: Macmillan, 1969).

33. The discussion of forts in Alabama is drawn from the invaluable information in Robert B. Roberts, *Encyclopedia of Historic Forts: The Military, Pioneer, and Trading Posts of the United States* (New York: Macmillan, 1988).

34. This information is drawn from *The American Almanac and Repository of Useful Knowledge* (Boston: Charles Bowen and New York: Collins & Hannay [and later by G. and C. & H. Carvill], 1830–61). The *Almanac*, cross-checked for specific years with *Reports of the Secretary of the Treasury of the United States* (in the early years often called *Letter from the Secretary of the Treasury*), is the main source used for the figures which follow, with the exception of figure 4, whose source is *Historical Statistics of the United States: Colonial Times to 1970*, vol. 2 (Washington, D.C.: Department of Commerce, 1976). Useful discussions of militias can be found in Lawrence Delbert Cress, *Citizens in Arms: The Army and the Militia in American Society to the War of 1812* (Chapel Hill: University of North Carolina Press, 1982); and John K. Mahon, *History of the Militia and the National Guard* (New York: Macmillan, 1983).

35. The search for a naval policy proved vexing. Considerations can be found in Linda Maloney, "The War of 1812: What Role for Sea Power?" and G. Terry Sharrer, "The Search for a Naval Policy, 1783–1812," both in *In Peace and War: Interpretations of American Naval History, 1775–1978*, ed. Kenneth J. Hagan (Westport, Conn.: Greenwood Press, 1978).

36. The historical discussion in this section draws from *American Military History*, Army Historical Series (Washington, D.C.: Center of Military History, U.S. Army, 1989); Marcus Cunliffe, *Soldiers and Civilians: The Martial Spirit in America, 1775–1865* (London: Eyre & Spottiswoode, 1968); William Addleman Ganoe, *The History of the United States Army* "New York: D. Appleton Century, 1942 [1924]); Donald R. Hickey, *The War of 1812: A Forgotten Conflict* (Urbana: University of Illinois Press, 1989); James A. Huston, *The Sinews of War: Army Logistics 1775–1953* (Washington, D.C.: Office of the Chief of Military History, U. S. Army, 1966); Marvin A. Kriedberg and Merton G. Henry, *History of Military Mobilization in the United States Army, 1775–1945* (Washington, D.C.: Department of the Army, 1955); Allan R. Millett and Peter Maslowski, *For the Common Defense: A Military History of the United States* (New York: Free Press, 1984); Raymond G. O'Connor, ed., *American Defense Policy in Perspective: From Colonial Times to the Present* (New York: John Wiley, 1965); John McAuley Palmer, *America in Arms: The Experience of the United States with Military Organization* (New Haven: Yale University Press, 1941); Russell F. Weigley, *History of the United States Army* (London: B. T. Batsford, 1969); and

Russell F. Weigley, *The American Way of War: A History of United States Military Strategy and Policy* (New York: Macmillan, 1973).

37. For a useful chronicle, see Robert W. Coakely, *The Role of Federal Military Forces in Domestic Disorders* (Washington, D.C.: Center of Military History, U. S. Army, 1988).

38. The Indians were made more vulnerable by the Jay Treaty of 1794, in which the British agreed to finally evacuate their frontier posts.

39. The Embargo Act of 1807 proscribed trade with all countries; the Non-Intercourse Act of 1809 restricted the prohibition to Britain and France; Macon's Bill No.2 of 1910 lifted the restrictions but provided that if either Britain or France repealed its restrictions and the other did not, the provisions of the 1809 Act would be restored.

40. For discussions, see K. Jack Bauer, *The Mexican War, 1846–1848* (New York: Macmillan, 1974); and John S.D. Eisenhower, *So Far from God: The U.S. War with Mexico, 1846–1848* (New York: Random House, 1989); and David M. Pletcher, *The Diplomacy of Annexation: Texas, Oregon, and the Mexican War* (Columbia: University of Missouri Press, 1973).

41. Tilly, in *Coercion*, famously pursued the theme that wars made states just as states made war.

42. Richard L. White, *"It's Your Misfortune and None of My Own": A History of the American West* (Norman: University of Oklahoma Press, 1991), 58. I am indebted to Guy Baldwin not only for this reference but for pointing to the intersection of models of a minimal bureaucratic American state that nonetheless, experienced unprecedented territorial growth. In his "Territorial Acquisition and Central State Expansion in Nineteenth-Century America: A Research Proposal" of (1994), Baldwin notes that "From the 1830s on, the American state maintained a substantially larger frontier military presence, directing it against Indians, but also Mexicans, Mormons, and Confederates. The presence fluctuated, but showed a long term rise through the 1870s as different phases of continental expansion produced threats of conflict" (13).

43. Cited in D. W. Meinig, *The Shaping of America: A Geographical Perspective on 500 Years of History*, vol 2, *Continental America, 1800–1867* (New Haven: Yale University Press, 1993).

44. Meinig, *Shaping*, 164.

45. Peter T. Manicas, *War and Democracy* (Oxford: Basil Blackwell, 1989), 126, 137, 148. On the role of parties, see Richard Hofstadter, *The Idea of a Party System* (Berkeley: University of California Press, 1965); John Aldrich, *Why Parties? The Origin and Transformation of Political Parties in America* (Chicago: University of Chicago Press, 1995); and Joel Silbey, *The American Political Nation, 1838–1893* (Stanford: Stanford University Press, 1991).

46. I do not mean to imply that antebellum state was a "garrison state" in Lasswell's sense, that is, state organized by specialists in violence. Harold D. Lasswell, "The Garrison State," *American Journal of Sociology* 46 (January 1941).

47. See Richard Hofstadter, "Reflections on Violence in the United States," in *American Violence: A Documentary History*, ed. Richard Hofstadter and Michael Wallace (New York: Knopf, 1970).

48. For a relevant discussion, see Janice Thompson, *Mercenaries, Pirates, and Sov-*

ereigns: State-Building and Extraterritorial Violence in Early Modern Europe (Princeton: Princeton University Press, 1994).

49. Between 1812 and the Civil War, as the obligatory militia declined in favor of a regular army and units of volunteers, the various schisms in civil society became quite apparent and later exploded in draft resistance during the Civil War, most visibly in the Draft Riots of 1863. For a useful overview of military-society relations in the era, see Margaret Levi, *Consent, Dissent, and Patriotism* (New York: Cambridge University Press, 1997), 58–66.

50. Greene, *Peripheries and Center*, 157–72.

51. Richard R. John, "Governmental Institutions as Agents of Change: Rethinking American Political Development in the Early Republic, 1787–1835," *Studies in American Political Development* 11, no. 2 (1997), 359; John M. Murrin, "A Roof without Walls: The Dilemma of American National Identity," in *Beyond Confederation: Origins of the Constitution and American National Identity*, ed. Richard Beeman, Stephen Botein, and Edward C. Carter II (Chapel Hill: University of North Carolina Press, 1987), 425; cited in John, "Governmental Institutions," 360.

52. John, "Governmental Institutions," 349.

53. Ibid., 373.

54. Ibid., 368.

55. Ibid., 378.

56. To be sure, he does briefly refer to the achievements of the military in the main body of his text (ibid., 370–71).

57. Alexis de Tocqueville, *Democracy in America* (New York: Harper & Row, 1966), 311–407.

Part III

WAR AND TRADE

Five

War, Trade, and U.S. Party Politics

MARTIN SHEFTER

WAR AND TRADE have fundamentally shaped and reshaped the American national state since its founding. The changing position of the United States in the international political and economic orders has influenced the entire "ensemble of institutions" in the United States, as J. P. Nettl puts it. Developments abroad have shaped institutions on both the *input* and the *output* side of the American political system. This chapter considers some major influences that international developments have had upon U.S. party politics.

There are at least three major ways in which international forces have affected American party politics since the nation's struggle for independence. First, international migration flows have regularly refashioned the nation's population, helping to make and remake the identities, loyalties, and antipathies of Americans. In their quest for support, party politicians have cultivated such sentiments. Second, international economic and military challenges have presented differing opportunities and threats to different segments of the population, generating cleavages that the nation's parties have represented. Third, throughout its history there has been considerable interaction between the character of the U.S. state and the structure of American party politics.[1] In responding to international challenges, national leaders often have altered the structure of, and the relationship among, U.S. government institutions, with important consequences for its political parties.[2] This chapter examines how these three international influences have shaped U.S. party politics since the late eighteenth century.[3]

The Great Powers and the Origins of American Politics

During the early history of European migrations to North America, international affairs were central in shaping the basic character of American government and politics. The initial European settlements in what was to become the United States of America were colonies of a foreign power — largely, of England. And politics in Britain's thirteen American colonies were profoundly influenced by competition between the home country and its chief foreign rival, that is, by conflicts between England and France.[4]

The Seven Years' War between the leading powers of the eighteenth century was fought in the American theater as the French and Indian Wars. Britain's triumph in 1765 led to the expulsion of France from the Atlantic coast of North America. This victory, in turn, eliminated the major benefit that many inhabitants of the thirteen colonies saw in English rule: God-fearing American Protestants no longer needed England to protect them from the French Papists.

To cover the costs of the French and Indian Wars, England levied a number of taxes that Americans found burdensome. These imposts led many colonists to insist that there should be "no taxation without representation," which became the rallying cry of those Americans who sought to sever ties with England. An important contribution to the success of the American War of Independence was the military support the colonists received from France. The rulers of France calculated that by helping to dismember the British Empire, they could weaken their major rival.

After the Americans (with French assistance) won their War of Independence, politics in the newly formed United States continued to be very much affected by struggles between the major European powers.[5] The first party system pitted Federalists against Democratic-Republicans. Federalists wished to strengthen ties between the American economy and the British market; hence they backed the treaty with Britain negotiated by President Washington's envoy, John Jay. Jeffersonian Republicans sympathized with the French Revolution and opposed Jay's treaty, believing that Americans involved in the commercial economy would benefit by selling their products in a wider market than Britain alone.

Jefferson's following also included forces known as "Old Republicans." Most Old Republicans were spokesmen for subsistence farmers, who opposed the economic policies advocated by Alexander Hamilton — U.S. secretary of the treasury and leader of the Federalists — which aimed at commercializing the U.S. economy. Since the number of Americans whose interests were served by the Federalist effort to increase ties between the American and British economies was smaller than the number operating entirely outside the international economy, the Jeffersonians were able to defeat the Federalists by constructing the world's first political party linked to a mass electorate.[6] The triumph of the Democratic-Republicans over the Federalists led to a period of no-party politics, the so-called "Era of Good Feelings." Virginia planter-politicians — most notably, Thomas Jefferson, James Madison, and James Monroe — were its dominant figures.[7]

In sum, the emergence of America's first national political movement, the American Revolution's "Party of Patriots," and the subsequent development of political parties to contest elections in the new nation, were greatly shaped by interactions between Americans, on the one side, and the world's great powers, on the other.

British Hegemony and America's "Party Period"

The "long eighteenth century" ended with Britain's defeat of Napoleon in 1815 and the rise of British hegemony over the industrializing world economy. The ensuing transformation of the international state system and the world economy was the context within which major changes occurred in American party politics.

The hegemonic position that Great Britain occupied in the nineteenth-century world economy was a boon to those Americans who produced and shipped the raw materials required by British industry and the food consumed by British workers. It also benefited Americans who transported, sold, or purchased the low-cost manufactured products of British industries.

The leading sector of Great Britain's economy during the nineteenth century was textile manufacturing. In the century's middle decades, Britain purchased almost half the world's raw cotton for its textile mills. The world's chief production zone for cotton was the U.S. South, and southern planters sold much of their crop to British manufacturers.

A major reason that New York City emerged as America's economic capital was its dominance of the trade between southern cotton growers and British manufacturers.[8] At the beginning of each growing season, New York merchants would advance loans to southern planters, enabling them to survive until their cotton was harvested. The merchants who provided this credit shipped cotton to Britain through the port of New York, and southern planters, in turn, used much of their profits to purchase British goods imported through New York. This alliance between New York and the South, based on trade with Great Britain, became central to the Democrats during the era extending roughly from 1828 to 1896, when mass-based, patronage-oriented political party organizations dominated government and politics in the United States. During this era the nation was governed by a "state of courts and parties," as political scientist Stephen Skowronek has termed it.[9] Historian Richard L. McCormick calls these years the "party period" in American political history.[10]

Martin Van Buren, a leading New York politician in the 1820s, forged a coalition behind the presidential candidacy of Andrew Jackson among Americans who traded with Great Britain. In addition to southerners and New Yorkers, another element of the Jacksonian coalition were midwestern farmers. Many of the crops these farmers produced were ultimately consumed by British industrial workers, and a central policy of the Jacksonians — suppression of the American Indians — was a key concern of farmers on the frontier of Euro-American settlement. The task of Indian removal was eased by the withdrawal of France and Spain from the alliances they had cultivated with American Indian tribes, as Aristide Zolberg notes in his chapter above.

The coalition that elected Andrew Jackson to the U.S. presidency was institutionalized as the Democratic Party. The Democrats of the second American party system strongly opposed protective tariffs. They also were committed to the westward expansion of both slave agriculture and freehold farming—policies that presupposed the international order of free trade and balance-of-power politics over which Great Britain presided as the world's hegemonic power.

If the industrial hegemony of Great Britain benefited many Americans, it posed a threat to others, the ones who made products that were undersold by British industry. Britain's manufacturers generally could beat the competition, so long as the contest was conducted on a level playing field, and for this reason, the British strongly advocated free trade.[11] For the same reason, some American politicians were able to mobilize support among U.S. manufacturers, their employees, and their suppliers by advocating protective tariffs. The tariff became a central Whig and Republican campaign appeal during the second and third American party systems, extending from the 1820s to the 1890s.

Tariffs raised enormous revenues, which the Whigs proposed to spend on an ambitious program of "internal improvements." In the "American system" advocated by Henry Clay, tariff revenues were used to subsidize the construction of transportation projects that facilitated domestic commerce and manufacturing. The Republicans, who succeeded the Whigs, also advocated using tariff revenues to finance public works, and after the Civil War, the GOP sought to dispose of the remainder of the politically embarrassing "treasury surplus" that the tariff generated by enacting America's first national social welfare program: pensions for veterans of the Union army, the widows of "old soldiers," and native-born northerners who claimed to be Union veterans or their widows.[12]

During the second and third American party systems, the Whigs and Republicans were spokesmen for U.S. manufacturing interests. They sought to create an industrial working class possessing the skills and discipline that would enable U.S. manufacturers to compete with their British rivals. This was the economic foundation of the Whig and Republican cultural program (temperance, public education, nativism). There is no need to settle here the issue of economic base versus ideological superstructure, that is, to determine whether cultural politics in nineteenth-century America reflected economic struggles that, in some sense, were more fundamental. Suffice it to say that there was an international economic dimension to the cultural conflicts emphasized by scholars associated with the "new political history."[13]

Conflicts between those Americans who benefited from British international hegemony and those who feared being undersold by British industry provided the economic and social foundation for the U.S. system of competitive party politics.

If Britain's economic hegemony created the central *cleavage* in the American party system, its military primacy influenced the basic *structure* of the nation's political parties. The era of Britain's military hegemony—which extended from its defeat of Napoleonic France in 1815 to Germany's challenge to Britain's dominance as the century ended—coincided almost precisely with the "party period" of American political history. During the last three-quarters of the nineteenth century, America's key political institution was a system of patronage-fueled party organizations that mobilized an extensive electoral base.[14]

That the U.S. party period coincided with Britain's international military hegemony was no mere coincidence: British military primacy made it possible for America's party organizations to dominate *all* governmental institutions in the United States. Patronage-oriented political parties so dominated American public life from the Jacksonian through the Progressive Eras that they even were able to intrude into the domain of the military. Parties mobilized not only popular support but also troops for America's nineteenth-century wars.[15] Politicians organized volunteer regiments through the same communications networks upon which they relied to reach voters. For example, during the Mexican War, Congressman Jefferson Davis relied upon the Democratic Party in his district to fill the ranks of the regiment he founded, the First Mississippi Rifles. More generally, the same party organizations that mobilized the world's most extensive mass electorate in the nineteenth century also helped to recruit soldiers in the Western world's bloodiest military conflict between 1815 and 1914, the American Civil War.

In addition to mobilizing soldiers to the military rank and file, parties influenced appointments to military commands. Such appointments rewarded public figures for mobilizing troops, providing them with incentives to organize military units. (E.g., the commanding officer of the First Mississippi Rifles was Congressman Jefferson Davis, who had founded the regiment.) During the Mexican War, the Democrats were so unhappy that both officers holding the highest rank (major general) in the army were Whigs that they attempted to revive the rank of lieutenant general—the only previous lieutenant general in the U.S. Army had been George Washington—and to appoint a prominent Democrat (Senator Thomas Hart Benton) to this rank. This illustrates Samuel Huntington's point that until the late nineteenth century military officership was not viewed as a distinct profession in the United States.[16]

During the Civil War, many politicians who mobilized troops were given major military commands. Among those appointed as generals in the Union

army were Speaker of the House Nathaniel Banks, Massachusetts state senator Benjamin Butler, Congressmen John McClernand and John A. Logan
from Illinois, and New York politicians John Dix and Daniel Sickles. In
what may have been the most significant Northern military offensive of the
war, the campaign to gain control of the Mississippi River at Vicksburg, the
commander of the Union forces, Ulysses S. Grant, found it necessary to
devote almost as much attention to contending with his nominal subordinate, John McClernand, as to countering the moves of his Confederate
adversaries.[17] Even after Grant's triumphs at Vicksburg and Chattanooga led
Congress to revive the rank of lieutenant general (so that Grant could be
appointed as the army's highest-ranking officer), the influence of political
generals made it difficult for the new general in chief to control the armies
nominally under his command. As James McPherson notes, "On the periphery of the main theaters stood three northern armies commanded by
political generals whose influence prevented even Grant from getting rid of
them: Benjamin Butler . . . Franz Sigel . . . and Nathaniel Banks."[18]

Because it was in Great Britain's interest to prevent other European states
from extending their sway in the Western hemisphere, the United States did
not have to rely on political generals such as these to defend itself from the
world's great powers. As Paul Kennedy observes, the United States in the
nineteenth century was protected by "the *cordon sanitaire* which the Royal
Navy (rather than the Monroe Doctrine) imposed to separate the Old World
from the New."[19] Because the United States was thus protected by Britain,
the world's hegemonic military power, political parties in the United States
were able, during the Party Period, to dominate not only civil but military
institutions.

The 1860s witnessed the most dramatic, but not the only, instance of a
noteworthy feature of early-nineteenth-century U.S. party politics: regional
minorities defeated in national politics threatening to secede from the
Union. The threat of secession was plausible, because the immediate neighbors of the United States were not major military powers likely to gobble up
the territory that seceded. In addition, as Aristide Zolberg observes, states
considering secession could anticipate that Britain would prevent the European powers from seizing them.

Southern advocates of extending slavery were not the first defeated minority in U.S. politics to speak of leaving the Union: New England threatened
to secede over the 1803 Louisiana Purchase (much of which would be
devoted to slave agriculture) as well as over the declaration of war against
Britain in 1812. And the southern states carried out their vow to secede in
1860, in part because southerners anticipated that they would get the support of Great Britain in their war of independence. They thought that the
British would have little choice but to back the Confederate states, because
Britain required access to southern cotton in order to retain its international
standing.

Building a New American State

The structure of the international economy and state system changed significantly at the turn of the twentieth century.[20] American productivity came to exceed Britain's in the 1890s, and manufacturers in continental Europe also began to present serious competition to their rivals across the English Channel. The international economic regime associated with British economic hegemony experienced strains: European tariffs started rising. And the pattern of politics that had emerged in the United States at least partly in response to British hegemony also faced serious challenges.

When U.S. producers had not been able to compete with British industries, national officials affiliated with the Whigs and Republicans had won support among American manufacturers and industrial workers by enacting high tariffs to exclude foreign goods from the home market. As American industry became the most productive in the world, many U.S. manufacturers sought to sell their output abroad as well as at home. But with rising European tariffs, American producers faced greater restrictions in foreign markets.

At the turn of the century, U.S. presidents—Republicans as well as Democrats—sought to adjust American commercial policy so as to increase exports. As David Lake argues, "the foreign policy executive" took the lead in "reconceptualizing the tariff" as an instrument for promoting American exports.[21] Both Republican and Democratic presidents sought to mobilize popular support for a commercial strategy that relied on negotiating with foreign nations to open markets. The tariff declined as a central focus of contention in American politics. At the same time, the Progressive movement (which was not especially concerned with questions of international trade) launched its challenge to the party organizations that had been constructed in the nineteenth century to engage in battles over the tariff.[22]

The turn of the century witnessed major changes not only in the world economy but also in the international state system. As George Modelski observes, of the state system of 1900: "Bismarck's empire, fueled by German nationalism put into question the stability of the European balance. . . . By 1900 it had become clear to many that *Pax Britannica* was well past its prime."[23]

These developments produced World War I, into which the United States was drawn by German submarine attacks on U.S. merchant ships, just as England's violations of the neutrality of American merchantmen had drawn the United States into the previous global war in 1812. Whereas political parties had played a key role in America's nineteenth-century wars, during World War I the Progressive Woodrow Wilson undertook to separate America's institutions of political and military mobilization. The Progressive ideal was to strengthen bureaucratic institutions at the expense of parties,[24] but the bureaucratization of the war effort in 1917–18 was incomplete. It is politically feasible for government agencies to operate in accord with the principles of "imperative coordination," as Max Weber terms it, only if there is broad support among politically influential forces for the policy being enforced. Absent such support, President Wilson administered the war effort through various nonbureaucratic alternatives to traditional party organizations.[25]

To secure the backing of business and other elements of American society whose cooperation was necessary to fight a total war, the Wilson administration established government agencies run by prominent leaders of the private sector. The most important of these agencies was the War Industries Board, staffed by business executives and chaired by a major Wall Street figure, Bernard Baruch.[26] Another example was the Food Administration, headed by Herbert Hoover, who had gained considerable prominence by running the Belgian relief effort early in the war.

A second feature of the mobilization for World War I was a great reliance upon mass media campaigns. The Committee on Public Information (CPI) produced songs (such as "Over There") and films (such as "The Beast of Berlin") intended to convince citizens that all "100 percent Americans" supported the Allied cause. But the CPI's reliance upon public relations was not unique. For example, absent any consensus that the war was unavoidable, civilian food rationing could not be considered. Instead, Herbert Hoover's Food Administration sought through the new techniques of public relations to persuade Americans to observe "meatless" Fridays and "wheatless" Wednesdays.

The way troops were mobilized illustrates how incompletely government functions that formerly had been administered through party organizations were bureaucratized during World War I. When the United States entered the war, politicians such as Theodore Roosevelt, adhering to earlier practices, sought to mobilize their followings as volunteer troops. TR proposed raising an army division (eventually an army corps), which would have required promoting Colonel Roosevelt and his associate Brigadier General Leonard Wood to positions as major generals.

But the U.S. Army and President Wilson would not countenance this. The army was becoming increasingly professionalized at the turn of the century and no longer would accept the appointment of political generals.[27] And President Wilson, who sought to mobilize the *entire* nation for total war, did not want the conflict to be regarded as a partisan venture.

Woodrow Wilson, the Progressive, established a set of government agencies (i.e., Selective Service Boards) to accomplish a task (military recruitment) that formerly had largely been achieved through party organizations. But the Selective Service system was not a centralized bureaucracy with field offices that implemented the policies and priorities of national officials.

Rather, draft boards were "little groups of neighbors," whose members drew on their local standing to reinforce their legal mandate. Unable to rely solely upon its own authority, the administration in Washington was compelled to accept whatever social discrimination was practiced by local draft boards. Nonetheless, in the eyes of Progressives, a virtue of the new system of military mobilization was that it bypassed the militia, whose roots were "firmly planted . . . in the party organization of the States," as the *New York Times* put it.[28]

The increase in the power of the American state during World War I, as a result of conscription, personal income taxation, taxes on the "excess profits" of corporations, and the mobilization of the economy for industrial warfare raised two questions after the hostilities ceased. With the return of peace, how much of its new power should Washington retain? And what sorts of policies would the government pursue?

As for the first question, the United States experienced a "general postwar reaction against active government."[29] Wartime policies brought government into the lives of ordinary Americans so intrusively that it reduced popular support for Progressivism. In 1912 candidates identified with the Progressive cause (Woodrow Wilson and Theodore Roosevelt) had won 75 percent of the vote, but following the war — that is, in the 1920s — the voters brought in three successive conservative GOP presidents and also "regular Republican" majorities in both houses of Congress.

A dramatic development overseas, the Russian Revolution, presented an answer to the second question that many Americans found unacceptable. Respectable citizens sought to ensure that Communism would not triumph in the United States. The postwar "red scare" smashed any radical tendencies in the American labor movement.[30]

World War I greatly strengthened firms capable of operating in global markets.[31] After the war, politicians affiliated with this economic sector (known as "internationalists") fought vigorously against the policies of the "isolationists."[32] From roughly 1918 to 1932, isolationists usually prevailed,[33] killing U.S. entry into the League of Nations and enacting restrictive trade legislation that escalated the U.S. stock market crash into the worldwide Great Depression of the 1930s.[34]

U.S. International Hegemony and the Imperial Presidency

The middle third of the twentieth century witnessed enormous changes in the international political and economic orders: the United States succeeded Great Britain as the world's hegemonic power. Germany's efforts to dominate Europe, which precipitated two world wars, were defeated in the 1940s by the United States, the United Kingdom, and the Soviet Union.[35]

After winning World War II, the United States and the Soviet Union became the world's dominant military powers. Each superpower led an alliance that confronted its rival in a Cold War extending over more than forty years. The two blocs were economic, as well as military, alliances. The United States largely ran the institutions (e.g., the World Bank, GATT, and IMF) that managed the capitalist world economy.

During the era of U.S. international hegemony after the Second World War, the president became *the* central figure in American government and politics. Richard Neustadt asserted at the time that there was a simple relationship between these developments: as the international crises confronting presidents became increasingly severe, presidents became more powerful relative to other actors in American politics.[36]

But, as Stephen Skowronek has argued, there was nothing automatic about the relationship between America's changing position in the international system and the growth of presidential power.[37] International crises were not simply presented to presidents by foreign powers. The United States played a key role in shaping the international system that generated the crises presidents were expected to manage. And forces outside the American political system did not provide presidents with the means of dealing with these problems. Presidents fashioned the tools they used to manage international challenges. As Skowronek puts it, presidents needed to "make" the politics they played.

The ways in which the White House operated internationally very much influenced the president's political standing. U.S. international successes from the mid-1940s to the mid-1960s had major consequences for American politics and government. Presidents were not unaware of these consequences, and domestic considerations almost certainly affected their conduct abroad.

In promoting the international political and economic policies associated with the *Pax Americana*, postwar presidents served the interests and won the support of several important domestic political forces. The owners, managers, and employees of American firms that were able to prevail over foreign firms in both domestic and world markets benefited greatly from an open international trading system. Commercial interests that shipped or sold American goods abroad and imported foreign goods into the U.S. market also profited from the free trade regime promoted by postwar presidents, as did financial institutions that financed this trade or invested overseas. And those Americans (many of them southerners) who made careers in the U.S. armed forces or sold weapons and supplies to the U.S. military also directly gained from American hegemony. During the two decades following World War II, presidents of both parties promoted policies these interests favored. Indeed, a bipartisan accord extended beyond simply the military, foreign, and trade policies associated with the *Pax Americana*. To avoid dividing the nation in the face of foreign foes, postwar presidents sought to strike compromises on domestic disputes that might threaten national harmony.

That both Democratic and Republican presidents sought to serve internationally oriented interests encouraged these powerful interests to support, in turn, efforts by presidents to assert their authority relative to other public officials and political institutions.[38] Following World War II, the forces of internationalism persuaded Congress to increase the powers of, and centralize control over, the U.S. national security state—creating the Department of Defense, the Central Intelligence Agency, the Atomic Energy Commission, and the National Science Foundation.[39]

Beginning with FDR, presidents relied increasingly on administrative mechanisms to assert their leadership.[40] World War II manifested and reinforced this tendency. To mobilize the American economy for war, Franklin Roosevelt, like Woodrow Wilson before him, established numerous agencies, staffed by dollar-a-year executives on loan from business. In particular, when war broke out in Europe, FDR created a War Resources Board (WRB), run by various industrial magnates. But organized labor and other liberal forces in the New Deal coalition objected to endowing business with so much power. Roosevelt responded to these concerns by replacing the WRB with the Office of Production Management (OPM), co-chaired by the president of General Motors and FDR's closest ally in the labor movement, Sidney Hillman.[41]

But Roosevelt himself was not completely comfortable with such a delegation of power. During his first two terms, the executive branch had acquired considerably greater administrative capacity than it had possessed on the eve of World War I. Through various new executive agencies, the White House obtained information about American industry that it had not previously commanded, and the Executive Reorganization Act of 1939 created an "institutionalized presidency" to manipulate these new levers of power.[42] Thus, in World War II the president himself was able to play a major role in mobilizing the nation for war.

Whereas World War I had destroyed Progressivism, the Second World War helped to institutionalize the New Deal. Political forces to the right and left of the New Deal were discredited by international developments during the 1940s. As World War II became America's most popular war, liberals were able to charge that the isolationism of the anti–New Deal Right prior to Pearl Harbor indicated insufficient commitment to the fight against fascism. And the Cold War enabled McCarthyites to charge leftists with being "soft on Communism."

As Edwin Amenta and Theda Skocpol brilliantly argue, World War II helped to institutionalize the New Deal by redefining its welfare aspirations.[43] The major social policy of FDR's first two administrations had been providing jobs to the unemployed, largely on public construction projects. People for whom such jobs were unsuitable (e.g., the elderly, widows) were to be provided with a uniform package of social benefits.

The economic boom following World War II greatly reduced the appeal of public works jobs. And during the postwar decades, the various segments of the unemployed came to be treated very differently. The federal government itself provided direct and relatively generous benefits to those unemployed persons who universally were regarded as worthy: retired workers, widows, crippled veterans. Public assistance for people who had inadequate incomes for other reasons was administered and partly financed by state governments, so that benefits varied considerably among the states, reflecting local views of the worthiness of different segments of the poor.

Locally oriented political forces were able to prevail on these matters for two reasons. First, although the New Deal modified, it did not completely remake, U.S. party politics. Certainly, it did not create the "more responsible two-party system" that liberal academics advocated at the time.[44] Rather than establishing a centralized party organization committed to a national program, FDR and his successors mobilized electoral support through America's patronage-oriented "traditional party organizations," as well as through local elites and other local institutions (e.g., trade associations, labor federations).[45] Elected officials, who relied upon such institutions for support, had to pay heed to local views concerning who deserved reasonably generous benefits and who should receive minimal public support.

A second reason why the character of New Deal social policies varied considerably across the nation was that the New Deal regime did not create a centralized national state to administer its social programs.[46] Most social policies of the New Deal—such as Unemployment Insurance, Aid to Dependent Children, public housing—were administered through state and local governments. In administering national policies, these institutions interpreted them in ways that accorded with the concerns of locally dominant political forces. The most dramatic example of the New Deal's capitulation to such local forces was its refusal to "interfere" in the southern racial order. To retain support among southern white voters and the officials they elected (most southern blacks were disfranchised at the time), FDR scrupulously avoided challenging the southern caste system.

International Sources of "Divided Government," 1968–92

International military, political, and economic developments played a significant role in undermining the political coalition that had dominated presidential elections during the first two decades of the Cold War. JFK and LBJ interpreted the doctrine of containing Communism to require U.S. intervention in Vietnam, and this drove many liberals—notably, younger middle-class liberals — away from the Democratic Party. On the other hand, some voting blocs that formerly had been strongly Democratic (e.g., southern whites, northern Catholics) now supported GOP presidents who were more inclined to make use of U.S. military power abroad.

Conflicts over Vietnam seriously disrupted the Democratic Party. In the aftermath of the party's divisive 1968 national convention, antiwar Democrats secured "reforms" that weakened the party's traditional "power brokers" and boosted the influence of liberal activists. This, in turn, helped the GOP secure a "lock" on the electoral college, controlling the presidency for twenty of the twenty-four years between 1968 and 1992.

During this quarter-century, the Democrats experienced deep divisions not only over military issues but also over race — a question that also had international dimensions.[47] World War II created jobs in war industries that encouraged millions of southern blacks to move to the North, where they could vote. To win their support, northern Democrats began to advocate black civil rights, a cause that FDR had pointedly avoided. The Cold War provided the Democrats with other reasons to aid blacks. Racial apartheid in the South embarrassed the United States in its competition for the "hearts and minds" of Third World peoples. This helps explain why Presidents Truman, Kennedy, and Johnson opposed racial discrimination, driving many southern whites from the Democratic Party.

Republican dominance of the presidency was further bolstered in the 1980s by international economic forces. President Reagan's 1981 tax cuts, in conjunction with his defense buildup, caused the American national budget deficit to balloon, placing upward pressure on U.S. real (i.e., inflation-adjusted) interest rates. In conjunction with Reagan's pro-business stance, this encouraged foreigners to invest in U.S. Treasury securities.[48] The flood of foreign capital into the United States reduced domestic interest rates by approximately five percentage points at the midpoint of the Reagan presidency,[49] contributing to the expansion of the U.S. economy and the reelection of Republican presidents in 1984 and 1988.

Foreigners needed to acquire dollars to purchase American securities. Hence, the rise in foreign investment increased the international exchange value of the dollar (it rose by almost 67 per cent) during the early 1980s. High dollars reduced the cost to Americans of imported goods, helping to increase the U.S. trade deficit from $12 billion in 1980 to $136 billion in 1985.[50]

The availability to American consumers of inexpensive, high-quality imported goods contributed to the sense of well-being among the GOP's middle-class constituents. Imports also imposed discipline on organized labor. Union leaders hesitated to insist that U.S. firms accept costly changes in wages and work rules, lest these firms transfer jobs abroad. This restraint was welcomed by the American business community, further encouraging Presidents Reagan and Bush to promote foreign trade.

The Reagan administration took steps to ensure that the flood of goods into America from Japan, the nation having the largest trade surplus with the United States, would help finance the U.S. budget deficit. In the mid-1980s, it negotiated the yen-dollar agreement, enabling Japan's banks to invest in high-yielding U.S. Treasury securities the profits that Japanese firms made selling their products in the American market.

In effect, the U.S. budget in the 1980s was partly financed by a "Toyota tax," equal to the interest payments on U.S. Treasury securities sold to Japanese investors.[51] Future generations will have to pay this tax, but the burden of this mode of public finance was borne most immediately and heavily by American workers left unemployed by a system that benefited members of the Reagan-Bush constituency as consumers and taxpayers.

The weakening of organized labor in the 1980s greatly increased the influence of liberal activists — feminists, environmentalists, Naderites — within the Democratic coalition. From the 1940s through the 1970s, organized labor had regularly fought with liberal activists over issues and candidates.(AFL president George Meany's support of the war in Vietnam was especially galling to liberal peace activists.) But in the face of Reaganite assaults, unions have sought to reach accommodations with other liberal forces, in the hope that labor will be supported by liberals on the issues it regards as most critical. For example, organized labor had opposed the Clean Air Act in 1978 but supported its renewal in 1990. And, in a tacit exchange, environmentalists in recent years have joined labor in seeking to impose restrictions on foreign trade.

All members of the liberal coalition opposed the Reagan-Bush fiscal policies of tax cuts and budget deficits. Large deficits limited funds for discretionary federal programs, thus reducing the flow of resources to the public agencies and nonprofit organizations that design and administer social programs.[52]

In these ways, Reaganite economic policies, which had international dimensions, threatened the livelihood of members of the liberal coalition: unionized labor, the clients of social programs, employees in the public and nonprofit sectors, and the racial minorities that are heavily served by or employed in these sectors. That is, the conservative Republican crusade against big government attacked the livelihood of groups at the core of the liberal coalition. This explains the bitterness of the conservative offensive and of the liberal counteroffensive against contemporary conservatism. These attacks and counterattacks have produced an era of acrimony in U.S. politics.[53]

"Globalization"

In 1991, the Soviet Union collapsed, and the Cold War passed into history. But America's triumph in the Cold War did not reduce the intensity of party conflict in U.S. domestic politics. To the contrary, partisan divisions in Congress deepened in the 1990s.[54] President Clinton often failed to seek compromises with his opponents, and a number of his initiatives were not supported by a single Republican in either the House or Senate.

At the same time, new modes of political combat — for example, a reliance upon scandals and character assassination — became routine in the United States. This mode of political warfare was initiated by the Democrats, who used it to drive Richard Nixon from the presidency in the Watergate affair. Subsequently, Democrats sought to discredit a number of Republican appointees with charges of financial or sexual misconduct. Republicans picked up this tactic in the late 1980s, driving from office Democratic Speaker of the House Jim Wright and House Democratic whip Tony Coehlo.

After Bill Clinton entered the White House, the GOP further escalated this mode of political warfare. Republicans charged Clinton himself, a half-dozen members of his cabinet, and top White House aides with criminal misbehavior, securing the appointment of seven independent counsels to investigate these allegations. Following the Republican capture of the House in November 1994, the Democrats retaliated by filing seventy-five charges of ethical misconduct against GOP Speaker Newt Gingrich. In short, efforts to humiliate one's opponents and drive them from public life became a regular feature of American politics in the 1990s.[55]

This recent intensification of political warfare in the United States has an international dimension. As Peter Gourevitch notes below, the 1990s saw a fragmentation of the consensus that had been forged after World War II with regard to America's role in the international political and economic orders. During the Cold War, opposition to the institutional order of the West (i.e., NATO, GATT, IMF) was regarded as politically unacceptable on both the right and the left. But beginning in the 1990s, this consensus faced serious challenge within both the Republican and Democratic Parties.

In the GOP, "neo-isolationists," such as Pat Buchanan, denounce specific international economic institutions and the entire "new world order" that they claim is being fashioned by the forces of internationalism. Another post–Cold War perspective that can be found among Republicans is "unilateralism," as Gourevitch terms it. Unilateralists argue that the United States should deploy military force on its own initiative, without seeking the prior approval of the United Nations or any other international authority. Unilateralists have been a significant force in the GOP since the presidency of Ronald Reagan. This helps explain why more and more southerners, many of whom have ties to the military, have become Republicans since 1980.[56]

Democrats also have manifested a variety of views on international issues over the past decade. President Clinton sought to strengthen the institutions that promote international trade, but a majority of Democrats in Congress sought to kill NAFTA, to deny the president "fast track" authority in trade negotiations, and to withhold permanent, normal trade relations (PNTR) from China. The most fierce opposition to free trade policies came from organized labor, but other liberal forces — Naderites, environmentalists — joined the fray, arguing that free trade hurts U.S. firms, which are subject to stricter consumer, environmental, and labor standards than those in force in the developing nations. They fear, therefore, that increases in foreign trade will heighten opposition to their proposals among American producers and employers.[57]

Human rights advocates are another liberal interest that has moved away from policies supported by Democrats during the Cold War. The Cold War had encouraged the United States to establish friendly relations with the dictators ruling many Third World nations, on order to keep these countries out of the Soviet orbit. Thus, during the Cold War, the United States supported a number of regimes that scarcely were paragons of liberal democracy. American presidents, both Democratic and Republican, provided rulers such as Ferdinand Marcos and Anastazio Somoza with aid, so that their countries would not "go Communist." In the 1970s, liberals sought to discredit the realpolitik of Henry Kissinger and held that the United States should avoid ties to regimes that violate human rights, a stance they maintain to the present day.[58]

The end of the Cold War greatly altered the relationship between U.S. domestic politics and foreign policy. When presidents considered the very survival of the United States to be at stake, their actions largely accorded with the precepts of Realism in international relations.[59] For example, FDR's concern about the Axis threat to the United States led him to denounce Mussolini for joining Hitler's 1940 invasion of France, even though it occurred on the eve of an election in which his party hoped to win Italian-American votes.[60] And President Reagan provided generous aid to Israel, although he could expect to win very few Jewish votes, because he regarded Israel as one of America's "strategic assets" in the Cold War: Israel's government helped the United States fight Soviet-backed regimes in Angola, Iraq, and Nicaragua, enabling Reagan to circumvent his opponents in Congress.[61]

The collapse of the USSR and the end of serious threats to U.S. national security enabled commercial and ethnic interests to exercise unprecedented influence over U.S. foreign policy. Regarding commercial interests, Samuel Huntington noted in 1997 that President Clinton "may . . . spend more time promoting American sales abroad than doing anything else in foreign affairs."[62]

As for ethnic politics, recent immigrants have increasingly come to regard themselves less as refugees than as members of a transnational diaspora. As such, they seek U.S. aid in furthering the interests of their people as a whole and its homeland.[63] It is true that refugees from the Soviet bloc exercised a measure of influence over U.S. foreign policy during the Cold War, supporting hard-line anti-Communist positions. But in recent years, domestic political pressures have gained in importance relative to national strategic calculations.

As U.S. foreign policy has come to be more oriented toward the concerns of commercial interests and ethnic diasporas, firms and governments that share these concerns have increasingly sought to influence U.S. behavior in the international arena. In 1996, for example, various overseas Chinese business interests with ties to the government of China (e.g., the Riady group) made very large contributions to U.S. election campaigns. A Riady aide was appointed to a major fund-raising post at the Democratic National Committee and channeled contributions from foreign citizens and governments to American candidates who favored increasing U.S. trade with China. Along with campaign contributions from domestic firms seeking foreign contracts, this helped President Clinton and the Democrats to raise roughly as much as their Republican opponents in 1996 — overcoming the financial advantage the GOP. long enjoyed as the "party of business" in American politics.

The Clinton administration justified its preoccupation with foreign trade with the ideology of "globalism." It argued that, with the growth of international trade, a precondition for creating jobs at home was increasing American sales abroad and that the government's prime responsibility, since the collapse of the Soviet threat, had become helping U.S. firms to compete overseas.

To be sure, during the Cold War, a number of nongovernmental forces and many foreign regimes had sought to shape U.S. foreign policy. Some coalitions of private interests and foreign governments (e.g., the "China lobby" of the 1940s) had considerable success. But there were important differences between these earlier efforts to influence U.S. foreign policy and those made in the decade following the collapse of the Soviet bloc.

From the 1940s through the 1960s, American foreign policy was shaped by powerful elites and by concerns about national security that have no counterparts today. Forces seeking to alter U.S. behavior in the middle decades of the twentieth century needed to show how the policies they advocated would meet threats to U.S. security posed by the Axis powers and then by the Soviet Union. They also found it necessary to contend with such imposing figures as Henry Stimson, George C. Marshall, Robert McNamara, and Henry Kissinger.[64] Interests seeking to shape U.S. foreign policy in recent years have faced a much less daunting task and have been able to work through many channels, such as the Department of Commerce, one or another congressional committee, and various Democratic or Republican party organs.

It is difficult to anticipate precisely how these influences will alter U.S. foreign policy in years to come. But one thing is certain: now, as in the past, changing institutions and alignments within the domestic U.S. party system can only be understood in the context of changes in the international political and economic orders.

Notes

1. Martin Shefter, *Political Parties and the State: The American Historical Experience* (Princeton: Princeton University Press, 1994).

2. See Martin Shefter, "International Influences on American Politics," chap. 16 in *New Perspectives on American Politics*, ed. Lawrence Dodd and Calvin Jillson (Washington, D.C.: CQ Press, 1994).

3. The impact on American party politics of international migration has been subject to more extensive analysis than the influence of other aspects of the international system. See, for example, Gary Gerstle, *American Crucible: Race and Nation in the Twentieth Century* (Princeton: Princeton University Press, 2001). Therefore, this chapter will focus less on migration than on warfare and international trade.

4. See Walter Dean Burnham, "Critical Realignment: Dead or Alive?" in *The End of Realignment: Interpreting American Electoral Eras*, ed. Byron Shafer (Madison: University of Wisconsin Press, 1991), 112–15.

5. Steven Watts, *The Republic Reborn: War and the Making of Liberal America, 1790–1820* (Baltimore: Johns Hopkins University Press, 1987).

6. John H. Aldrich, *Why Parties?* (Chicago: University of Chicago Press, 1995), chap. 3.

7. Richard P. McCormick, *The Presidential Game* (New York: Oxford University Press, 1982).

8. Martin Shefter, ed. *Capital of the American Century: The National and International Influence of New York City* (New York: Russell Sage, 1993), chap. 1.

9. Stephen Skowronek, *Building a New American State: The Expansion of National Administrative Capacities, 1879–1920* (New York: Cambridge University Press, 1982), chap. 1.

10. Richard L. McCormick, *The Party Period and Public Policy* (New York: Oxford University Press, 1986).

11. See Charles Kindleberger, *World Economic Primacy: 1500–1990* (New York: Oxford University Press, 1996), chap. 8.

12. Theda Skocpol, *Protecting Soldiers and Mothers: The Political Origins of Social Policy in the United States.* (Cambridge: Harvard University Press, 1992), chap. 2.

13. Paul Kleppner, *Parties, Voters, and Political Cultures* (Chapel Hill: University of North Carolina Press, 1979).

14. Joel Silbey, *The American Political Nation, 1838–1893* (Stanford: Stanford University Press, 1991).

15. I am indebted to Joel Silbey and Richard Jensen for discussions of the role that U.S. political parties played in military mobilization and appointments.

16. Samuel P. Huntington, *The Soldier and the State* (Cambridge: Harvard University Press, 1957).

17. Shelby Foote, *The Civil War: A Narrative* (New York: Vintage Books, 1987), vol. 2, chaps. 4–5.

18. James MacPherson, *Battle Cry of Freedom* (New York: Oxford University Press, 1988), 328.

19. Paul Kennedy, *The Rise and Fall of the Great Powers* (New York: Random House, 1987), 178

20. Aaron Friedberg, *Weary Titan: Britain and the Experience of Relative Decline, 1895–1905* Princeton: Princeton University Press, 1988).

21. David Lake, *Power, Protection, and Free Trade: International Sources of U.S. Commercial Strategy, 1887–1939.* (Ithaca: Cornell University Press, 1988).

22. John Coleman, *Party Decline in America: Policy and Politics in the Fiscal State* (Princeton: Princeton University Press, 1997), chap. 1.

23. George Modelski, "The Long Cycle of Global Politics and the Nation State," *Comparative Studies in Society and History* 20 (1978): 214–38.

24. Shefter, *Political Parties and the State*, chap. 3.

25. David Kennedy, "Rallying Americans for War, 1917–1918," in *The Home Front and War in the Twentieth Century*, ed. James Titus (Colorado Springs: U.S. Air Force Academy, 1984).

26. Robert Cuff, *The War Industries Board: Business-Government Relations during World War I* (Baltimore: Johns Hopkins University Press, 1973).

27. James Abrahamson, *America Arms for a New Century* (New York: Free Press, 1968).

28. Quoted in Kennedy, *Rise and Fall*, 150.

29. Morton Keller, *Regulating a New Society: Public Policy and Social Change in America, 1900–1933* (Cambridge: Harvard University Press, 1994), 209.

30. David Montgomery, *The Fall of the House of Labor* (New York: Cambridge University Press, 1987), chap. 8.

31. Peter Gourevitch, *Politics in Hard Times* (Ithaca: Cornell University Press, 1986), chap. 4.

32. Joan Hoff Wilson, *American Business and Foreign Policy 1920–1933* (Lexington: University Press of Kentucky, 1971).

33. Jeffrey Frieden, "Sectoral Conflict and U.S. Foreign Economic Policy," *International Organization* 42 (Winter 1988): 59–90.

34. Charles Kindleberger, *The World in Depression* (Berkeley: University of California Press, 1986).

35. Eric Hobsbawm, *The Age of Extremes, 1914–1991* (New York: Vintage, 1994).

36. Richard Neustadt, "The President at Mid-Century," *Law and Contemporary Problems* 21 (Autumn 1956): 608–45.

37. Stephen Skowronek claims that it is a modern conceit to believe that the problems that have confronted recent presidents are much more complex than those faced by their predecessors. I would argue that although the challenges facing previous presidents may indeed have been akin to those confronting their successors, as Skowronek claims, the institutions with which presidents have had to contend in recent decades have enjoyed greater autonomy than those confronting their predecessors. In this sense, the burdens borne by presidents during the second half of the twentieth century may, in fact, have been more onerous than those faced by the White House during the party period.

38. Samuel P. Huntington, "Congressional Responses to the Twentieth Century," in *The Congress and America's Future*, ed. David Truman (Englewood Cliffs, N.J.: Prentice-Hall, 1973).

39. Nelson Polsby, "Political Change and the Character of the Contemporary Congress," in *The New American Political System*, ed. Anthony King (Washington, D.C.: AEI, 1990), 30.

40. Sidney Milkis, *The President and the Parties* (New York: Oxford University Press, 1993).

41. Alan Brinkley, *The End of Reform: New Deal Liberalism in Recession and War* (New York: Alfred A. Knopf, 1995), chap. 8.

42. Michael J. Lacey and Mary O. Furner, *The State and Social Investigation in Britain and the United States* (New York: Cambridge University Press, 1993).

43. Edwin Amenta and Theda Skocpol, "Redefining the New Deal: World War II and Social Provision," chap. 2 in *The Politics of Social Policy in the United States*, ed. Margaret Weir, et al., (Princeton: Princeton University Press, 1988).

44. American Political Science Association Committee on Political Parties, "Toward a More Responsible Two-Party System." *American Political Science Review* 44, suppl. (September 1950).

45. David Mayhew, *Placing Parties in American Politics* (Princeton: Princeton University Press, 1989).

46. James Q. Wilson, "New Politics, New Elites, Old Publics," chap. 10 in *The New Politics of Public Policy*, ed. Marc Landy and Martin Levin (Baltimore: Johns Hopkins Univ Press, 1995).

47. Mary Dudziak, *Cold War Civil Rights* (Princeton: Princeton University Press, 2000).

48. In the mid-1980s, foreign investors annually purchased more than $30 billion of U.S. Treasury bills, notes, and bonds. In all, foreigners financed as much as one-fifth of the enormous American budget deficits of the 1980s. I. M. Destler and Randall Henning, *Dollar Politics* (Washington, D.C.: Institute for International Economics, 1989), 29.

49. Stephen Marris, *Deficits and the Dollar* (Washington, D.C.: Institute for International Economics, 1987), 44.

50. Jeffry Frieden, "Economic Integration and the Politics of Monetary Policy in the United States," in *Internationalization and Domestic Politics*, ed. Robert Keohane and Helen Milner (New York: Cambridge University Press, 1995), 108–136.

51. Benjamin Ginsberg and Martin Shefter, *Politics by Other Means: Politicians, Prosecutors, and the Press from Watergate to Whitewater* (New York: W. W. Norton, 1999), chap. 4.

52. Paul Peterson, "The Rise and Fall of Special Interest Politics," *Political Science Quarterly* 105 (1991): 539–56.

53. Another source of intense recent conflicts in U.S. politics has been the emergence of divisive "social issues." International influences did not directly produce these disputes, but recent trade policies have buttressed the influence of the middle class, which dominates organizations concerned with these issues. See James Q. Wilson, *Political Organizations* (Princeton: Princeton University Press, 1994), chap. 4.

54. Margaret Weir, ed., *The Social Divide: Political Parties and the Future of Activist Government* (Washington, D.C.: Brookings Institution Press, 1998), 8–10, 52.

55. Benjamin Ginsberg and Martin Shefter, "The Politics of Ethics Probes," *Journal of Law & Politics* 11 (Summer 1995): 433–44; Richard Posner, *An Affair of State: The Investigation, Impeachment, and Trial of President Clinton* (Cambridge: Harvard University Press, 1999).

56. The positions of the parties on racial issues in recent years have reinforced Republican voting by southern whites, while 90 percent of African-American voters in all regions of the country vote Democratic.

57. Environmentalists and Naderites also fear that international authorities might strike down as barriers to trade various regulations that they advocate. See David Vogel, *Trading Up* (Cambridge: Harvard University Press, 1995).

58. Kathryn Sikkink, "The Power of Principled Ideas," In *Ideas and Foreign Policy*, ed. Judith Goldstein and Robert Keohane (Ithaca: Cornell University Press, 1993).

59. It has been argued, however, that U.S. policy regarding Eastern Europe in the 1940s was shaped not only by strategic concerns but also by the quest for Polish-American votes.

60. James Schlesinger, "Fragmentation and Hubris," *National Interest*, Fall 1997, 6.

61. To be sure, the American-Israel Public Affairs Committee (AIPAC) contributes to candidates friendly to Israel, but President Reagan's Mideast policy was shaped more by strategic considerations than by the quest for such support. See Benjamin Ginsberg, *The Fatal Embrace: Jews and the State* (Chicago: University of Chicago Press, 1993), chap. 5.

62. Samuel P. Huntington, "The Erosion of American National Interests," *Foreign Affairs*, September/October 1997, 37–38.

63. Gabriel Sheffer, "Ethno-National Diasporas and Security," *Survival* 36 (Spring 1994): 60–79.

64. Opponents of the Vietnam War did, of course, ultimately manage to prevail over the U.S. foreign policy elite, but only by overturning the regime that had dominated American government and politics at the height of the Cold War.

Six

Patriotic Partnerships: Why Great Wars Nourished American Civic Voluntarism

THEDA SKOCPOL, ZIAD MUNSON, ANDREW KARCH, AND BAYLISS CAMP

NATIONALLY TELEVISED disasters at home and abroad have made the Red Cross a familiar embodiment of humane voluntarism. If contemporary Americans were asked about the history of this respected civic association, some might recall the founding role of nurse Clara Barton, that iconic symbol of feminine caring. But few would realize the debt owed by the Red Cross to official collaborations with the U.S. government during America's greatest wars.

The American Red Cross was founded in 1881 as an aftereffect of gargantuan voluntary relief efforts mounted during the Civil War.[1] Not just Clara Barton, but many other women and men who had been involved in efforts of the United States Sanitary Commission to care for wounded Union soldiers and succor both soldiers and civilians, agitated for years to persuade the U.S. Congress to charter this American wing of an international movement. Thereafter, the American Red Cross grew haltingly — until World War I, when it entered into a full-fledged partnership with the U.S. federal government and was able to spread a national network of more than thirty-five hundred chapters and suddenly recruit more than twenty million members.[2] As figure 6.1 displays, gains in chapter infrastructure brought by World War I proved permanent, even though Red Cross membership did not spike again until another period of official partnership during World War II.[3]

The place of wars in the Red Cross saga is unique in some ways, yet hardly exceptional in the annals of U.S. voluntary associations. As we show and seek to explain in this chapter, big wars have been surprisingly good for American civic voluntarism. The Civil War and the twentieth-century world wars spurred the creation of new associations and buoyed the fortunes of preexisting groups willing and able to join victorious wartime mobilizations. Each great conflict has also reshaped the associational universe, hurting some groups and discouraging some kinds of participants, even as most groups and vast numbers of Americans experienced new bursts of civic engagement.

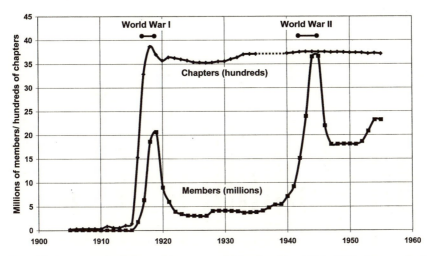

FIG. 6.1. American Red Cross Chapters and Membership, 1905–1955. Source: Red Cross annual reports and data from the national office.

We can survey the landscape using data gathered by the Civic Engagement Project at Harvard University. This ongoing project has identified and traced the histories of all of the very large voluntary membership associations in U.S. history, including (according to our findings so far) fifty-eight groups, apart from churches and political parties, that have ever recruited 1 percent or more of U.S. men and/or women as members (the basis for calculation is men, women, or both, depending on whether the association was formally or de facto restricted by gender). A full list of these membership associations appears in appendix A at the end of this chapter. By early in the twentieth century, the United States had more than twenty coexisting voluntary membership associations, each of which had already recruited at least 1 percent of all American men and/or women. Almost all of these associations were federations, in which regularly meeting local chapters sent representatives to regular state or regional and national meetings. Elsewhere we have established that local chapters of the very large voluntary federations listed in appendix A were central to organized voluntary activity in towns and cities across the country.[4] This means that the large membership federations on which this essay focuses were at the heart of local as well as national civil society. We make occasional reference to smaller associations whose histories provide a window into national dynamics. But most of our data and illustrations refer to the large membership associations listed in appendix A.

Figure 6.2 presents breakdowns at five-year intervals for group foundings and the cumulative incidence of associations exceeding the 1 percent mem-

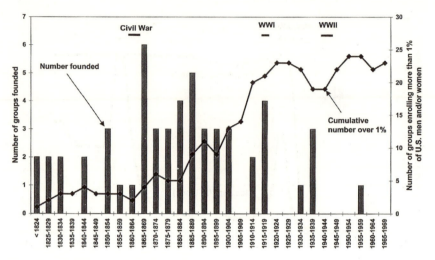

FIG. 6.2. Foundings and Cumulative Incidence of Large U.S. Membership Associations. Source: Harvard Civic Engagement Project data.

bership threshold. Note that the numbers of coexisting associations with memberships exceeding 1 percent of U.S. men and/or women moved noticeably upward immediately after the Civil War, as well as during and right after World Wars I and II. In this overview figure, periods of national economic depression coincide with downturns in numbers of coexisting large membership associations; and wars and their immediate aftermaths were certainly not the only times that numbers of large associations climb upward. Yet even without dissecting associational dynamics in greater detail, as we do below, we can see that America's big wars have been linked to upward swings in numbers of coexisting large associations. Figure 6.2 also underlines the dramatic impact of the Civil War on foundings of popular associations that would eventually grow very large. More such associations were launched in the five years right after the end of the Civil War than in any other five-year period in all of U.S. history. More broadly, the entire post–Civil War era, from the 1860s through the 1890s, was the seedbed time for modern America's prominent membership associations.[5]

The impact of great wars on foundings of major popular associations was not constant. Although the Civil War was followed by a disproportionate number of such foundings, World War I marked only a minor uptick of two such foundings, and no new large membership associations were launched right after World War II. This difference is partly due to the fact that, by the twentieth century, a large number of popularly rooted membership associations already existed. In addition, twentieth-century warfare spurred a distinctive kind of associational innovation in the United States, encouraging the creation of many new business and professional associations. As we will learn below, the ways in which America's great wars were fought — the specific kinds of partnerships each conflict forged between the government and voluntary associations — help to make sense of the patterns of associational foundings during and after each conflict.

In the remainder of this chapter, we explore and seek to explain the surprisingly favorable civic impact of the first two major wars in which the United States became embroiled: the Civil War of 1861–65 and World War I between 1917 and 1919. A complete analysis would, of course, give equal consideration to voluntary associations during and after World War II, while also probing the effects of pivotal smaller conflicts, such as the Spanish-American War and the war in Vietnam. But this is a chapter, not a book, and for students of U.S. civic development the nation's first two modern wars are fundamental. Punctuating the transition from the early republic of farmers and townspeople visited by Alexis de Tocqueville in the 1830s to the hegemonic industrial giant that the United States became by the mid–twentieth century, the Civil War was, by far, biggest and most destructive war the country has ever engaged in, a struggle that redefined the very meaning of U.S. nationhood and permanently reshaped American civil society. In turn, World War I marked the advent of the United States as a great global power, with a national government prepared to use unprecedentedly centralized means to marshal agricultural plenty and industrial might as well as military manpower, projecting U.S. might abroad to reshape the internecine struggles of the Old World. Two decades later, in World War II, the U.S. government and leading civic associations reenacted partnerships first worked out in 1917 and 1918. Both global wars thus encouraged and channeled American civic voluntarism, yet World War I, though brief, was, both institutionally and culturally, the more pivotal episode.

Perspectives on War and Democratic Civil Society

To explore the relationship of modern wars to the development of U.S. civil society is to revisit and challenge arguments originally made by the greatest student of American voluntarism, Alexis de Tocqueville. Ever quoting the great French visitor's fond observation that "Americans of all ages, all stations in life, and all types of dispositions are forever forming associations,"[6] scholars have repeatedly documented that the United States is an unusually civic democracy, where participation in voluntary groups rivals (indeed, usually surpasses) voting in competitive elections. But while treating Tocqueville's celebration of American voluntarism as timeless truth, scholars have ignored his ominous prognostications, ultimately mistaken, about what might happen if the United States found itself embroiled in major wars.

"All those who seek to destroy the freedom of the democratic nations must know that war is the surest and shortest means to accomplish this," wrote Tocqueville in *Democracy in America*.[7] Of course he penned this warning in the 1830s, well before the nation's great wars and in an era when it seemed that "fortune, which has showered so many peculiar favors on the inhabitants of the United States, has placed them in the midst of a wilderness where one can almost say that they have no neighbors. For them a few thousands soldiers are enough. . . ."[8] Tocqueville hoped that the American Republic could avoid the recurrent warfare that embroiled the great powers of Europe. As for civil war, Tocqueville considered the dissolution of the fledgling U.S. union possible but not probable; and if it did break up, he thought it might do so relatively peacefully. As of the 1830s, Tocqueville believed that the U.S. national government was steadily losing power and administrative coherence. He also felt that people in America, as in all commercially oriented democracies, had little taste for war.[9]

Tocqueville nevertheless feared for civic republicanism should the United States become involved in civil or international conflicts. "War almost always widens a nation's mental horizons and raises its heart . . . ," Tocqueville acknowledged, but "any long war always entails great hazards to liberty in a democracy."[10] Perceiving possibilities through the lens of French history, from the Old Regime through the Napoleonic denouement of the Revolution, he posited that protracted "war between the now confederate states" would inevitably bring "standing armies, dictatorship, and taxes."[11] Once democratic peoples are finally dragged into wars, Tocqueville astutely observed, they tend to fight wholeheartedly; and democratic soldiers are inclined to compete for place and advancement, thus pushing the swollen military of a democracy at war to look for ever renewed fields of combat. Besides, government would come to the fore, displacing civil society. "War does not always give democratic societies over to military government," Tocqueville argued, "but it must . . . almost automatically concentrate the direction of all men and the control of all things in the hands of the government. If that does not lead to despotism by sudden violence, it leads men gently in that direction by their habits."[12]

Despite knowing about America's martial experiences, twentieth-century analysts have said much less than Tocqueville about war and civic democracy. Presenting his "Biography of a Nation of Joiners" in 1943–44, at the height of World War II, historian Arthur Schlesinger, Sr. highlighted the civic impact of the American Revolution and the profoundly nationalizing impact of the Civil War, but he presented no systematic reasoning about war and voluntary associations and barely mentioned the twentieth-century world wars.[13] Some years later, Gabriel Almond and Sidney Verba published *The Civic Culture*, a classic social-scientific treatment of U.S. voluntarism based on interviews with representative samples of Americans and citizens of four other democratic nations.[14] Even though World War II must have been a life-defining experience for many of the men and women interviewed, the effects of war on civic engagement were not explored.

Nor have these effects been much examined since. To be sure, Robert D. Putnam acknowledges World War II as an important spur to civic voluntarism in mid-twentieth-century America.[15] But Putnam's attention to war is unusual among scholars and pundits debating the health of U.S. civil society today. As Christopher Beem shows in a wide-ranging survey, theorists of all persuasions focus on local communities and consider "governmental action . . . at best irrelevant to, and, at worst, inimical to, the production of social capital."[16]

Reasoning much as Tocqueville once did when he considered the likely impact of war on democratic civil society, Ladd and many other contemporary analysts rely on an *institutional displacement* understanding of the relationship between state activity and voluntarism. According to this zero-sum view, as government activity waxes, societal associations and voluntary participation must wane. In Peter Drucker's characteristic formulation, America's "voluntary group action from below" must be understood as flourishing in opposition to the "collectivism of organized government action from above."[17]

There is, however, another way to think about the possible interrelationships of state and society, a theoretical framework stressing *institutional synergy*. This approach makes better sense of variations across time and place in the impact of state structures and activities on civil society. "Instead of assuming a zero-sum relationship between government involvement and private cooperative efforts," writes sociologist Peter B. Evans in a recent synthesis of ideas from contemporary studies of economic development, "active government and mobilized communities can enhance each other's . . . efforts."[18] Such enhancement — harnessing governmental and social energies together — is most likely to happen when both governments and social communities have a joint stake in collective tasks that neither can perform entirely on their own.

Beyond a joint stake, two sets of conditions must also be present to create what Evans labels "state-society synergy." There must be "complementarity" between certain necessary inputs that can be provided by government agencies and other necessary inputs that can provided by social groups. In addition, posits Evans, cooperative action is facilitated by "embeddedness," by which he means social relationships that cut across the state/society divide, tying relatively cohesive governmental agencies to surrounding groups. According to Evans, governmental and social conditions favoring state-society synergy are not always there — not even when joint action would be helpful to both. To understand whether institutional synergy will occur, we need to examine a country's historical endowments of governmental institutions and organized social ties, both within communities and between communities and government.

Although these ideas about institutional synergy have been formulated in contemporary debates about economic development, they can guide our thinking about warmaking and the historical development of U.S. civil society. By definition, modern wars create a demand for joint action by state authorities and members of society. What makes a war "modern" is the attempt by a national government (or in a civil war, by a would-be national government) to mobilize involvement and support not just from soldiers but from all of society. Still, modern wars have obviously been fought in various ways — and with varying degrees of effectiveness — by different kinds of states in various societal contexts. For our purposes, the point of interest is the role of state organizations and voluntary associations in America's initial modern wars, the Civil War and World War I. How did preexisting governmental institutions and voluntary associations contribute to the prosecution of each of these great conflicts? Can the organized ways in which Americans mobilized for each war help us to understand the creation of new voluntary groups and the growth of existing voluntary associations during and after each major conflict?

Not just *how* each great American war was fought but the outcome — who won and who lost — had consequences for civic democracy. Wars are fought as organized mobilizations in institutional contexts, marked by given patterns in state and society. But they are also — preeminently — conflictual events, struggles that pit friends against enemies and result in winners and losers. Voluntary associations are built by networks of leaders and members who pursue shared purposes, while expressing and constructing shared identities — and few historical events have a more powerful effect on the sense of shared fate than wars. Groups that mobilize for war learn who is friend and who is foe; and the friends learn to cooperate, to struggle together. After victory in war, former combatants may have renewed energy and will to cooperate with their allies and friends. But groups that mobilize and then suffer defeat may well dissolve or fragment, as participants downplay their unsuccessfully realized identity.

Associationalism during and after wars is, in short, not only influenced by how a nation mobilizes for the conflict. It is also shaped by divisions of friend and foe and — above all — by victory and defeat. This may be especially true for nations whose citizens remain free to organize voluntary endeavors — or, like the American slaves, gain new freedoms as a result of a war. For free people, above all, the most "state-centered" of historical events, modern warfare, may be culturally as well as institutionally critical, because free people are able to express a variety of possible shared identities in associational life.

Although abstractly stated, these considerations about state-society synergy as an institutional process, and about shared identities reinforced by friendship and enmity, winning and losing, can readily be applied to associational trends in the United States during and after its first two great wars. We will consider each war in its own terms and also pay attention to the sequence of these great conflicts. Wars punctuate the biographies of nations, shaping and reshaping both state and civil society. In the United States, as we are about to see, modern civil society took distinctive shape through a particular sequence of great wars. During the course of urbanization and industrialization in just over a half century, America passed from a massive domestic conflict to an initial twentieth-century mobilization for large-scale international warfare. Civic associationalism was mobilized, refocused, and expanded at home, well before the U.S. state fully joined the world of international power politics.

The Civil War and Popular Voluntary Federations

No other feature of U.S. political development is more significant than this: America's most protracted, destructive, and transformative war happened not in the "modern" twentieth century but in the middle of the nineteenth century, at a relatively early stage in the country's urbanization and industrialization.[19] This gargantuan struggle was not a conflict with foreign states but an internecine struggle about the identity and shape of the American nation itself. As a military conflict, the Civil War stretched for forty-eight months, from April 1861 through April 1865. More than a third of adult men in the North served in the Union armies; and while estimates of the proportion of white southern men who fought for the Confederacy range from about 30 percent to nearly 75 percent, the most likely proportion is just over 40 percent. American casualties were many times higher in this war than in World Wars I and II, and the Civil War brought enormous destruction to the American homeland, especially in the South. Alexis de Tocqueville's expectation that a full-fledged war might be protracted and fierce proved quite prescient.

But Tocqueville's equally confident expectation that a protracted war between the states would undercut democratic civil society could hardly have been more mistaken. To be sure, memberships and energies were temporarily diverted from most U.S. civilian associations, as from many economic and family pursuits. This conflict hit a society of farms and small towns like an unending series of tornadoes, as local notables departed for military service along with workers and farm boys. Yet from the end of the Civil War, American associational life was reknit and magnified. Established groups experienced upsurges of membership and activities; and national, state, and local leaders undertook unprecedented rounds of voluntary organizing, setting off a civic boom that lasted through the early twentieth century.

To understand the remarkable civic developments that flowed from the Civil War—and to see why Tocqueville's worries for American civil society were not realized, despite the scale and ferocity of the conflict—we must survey voluntary associations and government prior to 1860, dissect the modalities of war mobilization, and explore the implications of victory and defeat for late nineteenth-century association building.

American Voluntary Associations before 1860

It is often imagined that American civil society through much of the nineteenth century was purely local, centered in "island communities" until, toward the end of the 1800s, large-scale industrialization brought extralocal organization and centralization.[20]; But this picture is misleading, and fails to underline the startling political, religious, and associational changes that occurred well before the advent of corporate industrialization, as America remade itself from a set of British colonies into a representatively governed federal republic.[21]

Except for churches, voluntary associations of any kind were indeed scarce in colonial America. But rapid change came along with the birth of the new nation. In the words of Arthur Schlesinger, Sr., the struggle for American independence from Britain taught "men from different sections valuable lessons in practical cooperation."[22] From the Sons of Liberty to the Committees of Correspondence, patriots learned to build federations for the anti-British resistance, tying the colonies together and linking local groups together within each colony. The War of Independence itself was fought, in the end, by an amalgamation of local and state militias working with George Washington's nascent professional officer corps.[23] Once independence was won, Americans came together to institute a unique federal constitution, which divided governmental prerogatives not just across functional branches but across three levels of sovereignty: local, state, and national. The Constitution mandated regular elections at all levels, and before long federated political parties emerged to manage competition for votes and offices across all three levels of government in the new Republic.[24] In the realm of party politics, therefore, American men soon learned to manage voluntary enterprises linked together in nation-spanning federal networks.

In this same era, people inspired by religious messages competed to spread federated networks of congregations across the land: Methodist and Baptist as well as Presbyterian, Congregational, and Episcopal.[25] By the 1830s, transdenominational moral crusades emerged as well. Aiming to close U.S. post offices on Sundays, the General Union for Promoting the

Observance of the Christian Sabbath coordinated petition drives across communities and regions. Meanwhile, the American Temperance Society and American Anti-Slavery Society organized representative federations that paralleled the three levels of U.S. governance, linking local face-to-face groups into state networks, and those in turn into associations with national labels and organizational centers. All such translocal voluntary movements took advantage of the national postal system to mail newspapers and petitions as well as letters. Unusually efficient and far-reaching for its day, the United States postal system made it possible for early Americans to link local voluntary groups into translocal movements and state and national organizations.[26]

Parallel developments were seen in the expanding world of ritualistic fraternal groups. Here the Odd Fellows were the pioneers. They reached further down the class structure for recruits than the Masons did, and between 1819 and 1843, the American "Independent" Order of Odd Fellows broke away from allegiance to Britain and developed a three-tiered lodge structure paralleling U.S. government institutions.[27] Other fraternal groups followed suit, including white nativist fraternals, like the Improved Order of Red Men; ethnic associations, like the Ancient Order of Hibernians and the German Order of the Harugari and Sons of Herman; and assorted temperance-promoting groups, especially the Order of the Sons of Temperance and the Independent Order of Good Templars.

Well before the Civil War, in short, the United States had a vibrant civil society centered in citizen-run membership associations as well as church denominations and political parties. This remarkably participatory civil society was translocally as well as locally organized, with voluntary federations flourishing parallel to — and on the same scale as — political parties and representative federal governing institutions. By the 1850s, it is true, tensions over slavery were sundering political parties and religious denominations. Yet Americans everywhere — and especially in the North — knew how to organize voluntarily for public purposes across localities and states, as well as within particular local communities.

Voluntarism in the Civil War

For the leaders of the Confederacy and the Union in 1861, the established associational skills of Americans turned out to be a very good thing. This was especially true for the Union. The early United States had but a modest national bureaucracy, mostly employed in the postal service. And as of 1861, the military consisted of only sixteen thousand men, mostly stationed in the West to fight Indians and led by a minuscule layer of aging professional officers, the best of whom (like Robert E. Lee) soon left to serve the

Confederacy. On both sides of the war between the states, military and relief efforts had to be created almost from scratch.[28] Government bureaus certainly tried to direct war-related activities — and, ironically, as Richard Bensel has shown, functioned in even more centralized ways in the South than in the North.[29] But there is no way that central governments alone could have fashioned armies or coordinated civilian relief efforts. Huge undertakings were put together quickly only because both men and women proved remarkably adept at assembling local volunteers and resources into state or regional assemblages, which in turn were amalgamated into the Union and Confederate militaries and their support organizations.

The Union army, for example, was initially composed entirely of organized groups of volunteers.[30] Typically, local communities or chapters of preexisting voluntary associations provided officers and men; then state governors combined such volunteer military units and contributed them to the armies controlled by President Abraham Lincoln and his generals. Federal military drafts commenced in the summer of 1862, after the first rush of enthusiasm had spent itself and the protracted and bloody nature of the war was well understood by everyone. But such drafts, culminating in America's first experiments with relatively universal conscription in 1863, mostly spurred local communities and states to find more volunteers and offer higher bounties to recruits and their families. In the final analysis, fewer than 15 percent of the Union army's nearly 2.5 million soldiers can be attributed, to the direct or indirect effects of federal conscription.[31] The Union military effort overwhelmingly consisted of voluntary mobilizations — and was remarkably equitable across class lines. Businessmen, professionals, and white-collar workers "led by example, not by prescript."[32]

As we have already glimpsed in the introductory sketch of the history of the Red Cross, civilian support for the Union effort was also achieved through organized voluntarism.[33] Ladies' aid societies provided military support and civilian aid in the hard-pressed South; and in the North prominent men and women stepped forward immediately in 1861 to form the United States Sanitary Commission, whose proliferating networks of volunteers, disproportionately women, raised money in "sanitary fairs" and made or assembled supplies to meet soldiers' medical and personal needs. Simultaneously, many northern chapters of the Young Men's Christian Association transformed themselves into arms of the United States Christian Commission, devoted to supplying military chaplains for the Union armies and material as well as spiritual assistance to the troops. Organizationally, both the Sanitary Commission and the Christian Commission were federations, assembled by combining local into state into regional or national efforts (or linking city projects into national or regional undertakings). Like the armies themselves, the great Civil War civilian relief efforts were (to use Peter Evans's terminology) "coproductions" of government and civil society, dependent on close cooperation between voluntary groups and government officials. Officials did not have established national bureaucracies through which they could act entirely on their own, but they did have contacts with civil associations and organizationally adept social leaders. The remarkable achievements of the Sanitary and Christian Commissions were very much indebted to the prewar experience Americans had gained in founding and running extralocally interlinked voluntary efforts. To save the Union, Lincoln's government needed voluntary commitment and organizational savvy, and fortunately, northern Americans were ready to do what was needed.

The Postwar Associational Surge

Given that the mobilizations of the Civil War were nested local-state-national efforts involving direct leadership by local notables, we can better understand why U.S. voluntary federations were poised for renewal and proliferation right after the war. To be sure, most previously established voluntary associations, even very large ones, suffered during the conflict.[34] Southern fraternalists and temperance reformers stopped attending national conventions, and voluntary chapters contracted, sometimes disbanding altogether as local notables and men departed for the battlefields. Yet America's great voluntary federations reknit themselves immediately after the conflict. At wartime national conventions of the Independent Order of Odd Fellows (IOOF), for example, chairs were left vacant for representatives of the southern "grand lodges" — and these gentlemen duly reappeared to reclaim their seats within months after Lee surrendered at Appomatox.[35]

U.S. voluntary federations revived and surged upward from 1865, as men leaving the armies rejoined the local chapters of voluntary federations and formed new ones (or, in some cases, arrived at home in chapters already formed in military camps). Figure 6.3 documents membership trends during and after the Civil War for associations that were already very large prior to the conflict, including the Masons, the Odd Fellows, and the temperance movement as a whole (summing memberships for the IOGT, the Sons of Temperance, and the Woman's Christian Temperance Union, the three leading federations that to some degree competed for adherents during the 1860s and 1870s). Also buoyed in the immediate aftermath of the Civil War were nascent federations such as the Improved Order of Red Men and the Junior Order of United American Mechanics. Here the YMCA is an especially telling case. Launched in North America in 1851, this evangelical Protestant men's movement was beginning to knit together a national network of "Ys" when the Civil War broke out. Between 1861 and 1865, southern chapters collapsed, while northern Ys reorganized themselves to participate in the Christian Commission tied to the Union army. But "in thus

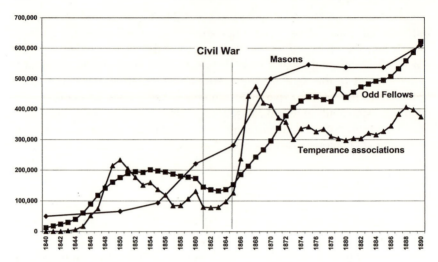

FIG. 6.3. Membership in Large Voluntary U.S. Associations before, during, and after the Civil War. Source: Harvard Civic Engagement Project data.

losing their life in a sense, they saved it," explains association historian Howard Hopkins (using unmistakably Christian imagery), "for they identified themselves in the public mind with the great cause to which the nation was committed" and positioned the YMCA movement to grow rapidly after the war.[36]

Beyond buoying memberships, the Civil War also sparked the founding of many new popular membership federations. Men and women from various communities and states met for the first time during this great national struggle, which clearly raised the horizons and emboldened the civic imaginations of many, inspiring them to launch ambitious new associational projects. Some, like the Red Cross, were attempts to continue Civil War undertakings in civilian formats. Others were fresh national projects, clearly intended to reknit the newly reunited country and deal with problems across regions.

Founded in Washington, D.C., in 1864 by a regionally disparate group of young clerks who met in the wartime civil service, the Knights of Pythias — which rapidly became America's third largest fraternal group (excluded only be the Masons and Odd Fellows) — was built around a ritual of mutually sacrificial brotherhood that allowed men to reexpress wartime ties and simultaneously symbolized regional reconciliation.[37] The Patrons of Husbandry, or National Grange, was launched in Washington, D.C., in 1867 by another group of clerks, led by Oliver Kelley, a Department of Agriculture official originally from Minnesota, who conceived the idea of a new national fraternity for farm men and women after he took a postwar official tour to assess the needs of farmers in the depressed agricultural economy of the South.[38]

Postwar conditions also stirred women, who were horrified at the drinking habits of returned soldiers and worried that wartime taxes on liquor had enhanced the influence of the liquor industry on government. Grassroots female protests against saloons spread in the Midwest in the early 1870s, and then leading women who met at a summer Sunday school camp called for the creation of the Woman's Christian Temperance Union (WCTU) in 1874.[39] "In union and in organization are . . . success and permanence, and the consequent redemption of this land from the curse of intemperance," proclaimed the "Call" to form the WCTU, in phrases resonant with the "Onward, Christian Soldiers" rhetoric of the Union cause.[40] The idea was to create a nationwide federation of female-led temperance unions paralleling all levels of government, in order permanently to institutionalize temperance activities that might otherwise prove hard to sustain. Typical of many activists in the new federation, the first president, Mrs. Annie Wittenmyer, had built her reputation and forged many connections as a key wartime leader in both the Sanitary Commission and the Christian Commission.[41]

As these examples suggest, northerners took the lead in building national U.S. membership federations in the post–Civil War era. America's mid-nineteenth-century fratricidal conflict not only spurred organized civic life, it also shifted its center of gravity to the north, at least among whites. Victory and defeat mattered. Before 1860, associations aspiring to national status were usually launched from great Eastern seaboard cities, and Baltimore was especially prominent in this regard, in part because it was a "hinge" between North and South. But from 1860 on, virtually all major voluntary associations were launched from northern cities, and the founding locations spread into medium as well as large cities in the Midwest and West. This was true not only for the very large federations listed in appendix A, but also for the vast preponderance of the hundreds of smaller federations launched in the late nineteenth century.[42]

Much evidence suggests that the defeat of the Confederacy undercut in the postwar white South the kinds of connections between local and supra-local associational life that nourished civic vitality across the rest of the nation. Local veterans' and memorial or aid groups formed in southern communities, but the United Confederate Veterans, to take one example, did not come together until 1889, whereas the leading Union veterans' federation, the Grand Army of the Republic, formed in 1866, ahead of virtually all the state and local camps that eventually proliferated within it. By the early twentieth century, to be sure, churches were unusually numerous in southern communities. But most churches were affiliated with the southern Baptist and Methodist denominations, while local chapters of nonchurch

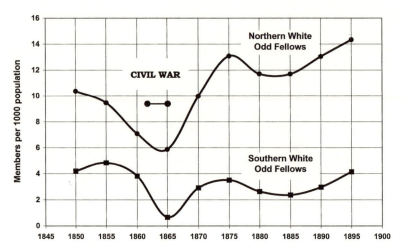

FIG. 6.4. White Odd Fellows Membership in the North and South before, during, and after the Civil War. Source: Annual reports of the Independent Order of Odd Fellows.

voluntary federations, virtually all of them headquartered in the North, were not as dense on the ground inside as outside the South.[43]

After the Civil War, white southerners joined or rejoined chapters of nationally organized membership federations at a lower rate than they had before. Striking evidence of this appears in figure 6.4, which traces southern and northern membership in the Independent Order of Odd Fellows (IOOF) per 100,000 population over the course of the nineteenth century. Notice that, prior to 1860, white southern and northern membership densities were converging somewhat, even though the South was a considerably less urbanized region. But white southern IOOF membership plunged drastically during the Civil War and afterward rebounded only modestly. Even as postwar population grew rapidly, northern per capita IOOF membership grew even more strongly after the war, surpassing the prewar highpoint by the early 1870s and continuing upward from there (with modest losses during the economic hard times of the late 1870s and early 1880s). In contrast, white southern IOOF membership did not come close to regaining its mid-1850s per capita level until the very end of the nineteenth century.[44]

Figure 6.5 offers yet another picture of the development of American Odd Fellows through the nineteenth century—this time adding African Americans to the picture. The only data available to us right now is on estimated lodge formation rather than membership trends, but this figure dramatizes the liberating impact of the Civil War and Union victory on African Americans. American blacks were excluded from the white-run In-

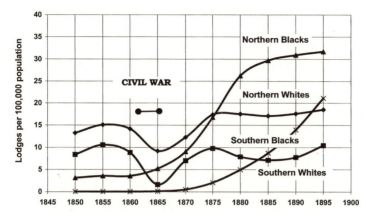

Fig. 6.5. White and Black Odd Fellows Lodges in the North and South before, during, and after the Civil War. Source: Annual reports of the Independent Order of Odd Fellows; estimates from lodge foundings and death rates in Charles H. Brooks, *The Official History and Manual of the Grand United Order of Odd Fellows in America* (Freeport, N.Y.: Books for Libraries Press, 1971 reprint of 1902 edition).

dependent Order of Odd Fellows, but in 1843 they founded their own parallel federation, the Grand United Order of Odd Fellows (GUO of OF).[45] Prior to the Civil War, the GUO of OF was run by northern free blacks, most gathered in lodges in the major East Coast cities of Boston, New York, Philadelphia, Baltimore, and Washington, D.C., but some in smaller cities as well. With the outbreak of the war about slavery, northern blacks stepped up their organizing, and after the 1863 Emancipation Proclamation, southern blacks immediately began to found lodges of their own. The hopes of the time were captured in such evocative names as "Star of Liberty Lodge" (founded 1863), "Free Virginia Lodge" (1864), "Frederick Douglass Lodge" (1865), "United Sons of the Morning Lodge" (1866), and "Abraham Lincoln Lodge" and "Republican Star Lodge" (both 1869) — and in the new name of one previously established lodge that petitioned in 1866 to change its name to "Freedom's Friend Lodge."[46] Northern and southern African Americans thus responded to victory and freedom with a surge of organizing and joining. Eventually, the numbers of African American GUO of OF lodges overtook white IOOF lodges in per capita terms.

The trends traced in figure 6.5 are truly remarkable, given that African Americans, especially in the South, were much poorer and much less educated than whites. Nor was the African American organizational explosion restricted to the Grand United Order of Odd Fellows. From the Civil War through the turn of the twentieth century, emboldened American blacks created dozens of new translocally organized fraternal, sororal, and mutual-aid associations, groups like the Order of Galilean Fishermen (founded in

Washington, D.C., in 1865); the Independent Order of St. Luke (founded in Baltimore in 1867); the Knights and Daughters of Tabor, International Order of Twelve (founded in Independence, Missouri, in 1872); the Independent Order of Immaculates (founded in Nashville, Tennessee, in 1872); the Knights of Pythias of North and South America, Europe, Asia, and Africa (founded in 1880 in Vicksburg, Mississippi); and the Mosaic Templars of America (founded in Little Rock, Arkansas, in 1883). Postwar African American federations were often launched from upper-South or border-state cities, symbolizing the new capacity of blacks to forge ties between northerners and southern brothers and sisters now released from slavery.

The Civil War, in short, not only gave a big push to American civic organizing but redirected the leadership of national endeavors toward northerners and empowered African Americans in unprecedented ways, while disheartening and disconnecting southern whites. For the most part, this meant that national association building was encouraged, because the North (tied to much of the dynamically expanding West) was the richer, faster-growing region in late-nineteenth-century America. But associational fortunes varied through the Civil War, and particular groups could end up being torn apart in the fierce crosswinds of this era. Inside the vast American temperance movement, for example, the Independent Order of Good Templars (IOGT) grew both during and just after the war, reaching amazing heights in the early 1870s.[47] From its birth, the IOGT had a policy of recruiting women as well as men and allowing women to be elected officers. During the war, American women intensified their temperance activism at a time when many men were in the military; so its gender-inclusive norms helped the IOGT to keep growing even during the war and gain important new ground in competition with the Sons of Temperance (which only slowly and reluctantly abandoned its policy of exclusively recruiting men). Remarkably, the IOGT also accepted African Americans, and such recruitment grew during and right after the Civil War, at a time when northerners alone were in charge of the national IOGT. But as white southerners returned to the federation after the Civil War, fierce fights broke out over the place of blacks in the association. In 1876, the IOGT split into two organizations, which came back together only in 1886. But by then, the IOGT's mass appeal was dwindling. Leadership in the American temperance movement had passed primarily to the female-led WCTU.

Thus, the Civil War not only fueled temperance crusades but furthered the feminization of this sector of U.S. civic life. Simultaneously, the lingering reverberations of a war fought mostly by volunteer brotherhoods encouraged the growth and formation, at least among whites, of male-dominated fraternal groups. Hundreds of fraternals, large and small, spread across America in the late 1800s.[48] These associations brought men across occupational strata together to enact regular rituals of cross-class brotherly solidarity and in many cases sponsored internal "military orders" devoted to drills and parades that surely must have resonated with wartime experiences for millions of late-nineteenth-century veterans and their sons.

American voluntarism flourished from 1865 through the turn of the twentieth century, and its predominant institutional form was the local-state-national federation, a form in place before the Civil War — indeed, a form that helped Americans mobilize, in partnership with government, to fight that war. Although post–Civil War associationalism was arguably more gender-segregated among whites, the postwar civic world was in many ways an expanded and more northern-centered version of prewar civic America. To be sure, as industrialization gathered force, business and professional groups and labor unions proliferated in the late 1800s and early 1900s. But class- and occupation-based groups never became as numerous or anywhere near as large as cross-class membership associations.[49] Because the Civil War was fought through voluntary mobilizations, it ended up revivifying and spreading an early form of the modern U.S. association: the nation-spanning, cross-class, membership federation. Popularly rooted membership associations expanded and proliferated, even as the United States became a more class-divided society with the advent of corporate industrialization.

State and Civil Society in America's First World War

Both the Civil War and World War II were bigger conflicts by far than America's first venture into European big-power warfare between 1917 and 1919. But despite its shorter duration, lower level of military involvement, and fewer casualties, World War I brought the most pivotal changes in U.S. methods of making war. State-society relationships forged during World War I became a "dress rehearsal" for similar undertakings on a greater and more sustained scale in the 1940s. Experiences during World War I also contributed centrally to shaping a modernized universe of U.S. voluntary membership associations, including both business and professional groups and popularly rooted federations closely attuned to national purposes, a configuration of groups that remained vibrant into the 1960s. In many ways, World War I set the civic mold for the United States as a global power.

A New Approach to Military Mobilization

Until 1917, U.S. wars were primarily fought by volunteers assembled from localities and states. In the Civil War, as we have seen, local leaders raised units and (often) served as officers of the men they recruited. Decades later, a similar approach was taken to mobilize units for the Spanish-American

War of 1897–98.[50] Theodore Roosevelt's Rough Riders epitomize this re-markably persistent American tradition. As late as 1916, public and Con-gressional sentiment still favored the militia-based system, and President Woodrow Wilson initially resisted "preparedness" advocates who pushed for a national draft and universal military training. But once the United States entered the stalemated European war in April 1917, Wilson did an about-face and asked Congress to enact a system of national conscription, to be based on registration by all adult men on June 5, 1917.[51] Suddenly faced with the need to enhance and manage national industrial and agricultural production while raising a large force for potential dispatch to the European battlefronts, Wilson sought to coordinate "selective service" in the military with retention of skilled manpower in key segments of the economy. Amer-ica's experiences in the Civil War and Britain's experience in the first years of World War I convinced the Wilson administration that reliance on locally assembled volunteer units would prompt indiscriminate enlistment by key civilian leaders and skilled workers, leaving the domestic economy without the leadership deemed necessary to fight a modern total war. President Wilson and his War Department aimed for a more rationally coordinated approach.[52]

Given the fundamental breaks with the past embodied in national con-scription and a nationally managed war economy, historians have told the story of World War I in terms of governmental centralization and functional coordination between government and organized economic sectors.[53] Part-nerships between government and voluntary associations have certainly been highlighted in standard accounts, but historians have focused almost exclusively on business, professional, labor, and farm associations. The presi-dent, the War Department, the Treasury, the Department of Agriculture, and other parts of the federal executive convened coordinating agencies — such as the Council of National Defense, the War Industries Board, and the Food Administration — each of which in turn formed partnerships with key economic actors.[54] In Ellis Hawley's phrase, an "associative state" began to take shape, based on partnerships between federal agencies and business groups, with some participation by the leadership of the American Federa-tion of Labor.[55] "State-society synergy" has certainly been portrayed as cen-tral to U.S. mobilization for World War I, but this synergy appears to have taken a fundamentally different form than the partnerships between govern-ment and cross-class citizens' associations which predominated during and after the Civil War.

This is the orthodox account, and much of it makes sense. Socio-economically, America was transformed between the Civil War and World War I from a nation of farms and small towns where 53 percent of the work force was in agriculture, to an urban and industrial giant where more than half of Americans lived in cities of various sizes. Only 27 percent "remained engaged in agriculture," and the work force consisted "increasingly of employees rather than the self-employed."[56] Associations grounded in occupational or class identities proliferated from the 1880s on.[57] As the United States moved into global power politics, federal authorities had much to gain by forming ties to—and fostering cooperation among—nationally influential business, professional, and labor leaders.

Associational Foundings

The conventional historical, focus on government partnerships with business and professional associations also accounts for a striking difference between the associational aftereffects of the Civil War and World War I. In the former case, as we have seen, wartime mobilizations encouraged leaders to launch new cross-class membership federations, in effect imitating and extending the kinds of organizational networks through which the Civil War itself was fought. But the upsurge in association building that accompanied and followed World War I (and World War II as well) encouraged the founding of new business and professional societies—that is, exactly the *new kinds of groups* that public officials closely cooperated with in order to manage twentieth-century warfare in more rationalized fashion.

There is no listing yet available of the founding dates of all national U.S. business and professional associations past and present, but chroniclers agree that such groups proliferated gradually from the late nineteenth century onward and then more than doubled during and right after World War I, going from mere hundreds to between one and two thousand in number and assuming "many of the characteristics that are typical today."[58] As would happen again in 1933–34 (when the first New Deal required business cooperation) and during World War II (when the federal government worked closely with business and professional elites), World War I was a time when experts and managers were brought together on officially sponsored government boards and committees. In 1917, for example, as federal officials mounted unprecedented national propaganda campaigns, and encouraged the founding of the American Association of Advertising Agencies; and in 1919, at the conclusion of a war that involved orchestrated food conservation campaigns, the National Restaurant Association was born. In some cases, federal officials pulled together more specifically elite associations than those prevalent before the war, as the birth of the National Federation of Business and Professional Women illustrates. When "Secretary of War Newton D. Baker issued a call to make . . . woman power available for the war effort, . . . it was found that women were organized in so far as religious, cultural, and fraternal groups were concerned, but that business and professional women were an unorganized group." National war mobilization committees thus brought leading women professionals together; and even though the Armistice intervened before plans came to fruition, the Secretary of War continued to sponsor meetings and paid regional organizers until the National Federation was instituted in July 1919.[59]

While mobilization for World War I encouraged the formation of hundreds of new business and professional associations, it served as midwife to only two of the large popularly rooted voluntary federations listed in appendix A. Significantly, the American Farm Bureau Federation (AFBF) and the American Legion were directly encouraged by World War I officials seeking to fill what they saw as lacunae in the existing universe of popular membership federations.

The formation of the AFBF was facilitated because federal authorities wanted new, reliable associational partners for managing relations with commercial farmers at a time when agricultural production was critical to the war effort.[60] Federal officials did not find preexisting farmers' associations appealing: some were too radical, and the National Grange had opposed the original 1917 military draft and was dismissed as a "secret" fraternal organization. Prior to 1917, federally appointed county agricultural agents had fostered "farm bureaus," and they encouraged their rapid spread during the war. In turn, Hoover's Food Administration, along with other state and national authorities promoted farm bureau coordination, setting the stage for nongovernmental leaders to found the national Farm Bureau as an independent voluntary association in 1919.

Meanwhile, officers of the American Expeditionary Force sponsored the American Legion as a new national federation of World War I veterans, issuing a plan while the armies were still in France that called for officers and soldiers returning home to set up Legion posts in every community and state.[61] The military and civilian elites who launched the Legion were determined to create a nationally influential, cross-class association open to all veterans. In their vision, the Legion would replace the earlier Grand Army of the Republic (GAR) — which, of course, was a geographically uneven association restricted to Union veterans of the 1861–65 war and was destined to die with them. Remarkably, the entire federation edifice was put in place during 1919, proving the potency of marrying official sponsorship and an established armed forces communications network to a familiar model of cross-class civic associationalism.

Popular Federations in World War I

But the Legion and the Farm Bureau were atypical instances of official encouragement of new popular voluntary federations in conjunction with the world wars. In most spheres, such innovations were unnecessary, be-

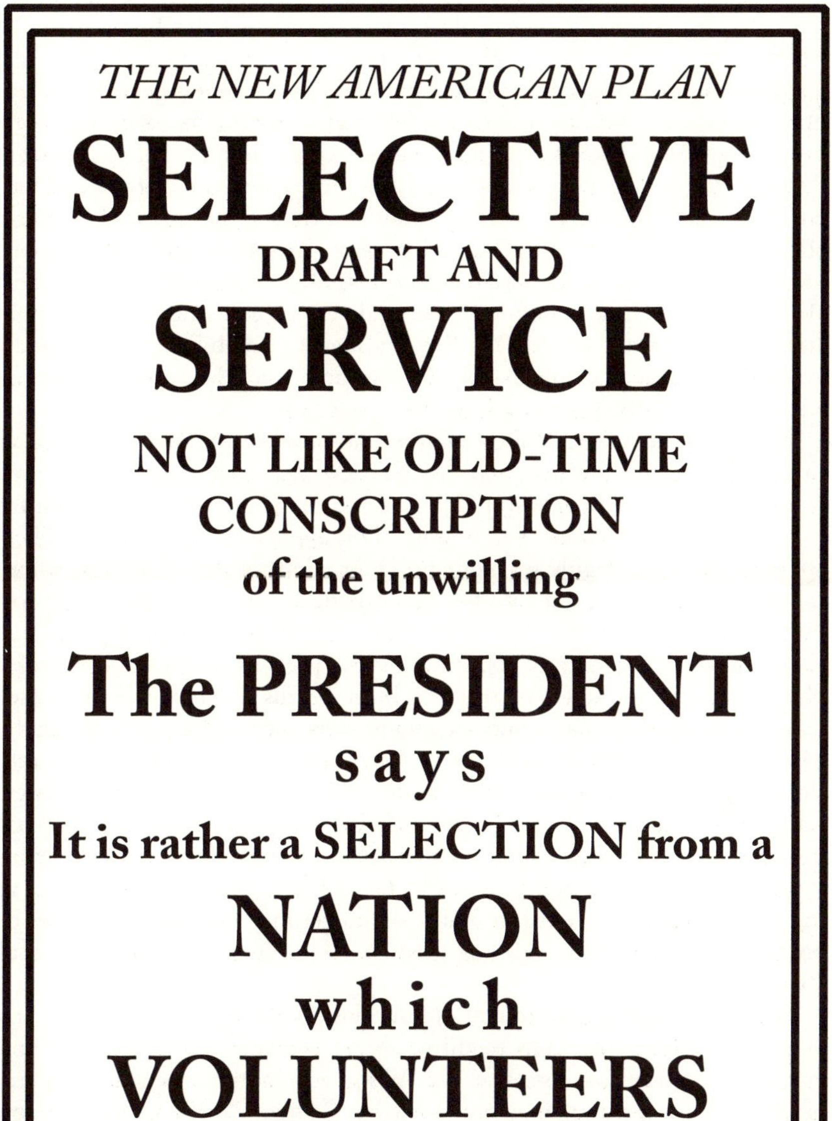

THE NEW AMERICAN PLAN

SELECTIVE

DRAFT AND

SERVICE

NOT LIKE OLD-TIME
CONSCRIPTION
of the unwilling

The PRESIDENT
s a y s
It is rather a SELECTION from a
NATION
w h i c h
VOLUNTEERS
IN MASS

FIG. 6.6. U.S. Selective Service Poster, 1917. Redrawn from a copy.

cause twentieth-century American civil society was *already* networked with a rich array of popularly rooted, cross-class voluntary federations, many of which were able and very willing to enter into wartime partnerships with government. Because of the conventional focus on business-government cooperation during World War I, another major part of the story has been overlooked. Mobilization for this conflict could not be achieved solely through cooperation between business and professional associations and federal agencies. Millions of ordinary Americans had to be involved, through efforts reaching out to families and communities throughout the nation. Executive agencies and coordinating committees certainly proliferated in Washington, D.C., and defined bold goals to project American economic and military power abroad. Yet the goals of war mobilization far outran available bureaucratic means—as, for the first time, the American people were asked to participate in a huge European war.

When officials of the Wilson administration asked millions of American men to register for the new Selective Service system on June 5, 1917, they were not at all sure people would respond to the president's exhortation for everyone to come forward "voluntarily." This approach was taken in deliberate contrast to the highly problematic Union draft of the Civil War, where military officials went out into the countryside to run men down. Yet "voluntary" registration had to be backed not just with national propaganda but also with much community hoopla and social pressure, and local civic notables had to be recruited to run the local boards through which further registrations and actual draft selections were accomplished.[62] Similarly, when Treasury Secretary William McAdoo chose to make sales of "Liberty Bonds" a major part of his scheme for financing the war with cheap money, millions of Americans had to be persuaded to buy these unfamiliar financial instruments. And when Food Administrator Herbert Hoover wanted consumers to conserve scarce food stocks for military supply and shipment to starving Europe, he needed to find a way to get the word out to millions of ordinary households, persuading housewives to prepare "meatless" and "wheatless" meals.

The U.S. national government did not possess the capacity to handle any of these administrative tasks requiring direct contacts with individuals and families. Historians have stressed the Wilson administration's innovative use of propaganda techniques coordinated by George Creel's Committee on Public Information, which inundated the country with newsreels, posters, and pamphlets.[63] But what about the actual dissemination of such messages? Newsreels could be sent to movie theaters, but this was not yet the era of instant electronic communication through televisions or radios in every home. Organized social intermediaries mattered in what social scientists used to call the "two step flow of communication": from authoritative central sources to local "opinion leaders," and from them to ordinary citizens.[64]

Not surprisingly, America's World War I managers turned to the great voluntary federations for help. The federal government relied on partnerships with voluntary associations — and it needed groups with extensive networks and popular roots, not just the sorts of business and professional associations on which scholars have concentrated so much attention. Knit together in the decades following the explosion of associational births in the post–Civil War period, an elaborate associational infrastructure, reaching into towns and states across the nation, made it possible for the United States to mobilize for World War I. Organized popular campaigns involving the national, state, and local bodies of more than two dozen leading voluntary federations (and many smaller federations as well) figured in every aspect of war mobilization, from drafting, training, and supporting troops, to raising money to pay for the war, to heightening industrial and agricultural production, to conserving resources in order to maximize their deployment abroad. The best place to learn about these efforts is not in scholarly treatments of World War I, which tend to be top-down accounts focused on business and federal managers, but from the ubiquitous reports prepared soon after 1919 by chroniclers proud of the wartime efforts of "their" states or communities.[65]

At the official core of the popular war mobilization were new versions of the same kinds of partnerships that constituted the civilian contribution to fighting the Civil War. Picking up right where they left off in earlier conflicts, the YMCA and the Red Cross were immediately commissioned by the War Department to organize and fund services ranging from the recreational to the spiritual, supporting the newly mobilized soldiers in training camps, in transit, and on the European fronts.[66] YMCA "huts" went everywhere with the troops and were advertised to potential donors as "homes away from home" (figure 6.7). Associations engaged in war relief also supported families and communities on the home front.

World War I brought an important new twist to government-association partnerships for military and civilian support. This time, non-Protestant voluntary associations also got officially involved. By the 1890s, at a time of heightened ethno-religious tensions between Protestants and Catholics, the Knights of Columbus (K of C) was emerging as an influential and ambitious nationwide Catholic fraternal group (figure 6.8). Tied to the Church but led by laymen, the Knights stressed their patriotic credentials. This fraternal group's name and ceremonies celebrated the Catholic explorer and discoverer of America, Christopher Columbus, and the K of C added a patriotic higher "degree" to its group ritual in the 1890s. By the early twentieth century, Knights of Columbus leaders were confident enough to begin to challenge Protestant hegemony in national affairs.[67] During the 1916 U.S. military incursion into Mexico, local K of C councils persuaded military authorities to allow them to join the YMCA in setting up centers offer-

THE Y. M. C. A. Hut is home to-day for two million boys over there, and for another million on this side. Your money helped to build the Huts; and is helping to keep them the bright spot in the soldiers' and sailors' lives.

Follow your money through the pages of this book, and see how many different good things it is doing for our boys.

FIG. 6.7. Young Men's Christian Association Hut for U.S. Troops during World War I. From a leaflet, 1918. Source: Personal collection of Theda Skocpol.

FIG. 6.8. Knights of Columbus Hall for U.S. Troops during World War I. Postcard, 1917. Source: Personal collection of Theda Skocpol.

ing comforts and religious services to American troops. With the outbreak of World War I, national K of C leaders pointed to this example and stressed to the Wilson Administration that one-third of Americans were Catholics, and Catholic soldiers should not be subjected to the Protestant evangelism that YMCA volunteers dispensed along with social services. This came at a juncture when the newly instituted military draft was reaching out to take many Catholic working-class men, and some leading Knights had strong ties to the Democratic Party. So no doubt for political as well as administrative reasons, President Wilson and the War Department agreed to give the Knights of Columbus official standing, along with the YMCA, in the wartime support apparatus run by voluntary associations.

Protestant fraternal groups, including the prestigious Masons, protested the "favoritism" allegedly being shown the leading Catholic fraternal federation. But the War Department held firm, stressing that the K of C was acting as a social service agency, not a fraternal brotherhood, and pointing out that its "huts," like those of the YMCA, would be open to all soldiers.[68] To highlight the interdenominational nature of the new arrangements, the War Department invited the Young Men's Hebrew Association to join with the YMCA, K of C, Salvation Army, Young Women's Christian Association

FIG. 6.9. Window Poster for the U.S. "United War Work Campaign," November 1918. Source: Personal collection of Theda Skocpol.

(YWCA), and other officially supported voluntary associations in what soon became the "United War Work Campaign" (figure 6.9). Along with the American Federation of Labor and the farm bureaus, which were crucial partners in ensuring heightened economic production, the associations of the War Work Campaign were at the official heart of government-society partnerships during World War I.

When other voluntary associations wanted to help the troops, federal agencies told them to channel their volunteers and monetary contributions through the groups officially commissioned to take the lead. Thus the Benevolent and Protective Order of Elks ended up conducting a national fundraising campaign for the Salvation Army;[69] and the General Federation of Women's Clubs, informed that it could not send members directly to France, placed volunteers wearing "GFWC" arm patches in units run by the YWCA (which, along with the YMCA, was officially designated to serve the troops).[70] The national managers of America's wartime mobilizations may have badly needed the enthusiasm and contributions of many voluntary associations, but they also aimed for efficiency and wanted to avoid duplication of efforts. So they required associations to work together and limited the number that could officially gain direct access to military encampments and fronts. This was in important respects a departure from voluntarist traditions in the past, when local communities and particular associations tended to maintain direct ties to units of "their men" in the military, without going through central authorities either to gain information or to make deliveries.[71] Especially where access to military units was concerned, the state-society synergy of World War I was more rationalized than the Civil War mobilization.

Even so, there remained many routes that federations could take to get into the heart of the World War I mobilizations on the home front. Domestic efforts were not completely rationalized—in large part because each federal committee and agency forged its own associational partnerships. The Treasury Department tapped the Boy Scouts to help conduct national Liberty Loan drives.[72] Promising to avoid European-style food "dictatorship" and instead "assemble the voluntary effort of the people," Food Administrator Herbert Hoover convened fraternal and women's group leaders to request their help in persuading families to cut back use of wheat, sugar, fats, and meat.[73] And only fifteen days after Congress declared war in April 1917, the Council of National Defense decided to set up a Woman's Committee, which quickly tapped leaders of national women's federations.[74] Prominent "organization women," especially from the General Federation of Women's Clubs, the National American Woman Suffrage Association, and the Daughters of the American Revolution, immediately brought their federations' networks into the war effort. In state after state, Federated Women's Club leaderships essentially converted themselves into instruments of war

TABLE 6.1
Federated Groups Engaged in World War I Food Drives in Iowa

Federated Groups	Number
Church Congregations	
Methodist	783
Catholic	480
Lutheran	337
Christian	324
Congregational	237
Baptist	221
Presbyterian	202
German Lutheran	121
German Evangelical	56
Swedish Lutheran	53
Episcopal	40
Evangelical Lutheran	19
Total	2873
Association Chapters	
United Commercial Travelers	34 lodges
Travelers Protective Association	14 lodges
Iowa State Traveling Men's Association	235 lodges
Gideons	324 lodges
Knights of Pythias	235 lodges
Benevolent and Protective Order of Elks	32 lodges
Loyal Order of Moose	50 lodges
Knights of Columbus	47 lodges
Ancient Order of United Workmen	118 lodges
Fraternal Order of Eagles	25 lodges
Independent Order of Odd Fellows	685 lodges
Brotherhood of American Yeomen	500 lodges
Homesteaders	140 lodges
Woodmen of the World	400 lodges
Modern Woodmen of America	982 lodges
Masons	531 lodges
Sons of Herman	1500 lodges
Foresters	22 lodges
Royal Neighbors of America	575 lodges
Order of the Eastern Star	419 lodges
Woodmen of the World Circle	190 lodges
Rebekahs	600 lodges
Pythian Sisters	144 lodges
Women's Clubs	600 clubs
Woman's Christian Temperance Unions	400 unions
Daughters of the American Revolution	75 chapters

TABLE 6.1 *Continued*

Federated Groups	Number
Colonial Dames	100 chapters
Grand Army of the Republic	600 posts
Sons of the American Revolution	25 chapters
Ad Men's Clubs	14 branches
Rotary Clubs	14 clubs
Total	9630

Source: Ivan L. Pollock, *The Food Administration in Iowa*, vol. 1 (Iowa City: State Historical Society of Iowa, 1923), 188–89.

mobilization, able to reach millions of individual homes through clubs in thousands of local communities.[75]

In fact, local chapters of all kinds of voluntary membership federations became crucial nodes in war mobilization drives. Reproducing lists from a chronicle of war activities in Iowa, for example, table 6.1 indicates the re-markable range of networks, between both church congregations and volun-tary chapters that were reported as contributing to food conservation cam-paigns in that one state. Without including the public schools, which were invariably mobilized for war drives, some 43 federated networks and more than 12,500 congregations and chapters were reportedly involved in food conservation drives in just this state. Iowa may well have been one of the most civically engaged states, but it was not unique. Voluntary association reports and other state and community histories tell the same tale, again and again. Drives to purchase Liberty Bonds were regular undertakings for associational chapters, often involving competition among local or state units within the membership federations. Women's groups routinely spear-headed food conservation drives, worked on behalf of the United War Work associations, or convened to knit socks or wrap bandages for the Red Cross. Male fraternal and veterans' groups championed draft registration and mili-tary recruitment, participated in patriotic parades and pageants, and raised funds to help soldiers and their families. "For the temple units, it was pa-rade, parade, parade," recounts the group's official history about the wartime contributions of the Ancient Arabic Order of the Nobles of the Mystic Shrine.[76]

At their most attenuated, group efforts shaded into primarily symbolic association with the war effort. Of course, even symbolic participation re-quired that voluntary associations lend their internal communications to the shaping of public opinion in support of America's newfangled engagement in a European war. For federal authorities, running the war effort through partnerships with voluntary associations and societal institutions had great advantages. "A national bureaucracy might possibly have handled the local problems of war administration more efficiently . . . ," explained historian Preston William Slosson in a 1931 retrospective, "but it could not have enlisted an equal degree of popular enthusiasm. The fact that nearly every prominent citizen could wear some sort of button or badge, that homes and business houses could hang out flags with a star for each person serving in France, that the operation of the draft was in the hands of local civilian boards, that food-saving posters could be placed in every kitchen window, that every child could collect thrift stamps, made the war national as no congressional resolution or presidential proclamation could have."[77]

Voluntary associations had their own reasons for trumpeting war service and also benefited from the effort. Federations gained visibility and legitimacy with the general public — and this was surely valuable to associations dependent on membership recruitment and dues. Wartime service also allowed voluntary groups to provide praise and status inducements to leaders and members. Engagement with the war was a way to honor "manly" patriotic service in fraternal lodges and feminine caring in women's clubs and auxiliaries. Idealizations of patriotism, community service, and brotherhood and sisterhood across class lines were already standard in American civic culture — drummed in constantly in the rituals and programs of voluntary chapters as well as churches. Thus, as World War I was fought in large part through alliances between government and voluntary membership federations, the wartime mobilizations both drew upon and reinforced longstanding civic ideals and norms about status and leadership in voluntary federations.[78]

Winners and Losers

Earlier we pointed to aggregate trends suggesting that coexisting numbers of large voluntary federations increased during and after World War I. But the events of 1917 to 1919 also had a differential impact on various American voluntary associations, very much depending on whether groups appeared as friend or foe of the U.S. war effort, and in part as well on how close a partnership each association's national leadership forged with government during the mobilization.

For associations that found themselves outside the official pale, World War I was a very dark time. A new kind of nationalistic endeavor, this war was conducted by U.S. authorities uneasy about managing a society divided by class, ethnicity, and politics. Ironically, because federal authorities were so reliant on public mobilization and partnerships with voluntary associations, they were quick to perceive opposition and fierce in orchestrating popular, as well as legal, repression of possible opponents. Associations thus had sharply divergent experiences, depending on whether the government saw them as friend or foe of the war effort. Even as World War I proved propitious for the American Federation of Labor, whose president, Samuel Gompers, accepted appointments to national boards, it brought disarray, destruction, and massive membership loss to the Socialists and the International Workers of the World, whose leaders were often jailed, deported, or held up for public scorn.[79] Similarly, while many ethnic-American associations (including Polish and Italian groups) joined the war effort just as enthusiastically as Anglo-Protestant groups, other associations suddenly found themselves on the wrong ethnic side of the international alignment of friends and enemies, while still others could not muster enthusiasm for a war that tied the United States to England.

Many Irish-American associations fell into the unenthusiastic category. Because nationalist resentment of England ran high in Ireland, sympathetic Irish-American groups tended not to like the U.S. alliance with Britain — and they paid a price for sympathy with their ancestral homeland. The Ancient Order of Hibernians, for example, was growing until World War I, but then went into a decline and never regained the same momentum. Yet the fate of the Hibernians, and the difficulties of other Irish-dominated associations that stood back from the war effort, contrast sharply with the rising fortunes of the Knights of Columbus (which, despite its name, was also Irish-dominated). As we have seen, the Knights of Columbus strongly supported the war effort and was made an official partner with the War Department. During and after the war, the Knights of Columbus gained members and prestige, partially at the expense of other Irish and Catholic associations.

Fates worse than stagnation awaited ethnic associations that became identified with "the Hun," as official propaganda labeled the imperial German enemy in World War I. Constituting more than a tenth of the population (along with the nation's other two very large minorities, Irish and African Americans), German Americans had developed since the early 1800s a flourishing world of ethnically identified Catholic and Protestant churches, singing societies and sports clubs, fraternal groups, and associations devoted to cultural assertion and defense. In the early twentieth century, German language and culture continued to flourish in the United States, even though many German immigrants had assimilated and spoke English quite well. Not only did the Germans have their own distinctive groups; major U.S. fraternal orders, like the Odd Fellows and Knights of Pythias, had long histories of welcoming German-speaking lodges into their midst. But the visibly distinctive associational world of German Americans was largely destroyed during World War I.[80]

Straightforward national repression was part of the story. Formed in 1901 to foster German culture and advocate for the civil rights of German Americans, the German-American National Alliance was immediately targeted when the United States went to war with Germany. In early 1918, Congress investigated the alliance as a potentially subversive group; and as members deserted and units closed down, the organization disbanded and donated its remaining funds to the Red Cross.[81] Meanwhile, other German-American voluntary groups faced pressures and threats. Non-German Americans sometimes attacked and criticized them, and even if they did not, German Americans were anxious to distance themselves from ethnic markers. Suddenly, German churches and societies changed their names. Fraternal groups rescinded their longstanding policies allowing foreign-language lodges. Group badges that used to sport the black, red, and gold of the German Empire suddenly turned red, white, and blue. And some groups did not survive, at least not nationally. The Sons of Herman, for example, had flourished since the 1840s as a fraternal, insurance, and cultural self-defense association. But after the tribulations of World War I, the national Sons of Herman disbanded in 1921, leaving organizations only in particular states, like Texas, where local infrastructure remained strong.

That groups identified with the foreign enemy (or hostile to foreign friends) suffered from 1917 to 1919 is, in a sense, not surprising. Of more interest are the fortunes of large U.S. membership associations that supported the official war effort in varying ways and degrees. Using the information we have been able to find for twenty-four of the thirty voluntary membership federations that came into existence no later than 1919 and whose membership exceeded 1 percent of the U.S. adult population between 1910 and 1930, figure 6.10 displays associational membership trends from 1915/16 to 1920/21.[82] Associations are classified along a continuum, according to how involved they were with the federal government during World War I (see appendix B for category definitions).

At the top of the continuum, two "Officially Sponsored" groups, the American Legion and the Farm Bureau, formed in 1919 after much encouragement by federal officials. And at the opposite extreme, the German Alliance was "Identified with the Enemy" and targeted for repression by the federal government. Obviously, the "Officially Sponsored" groups suddenly achieved very large memberships during their time of close involvement in the war effort; and equally clearly the German Alliance lost its membership, indeed its very organizational life, as a result of its identification with the wartime enemy. Most associations fall these extremes, however. In general, groups that were more involved in the national war effort experienced greater membership increases, but there are interesting nuances, too.

"Official Partner" associations include the Red Cross and the YMCA and K of C, the two large federations among the United War Work designees. These were unquestionably the voluntary membership federations most closely involved in the war effort, supporting troops abroad and in the field

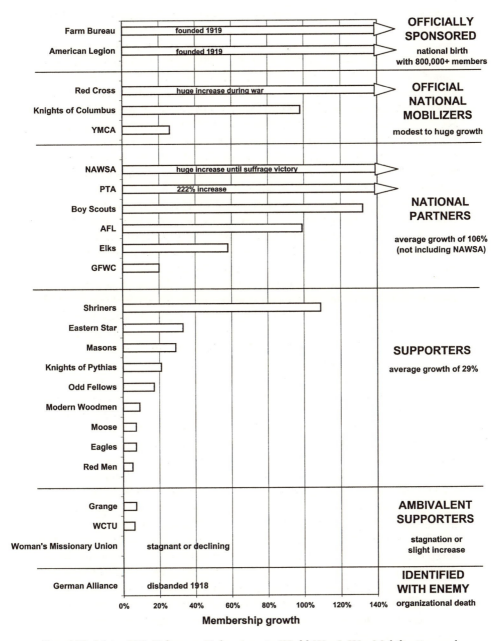

FIG. 6.10. Major U.S. Voluntary Federations in World War I: War Mobilization and Membership Growth, 1915/16 to 1920/21. Source: Harvard Civic Engagement Project data.

as well as troops and other Americans at home. All three gained membership over the wartime period, yet the Red Cross (which included donors as
well as chapter participants) experienced an extreme spike restricted to the
emergency itself (see figure 6.1), and the YMCA experienced only modest
membership growth during its intense period of service to U.S. troops. As
the association that gained the greatest new national visibility and legitimacy
in World War I, the Knights of Columbus experienced an immediate membership payoff. For the Red Cross and the YMCA, the national legitimacy
brought by World War I was not new, and the tasks they had to accomplish
were enormous. Both of these associations gained more in terms of institutional heft than membership. The Red Cross achieved an enduring and
nationwide structure of local chapters that could continue to foster giving
and volunteering through peace and war. The YMCA, meanwhile, moved
into a postwar building boom, and during and after the war chapter secretaries became more professionalized, as YMCAs in general made a transition from evangelism among Protestant group members toward community
social service, the function "Ys" serve today.[83] Synergy with the U.S. government in the prosecution of World War I paid off for the Red Cross, the
YMCA, and the Knights of Columbus alike, but if we measure associational
health strictly in terms of enduring membership gains, then the K of C—
which enjoyed official status but did not give as much effort or treasure to
the war as the Red Cross and the YMCA—benefited the most.

That synergy may work best for voluntary membership groups when it is
enthusiastic and nationally visible, yet something less than a complete embrace by the state, seems borne out by the experiences of federations classified as "National Partners," "Supporters," and "Ambivalent Supporters" in
figure 6.10. Groups in these categories either held their own or gained
ground during World War I, in rough correlation to how closely their national leaderships and organizations tied in to official war efforts.[84]

Little more than holding their own were "Ambivalent Supporters" opposed to war or the military draft before 1917. These groups endorsed the
U.S. effort after Congress declared war, and their local chapters participated
in the major domestic drives. But national federation leaders remained focused on prewar objectives throughout. In contrast, "Supporter" groups favored the war, and their national leaders consistently urged state and local
chapters to respond to government requests, while they concentrated on
raising funds to help soldier-members and their family dependents. Supporter associations gained members, but to widely varying degrees, and for the
most part they did not expand as much (in percentage terms) as the "National Partner" groups.

Partners entered into close working relationships with the federal government but were not officially designated to carry the full burden in any area.
In return for their major contributions—such as lending national officers to

federal war boards, committing state and local networks to run war campaigns, and amassing resources to donate to the national military effort — the partner associations gained enhanced institutional solidity and national respect, which certainly helped them gain members. When World War I came to an abrupt end with the German collapse in 1918, moreover, the national headquarters of several partner federations were left with "surplus" funds gathered as intended contributions to the nation. Some also received back from the federal government buildings that they had donated during the war.

Overall, the voluntary federations most closely involved with World War I mobilization seem to have significantly built up their national organizations and finances as well as their memberships. These buildups may have put such groups in the best position to ride through the economic dips of the 1920s and the Great Depression of the 1930s, which subjected most dues-based popular associations to great stress. Overall, there were twenty-nine voluntary associations that enrolled 1 percent or more of U.S. men and/or women as members (at least briefly) during the 1910s or 1920s, and of these only seventeen (about 59 percent) were still enrolling over 1 percent in the 1940s. In line with this macroscopic picture of associational turnover, six out of nine of the associations listed as "Supporters" in figure 6.10 and only one out of the three "Ambivalent Supporters" remained in the ranks of membership associations surpassing the 1 percent mark in the 1940s. But ten of the eleven associations classified as "Officially Sponsored," "Official National Mobilizers," or "National Partners" remained in (or in the case of the Boy Scouts, entered) the ranks of America's largest membership federations by the 1940s.[85]

Not only did they ride through the Great Depression and flourish into the 1940s, the associations most involved in the U.S. mobilizations for World War I again became closely involved in national mobilizations for World War II — and expanded anew in the aftermath of America's victory in that conflict. Partners with the U.S. national state in the mobilizations to fight and win two global wars, the leading voluntary membership associations of the 1910s and 1940s were essential to the nation's warmaking capacities. And America's biggest wars proved surprisingly good for them, too, enabling these associations to remain at the heart of local and national civil society through much of the twentieth century.

Avoiding Tocqueville's Nightmare

Neither the prolonged and destructive Civil War nor the internationally entangling World War I fulfilled Alexis de Tocqueville's worst fears about the likely impact of big wars on democratic civil society. To be sure, each of these great wars damaged particular groups and undercut certain identities and spheres of association in American civil society. Defeated white southerners lost much of their civic vigor after the Civil War. German Americans rushed to blend in to undifferentiated groups once the United States locked into twentieth-century wars with their ancestral homeland. And groups that countered the U.S. state, even symbolically, or challenged any powerful institution in times of national mobilization for war, could find themselves disorganized out of existence. In all of these ways, America's first modern wars were, at the very least, disheartening, for some voluntary joiners and organizers. On balance, however, America's civic vigor was greatly enhanced after the national fratricide of the1860s and through the plunge into global conflict in 1917. Hearts were raised for those who joined in victorious shared endeavors, and mental horizons were broadened by the sheer scale of cooperation Americans managed to achieve in both the Civil War and the Great War.

Raised hearts and widened horizons were wartime benefits that Tocqueville acknowledged, but he feared that a war-swollen state would, inevitably, displace self-organized civil society. In this fear, Tocqueville misunderstood, quite fundamentally, the bases for complementarity between state power and an engaged civil society in the United States. He did not comprehend the institutional and organizational underpinnings of the apparently spontaneous civic voluntarism he so often celebrated. And he did not understand, or foresee, that the genius of American associationalism would lie in representative membership federations that could serve as two-way bridges across communities and between leaders and led. Because they were translocally as well as locally organized, such voluntary federations could be, at once, significant counterweights to, and powerful partners of, the U.S. federal government.

Along lines more explicable in terms of Peter Evans's ideas about state and society, both the Civil War and World War I were fought by intricately organized and balanced partnerships. Government agencies were unable to go it alone or assert full preeminence, and voluntary federations were available to mobilize popular energies for war. In turn, because America's first great wars were fought through synergistic partnerships between state and society, not through displacement of society by the war-swollen state, these great conflicts ended up nourishing rather than undercutting organized civil society, at least from the perspective of the vast majority of groups prepared to cooperate with national endeavors.

In the Civil War and the Great War, and ultimately in World War II as well, state authorities needed organized civil society, and America's civically capable people responded, deploying federated associations to meet the wartime challenges. From Abraham Lincoln to Woodrow Wilson to Franklin Roosevelt, U.S. leaders called upon a well-organized and participatory civil society to help fight great wars at home and abroad. In consequence of how these conflicts were fought, Americans managed to direct the fierce fires of civil and international war to forge a stronger civil society. Americans used times of war, and the immediate aftermaths of victory, to reinforce a dense network of popularly rooted membership federations, rich in organizational resources and shared values and able to withstand, for a remarkably long time, the class divisions and economic crises of industrial capitalism.

Notes

1. William Quentin Maxwell, *Lincoln's Fifth Wheel: The Political History of the United States Sanitary Commission* (New York: Longmans, Green, 1956), chap. 13.

2. Charles Hurd, *The Compact History of the Red Cross* (New York: Hawthorne Books, 1959).

3. The Red Cross defines "members" as either chapter-based volunteers or donors (of even tiny sums).

4. For further discussion of the large voluntary membership associations at the core of this chapter's analysis, see Theda Skocpol et al., "How Americans Became Civic," in *Civic Engagement in American Democracy*, ed. Theda Skocpol and Morris P. Fiorina (Washington, D.C., and New York: Brookings Institution Press and Russell Sage Foundation, 1999), 27–80. For systematic evidence that these associations were also central to local associational life, see Theda Skocpol, Marshall Ganz, and Ziad Munson, "A Nation of Organizers: The Institutional Origins of Civic Voluntarism in the United States," *American Political Science Review* 94, no. 3 (2000): 527–46, especially tables 3 and 4.

5. An event-history hazard analysis of the spread of state-level units of voluntary federations across the continental United States reveals that a state's involvement in the Union war effort had a continuing favorable impact on associational formation for many decades after the war. See Jocelyn B. Crowley and Theda Skocpol, "The Rush to Organize: Explaining Associational Formation in the U.S. States, 1860s–1920s," forthcoming in the *American Journal of Political Science*, October 2001.

6. Alexis de Tocqueville, *Democracy in America*, vols. 1 and 2, ed. J. P. Mayer, trans. George Lawrence (Garden City, N.Y.: Doubleday, Anchor Books, 1969 [1835, 1840]), 513.

7. Ibid., 650.

8. Ibid., 646.

9. Ibid., vol. 2, chap. 22.

10. Ibid., 649.

11. Ibid., 395.

12. Ibid., 650.

13. Arthur M. Schlesinger, "Biography of a Nation of Joiners," *American Historical Review* 50, no. 1 (1944): 1–25.

14. Gabriel A. Almond and Sidney Verba, *The Civic Culture: Political Attitudes and Democracy in Five Nations* (Princeton: Princeton University Press, 1963).

15. Putnam's analysis is framed in social psychological terms, stressing the impact

of wartime efforts and solidarities on the outlooks and habits of Americans who were young adults at the time, and subsequently became the most civic generation of the late twentieth century. See Robert D. Putnam, "Tuning In, Tuning Out: The Strange Disappearance of Social Capital in America," *PS: Political Science & Politics* 28, no. 4 (1995): 664–83; and Putnam, *Bowling Alone: The Collapse and Revival of American Community* (New York: Simon & Schuster, 2000), especially 267–72.

16. Christopher Beem, *The Necessity of Politics: Reclaiming American Public Life* (Chicago: University of Chicago Press, 1999), 197. Typical is a study by Everett Carl Ladd, *The Ladd Report* (New York: Free Press, 1999) that says nothing about the impact of wars and argues that what government has *not* done has been the key to American civic vitality. "Surely the flourishing of all sorts of religious organizations in America is the product not of government action but of *deliberate inaction,*" declares Ladd (10, 12), who "guesses" that the U.S. government's historic role in shaping all facets of civic engagement "has been minimal," except to guarantee political freedoms and allow citizens to organize spontaneously.

17. Peter F. Drucker, *The Ecological Vision: Reflections on American Civilization* (New Brunswick, N.J.: Rutgers University Press, 1993), 9.

18. Peter B. Evans, "Government Action, Social Capital, and Development: Reviewing the Evidence on Synergy," in *State-Society Synergy: Government and Social Capital in Development,* ed. Peter B. Evans, Research Series, no. 94 (Berkeley: International and Area Studies Center, University of California at Berkeley, 1997), 178. The following discussion draws from Evans's arguments in the chapter as a whole.

19. For comparisons of the destructiveness of major U.S. wars, see the statistics and references in Theda Skocpol, *Protecting Soldiers and Mothers: The Political Origins of Social Policy in the United States* (Cambridge: Harvard University Press, 1992), 103–4. We are also grateful to Meyer Kestnbaum of the Department of Sociology at the University of Maryland for sharing his estimates of the proportion of southerners who served in the Confederate Army.

20. For a classic formulation along these lines, see Robert H. Wiebe, *The Search for Order, 1877–1920* (New York: Hill & Wang, 1967).

21. The following discussion draws especially upon Richard D. Brown, "The Emergence of Urban Society in Rural Massachusetts, 1760–1820," *Journal of American History* 61, no. 1 (1973): 29–51.

22. Schlesinger, "Nation of Joiners," 5.

23. Meyer Kestnbaum, "Partisans and Patriots: National Conscription and the Reconstruction of the Modern State in France, Germany, and the United States," (Ph.D. diss., Harvard University, 1997), chap. 4.

24. Martin Shefter, *Political Parties and the State: The American Historical Experience* (Princeton: Princeton University Press, 1994), 61–71.

25. Donald G. Mathews, "The Second Great Awakening as an Organizing Process, 1780–1830: An Hypothesis," *American Quarterly* 21, no. 1 (1969): 23–43; and Roger Finke and Rodney Stark, *The Churching of America, 1776–1990* (New Brunswick, N.J.: Rutgers University Press, 1992), chap. 3.

26. Richard R. John, *Spreading the News: The American Postal System from Franklin to Morse* (Cambridge: Harvard University Press, 1995).

27. Full development of this argument and citations are to be found in Skocpol, Ganz, and Munson, "A Nation of Organizers."

28. This discussion draws on "Amateurs Go to War," chap. 10 in James M. McPherson, *Battle Cry of Freedom: The Civil War Era* (New York: Oxford University Press, 1988).

29. Richard Bensel, "Southern Leviathan: The Development of Central State Authority in the Confederate States of America," *Studies in American Political Development* 2 (1987): 68–136.

30. James W. Geary, *We Need Men: The Union Draft in the Civil War* (DeKalb: Northern Illinois University Press, 1991), chap. 1.

31. Ibid., chap. 7.

32. Ibid., 89, table 4. If anything, white collar and professional men were overrepresented in the Union military effort. Because Union drafts allowed people to pay substitutes, many assume that modern selective service methods are more equitable. But in practice, Geary (170) concludes, "northern conscription was fairer than most of the methods used in raising America's armies in the twentieth century."

33. Maxwell, *Lincoln's Fifth Wheel*; McPherson, *Battle Cry of Freedom*, 323, 480–85; C. Howard Hopkins, *History of the Y.M.C.A. in North America* (New York: Association Press, 1951), 89–94; and Linus Pierpont Brockett, *The Philanthropic Results of the War in America. Collected from Official and Authentic Sources by an American Citizen* (New York: Sheldon, 1864).

34. There were a couple of major voluntary groups that held their own even during the war. Because it welcomed women, the Independent Order of Good Templars fared better than alternative temperance associations. And the Masons also did well, probably because they were the most prestigious fraternal group and various state "grand masters" allowed lodges to form within the Confederate and Union armies. For more on the special attractiveness of Masons for white southerners, see note 44 below.

35. Theodore A. Ross, *Odd Fellowship: Its History and Manual* (New York: M. W. Hazen, 1888), 158–79.

36. Hopkins, *History of the Y.M.C.A.*, 90.

37. James R. Carnahan, *Pythian Knighthood: Its History and Literature* (Cincinnati: Pettibone Manufacturing Company/Fraternity Publishers, 1890), chaps. 5–6.

38. Sven D. Nordin, *Rich Harvest: A History of the Grange, 1867–1900* (Jackson: University of Mississippi Press, 1974), 4.

39. Ruth Bordin, *Woman and Temperance: The Quest for Power and Liberty, 1873–1900* (Philadelphia: Temple University Press, 1981).

40. The "Call" is reprinted in Helen E. Tyler, *Where Prayer and Purpose Meet: The WCTU Story, 1874–1949* (Evanston, Ill.: Signal Press, 1949), 18.

41. "Life Sketches: Annie Wittenmyer" (Evanston, Ill.: National Woman's Christian Temperance Union, undated pamphlet).

42. This is based on an analysis of founding locations for hundreds of fraternal, patriotic, labor, and women's auxiliary associations cited in Albert C. Stevens, *The Cyclopedia of Fraternities* (New York: Hamilton Printing and Publishing Company, 1899), as well as additional groups included in Arthur R. Preuss, *A Dictionary of Secret and Other Societies* (St. Louis, Mo.: Herder, 1924), and Sophinisba Breckinridge, *Women in the Twentieth Century: A Study of Their Political, Social, and Economic Activities* (New York: McGraw-Hill, 1933), chap. 2.

43. On the prevalence of churches as compared with other voluntary groups in

the South, see Gerald Gamm and Robert D. Putnam, "The Growth of Voluntary Associations in America, 1840–1940," *Journal of Interdisciplinary History* 29, no. 4 (1999): 538, n. 29.

44. Southern whites held back from voluntary federations centered in the North. This interpretation is strengthened by the contrasting trajectory of Masons during and after the Civil War. In that fraternal universe, southern whites joined more often than northern whites before the Civil War, and on a per capita basis southern white Masons did *not* fall behind northern white Masons during or after the great conflict. Yet there was a crucial institutional difference between the Masons and the Odd Fellows, one which surely made Masons more attractive to southerners throughout the nineteenth century, marked as it was by regional divisions. Basic ("blue-lodge") Masons were organized into state grand lodges with no national center; and the higher-level "Scottish" jurisdiction, into which white southerners disproportionately flooded, was divided into regional wings, with the Southern Jurisdiction both autonomous and predominant. During an era of American history when the symbolism of Union triumphalism ran strong in most national voluntary federations, southern Masons did not have to subordinate themselves to northern organizational centers or attend national conventions run by their former enemies.

45. The African American Odd Fellows started in lodges chartered in the United States by a different branch of English Odd Fellows than the branch that chartered most of the original white lodges. Interestingly, the GUO of OF retained its allegiance to the English center, even as it grew in America under the guidance of its own national committee.

46. Charles H. Brooks, *The Official History and Manual of the Grand United Order of Odd Fellows in America* (Freeport, N.Y.: Books for Libraries Press, 1971 [1902]), 90, 94, 96, 97, 105.

47. This account of the IOGT draws especially on David M. Fahey, *Temperance and Racism* (Lexington: University of Kentucky Press, 1996).

48. Stevens, *Cyclopedia of Fraternities*; and Mary Ann Clawson, *Constructing Brotherhood: Gender, Class, and Fraternalism* (Princeton: Princeton University Press, 1989).

49. See figure 2 in Gamm and Putnam, "Growth of Voluntary Associations."

50. Gerald Linderman, "The Spanish-American War and the Small-Town Community," in *The Military in America: From the Colonial Era to the Present*, rev. ed., ed. by Peter Karsten (New York: Free Press, 1986), 275–94.

51. John Whiteclay Chambers II, "Conscripting for Colossus: The Progressive Era and the Origin of the Modern Military Draft in the United States in World War I," in *The Military in America*, 297–311.

52. David M. Kennedy, *Over Here: The First World War and American Society* (New York: Oxford University Press, 1980), 146–50.

53. Examples include Kennedy, *Over Here*; Ronald Schaffer, *America in the Great War: The Rise of the War Welfare State* (New York: Oxford University Press, 1991); and Ellis W. Hawley, *The Great War and the Search for Modern Order: A History of the American People and Their Institutions, 1917–1933* (New York: St. Martin's Press, 1979).

54. For accounts of key federal coordinating bodies, see Franklin H. Martin, *Digest of the Proceedings of the Council of National Defense during the World War*

(Washington, D.C.: U.S. Government Printing Office, 1934); Robert D. Cuff, *The War Industries Board: Business-Government Relations during World War I* (Baltimore: Johns Hopkins University Press, 1973); and William C. Mullendore, *History of the United States Food Administration, 1917–1919* (Stanford, Calif.: Stanford University Press, 1941).

55. Hawley, *Great War*, chaps. 2 and 6.

56. Ibid., p. 3.

57. Gamm and Putnam, "Growth of Voluntary Associations," 526.

58. W. Lloyd Warner, ed., *The Emergent American Society*, Volume 1, *Large-Scale Organizations* (New Haven and London: Yale University Press, 1967), 317–25. See also *National Trade and Professional Associations of the United States, 1966* (Washington, D.C.: Potomac Books, 1966), v–vii; and Joseph F. Bradley, *The Role of Trade Associations and Professional Business Societies in America* (University Park: Pennsylvania State University Press, 1965), chap. 2.

59. *A History of the Oklahoma Federation of Business and Professional Women, 1919–1993* (Oklahoma Federation of Business and Professional Women, n.d.), 11–12. As this history recounts, regional organizers stimulated the concurrent emergence of town clubs and state federations along with the national group.

60. Orville Merton Kile, *The Farm Bureau Movement* (New York: Macmillan, 1921), chaps. 8–9.

61. Thomas A. Rumer, *The American Legion: An Official History, 1919–1989* (New York: M. Evans & Company, 1990), 5–56; and William Pencak, *For God and Country: The American Legion, 1919–1941* (Boston: Northeastern University Press, 1989), chaps. 2–4.

62. Members of military veterans' associations and fraternal groups—typically, men of local prominence men who were also church members and participants in community service, business, or professional associations—became the volunteer managers of the local draft boards that ran America's twentieth-century Selective Service system. See table 3.5 in James W. Davis, Jr., and Kenneth M. Dolbeare, *Little Groups of Neighbors: The Selective Service System* (Chicago: Markham Publishing Company, 1968), 68.

63. James R. Mock and Cedric Larson, *Words That Won the War: The Story of the Committee on Public Information 1917–1919* (Princeton: Princeton University Press, 1939).

64. Paul F. Lazarsfeld, Bernard Berelson, and Hazel Gaudet, *The People's Choice* (New York: Columbia University Press, 1948).

65. We cannot list all the reports of this kind that we have consulted, but it is worth noting that the best resource for understanding both the national and local contributions of voluntary federations to the war effort is a seven-volume series called "Iowa Chronicles of the World War," edited by Benjamin F. Shambaugh and published between 1919 and 1923 by the State Historical Society of Iowa. One scholarly study that does stress state and local voluntary activities is William J. Breen, *Uncle Sam at Home: Civilian Mobilization, Wartime Federalism, and the Council of National Defense, 1917–1919* (Westport, Conn.: Greenwood Press, 1984).

66. On the YMCA efforts in World War I, see Hopkins, *History of the Y.M.C.A.*, 485–504; and Frederick Harris, Frederic Houston Kent, and William J. Newlin, *Service with Fighting Men: An Account of the Young Men's Christian Associations in*

World War I, 2 vols. (New York: Association Press, 1922). On the Red Cross, see Henry P. Davison, *The American Red Cross in the Great War* (New York: Macmillan, 1920); and Earl S. Fullbrook, *The Red Cross in Iowa*, vol. 1 of *Iowa Chronicles of the World War* (Iowa City: Historical Society of Iowa, 1922), chap. 3.

67. This account draws upon Christopher J. Kaufman, *Faith and Fraternalism: The History of the Knights of Columbus, 1882–1982* (New York: Harper & Row, 1982), chaps. 4 and 6–9; and Maurice Francis Egan and John B. Kennedy, *Knights of Columbus in Peace and War*, vol. 1 (New Haven: Knights of Columbus, 1920).

68. Kaufman, *Faith and Fraternalism*, 204–5.

69. James R. Nicholson, Lee A. Donaldson, and Raymond C. Dobson, *History of the Order of Elks, 1868–1978*, rev. ed. (Chicago: Grand Secretary's Office, 1978), 248–49.

70. Mildred White Wells, *Unity in Diversity: The History of the General Federation of Women's Clubs* (Washington, D.C.: General Federation of Women's Clubs, 1953), 231–32.

71. Linderman, "Spanish-American War and Small-Town Community."

72. Mitch Reis, *The Boy Scouts of America during World War I & II* (private publication, 1984), chap. 1.

73. Mullendore, *History of Food Administration*, 94–95; and Nicholson, Donaldson, and Dobson, *History of Order of Elks*, 246–47.

74. Clarke, *American Women and the World War*.

75. Ibid., part 2, "State Organizations"; Breen, *Uncle Sam at Home*, chaps. 7–8; and Ivan L. Pollock, *The Food Administration in Iowa*, vol. 1 (Iowa City: State Historical Society of Iowa, 1923), 54. As Pollock recounts, the leader of the food pledge campaign and chair of the Woman's Committee of the Iowa State Council of National Defense was Mrs. Francis E. Whitley, who "had just completed a term as president of the Federation of Women's Clubs of the State and had been an active member and officer of the federation for many years prior to this time. Consequently, she had a wide personal acquaintance among members of the women's organizations throughout the State. In a very short time, she had a district chairman in each of the eleven congressional districts, and with the aid of these district chairmen she selected a woman in each county to act as county chairman. . . . During the food pledge campaign the women perfected their organization until it extended out into every school district and voting precinct."

76. Orville Findley Rush and (original author) Fred Van Deventer, *Parade to Glory: The Story of the Shriners and Their Caravan to Destiny*, rev. ed. (Iowa: Imperial Council, AAONMS, 1980), 166.

77. Preston William Slosson, *The Great Crusade and After, 1914–1928*, vol. 12 of *A History of American Life* (New York: Macmillan, 1931), 63–64.

78. U.S. voluntary federations found it so easy to adapt longstanding values to wartime efforts that some merely bent the war emergency to their usual goals. The Woman's Christian Temperance Union, for example, took the war as a set of new opportunities to push for prohibition, which they ultimately achieved through the Eighteenth Amendment to the Constitution, while also pressing authorities to curtail the production and distribution of alcohol (as a food conservation measure at home and to safeguard the morals of troops in camps and abroad). See Elizabeth Putnam Gordon, *Women Torch Bearers: The Story of the Woman's Christian Temperance Union*, 2d ed. (Evanston, Ill.: Woman's Christian Temperance Union, 1924), chaps.

5–6. The Loyal Order of Moose, moreover, was heavily invested prior to the war in building and sustaining a national children's orphanage at Mooseheart, Illinois—a massive undertaking that required regular contributions from local lodges. When World War I came along, Moose lodges contributed to Liberty Loans and honored their many soldier-members, but the national Moose leaders became only modestly involved in national war-support activities. This is the conclusion one can draw from a complete reading of Guy H. Fuller, *Loyal Order of Moose and Mooseheart* (Mooseheart, Ill.: Mooseheart Press, 1918). The national headquarters did, however, take the occasion to recast its message about Mooseheart: it was now presented as an institution that would help to care for soldiers' orphans after the war. Supreme Lodge of the World, Loyal Order of Moose, Letter appealing for War Emergency Contribution, September 15, 1917, sent from Mooseheart, Illinois (personal ephemera collection of Theda Skocpol). This letter included a flyer/poster portraying "Some of the children now at Mooseheart" and asking "What will become of the widows and orphans after this Great War?"

79. William Preston, Jr., *Aliens and Dissenters: Federal Suppression of Radicals, 1903–1933*, 2d ed. (Urbana: University of Illinois Press, 1994 [1963]), chap. 4.

80. Frederick C. Luebke, *Bonds of Loyalty: German-Americans and World War I* (DeKalb: Northern Illinois University Press, 1974), chaps. 9–10.

81. Senate Committee on the Judiciary, *National German-American Alliance: Hearings before the Subcommittee of the Committee on the Judiciary . . . on S. 3529*, 65th Congr., 2d sess. February 23–April 13, 1918; and Luebke, *Bonds of Loyalty*, 269–70.

82. Four groups (Maccabees, Christian Endeavor, American Automobile Association, American Bowling Congress) are not included, because we so far lack detailed membership data or information on wartime activities. In addition, the Ku Klux Klan is omitted, because reliable year-by-year membership trends are unlikely ever to be available; and the Woodmen of the World, because it split into separate jurisdictions around 1920 and we have not yet been able to develop consistent membership trends. There is no reason to believe that including any of these associations would substantially alter the picture presented in figure 6.10.

83. Hopkins, *History of the Y.M.C.A.*, chaps. 12–15.

84. To fully explain percentage shifts in memberships, however, we would need a more fine-grained analysis of the timing and modalities of associational involvements in war campaigns. And we would have to take idiosyncratic factors into account as well. The PTA, for example, was both sharply on the rise and had a national recruitment drive in place when the war struck. And the Shriners seem to have done better than other supportive fraternal groups, in part because they conducted recruitment drives inside the military and in part because, as a nationally visible group open only to high-degree Masons, Shriners were at this time reaping the fruits among older men of membership surges experienced around 1900 by southern and northern Masonic lodges.

85. The only group that did not carry forward was NAWSA, an association that attained very large size only fleetingly and then went out of existence after female suffrage was established in 1921, giving birth in its stead to the smaller yet persistent League of Women Voters. The League vastly expanded after World War II, as displayed in trends graphed in Putnam, *Bowling Alone*, 442.

Appendix A

Large Membership Associations in U.S. History
Civic Engagement Project

Common Name	Founding Date	Ending Date
Ancient and Accepted Free Masons	1733	
Independent Order of Odd Fellows	1819	
American Temperance Society	1826	1865
General Union for Promoting Observance of the Christian Sabbath	1828	1832
American Anti-Slavery Society	1833	1870
Improved Order of Red Men	1834	
Washington Temperance Societies	1840	c1848
The Order of the Sons of Temperance	1842	c1970
Independent Order of Good Templars	1851	
Young Men's Christian Association	1851	
Junior Order of United American Mechanics	1853	
National Teachers Association / National Education Association	1857	
Knights of Pythias	1864	
Grand Army of the Republic	1866	1956
Benevolent and Protective Order of Elks	1867	
Patrons of Husbandry (National Grange)	1867	
Ancient Order of United Workmen	1868	
Order of the Eastern Star	1868	
Knights of Labor	1869	1917
National Rifle Association	1871	
Ancient Arabic Order of the Nobles of the Mystic Shrine	1872	
Woman's Christian Temperance Union	1874	
Royal Arcanum	1877	
Farmers' Alliance	1877	1900
Maccabees	1878	
Christian Endeavor	1881	
American Red Cross	1881	
Knights of Columbus	1882	
Modern Woodmen of America	1883	
Colored Farmers' National Alliance and Cooperative Union	1886	1892

(Continued)

Common Name	Founding Date	Ending Date
American Federation of Labor (AFL-CIO after 1955)	1886	
American Protective Association	1887	c1911
Woman's Missionary Union	1888	
Loyal Order of Moose	1888	
National American Woman Suffrage Association	1890	1920
Woodmen of the World	1890	
General Federation of Women's Clubs	1890	
American Bowling Congress	1895	
National Congress of Mothers / National Congress of Parents and Teachers (PTA)	1897	
Fraternal Order of Eagles	1898	
German American National Alliance	1901	1918
Aid Association For Lutherans	1902	
American Automobile Association	1902	
Boy Scouts of America	1910	
Veterans of Foreign Wars of the United States	1913	
Ku Klux Klan (second)	1915	1944
Women's International Bowling Congress	1916	
American Legion	1919	
American Farm Bureau Federation	1919	
Old Age Revolving Pensions, Ltd. (Townsend movement)	1934	1953
Congress of Industrial Organizations	1938	1955
National Foundation for Infantile Paralysis / March of Dimes	1938	
Woman's Division of Christian Service / United Methodist Women	1939	
American Association of Retired Persons	1958	
Greenpeace USA	1971	
National Right to Life Committee	1973	
Mothers Against Drunk Driving	1980	
Christian Coalition	1989	

Major U.S. Voluntary Federations in World War I

Officially Sponsored
U.S. Department of Agriculture officials, including County Extension agents, encouraged the spread and interconnection of farm bureaus during the war. American Expeditionary Force military officers helped to launch the American Legion at the end of the war.

Official National Mobilizers
The Red Cross was charted by Congress in part to manage aid to soldiers and wartime relief efforts. Seven other voluntary associations, including the Young Men's Christian Association and the Knights of Columbus, were designated as official relief agencies during the war.

National Partners
The national leaderships of these associations served on war advisory boards and/or directed their association's organizational networks and financial resources to provide major contributions to federal war efforts.

Supporters
All of these associations endorsed the U.S. war effort and encouraged local and state units to contribute to food conservation efforts, Liberty Loan drives, Red Cross drives, and the war relief efforts of the officially designated associations. The national undertakings of these groups were primarily directed to aiding their own soldier-members.

Ambivalent Supporters
Devoted to international peace or opposed to military conscription prior to the U.S. decision to enter World War I, these associations accepted the war, once declared, and local units participated in civilian drives. But national leaders emphasized other priorities throughout the conflict.

Identified with Foreign Enemy
Formed in 1901 to defend German Americans from nativist attacks and assert the value of German culture, the German American National Alliance (along with other German-American voluntary associations) was caught in the anti-German fervor of World War I. Congress investigated the group, and it disbanded in 1918.

Seven

Trade and Representation: How Diminishing Geographic Concentration Augments Protectionist Pressures in the U.S. House of Representatives

RONALD ROGOWSKI

ACROSS economically advanced democracies, the size of electoral constituencies varies almost perfectly with exposure to international trade: the more trade-dependent the economy, the greater the share of the electorate its average constituency will include (Rogowski 1987; cf. Katzenstein 1985, Mansfield and Busch 1995; for a dissenting view, see Boix n.d. and Boix 1999). At the extreme — reached, for example, in the Netherlands, the entire country is a single electoral district.

The reason is not far to seek. Smaller constituencies, it is generally conceded, exaggerate the power of parochial interests, most notably with respect to trade policy (Katzenstein 1985; Rogowski 1987; Mansfield and Busch 1995; but see also Boix n.d., 3–5). One result is that trade-exposed countries with small constituencies pay a high price in vulnerability to protectionism (until its recent reform, New Zealand was the classical case). In the U.S. context, generations of students have observed that the House is normally more protectionist than the Senate, and the Senate more protectionist than the presidency (Lohmann and O'Halloran 1994).

Small-district systems increase not only the mean of protectionism but its variance: such systems, by translating small shifts of popular votes into large shifts of seats (Taagepera and Shugart 1989), typically induce greater volatility and more frequent reversals of policy (Powell 1982, esp. chap. 10; Lijphart 1984; Rogowski 1987). Moreover, small-district chambers with weak party discipline and many safe districts award protection yet more freely (McGillivray 1997).

In light of all these findings, several mysteries arise with respect to the United States:

- Why did the U.S. House of Representatives — elected from 435 districts, weak in party loyalty, and notoriously safe for most of its incumbents — acquiesce in policies of ever freer trade between 1934 and 1997?

- Why was the House's acceptance of freer trade during those years so unvolatile, and why was trade so rarely a salient, let alone a decisive, issue in marginal constituencies?
- Why has the House shifted only in recent years — well *after* the main surge in U.S. exposure to trade (in the 1970s) and after an unbroken series of international agreements that had made free trade almost irreversible — to a pronouncedly more protectionist stance, seen most notably in the near defeat of NAFTA and the ultimate rejection of renewed "fast track" authority?
- Finally, why have protectionist sectors' relative activity and influence changed so radically over time? (Why, for example, is steel today far less important, than it was thirty years ago, and sugar far more so)?

A significant part of the answer, I shall argue here, is the peculiar but changing pattern of *geographic concentration* of economic activity in the United States. As economists and economic historians have consistently noted, economic sectors have tended to "cluster" geographically in the U.S. more than they do in virtually any other industrial democracy (Krugman 1991, 75–83 and appendix D): no European country, for example, really possessed its own Detroit or Pittsburgh. As I shall show below, extreme geographic concentration mitigates a small-district system's tendencies toward overrepresentation and volatility. On the other hand average geographical concentration of U.S. industry peaked around 1920 and has been declining ever since, the decline being particularly rapid since about 1960 (Kim 1992, chap. 1): even America, one might say, no longer has a Detroit, for Michigan now shares automobile manufacturing with such distant locales as South Carolina and Alabama. This accelerating *de*concentration of economic geography, coupled with growing exposure of the U.S. economy to international markets (Leamer 1996), has led (and will lead) to increased overrepresentation of protectionist interests, to more frequent polarization of marginal districts around trade-related issues, and to greater volatility of trade policy. Any weakening of the presidency will exacerbate these tendencies, and one may even question whether the United States can maintain its trade-opening hegemonic policies under its traditional institutions of governance.

How, in general, does the geographic concentration of economic interests affect their representation in small-district systems? The two answers usually offered to this question are mutually contradictory; fortunately, both appear to be wrong. On the one hand we are told that highly *dispersed* interests (sugar, dairy farming) are most powerful, because they influence many congressional districts; on the other, that highly *concentrated* interests (aircraft, automobiles) have greatest "clout" by virtually dictating the position of a few (often quite senior) representatives. As I shall demonstrate formally, holding size of the interest group constant and letting only dispersion vary, it is in fact the *moderately dispersed* interest that logically will win greatest congressional support; and, not coincidentally, it is at moderate levels of dispersion that the most constituencies will be contested and policy will be most volatile. In general, then, moving from extreme geographic concentration to somewhat greater dispersion will mean increased interest-group influence, more vigorous contestation of policy, and greater volatility of outcomes.

If geographical concentration plays the role that I hypothesize here, it may offer a partial explanation for the riddle that, while the long-term link between trade exposure and electoral system seems quite strong, the short-term one — between increasing exposure to trade and a shift to larger constituencies — seems comparatively weak (Boix 1999). As I indicate below, countries that initially had moderately dispersed patterns of industrial activity may have faced strong pressures to alter their electoral systems; those, like the United States, with initially more concentrated patterns faced weaker pressures.

Far more speculatively, I shall advance the conjecture that a country's *geographic patterns of industrial concentration* may themselves be strongly influenced by exposure to international trade. Clearly, a major impetus to geographic concentration is easy internal mobility of factors of production, and the virtual absence, after 1789, of internal barriers to migration or investment within the United States did much to promote our extraordinarily concentrated pattern of industrial activity (cf. Krugman 1991, esp. chap. 2). If one controls for internal mobility, however, a country's industrial activity may well be more *dispersed*, the greater its exposure to international markets. Why?

The observation that "the division of labor is limited by the extent of the market" is as old as Adam Smith (1996 [1776], 1: 3), and as true as it is old. All else equal, an economy with a wider market will exhibit greater specialization. And if, as Sukkoo Kim (1992, esp. chap. 2) contends, industrial location within countries is well predicted by the factor endowments of the localities, wider markets permit even finer-grained exploitation of differences in such endowments, and thus greater dispersion of economic activity. In the simplest example, an agriculture that once focused entirely on grain may become one that includes truck, flowers, and wine.

In this chapter, I shall be able to provide only some of the building blocks for a larger argument. More concretely, this essay:

1. develops a rigorous measure of dispersion of interests across voting constituencies;
2. shows, by a deductive model,
   a. that a (minority) interest's influence will be negligible under conditions of total dispersion; but, as concentration increases, will rise to a maximum and then decline;

    b. that the competitiveness and volatility of trade policy will similarly maximize at moderate levels of dispersion;

    c. that interest-group influence increases with the number of districts from which representatives are elected (i.e., is least where districts are fewest); and

    d. that, all else equal, volatility of policy increases with party discipline, decreases with party indiscipline;

3. examines, for representative sectors of the U.S. economy, the actual distribution of employment across U.S. congressional constituencies, to distinguish highly concentrated sectors (tobacco products, aircraft, textiles) from ones that are only moderately concentrated (dairy products, lumber) or highly dispersed (commercial printing).

Obviously, what remains to be done is:

4. to trace in greater detail, using older data from the Census of Manufactures and the Census of Agriculture, historical processes of concentration and deconcentration in the U.S. economy;

5. to examine links between historical changes in dispersion and exposure to international trade; and

6. to link interests groups' political influence, across sectors and over time, to their geographic dispersion.

The heart of the present discussion is the formal model and its comparative statics. The model is complex, perhaps more than is needful, but its chief intuitions can be presented graphically, in a way that I hope is both transparent and convincing. This I attempt to do in the body of the essay, relegating the formal presentation to an appendix.

Analytical Model and Implications

Conventionally, students of politics take the distribution of voters as given and examine the effects of electoral laws (Rae 1971; Taagepera and Shugart 1989). The present analysis takes the electoral system — not only the method of election but also the construction of districts — as fixed and examines the effect of varying the distribution of voters among districts. More precisely I want to examine the effects of *interest-group concentration*: how compressed or dispersed, among geographical districts, a group's (or a party's) support is.

Let a total electorate of V voters be divided into S geographical districts of equal population,[1] so that each district contains precisely V/S voters. Some group A contends for votes and is supported nationally by share p (> 0) of the voters; hence A's total vote is pV. We stipulate that A is a minority; that is, $p < .5$. For convenience of notation, we rank-order the S districts according to their support for group A, so that V_1 denotes the electorate of the district in which A receives the highest vote share, V_2 that in which it receives the second highest, and so on. Correspondingly p_1 is A's vote share in its strongest district, p_i its share in its ith strongest district; and of course by construction $p_1 \geq p$ and $i < j \rightarrow p_i \geq p_j$. Obviously $\Sigma p_i V_i = pV$; that is, the votes received by the group in the various districts must sum to the national total.

Now, note that nothing logically requires districts contiguous in this rank ordering to be *geographically* adjacent: the district that contains the second-highest share of supporters of automobile quotas may lie a thousand miles from the one with the highest share.[2] Nature, however, usually distributes support (and employment) more coherently. Typically we observe some center, or "stronghold," of support, whether based on economic interest (steel, autos, tobacco), religion (Southern evangelicals, urban Catholics), or ethnicity (Irish- or African-American voters); and as we move away from that stronghold, support trails off for some distance, then drops abruptly. We may think of this as a model in which support "percolates" from the stronghold into adjacent areas, nature choosing randomly at each interval the precise area of further accretion (cf. Krugman 1996a).

As a reasonable representation of such processes of accretion, which can be observed in such varied phenomena as city size, earthquake severity, and word usage (Zipf 1949; Krugman 1995, 1996a, 1996b), we posit

$$p_i = p_1/i^\alpha \mid \alpha \in (0,1) \tag{1};$$

which transforms monotonically into the convenient linear form

$$\log (p_i) = \log (p_1) - \alpha \log (i) \tag{2}$$

and may be readily displayed graphically as in Figure 7.1.[3]

Holding p, the national share of support, constant, I shall take higher p_1 or higher α (in the linear form, higher intercept or a more negative slope) to signify greater geographical concentration of partisan strength.[4] A higher p_1 denotes greater support in "core" constituencies; a larger value of α, a steeper "drop-off" from those peak areas of support. (Conversely, $\alpha \rightarrow 0$ signifies almost equal support in every constituency in which the party wins votes.)

For any given $p < 1$ (and here we have stipulated $p < .5$), a high enough p_1 and a low enough α entail the possibility that group A will "run out" of votes before the point at which $V p_1/i\alpha < 1$, implying a sharp discontinuity, or "drop-off," of votes (such a case is illustrated in figure 7.1, where the discontinuity is indicated by the "votes exhausted" point on the horizontal axis).[5] Again, this seems to fit the facts of such real-world cases as the (formerly) "solid South" or the ethnic neighborhoods of major cities: after tailing off for some distance beyond the "core," support suddenly disappears

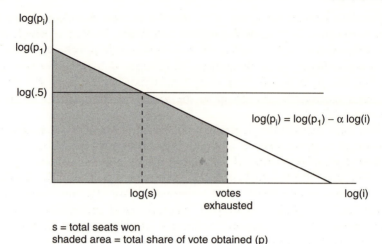

s = total seats won
shaded area = total share of vote obtained (p)

Fig. 7.1. Log-Log Graph of Typical Dispersion of Voter Support.

altogether. We shall see below that such precipitous declines are also typical of how sectoral employment is distributed among U.S. congressional districts.

We can arbitrarily define some threshold value of p_i above which A dominates the district. Without loss of generality, we examine here the case in which it controls all those, and only those, districts in which it wins a majority, that is, where $p_i > .5$.[6] Hence, where $p_1 \leq .5$, A wins no seats at all; where $p_1 > .5$, A's total number of seats (label this number s) will be specified by the highest value of i for which $p_1/i\alpha > .5$, equivalent to

$$s = \max \{i\} \text{ s.t. } i < (2p_1)^{1/\alpha} \qquad (3).$$

Graphically, this amounts to the value of i at which the downward-sloping line described by $\log (p_1) - \alpha \log (i)$ cuts the horizontal line for which $\log pi = \log .5$ (figure 7.1). If, however, group A is so evenly distributed across its stronghold districts as to exhaust its national pool of voters before it crosses that line, it gains all its seats in "stronghold" districts, then dropping abruptly into insignificance (figure 7.2).

Consider as the canonical case the one represented in figures 7.1 and 7.2, and think through what happens as support becomes more concentrated by either measure. (The formal treatment of comparative statics is presented in the appendix.) If α increases (i.e., the line slopes more steeply) from some starting point like that represented in figure 7.2, total support (represented by the shaded area) is at first squeezed to the right, into more areas in which A has a majority: *more* districts are captured (see figure 7.3). This continues until some supporters are edged into districts in which A's share falls below

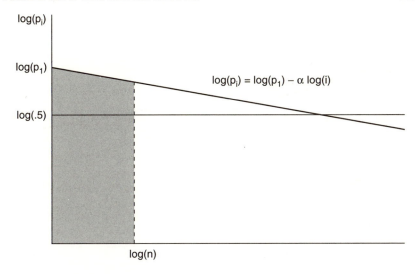

FIG. 7.2. Exhaustion of Support in Safe Majority Districts.

50 percent. Now what is determinative (just as in figure 7.1) is the point at which the sloping line crosses the horizontal log (.5) line; and, as α further increases, that manifestly shifts to the left: now *fewer* districts are won.

Note also that at first (see again figure 7.2) no districts are marginal. As α rises above some critical level, more and more districts are pushed into whatever band around the .5 line[7] we choose to designate as "marginal" (.5 $\pm$ δ, δ arbitrary); then a maximum is reached, and as α further increases (the downward-sloping line cuts through the band at an ever steeper angle), the number of marginal districts again *diminishes* (see figure 7.4). Normally, also, such a change in geographical concentration makes a *different set* of districts competitive.

The same process ensues as p_1 (our other indicator of increasing concentration) increases from some initially low level but α is held constant: (see figure 7.1) the line rises but retains its original slope, pushing to the right the point at which it cuts the .5 line; which means that A gains *more* districts. At the same time, the "votes exhausted" line moves steadily left, eventually meeting the downward-sloping one *above* the .5 line (figure 7.2). A's votes are then concentrated in districts where it has more than a majority, and as p_1 rises further, the group's total parliamentary representation declines. Marginality responds in the same way as p_1 rises: when p_1 is very low (below some arbitrarily defined level of marginality: .5 − δ), no constituen-

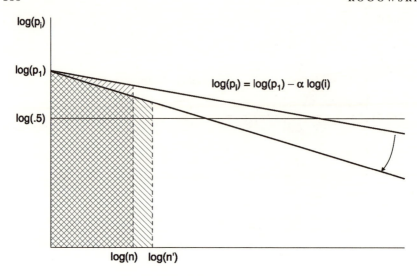

n = number of seats won initially
n' = number of seats after shift
shaded area = total share of vote obtained (p)

FIG. 7.3. Increase in Number of Districts Won as Slope Becomes More Negative.

cies are won and none are marginal. From the point at which p_1 edges into "marginal" territory, the number of competitive districts begins to rise. As p_1 itself rises above $.5 + \delta$, the number of marginal districts holds constant for some interval. Finally, as p_1 rises high enough, the number of competitive districts again declines, finally falling to zero.

By either definition, increasing geographical concentration of support — provided that *national* support, here designated as p, is held constant — first expands, then contracts, both parliamentary representation and the share of constituencies that is seriously contested. Clearly

    a. *representation* is maximized at an intermediate level of concentration: to be precise, the point at which the "votes exhausted" line's point of contact with the downward-sloping distribution line precisely meets the .5 horizontal line; and

    b. the number of *competitive districts* is maximized at:

        i. the lowest value of α at which the downward-sloping line cuts through the whole band of marginality and

        ii. over a broader range of values of p_1, from $p_1 = .5 - \delta$ to the point at which rising p_1 draws the intersection of the "votes exhausted" line and the downward-sloping one above the horizontal $.5 - \delta$ line.[8]

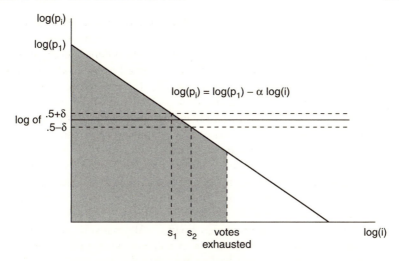

$s_2 - s_1$ = number of marginal seats
shaded area = total share of vote obtained (p)

FIG. 7.4. How Concentration Affects the Number of Marginal Constituencies.

As McGillivray (1997) and others have argued, nationally *disciplined* parties will devote to marginal constituencies the bulk of their campaign expenditures, their most attractive candidates, and — perhaps most crucially — the overwhelming majority of the "pork" and patronage that government commands. Thus, assuming declining marginal impact but rising marginal cost of favors granted, we can anticipate, ceteris paribus, more "pork" and greater distortions in small-district systems with a higher share of marginal constituencies — again, those at a "middle" level of geographic concentration.

A related point is *volatility* of electoral outcomes, that is, how many seats change hands in response to any given shift in national vote share. A reasonable assumption about the behavior of p_1 over time, and one that is consistent with the observed regularity of "nationally uniform swing" between parties,[9] is that p_1 is some fixed linear function of p, the group's share of the national vote at any given time. But then volatility must vary inversely with α; that is, the "flatter" the slope of the log-log line, the more seats will typically change hands as p_1 moves up or down. (Obviously, in the extreme case, $\alpha = 0$, a group loses *all* of its seats if it loses any.)

Parliamentary *power*, however, may be even more volatile: where only two highly disciplined parties contend (the "Westminster" archetype; cf. Lijphart 1984, chap. 1), the one with more seats holds virtually all power. Even where no group holds an absolute majority, however, Banzhaf (1966) has shown (cf. Hosli 1993) that where strong intragroup discipline prevails, so that each group votes as a bloc, power is roughly proportional to the *square* of each group's number of seats, not to the number of seats itself. For example, if in a 100-seat assembly three disciplined groups have respectively 25, 15, and 5 seats, while the other 55 members vote independently, the disciplined groups' respective "power indices" — defined as their odds of prevailing in a random contested vote — are not .25, .15, and .05, respectively, but roughly .67, .24, and .025; and the unorganized individual members have power indices not of .01 but of barely greater than .001.[10] Only where MPs were largely *undisciplined* would shares of power approximate shares of seats, and hence power be no more volatile than seats.

More to the point, any tendency toward increased volatility of policy will be exacerbated if, at the same time, parties or interests become more disciplined;[11] and party discipline is (as any student of electoral laws knows) *endogenous*, that is, powerfully affected by statutorily regulated methods of nomination, election, and campaign finance. Alternatively, one could seek stability through *irrevocable delegation* of policy-making authority, to courts, commissions, or supranational bodies, for example. This path was taken for monetary policy, through the creation of independent central banks.

Less evident in the depictions above is a final important issue: how the *total number of districts* affects a group's parliamentary representation. At one extreme the answer is clear: if the entire nation were a single majoritarian constituency — for example, directly electing a powerful president — group A (stipulated throughout the present discussion to be a national minority) could never win. If the country comprised two constituencies, A could win at most one; if it comprised three constituencies, A — provided it commanded just over a third of the national vote — could, under ideal circumstances, win two.[12] In the language of the graphs, we are talking about two things. First, having fewer districts constrains the extent to which p_1 can exceed p. (Where the whole country is one district, of necessity $p_1 = p$.) Second, the smooth curve imputed in figures 7.1 through 7.3 must, for any finite number of constituencies, be in actuality a "stairstep" line; and, as constituencies become fewer, a line with much sharper discontinuities that the model above does not adequately address.[13] The general rule, however, is intuitively clear: the fewer the constituencies, the less the minority's potential influence.

The preceding abstract analysis suggests the likely consequences if, as the closest students of U.S. industrial geography have concluded (see above, p. 182), economic activity — and consequent support for sectorally favorable policies — is becoming steadily more dispersed geographically, from an initially high level of concentration. The theory would lead us to expect:

1. *Different* industries will become politically powerful, as sectors that once enjoyed optimal dispersion now become too dispersed, while ones that were once suboptimally concentrated come closer to the optimum. (I give concrete examples below.)

2. Assuming that the modal U.S. industry has in the past been too concentrated to maximize its influence, *more* sectors will become politically salient, increasing the cross-pressures on representatives.

3. On the same assumption, more districts will become *marginal* contending parties or economic interests; that is, the number of competitive districts (and not just the level of national competition) will increase.

4. Policy will become *more volatile*, and any increase in congressional party discipline will exacerbate that tendency.

5. The tendencies toward greater pressure-group influence, more marginal constituencies, and greater policy volatility will be most pronounced in the House (with its small constituencies), less so in the Senate, least in presidential contests.[14]

On the other hand, we may note parenthetically, economic integration within the European Union — including free movement of capital and labor — may well *concentrate* interests geographically far beyond their previously moderate level (Krugman 1991). Such a development is likely to entail (again) a shift in which interests are politically powerful, both at Brussels and within the member states, but even more markedly should lead to an overall *weakening* of interest-group representation in those few but highly significant states (among them France, Italy, and the United Kingdom) that currently elect their parliaments by small-district systems.

Empirics: U.S. Data

As a preliminary test of the model's usefulness, I have analyzed the distribution, across U.S. congressional districts (CDs), of employment in twenty-four representative sectors of economic activity: ten two-digit SIC (Standard Industrial Classification) categories, ten three-digit ones, and four more comprehensive classifications (as explained below).[15] A typical log-log scatterplot in a moderately dispersed sector is that for "Chemicals and Allied Products," SIC 28, presented in figure 7.5. Here and in all similar plots, the horizontal axis is (natural) log of rank order of congressional district (from highest to lowest employment in the sector), the vertical is log of number of persons employed in the sector in the given CD.[16] Note the almost linear pattern through the highest and middle-ranked districts, followed by a precipitous drop-off — in this case, at roughly the 300th district, since $\ln(300) = 5.7$.

A more concentrated pattern among two-digit classifications is that of "Textile Mill Products," SIC 22 (figure 7.6); a more dispersed one, "Fabricated Metal Products," SIC 34 (figure 7.7). Note that in the latter case the drop-off is even more pronounced; in the former, more subdued. While simple OLS regression (whose least-squares lines are displayed in the figures) manifestly overestimates the (negative) slope α in the less concentrated

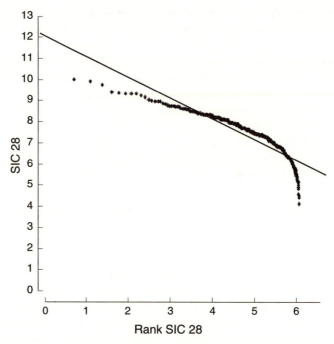

Dependent Variable: SIC 28, Chemicals and Allied Products

Source	DF	Sum of Squares	Mean Square	F Value	Pr > F
Model	1	367.055	367.055	2118.03	<.0001
Error	433	75.039	0.173		
Corrected Total	434	442.094			

R-Square: 0.830
Adj R-Sq: 0.830

Variable	DF	Parameter Estimate	Standard Error	t Value	Pr > |t|
Intercept	1	12.084	0.110	110.04	<.0001
Rank SIC 28	1	−0.975	0.021	−46.02	<.0001

FIG. 7.5. Geographic Distribution of Employment: Chemicals and Allied Products. Source: *1992 Economic Census* (U.S. Department of Commerce, 1997), SIC 28. Throughout figures 7.5–7.14, the vertical axis is log of employment in the given congressional district (CD); the horizontal axis is log of the rank of the given CD. I.e., log for the district with the highest level of employment in the industry will be $1(=0)$; log for the district with the second highest level of employment will be $2(=.693)$; and so on.

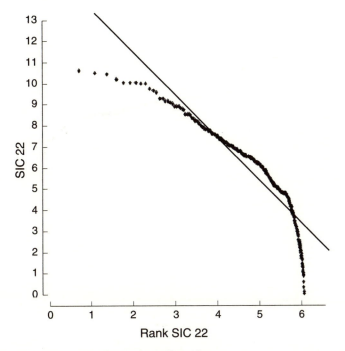

Dependent Variable: SIC 22, Textile Mill Products

Source	DF	Sum of Squares	Mean Square	F Value	Pr > F
Model	1	1560.860	1560.860	2142.63	<.0001
Error	431	313.974	0.728		
Corrected Total	432	1874.833			
R-Square: 0.833					
Adj R-Sq: 0.832					

Variable	DF	Parameter Estimate	Standard Error	t Value	Pr > |t|
Intercept	1	15.516	0.226	68.80	<.0001
Rank SIC 22	1	−2.015	0.0435	−46.29	<.0001

FIG. 7.6. Geographic Distribution of Employment: Textile Mill Products. Source: 1992 *Economic Census* (U.S. Department of Commerce, 1997), SIC 22.

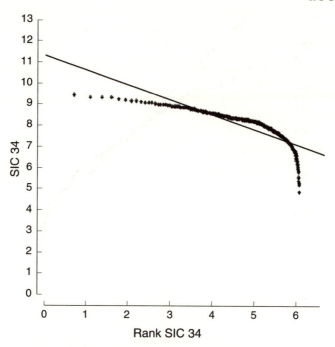

Dependent Variable: SIC 34, Fabricated Metal Products

Source	DF	Sum of Squares	Mean Square	F Value	Pr > F
Model	1	191.638	191.638	1051.02	<.0001
Error	433	78.951	0.182		
Corrected Total	434	270.589			

R-Square: 0.708
Adj R-Sq: 0.708

Variable	DF	Parameter Estimate	Standard Error	t Value	Pr > |t|
Intercept	1	11.381	0.113	101.03	<.0001
Rank SIC 34	1	−0.704	0.022	−32.42	<.0001

FIG. 7.7. Geographic Distribution of Employment: Fabricated Metals Products. Source: *1992 Economic Census* (U.S. Department of Commerce, 1997), SIC 34.

cases, these slope estimates are nonetheless good first approximations of the degree of geographic concentration.[17] Ordering our illustrative ten two-digit sectors from most to least concentrated, we have:

Sector	|α|	SIC
Tobacco	2.68	21
Textile mill products	2.02	22
Transportation equipment	1.25	37
Primary metals	1.21	33
Apparel	1.10	23
Lumber and wood products	1.10	24
Chemicals	.97	28
Electrical and electronic equipment	.87	36
Industrial machinery	.79	35
Fabricated metal products	.70	34

Another useful way of interpreting the graphs is to imagine a horizontal line extending from slightly above 9.0 on the vertical scale, a threshold that puts the sector's employment at around 4 per cent of the electorate of a typical congressional district. (A log of 10.0 puts the sector's employment at over 10 per cent of the eligible vote.) In a concentrated sector like textiles (figure 7.6), that horizontal line cuts the linear part of the distribution; the drop-off comes only *after* this threshold of political significance has been crossed, meaning that further dispersion of this industry would *increase* its political influence. In a highly dispersed sector like fabricated metals (figure 7.7), few districts lie above the 9.0 threshold; further dispersion would pull all districts below the threshold, thus *weakening* the sector politically.

The selected three-digit classifications present similar patterns. Figure 7.8 portrays a geographically concentrated sector, "Aircraft and parts" (SIC 372); figure 7.9, the less concentrated "Dairy products" (SIC 202); figure 7.10, the yet more dispersed "Commercial printing" sector (SIC 275). Again the drop-off is most abrupt in the most dispersed sector, least so in the most concentrated one. Further geographical dispersion apparently would increase the aircraft sector's influence but might well dissipate that of dairy and printing workers. With the previous caveats, the OLS estimates of α plausibly rank the ten sectors from most to least concentrated as follows:

Sector	|α|	SIC
Aircraft and parts	2.27	372
Guided missiles and parts	2.06	376
Sugar products	1.75	206
Motor vehicles	1.62	371
Electronics	1.48	367

Sector	$|\alpha|$	SIC
Grain mill products	1.28	204
Toys and sporting goods	1.21	394
Dairy products	1.03	202
Plastics	.83	308
Commercial printing	.63	275

Finally, to view how more populated categories of economic activity are distributed across congressional districts, we merged smaller two-digit categories into four large ones: (1) hired farm workers, regardless of sector; (2) all manufacturing; (3) all services; and (4) all retail trade. As might be expected, farm work is most concentrated, retail trade most dispersed; but these larger categories (figures 7.11 through 7.14) replicate the general pattern. Estimates of α were as follows:

Sector	$|\alpha|$
Hired farm workers	1.66
All services	.46
All manufacturing	.44
All retail trade	.24

Ignoring the absolute size differences among the twenty-four sectors examined — and ignoring also the unequal representation provided by the Senate — we should probably expect the most dispersed to be least powerful politically, the most concentrated to enjoy middling power, and the moderately dispersed (again, all else equal) to be most influential. While casual inspection of the estimates just presented seems to support that conjecture — services, printing, and plastics are relatively weak; tobacco, textiles, and aircraft are regionally strong; sugar, motor vehicles, and primary metals (e.g., steel) are congressional great powers — more systematic analysis is obviously required.

And what if, as many suspect, dispersion in general is increasing (i.e., $|\alpha|$ is declining), perhaps because of the growth in international trade? Grant, first, that some sectors will stay concentrated, by reason of climate or terrain (tobacco, sugar) or of regional economies of scale (aircraft, a sector likely to become even more concentrated). But I conjecture that in more typical cases, previously concentrated industries will augment their power: motor vehicles, textiles. On the other hand, moderately concentrated sectors — electronics, apparel, chemicals — are more likely to lose influence from further dispersion.

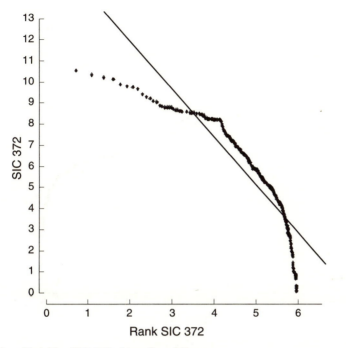

Dependent Variable: SIC 372, Aircraft and Parts

Source	DF	Sum of Squares	Mean Square	F Value	Pr > F
Model	1	1774.978	1774.978	1679.55	<.0001
Error	391	413.216	1.057		
Corrected Total	392	2188.194			
R-Square: 0.811					
Adj R-Sq: 0.811					

Variable	DF	Parameter Estimate	Standard Error	t Value	Pr > |t|
Intercept	1	16.490	0.281	58.66	<.0001
Rank SIC 372	1	−2.265	0.055	−40.98	<.0001

FIG. 7.8. Geographic Distribution of Employment: Aircraft and Parts. Source: *1992 Economic Census* (U.S. Department of Commerce, 1997), SIC 372.

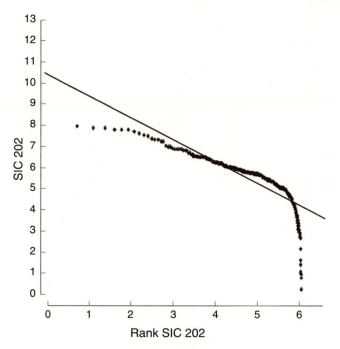

Dependent Variable: SIC 202, Dairy Products

Source	DF	Sum of Squares	Mean Square	F Value	Pr > F
Model	1	403.283	403.283	909.43	<.0001
Error	425	188.466	0.443		
Corrected Total	426	591.749			
R-Square: 0.682					
Adj R-Sq: 0.681					

Variable	DF	Parameter Estimate	Standard Error	t Value	Pr > |t|
Intercept	1	10.457	0.177	59.14	<.0001
Rank SIC 202	1	−1.0321	0.034	−30.16	<.0001

Fig. 7.9. Geographic Distribution of Employment: Dairy Products. Source: *1992 Economic Census* (U.S. Department of Commerce, 1997), SIC 202.

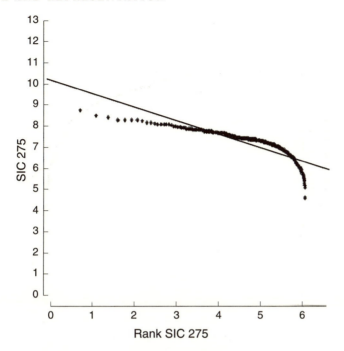

Dependent Variable: SIC 275, Commercial Printing

Source	DF	Sum of Squares	Mean Square	F Value	Pr > F
Model	1	155.142	155.142	1230.50	<.0001
Error	433	54.593	0.126		
Corrected Total	434	209.735			
R-Square: 0.740					
Adj R-Sq: 0.739					

Variable	DF	Parameter Estimate	Standard Error	t Value	Pr > |t|
Intercept	1	10.188	0.0937	108.76	<.0001
Rank SIC 275	1	−0.634	0.018	−35.08	<.0001

FIG. 7.10. Geographic Distribution of Employment: Commercial Printing. Source: *1992 Economic Census* (U.S. Department of Commerce, 1997), SIC 275.

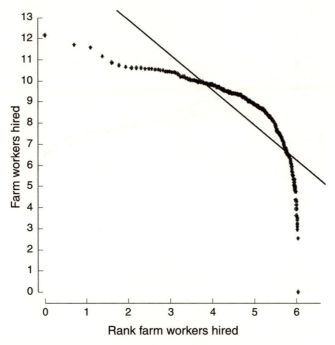

Dependent Variable: Farm Workers Hired, All Sectors

Source	DF	Sum of Squares	Mean Square	F Value	Pr > F
Model	1	1113.000	1113.000	555	<.0001
Error	427	857.042	2.007		
Corrected Total	428	94.022			

R-Square: 0.565
Adj R-Sq: 0.564

Variable	DF	Parameter Estimate	Standard Error	t Value	Pr > |t|
Intercept	1	16.212	0.363	44.6	<.0001
Rank Farm Workers Hired	1	−1.657	0.070	−23.5	<.0001

FIG. 7.11. Geographic Distribution of Employment: Agriculture. Source: *1992 Census of Agriculture* (U.S. Department of Commerce, 1995), Farm workers hired, Code 5002.

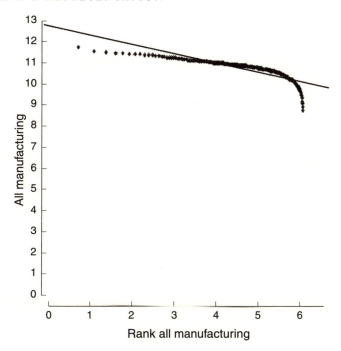

Dependent Variable: All Manufacturing

Source	DF	Sum of Squares	Mean Square	F Value	Pr > F
Model	1	75.569	75.569	1013.61	<.0001
Error	433	32.282	0.0746		
Corrected Total	434	107.851			

R-Square: 0.701
Adj R-Sq: 0.700

Variable	DF	Parameter Estimate	Standard Error	t Value	Pr > |t|
Intercept	1	12.787	0.072	177.52	<.0001
Rank All Manufacturing	1	−0.442	0.014	−31.84	<.0001

FIG. 7.12. Geographic Distribution of Employment: All Manufacturing. Source: *1992 Economic Census* (U.S. Department of Commerce, 1997), Manufacturing employment, Code 9001.

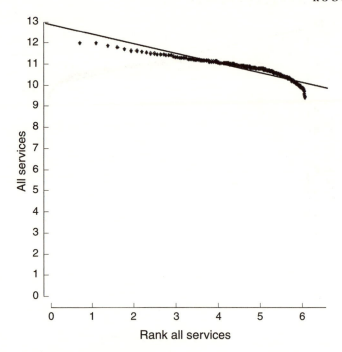

Dependent Variable: All Services

Source	DF	Sum of Squares	Mean Square	F Value	Pr > F
Model	1	80.266	80.266	2526.61	<.0001
Error	433	13.7569	0.032		
Corrected Total	434	94.022			

R-Square: 0.854
Adj R-Sq: 0.853

Variable	DF	Parameter Estimate	Standard Error	t Value	Pr > |t|
Intercept	1	12.908	0.047	274.53	<.0001
Rank All Services	1	−0.456	0.009	−50.27	<.0001

Fig. 7.13. Geographic Distribution of Employment: All Services. Source: *1992 Economic Census* (U.S. Department of Commerce, 1997), Service employment, Code 9004.

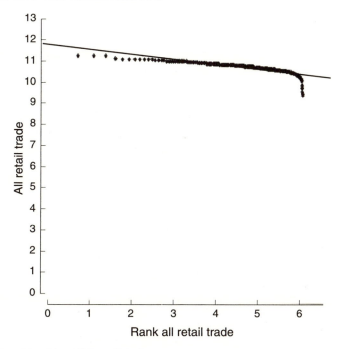

Dependent Variable: All Retail Trade

Source	DF	Sum of Squares	Mean Square	F Value	Pr > F
Model	1	21.340	21.340	936.94	<.0001
Error	433	9.862	0.0228		
Corrected Total	434	31.202			

R-Square: 0.684
Adj R-Sq: 0.683

Variable	DF	Parameter Estimate	Standard Error	t Value	Pr > |t|
Intercept	1	11.816	0.040	296.79	<.0001
Rank All Retail Trade	1	−0.235	0.008	−30.61	<.0001

FIG. 7.14. Geographic Distribution of Employment: All Retail Trade. Source: *1992 Economic Census* (U.S. Department of Commerce, 1997), Retail employment, Code 9003.

Conclusion

Only in small-district electoral systems does the geographical concentration
or dispersion of interests affect their institutional power. In general, the most
dispersed interests must logically be least powerful; group power, however,
increases with growing concentration up to a certain point, then declines
again with further increases in concentration. Similarly, the number of constituencies that an organized group can influence, and hence the volatility
of policy on its chosen issue, will be maximized at moderate levels of geographic concentration.

A preliminary analysis of congressional district data gleaned from the
Census of Agriculture and the *Economic Census* seems to confirm the
usefulness of the new measure of dispersion advanced here and allows comparison of representative sectors, from most concentrated (tobacco, textiles,
aircraft) to most dispersed (metal products, commercial printing, services).
Among the sectors shown to be at moderate levels of dispersion are ones
conventionally counted among the most powerful: sugar, motor vehicles,
and steel.

If, as some leading students of economic geography have argued, the U.S.
economy, once highly concentrated, is now dispersing—and further research is indicated on that point, along the lines developed here—we have
a partial answer to the riddles raised at the outset of this essay. Precisely
because most U.S. interests were so concentrated geographically, protectionist sectors were not as overrepresented as one would have expected in a
small-district system.[18] Deconcentration increases protectionist influence; it
means increased pressure-group activity, more district-level contests among
pressure groups, a shift of power to interests that were formerly more concentrated, and increased volatility of policy.

Paradoxically, all of this probably implies a shift to *greater* protectionism
at precisely the historical juncture where the United States appeared to have
almost achieved its hegemonic goal of global free trade. One consequence,
at least among the presumed free-trading majority, may be a more intense
search for alternatives to the small-district system.

Notes

For especially helpful comments on earlier drafts I want to thank, without implicat-
ing, Ira Katznelson, Robert Keohane, and Martin Shefter. Daniel Kotin provided
invaluable research assistance. Later stages of the work were supported in part by
NSF grant 9819307.

　1. This "one person, one vote" assumption greatly simplifies the formal argument
without significant loss of generality. It has the further advantage of verisimilitude:

few democracies still tolerate egregious malapportionment in powerful legislative bodies, the U.S. Senate being the major exception.

2. For this reason Busch and Reinhardt (1999a, 1999b) distinguish between *political* and *geographic* concentration.

3. Almost certainly, however, the analysis presented here applies to any monotonically decreasing distribution. Here we restrict the range of α to simplify the math, but the basic logic hold for $\alpha > 1$, the value that is empirically estimated in several cases of high concentration.

4. Below, I suggest that α is the better overall measure of dispersion in comparing sectors, but that is immaterial to the central comparative-statics task of ascertaining effects of change in dispersion.

5. In other words, the constraint $\Sigma p_i V_i = pV$ now binds.

6. In point of fact, some SMD systems choose representatives by plurality (the U.S. and U.K.), and one could imagine a system that required a supermajority (e.g., 60 per cent) for election. More practically, politicians pay keen attention to groups that command even a significant minority of their constituents' votes: certainly 5 per cent exert influence in a closly contested district, a point I revisit briefly in the empirical section.

7. Or other arbitrary benchmark of influence: see previous note.

8. Incidentally, it is easy to see what an astute pro-A gerrymanderer would attempt to do: carve districts so that p_1 is just above $.5 + \delta$ and $\alpha = 0$. In other words, pack all one's own support into districts where A has a "safe" (but barely safe) majority.

9. This has been observed with considerable consistency in the United Kingdom, going back at least to the pioneering work of Butler and Stokes 1971.

10. For example, for the first group the power index is approximated by $25^2/(25^2 + 15^2 + 5^2 + 55(1^2))$. As has frequently been noted, it is this exaggeration of power through bloc voting that gives to the larger American states their huge influence in the Electoral College: California's power index in electing U.S. presidents is not .1 (54/535, its share of the electoral vote) but about .29.

11. These considerations lead me to a tentative conjecture: that as electoral outcomes grow more volatile (and particularly as α declines), agents with strong interests in stability and predictability (most notably, investors) will favor a *weakening of party discipline* as one way of damping down the volatility of policy. They may, of course, advocate instead a total revision of the electoral system, in the direction of proportional representation (cf. Rogowski 1987), but in this essay we are confining ourselves to consideration of small-district systems.

12. By assumption districts are of equal population; each contains a third of the total electorate. Hence, a majority in each is just over $1/2 \times 1/3 = 1/6$ of the total electorate.

13. Suppose, for example, that there were only three constituencies, that p were .3, and that p_1 were .6. Then at most p_2 could be .3. Since each constituency must include 1/3 of the electorate, the first would consume $1/3 \times .6 = .2$ of the total .3 share of support nationally. The remaining .1, if contained entirely in the second constituency, would amount to $.1/(1/3) = .3$ of that constituency's votes.

14. But not absent. Recent events force us to recall that U.S. presidents are not directly elected but pursue Electoral College votes — above all in large, marginal states.

15. Data are from 1992 *Census of Agriculture* (U.S. Department of Commerce 1995) and 1992 *Economic Census* (U.S. Department of Commerce 1997). These provide data at the county level and have been consolidated, or where apropriate disaggregated, to congressional-district level by my research assistant, Daniel Kotin. The basic key linking counties to congressional districts is available from U.S. Department of Commerce and CIESIN 1998.

16. A linear transformation of percentages, given that (with rare exceptions) post–*Baker v. Carr* congressional districts are of equal population.

17. The *r*-squared figures indicate the poorer fit of the linear regression in the more dispersed cases. An obvious next step is to find precise breakpoints in these cases and to estimate the slope only of the pre–drop-off part of the line.

18. The exception was probably agriculture, but most of American agriculture — as one would expect in a land-abundant country — was free-trading.

References

Bailey, Michael A., Judith Goldstein, and Barry R. Weingast. 1997. The Institutional Roots of American Trade Policy. *World Politics* 49: 309–38.

Banzhaff, John F., III. 1966. Multi-Member Electoral Districts — Do They Violate the "One Man, One Vote" Principle? *Yale Law Journal* 75: 1309–38.

Boix, Carles. n.d. Trade, Politics and Proportional Representation: A Reinvestigation of Rogowski's "Trade and the Variety of Democratic Institutions." Available from Boix, Department of Political Science, University of Chicago.

———. 1999. Setting the Rules of the Game: The Choice of Electoral Systems in Advanced Democracies. *American Political Science Review* 93: 609–24.

Busch, Marc L., and Eric Reinhardt. 1999a. Industrial Location and Protection: The Political and Economic Geography of U.S. Nontariff Barriers. *American Journal of Political Science* 43: 1028–50.

———. 1999b. Geographic Concentration and Political Mobilization: The Spatial Determinants of Collective Action in Trade. Paper delivered at annual meeting of the American Political Science Association, Atlanta, Ga., 2–5 September.

Butler, David, and Donald Stokes. 1971. *Political Change in Britain*. 2d ed. New York: St. Martin's Press.

Hosli, Madeleine. 1993. Admission of European Free Trade Association States to the European Community: Effects on Voting Power in the European Community Council of Ministers. *International Organization* 47: 629–43.

Kim, Sukkoo. 1992. *Trends in U.S. Regional Manufacturing Structure, 1860–1987*. Ph.D. diss., University of California at Los Angeles.

Krugman, Paul R. 1991. *Geography and Trade*. Cambridge, Mass.: MIT Press.

———. 1995. *Development, Geography, and Economic Theory*. Cambridge, Mass. and London: MIT Press.

———. 1996a. *The Self-Organizing Economy*. Cambridge, Mass. and Oxford: Blackwell Publishers.

———. 1996b. Confronting the Mystery of Urban Hierarchy. Paper presented at NCER-NBER-CEPR Trilateral Conference on Economics of Agglomeration, Tokyo, 11–12 January.

Leamer, Edward E. 1996. Wage Inequality from International Competition and Technological Change: Theory and Country Experience. *American Economic Review* 86: 309–14.

Lijphart, Arend. 1984. *Democracies: Patterns of Majoritarian and Consensus Government in Twenty-One Countries.* New Haven and London: Yale University Press.

McGillivray, Fiona. 1997. Party Discipline as a Determinant of the Endogenous Formation of Tariffs. *American Journal of Political Science* 42: 584–607.

Rae, Douglas. 1971. *The Political Consequences of Electoral Laws.* 2d ed. New Haven: Yale University Press.

Rogowski, Ronald. 1987. Trade and the Variety of Democratic Institutions. *International Organization* 41: 203–23.

Smith, Adam. 1976 [1776]. *The Wealth of Nations.* Chicago: University of Chicago Press.

Taagepera, Rein, and Matthew Soberg Shugart. 1989. *Seats and Votes: The Effects and Determinants of Electoral Systems.* New Haven and London: Yale University Press.

U.S. Department of Commerce, Bureau of the Census. 1995. *1992 Census of Agriculture.* Geographic Area Series 1B: U.S. Summary and County Level Data. Compact disc 92-AG-1B. Washington, D.C.: Bureau of the Census.

U.S. Department of Commerce, Bureau of the Census. 1997. *1992 Economic Census.* Report Series. Vol. 1. Compact disc. EC92-IJ. Washington, D.C.: Bureau of the Census.

U.S. Department of Commerce, Bureau of the Census, and Consortium for International Earth Science Information Network (CIESIN). 1998. *MABLE/Geocorr v. 2.5, Geographic Correspondence Engine.* http://www.census.gov/plue/geocorr/.

Wolfram, Stephen. 1999. *Mathematica.* Version 4.0.1.0. Wolfram Research, Inc.

World Bank (International Bank for Reconstruction and Development). 1993. *World Development Report 1993: Investment in Health.* Oxford: Oxford University Press.

Zipf, George Kingsley. 1949. *Human Behavior and the Principle of Least Effort: An Introduction to Human Ecology.* Cambridge, Mass.: Addison-Wesley Press.

Appendix

As in the text, we posit that group A's share of votes in the ith district is specified as

$$p_i = p_1/i^\alpha \mid \alpha \in (0,1) \tag{1}$$

and its linear transformation

$$\log(p_i) = \log(p_1) - \alpha \log(i) \tag{2}$$

(see figure 7.1); and, assuming that majority support in a district is necessary and sufficient for election, group A's total parliamentary support is specified, supposing that it is a majority in at least one district, by

$$s = \max\{i\} \text{ s.t. } i < (2p_1)^{1/\alpha} \tag{3}.$$

But the sum of a group's district votes cannot exceed its national total, pV, where p is its national share and V is the total number of voters. Where districts are numerous, the sum of district votes will be well approximated by

$$p_1 \frac{V}{S} \int_1^n i^{-\alpha}\, di = \frac{V}{S}\frac{p_1}{(1-\alpha)}(n^{1-\alpha} - 1) \tag{4}.$$

Equating the two, we find that A can gain votes in no more than n districts, n specified now by α, p, p_1, and S according to the formula

$$pV = \frac{Vp_1}{S(1-\alpha)}(n^{1-\alpha} - 1) \Rightarrow \frac{pS}{p_1}(1-\alpha) = n^{1-\alpha} - 1$$

$$\Rightarrow n = \left[\frac{p}{p_1}S(1-\alpha) + 1\right]^{\frac{1}{1-\alpha}} \tag{5}.$$

If n is less than s — that is, the party gains votes only in districts where it holds a majority — obviously at most n seats will be won (see again figure 7.2). Hence (3) binds if $s < n$; otherwise, $s = n$ as defined in (5).

Now it turns out that $\partial s/\partial p_1$ is positive, $\partial n/\partial p_1$ negative; hence, if initially $n < s$, as p_1 declines (holding α constant), A's yield of seats first ascends, then declines. Similarly, we shall see that in the relevant range $\partial n/\partial \alpha$ is positive, $\partial s/\partial \alpha$ negative; hence, still from an initial point where $n < s$ as α rises, still from an initial point where $n < s$, A again experiences first an increase, then a decrease, in its yield of seats. Using either definition of geographic concentration of support, we find that the number of seats a group can win under a single-member district system — and hence, we infer, its parliamentary influence — is maximized at some "middling" level of concentration.

Our detailed task is thus to establish what happens to the A's number of seats, under these respective specifications, as p_1 and α change. Working from (3) and supposing for simplicity (but without loss of generality) that s exactly equals $(2p_1)^{1/\alpha}$, we can see that

$$\frac{\partial s}{\partial p_1} = \frac{1}{\alpha} (2p_1)^{\frac{1-\alpha}{\alpha}} \tag{6},$$

evidently positive for all admissible values of p_1 and α; and, a bit more opaquely,[1] that

$$\frac{\partial s}{\partial \alpha} = - \frac{(2p_i)^{\frac{1}{\alpha}}}{\alpha^2} \ln (2p_1) \tag{7},$$

which, equally clearly, is negative throughout the relevant domain.[2] Thus we see that, where (3) specifies A's seat yield, the yield is increasing in p_1 and decreasing in α.

When the number of seats won is specified instead by (5), we have

$$\frac{\partial n}{\partial p_1} = - \frac{pS}{p_1^2} \left[\frac{pS(1 - \alpha)}{p_1} + 1 \right]^{\frac{\alpha}{1-\alpha}} \tag{8},$$

clearly negative throughout. For the much hairier partial with respect to α, it helps (me, at least) to write (5) as

$$n = e^{(1-\alpha)^{-1} \log[\frac{pS}{p_1} (1-\alpha)+1]} \tag{9}$$

and to apply the chain and multiplicative rules of differentiation to yield first

$$\frac{\partial n}{\partial \alpha} = \left[\frac{pS}{p_1} + 1 \right]^{\frac{1}{1-\alpha}} \left[\left(\frac{1}{1-\alpha} \right) \frac{1}{\frac{pS}{p_1}(1-\alpha)+1} \left(-\frac{pS}{p_1} \right) \right.$$
$$\left. + \left(\frac{1}{1-\alpha} \right)^2 \log \left[\frac{pS}{p_1}(1-\alpha) + 1 \right] \right]$$

and, with some moderately heavy lifting,

$$\frac{\partial n}{\partial \alpha} = \left(\frac{1}{1-\alpha} \right) \left[\frac{pS}{p_1}(1-\alpha) + 1 \right]^{\frac{1}{1-\alpha}} \left[\frac{\log \left[\frac{pS}{p_1}(1-\alpha) + 1 \right]}{1-\alpha} \right] \tag{10}.$$

$$\left. - \frac{pS}{p_1} \frac{1}{\left[\frac{pS}{p_1}(1 - \alpha) + 1 \right]} \right] \qquad (10). \; cont.$$

The sign of this evidently depends on that of the bracketed expression; and its positive term turns out to outweigh its negative one only if

$$\log \left[\frac{pS}{p_1}(1 - \alpha) + 1 \right] > \frac{\frac{pS}{p_1}(1 - \alpha)}{\frac{pS}{p_1}(1 - \alpha) + 1} \qquad (11).$$

For simplicity of notation define

$$Q = \frac{pS(1 - \alpha)}{p_1} + 1 \quad ;$$

then (12) amounts to

$$\log (Q) > \frac{Q - 1}{Q} = 1 - 1/Q \qquad (12),$$

equivalent to

$$\log(Q) + 1/Q - 1 > 0 \qquad (13).$$

But this inequality is almost self-evidently satisfied for all (positive) values of Q save $Q = 1$, at which point the LHS is equal to zero.[3]

Thus we have in general $\partial n/\partial \alpha \geq 0$. As α increases, A's share of seats first rises, then (as seats come to be specified by (3), bringing into force the fact that $\partial s/\partial \alpha < 0$) declines. By both routes we see that, under SMD, a party's share of seats (holding fixed its share of the overall vote) is maximized at some moderate level of geographic dispersion.

Notes

1. Recall that, where $f(t) = b^t$, $f'(t) = b^t \ln(b)$.
2. By assumption, $p_1 > .5$.
3. The quickest way to see it is simply to take the first-order condition for a minimum, $1/Q - 1/Q^2 = 0$; this is plainly satisfied only when $Q = 1$.

Eight

International Forces and Domestic Politics: Trade Policy and Institution Building in the United States

JUDITH GOLDSTEIN

COMMERCIAL-POLICY making occurs in a political juncture in which decision makers weigh a nation's economic interest against the needs of particular domestic actors. The outcome is rarely optimal in terms of economic efficiency; that is, trade policies rarely reflect the economic opportunities presented to states by access to international markets. Rather, the degree of trade openness is more often a function of the relative power and interests of national actors. Interests in world markets vary over time and over groups, and the policies of representative governments vary in accord with these changing domestic interests. Although trade openness or free trade may be in the collective's best interest, democratic governments will pursue trade openness only to the degree that powerful interests within the collective support it.

International relations scholars have long agreed that representative governments find it difficult to support open trade. Still, although acknowledging domestic political factors, they more often find the source of the dilemma outside, rather than internal to, the nation-state. The problem is one of potential opportunism. Rational governments may prefer a liberal trade policy but fear that other nations will opportunistically renege on any agreement. The absence of international governance structures makes it difficult to garner cooperation for a joint policy of lowering trade barriers. The problem is captured in the game theoretic metaphor of "the prisoner's dilemma" (PD). Cooperation would lead all nations to lower trade barriers and therefore obtain the economic efficiency gains from trade. But the defining element of the game is a structure in which nations prefer unilateral defection to unrequited cooperation. Both would be better off with lower barriers, but each fears that the other will renege; each fears becoming the sucker.[1] The outcome is that neither side has an incentive to negotiate trade treaties. The theoretical solution to the problem is reciprocal play. Nations whose cooperative efforts are met by similar policies in other countries will do better in the long term.

The PD metaphor focuses analysis on an important problem associated with international trade, that is, the problem of ex post opportunism. Nations would like to conclude trade agreements, since they make each better off; in the absence of some institution that will change the incentive structure, however, cooperation will not occur. Even if nations want to cooperate, it is difficult in a state of nature to make a credible commitment not to act opportunistically in the future. Following this logic, scholars have argued for the need for some international regime to facilitate the creation of more welfare-enhancing trade policies. The function of such an institution is to lower transaction costs, provide information, and/or monitor cheating of those participating in the agreement.[2]

This line of argument assumes the interests of all nations to be pro-trade and focuses analysis on conflicts deriving from the absence of courts or enforceable law in the international system. The assumption of single-peaked domestic preferences, however, is problematic. Farmers in France and chip makers in the Silicon Valley fare differently in liberal markets and will attempt to assure that their interests are served by the choice of commercial policy. Further, logic suggests that the voices of import-competing groups should be louder and more numerous than those of groups who will benefit from trade openness. Mobilization is a result of many factors, including the cost of mobilizing and the potential gains from collective action. Given the concentrated benefits import-competing groups garner from a trade barrier and the diffuse costs they engender to consumers, those who stand to lose big, that is, the import-competing group, will have a greater incentive to organize.[3] In the absence of the articulation of the free-trade position by exporters or other interested parties, governments will find it difficult to open their borders to trade.[4]

In all democracies trade policy is determined by some balancing of the interests of those affected by international market forces. Although the relative power of these groups is important in an explanation of outcomes, governance structures play as critical a role in aggregating groups' various interests. Just as international institutions affect the incentives of nations to sign commercial trade agreements, domestic institutions will have an influence on what groups get their interests translated into national policy and thus their incentives to organize. For example, the electoral process could lead to the under- or overrepresentation of certain groups. In the case of Japan overrepresentation of agricultural workers leads policy to be more in line with farmers' interests than one would expect, given Japan's natural endowments. Because institutions can bias outcomes, leaders who favor a particular trade policy will attempt to structure domestic as well as international institutions in ways that will ultimately support their preferred policy.

The need for institutional support to maintain liberal trade is no where more apparent than in the United States. Given the small size of its electoral units, the problem of maintaining a free trade coalition in the United States is formidable. As districts increase in size, leaders are more willing to think about the "general" good, basically because they are able to make trade-offs between competing groups with crosscutting interests. Thus, the U.S. president with the largest constituency has historically been more willing to support free trade than has Congress. In the Congress, similarly, the Senate is more free trade–oriented than the House. With very small districts, House members have greater difficulty ignoring organized groups in their districts. Even though a majority may exist that will benefit from trade liberalization, the voice of import-competing groups is more likely to determine the votes of these representatives. The outcome is a logroll in which all interests are accommodated; the cost is a suboptimal collective policy.[5]

This essay examines this process of institutional design in the context of U.S. trade policy. The Constitution grants the House of Representatives primary responsibility over commercial policy, by giving it the right to set tariffs. Small districts partially explain why the United States kept tariffs high, even after becoming the low-cost producer in both industrial and farm products. As well as district size, direct congressional control of tariff levels, legislative oversight of the bureaucracy, and an independent judicial system all make it difficult for the United States to both negotiate and comply with trade treaties.

High barriers to trade may not have been optimal throughout the nineteenth century, but they did not undercut American growth. By the end of the first quarter of the twentieth century, however, high barriers to trade had become dysfunctional. The response of leaders to mounting domestic and international pressure was institutional reform. Starting in the mid-1930s, the weight of pro-protection interests was mitigated through a series of changes in the trade policymaking process, both domestic and international.[6] To a great extent, the liberalization in commercial policy that occurred in the post–World War II years demonstrates the malleability of U.S. institutions. American commercial policy is more open than at any previous time in history, and leaders have turned not only to domestic solutions, such as institutional redesign, but also to international agreements as a means to solve the domestic institutional dilemma created by the original constitutional mandate. Still, as I argue below, this remaking of institutions was never fully successful; liberal trade policy operates in the shadow of pro-protection institutions.

To demonstrate the Janus face of American institutions, I will look at three examples of institutional "fixes" to the trade-policy making system: delegation to the president of authority to set tariffs, fast-track legislation, and the evolution in judicial jurisdiction on certain trade issues. The first two involve a form of congressional hand tying; they were institutional solutions to the problem of pressure-group politics. In both cases, Congress gave agenda power to the president to write legislation that would be voted under a closed rule. Since presidents have a greater propensity to favor trade openness, agenda control assured that the legislation would provide greater free trade than any legislation initiated by Congress. But delegation alone cannot explain repeated congressional willingness to allow the president control over trade policy. An international component was also involved. President used their agenda control to bring back "bundled" agreements, thus enlarging the number of groups likely to favored the treaty. Trade agreements did not unilaterally open the American market to competition. Rather, they tied enlarged exporter access to foreign markets with lower tariffs at home. To get a big enough bundle required the United States to get all major countries to the negotiating table simultaneously, which explains America's continuing commitment to the GATT/WTO regime. The third "fix" involves the courts. Here the president is constrained not only by social pressure but also by the power of the judicial branch to reinterpret congressional legislation. Presidents have responded by attempting to rein in the courts, using domestic and international means. In a concluding section, I revisit the logic that motivates this essay and consider the more general interaction between international forces and domestic institutional design.

Delegating Trade Authority to the President

The constitution grants Congress the right to set duties as a means to raise federal revenues. Throughout the nineteenth century, however, tariffs were less about revenue than about the development of the American economy. Congress was split by both ideological and regional disagreements over the tariff: the South supported low tariffs while the manufacturing states demanded protection of their "infant" industries.

The Civil War and industrialization quieted debate for a short while. As the United States moved into the second half of the nineteenth century, however, a growing coalition of American producers began to demand access to cheaper products and/or foreign markets. But while the rest of the world, under British leadership, was liberalizing trade, American attempts to negotiate access to her market were repeatedly thwarted. The United States negotiated trade pacts, such as its first explicitly reciprocal trade agreement in 1844 with the German Zollverein, but this treaty, like every successor, was rejected by the Senate on the grounds that the president had no constitutional right to enter into commercial agreements with other nations. Only Congress could initiate revenue measures. The result was a tariff wall that could not be breached.

High protective barriers may have made some sense in 1844 but made for poor economic policy fifty years later. The completion of the transnational rail system made the United States the low-cost producer of many farm products, and by 1900 it was the world's greatest manufacturing nation. These changes in economic standing should have led to a change in trade policy, reflective of the opportunity costs of noninvolvement in world markets. Still, it took thirty-five years and the Great Depression for the United States to change its trade policy. Although the Democratic Party advocated a lower tariff throughout the nineteenth century, there could be no trade reform while Congress maintained sole control over tariff setting. Small congressional constituencies, the organization of congressional committees, and House rules that encouraged logrolling made it difficult to either lower tariffs unilaterally or agree to reciprocal reductions.

In 1934 Congress ushered in a new era of trade policy by passing the Reciprocal Trade Agreements Act. This legislation amended the 1930 Smoot-Hawley Tariff Act and allowed the president to negotiate reciprocal trade agreements with foreign governments. In exchange for greater access to foreign markets, the president was authorized to reduce U.S. duties by up to 50 percent. No specific duties were established or changed by the act and no congressional approval of the agreements was required.[7] Defending this delegation of power to the president, Roosevelt's secretary of state, Cordell Hull, argued to the House Ways and Means Committee that delegation was necessitated by international politics: "It is manifest that unless the Executive is given authority to deal with the existing great emergency somewhat on a parity with that exercised by the executive departments of so many other governments for purposes of negotiating and carrying into effect trade agreements, it will not be practical or possible for the United States to pursue with any degree of success the proposed policy of restoring our lost international trade."[8]

Saying that executive control over trade was a functional necessity says little about the timing or the form of that delegation. Hull had argued for liberalization since he arrived in Congress, and he and others had repeatedly suggested an enlarged role for the president.[9] But it was not till 1934 that he got what he wanted.

Explaining the change in Congress's role in trade policy has engendered much scholarly debate but limited intellectual consensus. A number of scholars see efficiency reasons behind the change. For example, Bauer, Pool, and Dexter and Schattschneider point out that the task of setting tariffs, was onerous for elected officials, given the level of world trade.[10] While revision of tariff schedules had never been a simple matter, the process had, with the passage of the Smoot-Hawley Tariff Bill of 1930 degenerated into a frenzy of special interest lobbying and deal making. Destler agrees that the now complex tariff schedule changed the nature of the congressional task, adding that members of Congress chose to delegate in order to "protect themselves from the direct one-sided pressure from producer interests that had led them to make bad trade law."[11] Other scholars point to the role of ideology, the rise of the United States to world power and idiosyncratic factors associated with the Roosevelt presidency.[12]

Analyses also differ over the effect of the change in institutional control on American policy. The most conventional view is that the RTAA allowed Congress to wash its hands of tariffs. With members of Congress — and the special interests they represented — out of the way, the president was freed to pursue rational liberalization of U.S. trade policy. This view is difficult to defend. While congressional activity on tariffs declined dramatically after the passage of the RTAA, it remained substantial; at every step along the path of trade liberalization, Congress played a central role. Congress extended the RTAA ten times between 1934 and 1962 and was active in almost every extension.[13] For example, in 1937 an amendment to limit reductions on agricultural duties to whatever level would be necessary to equalize production costs initially passed the Senate and was only defeated on a revote.[14] In 1948, 1951, and 1955, Congress added peril point provisions, which scaled duties to the minimum rates necessary to protect domestic producers against imports. In 1953, Republicans in Congress agreed to a one-year renewal only when the president promised not to enter into any new trade negotiations. Simply, there is little evidence to support the conventional view of a willing Congress wary of interest groups and an ideological free-trade president pushing a liberal vision. Still, although Congress did not remove itself from the trade policy process, the legislative role certainly shifted after 1934.

Congress's decision to change its role in tariff making remains one of the most interesting puzzles in American political history. At the time, there was no ground swell of support for tariff reductions. Roosevelt himself was no staunch free trader. While he associated himself with the Wilsonian international wing of the Democratic Party, at times he sounded very much like a protectionist. In the 1932 presidential campaign, he announced that his trade doctrine was "not widely different from that preached by Republican statesmen and politicians" and that he favored "continuous protection for American agriculture as well as American industry."[15]

What then explains the shift in congressional behavior after 1934, and what role, if any, was played by American involvement in world markets?[16] Although 1934 was an international "watershed," it did not mark America's first show of interest in world trade. U.S. trade had expanded greatly with the completion of the transnational railroad and rapid industrialization. Reflecting these interests, U.S. government officials had repeatedly attempted to expand America's economic opportunities through bilateral trade deals. These attempts, however, were never stable: initial deals were not endorsed by Congress, and this had the effect of discrediting subsequent U.S. attempts at negotiation.

This is not to say that the tariff schedule was immutable. Throughout the nineteenth and early twentieth centuries, the tariff schedule was repeatedly tinkered with, its height a reflection of congressional party control. Periods of low tariffs lasted only as long as the Democrats were in power: a shift in party control of government usually meant a change in the tariff schedule. The Democratic Party's traditional commitment to low rates in the nineteenth century reflected the interests of its constituents: Southern agricultural producers involved in world markets suffered from America's tariff position. The interests of the Democratic constituency, however, shifted in the twentieth century, partially from the influx of urban workers into the party. The party's position on tariffs changed accordingly in the early decades of the century. In 1913, the Democrats defended unilateral tariff reductions; by the time of the 1932 presidential race, however, Roosevelt's advisers roundly criticized a similar proposal by Hull. When Roosevelt vetted a draft of a speech calling for a flat 10 percent reduction in tariffs, Democratic Senators Pittman (Nev.) and Walsh (Mont.) advised him that support for such a measure was politically dangerous.[17] Further, the passage of the 1930 Smoot-Hawley tariff had made it clear that Democrats were as prone to "pork barrel" politics as were their Republican colleagues.

Although unilateral tariff reductions were no longer viable, tariff reform remained an important issue for the Roosevelt administration. A logical alternative was to negotiate bilateral agreements, thereby increasing the numbers of participants who benefited from a tariff cut. Using the treaty process as a means to lower tariffs, however, presented a second and almost as intractable problem: such agreements would need to be supported by a two-thirds majority in the Senate. Since before the Civil War, the executive office had regularly used its foreign policy–making powers to negotiate such trade agreements, but these agreements regularly failed to garner a supermajority in the Senate. In short, although there was support in the Democratic Party for trade reform, the inability to get House approval for unilateral tariff reductions and the inability to find Senate support for bilateral trade agreements made tariff reform impossible. This dilemma explains the institutional reforms that occurred under Roosevelt's administration. In essence, Roosevelt's 1934 trade act was an attempt to "fix" two problems: (1) the need for supermajorities in the Senate in order to ratify trade treaties and (2) the impossibility of mustering a majority in the House for tariff reductions, since the method — of voting — in seriatim, item by item — foreclosed the possibility of trade-offs among constituencies.

The Roosevelt program finessed these problems by coupling U.S. domestic policy more closely with the policies of our trading partners. After 1934, the United States only reduced tariffs upon negotiating a bi- or multilateral agreement with trading partners. By coupling losses and potential gains, a broader range of tariff cuts were made acceptable to a majority in Congress.

Congressional representatives found trade liberalization more palatable, because the tying of import reduction to export access gave voice to new groups whose interest lay with trade expansion. The strategy of coupled reductions, as a way to expand the free trade coalition was successful, however, only because of two other procedural changes.

First, reciprocal tariff reductions brought the executive office into tariff-policy making more centrally than at any previous time. Since the president is the chief foreign policy officer, the negotiation of all treaties, including trade agreements, are in the executive domain; this presidential authority took a new form after 1934. Because of the uncertainty of specific concessions from trading partners, the president had to be given broad authority, that is, in the absence of a particular negotiation, it was impossible to specify, ex ante, which industries would see tariff cuts. In essence, the president was given a "hunting license" to enter into talks with other nations and bring back the best trade deals possible. The only constraint on his discretionary power was that he could not lower the tariff schedule more than 50 percent. This form of delegation could muster majority support in the House because it engendered less social resistance. Social organization engenders costs. Groups weigh the potential gains and losses of state action against the costs of participation in the political process. Given the costs of collective action, and the certain and concentrated losses to import-competing industries if trade barriers are reduced, the voice of these industries and not the voice of those who benefit from trade liberalization traditionally dominated the debate on tariff policy. Changing the balance between import-sensitive industries and exporters was the requisite for a stable policy of trade liberalization. The 1934 system shifted that political balance by having representatives vote on trade talks behind a "veil of ignorance": they did not know beforehand exactly which industries would or would not be affected by tariff cuts. Because no import-sensitive group knew whether it would be included in the final package, there was far less of an incentive to organize against the legislation. The new system not only discouraged political activity by import-sensitive groups but also encouraged the organization of export groups, who now had an interest in tariff votes. Second, and as key, the form of delegation finessed the problem of Senate approval of treaties. Since authority was mandated within specific limits, the agreement only returned to Congress for approval if the president over-stepped his authority.

The ability to "bundle" import losses with export gains, the grant of ex ante authority to negotiate, and the circumscription of supermajority support for trade treaties were "international" solutions to the pro-protection bias in the design of American institutions. The essence of the solution, reciprocal tariff reductions, was not a new idea. The United States had attempted to link domestic policy with international concessions in the nineteenth century, but these agreements needed Senate approval, creating a disincentive for nations to come to the bargaining table. After 1934, reciprocity, in the absence of a congressional veto, created an incentive for foreign states to enter into agreements with the United States in order to get access to the U.S. market. Multilateral agreements created multiple opportunities for trade-offs among import and export interests at home. Lowered tariffs led to more trade. The more groups in each district that were involved in world trade, the easier it was to renew the trade agreements program. The number and complexity of "bundled" agreements added to their stability, since it became increasingly difficult to renege on an agreement without affecting some set of politically active export industries. Over time, this involvement in the world economy led to a more fundamental shift in preferences among constituents.

This process of changing preferences explains why the institutional solution of trade delegation was so successful. Tariffs declined precipitously and trade expanded dramatically during the tenure of the RTAA. In 1934 American duties averaged over 46 percent; by 1962, they had fallen to 12 percent. World trade increased from $97 trillion at the war's end to $270 trillion at the time of the 1962 Trade Act. U.S. exports went from $2.1 billion in 1934 to $3.3 billion in 1937 and from $9.8 billion in 1945 to over $20 billion in 1962.[18]

While some of the increase in trade should be attributed to the emergence of the world economy from depression, two factors point to the substantial role of the RTAA. First, the RTAA allowed the president to take the lead in fighting for more international openness. After the Smoot-Hawley Tariff Act of 1930, a retaliatory spiral of beggar-thy-neighbor policies had left the world with monumentally high tariffs. Given the protectionist pressures inherent in democracies, there is reason to believe that without the RTAA, tariffs would have moved downward at a far slower pace. Second, evidence suggests that U.S. trade grew more rapidly with treaty nations than with nontreaty nations. For example, in the first three years of the program, exports to the twenty-two nations with which the United States had trade agreements increased by 61 percent, as compared with a 38 percent increase in exports to other nations.[19]

The shift in institutional design did more than lower tariffs. By 1962, it had caused a significant change in the partisan character of U.S. trade policies. Where trade policy virtually defined the American parties in the late nineteenth and early twentieth centuries, it all but disappeared from the political arena by the early 1960s. This change eliminated the swings in trade policy so closely associated with changes in political control of government.[20] Although party voting on trade issues remained strong through the close of World War II, thereafter, the parties came to look increasingly similar in their voting behavior.[21]

By the early 1970s, however, the key trade issues concerned nontariff barriers (NTB), not tariffs. As world tariff levels declined, other aspects of nations' trading practices—from procurement policies to subsidies—became the major impediments to world trade. While Congress had agreed to preapprove tariff reductions, thereby allowing the president to negotiate tariff treaties, such a procedure was impractical for NTBs. The nature of international agreements now entailed that a treaty be returned to the legislature for approval of changes in domestic law. Although the general political problem was the same—that is, protectionist groups still had asymmetrical power to veto legislation—the solution of prestipulating the president's authority was now impractical.

The inability of U.S. officials to commit the nation to trade agreements, due to Congress's regaining its "last mover" advantage, became quickly evident to America's trading partners in the later 1960s. Negotiators returned from the Kennedy Round of multilateral trade talks with a treaty that cut tariffs by more than the 50 percent precommitted by Congress and that included other provisions, most notably, an international antidumping accord and a promise to eliminate the system of customs appraisals called the American Selling Price (ASP). Congress balked. On the issue of dumping, Congress exacerbated the problem by taking the position that whenever the codes conflicted with American dumping law, U.S. practices would always prevail. Congress simply refused to eliminate ASP, even though the pricing scheme was widely recognized as antiquated.

Congressional recalcitrance presented the Nixon administration with a dual problem as it prepared for what became known as the Tokyo Round of trade talks. On the one hand, the administration had to gain authority from Congress to initiate talks. On the other, America had lost credibility, so other nations had no incentive to come to the negotiating table. Once again, an institutional fix was attempted. Returning to the RTAA model, the Nixon administration proposed a simple extension of their delegation authority to NTBs. Under the plan, Congress would authorize talks on nontariff barriers; when the president signed an agreement, the necessary changes in domestic statutes would go into effect, unless either house of Congress vetoed the agreement within ninety days.

Although the House was willing to go along with the "veto" provision, the measure found little support in the Senate. Commenting that this was "not the way we make laws," Herman Talmadge of Georgia got his fellow members of the Finance Committee to demand nothing less than that no agreement negotiated by the administration go into effect without an affirmative vote.[22] Such a demand was tantamount to stopping the trade negotiating process. Recognizing the difficulty with this position, but refusing to undermine their own control over domestic laws, the Senate expressed willingness to compromise. The institutional fix called "fast track" became the compromise, operating under the guidance of the office of the Special Trade Representative. When in operation, fast-track procedures stipulate that the president can negotiate NTB concessions but must consult with relevant congressional committees throughout the talks. At least ninety days beforehand, the president gives Congress notice of intent to enter into a nontariff barrier agreement. Both houses of Congress are required to act within sixty days of his submitting the implementing legislation. In return for consultation, Congress votes under a closed rule: no changes are allowed either in committee or on the floor.

Fast-track authorization worked as envisioned for the Tokyo Round agreements. It allowed the United States to credibly commit to whatever agreements were signed, and in 1979 the implementation legislation to support the agreements passed with overwhelming and bipartisan support. Destler suggests that the success of this institutional innovation was due to its serving dual purposes. It allowed the United States to regain its credibility and the inclusion of particular congressional members into the trade agreement–making process served to undermine the power of certain disaffected groups. Just as important, however, was that the new procedures "allowed the new open Congress to replicate its closed predecessor."[23] While much of Congress was undergoing a "democratization," due to the arrival of the post-Watergate cohort, fast-track procedures reinforced the purview of the two key committees in making trade policy. Challenged through new procedures such as multiple referral, the Ways and Means Committee and the Finance Committee found in fast track a means to reassert their traditional control. And while the median representative still had little influence on trade negotiations, committee members found themselves both participating in trade talks and, more importantly, the drafting of the implementation legislation.

The means by which Finance and Ways and Means retained their control over trade was through a shadow process of writing trade legislation. Although they had formally given up their right to challenge legislation once it entered Congress, continued acceptance of a closed vote procedure was predicated on the committees having informal control over legislation. Thus, before the 1979 act came up for a formal vote, it had gone through nine "non-markup" sessions by the Senate Finance Committee and sixteen such unofficial sessions by the House Ways and Means Subcommittee on Trade. What followed was a "nonconference" and on agreement on a final bill. All meetings were closed to the public and, to a great extent, cut off from the rest of the House and Senate. It is true that the bill, as finally submitted to Congress by the president, was nonamendable, but its form was clearly determined by the members who sat on the two committees. The process made it nearly impossible for proponents of specific protectionist interests to get a voice, much less legislation, for their constituents, for the new arrangement had created powerful interests in the committees themselves supporting the trade negotiation process. Not surprisingly, members of the committee included an extension of fast-track authority in the 1979 act, thereby reinstituting their considerable influence over trade. When Congress agreed in principle to bilateral free trade agreements with Israel and Canada, the committees were more than willing to authorize negotiations under fast-track procedures. Likewise, the NAFTA accord was negotiated in the shadow of a closed congressional voting process.

Fast-track authorization expired in 1995. The response of other nations was as expected from a systemic analysis: ongoing trade talks were immediately halted, and no new ones were initiated. Thus, for example, negotiations over Chile's accession to the North America Free Trade Agreement ended, even though Chile had completed substantial revisions in its own commercial practices in anticipation of joining the accord. The breakdown of the fast-track "fix" underscores a point made above: agenda control is always constrained by the underlying preferences of Congress as a whole. The agenda control given to committees through fast-track legislation was a strategy that enabled Congress as a whole to "hide" from powerful groups. Getting approval for fast-track legislation and new trade initiatives, however, requires a congressional majority in support of an open trade policy. Such a majority, although stable in the decades after World War II, started crumbling as America's trade balance deteriorated. Agenda control through delegation and/or fast-track authorization can manipulate, but not change, the preferences of the legislature.

As suggested at the start of this essay, institutions have a powerful effect on the aggregation of interests. Explanations of trade liberalization, however, should not ignore the underlying preferences of representatives and their constituents. In the United States, trade openness was accomplished not by Congress successfully ignoring constituents but by presidents using their negotiating authority to bundle export gains with import losses, and thus create majority support. Presidents retained support for the trade program by assuring that over half of the districts had interests tied to trade expansion. It is the president's "bundling" of international and domestic tariffs which led members of Congress to be more willing to trade-off the political risk of opening their home market for the political benefit of increased access to foreign markets. This preference change is both a cause and an effect of the internationalization of the world economy after World War II: initial U.S. efforts to lower its tariffs were sustained only because of the positive feedback effects of increased trade on the American economy.

The Evolution of Trade Courts

As suggested above, the interaction between Congress and the president — the former having the constitutional prerogative to set tariffs and the latter controlling much of the contemporary institutional trade apparatus — is a central element in determining U.S. trade policy. The third branch of government, however, also influences trade policy. While Congress can oversee the executive's trade measures through its legislative, appointment, and budget authority, the judiciary is often the true "veto player" in deciding aspects of U.S. trade policy. The power of the courts derives from a number of sources. Most centrally, the courts are key actors because congressional legislation on many aspects of American trade policy — such as antidumping law, countervailing-duty legislation and Section 301 protections granted to producer groups — fail to specify clear criteria on the conditions for government action. This discretion creates incentives for private actors to take their case to the court as a means of influencing policy.

The evolution of the American system of trade courts provides another example of how institutional design is affected by America's involvement in the world. The current system of judicial review dates to the creation of the Board of General Appraisers in 1890, originally an administrative body within the Treasury Department. In inception, the board had few adjudicator functions. Rather, it resolved disputes over the classification and value of imported products. Its goal was to assure an uninterrupted stream of revenue for the federal government.[24]

The Customs Court was formally created in 1926 under article 1 of the Constitution. Not unusual for such specialized courts, the function of the body remained administrative, that is, the court handled disputes over Treasury Department decisions on tariff classification. In 1956, however, the status of the court changed and Congress reestablished it under article 3 of the Constitution. Among other things, judges would now have life tenure and would not be punishable through salary manipulation. Still, the powers of the court remained close to those of the original Board of General Appraisers. The court had narrow jurisdiction and limited power to give relief, even in justified complaints. If the court found error in a tariff classification case, they could do little more then send the case back to the Customs Bureau. Few individuals had standing in the court (only the party that had filed a protest with the Customs Service), and even then the defendant was the United States government, which simultaneously decided on what was open for suit.[25] The operating assumption of the court was that the administrative agency was correct; plaintiffs bore the burden of proof in litigation. Thus, for instance, a plaintiff claiming that the Customs Service had assigned a product an incorrect, tariff code needed to prove not only that the assigned classification was wrong but that an alternative one was right.[26]

In response to changes in America's interest and involvement in world trade, the Customs Court evolved into an institution more akin to other federal courts. In 1970, Congress legislated significant procedural reform. The Trade Act of 1974 then enhanced the court's jurisdiction by amending provisions of the Anti-Dumping (AD) Act of 1921 and the countervailing duty (CVD) statute so as to allow manufacturers, producers, and wholesalers the right to expanded court determinations. This augmentation of the court's docket forced the court to spend more time on AD and CVD cases and presented Congress with new problems arising from the adjudication of these cases.

Congress responded in 1979 with further reforms. The primary change was administrative: the Commerce Department gained responsibilities previously held by the Treasury Department. But also, by tinkering with administrative procedures and expanding the number of determinations made by the agency, Congress increased the number of AD and CVD case appeals. Thereafter, a case would have a preliminary determination, a determination of either dumping or subsidization, and finally, an injury determination. The legislation specified new causes of action and stated that any interested party had standing to sue. Thus, for example, unions and trade associations for the first time could initiate dumping and/or countervailing duty actions.[27] In addition, the 1979 act shortened the time period in which determinations could be made, which had the unintended effect of promoting administrative mistakes that would warrant appeal.

The reforms of 1979 set the agenda for the 1980 Customs Court Act. The stated purpose of the act was to eliminate jurisdictional conflicts between the Customs Court on the one side, and federal, district, and appellate courts on the other side, and also to make the court more available to people with a grievance against a government agency administering import relief. Thus, the Customs Court Act of 1980 gave a new court, the Court of International Trade (CIT) exclusive jurisdiction over all civil actions arising from import transactions. The CIT was granted the power of a district court to award monetary remedies and injunctive relief.

As mandated by the Customs Court Act of 1980, the CIT has nine judges, appointed by the president and confirmed by the Senate.[28] By statute, the court is bipartisan: no more than five individuals can be from the same political party. The president appoints the chief justice, who controls the assignment of cases. If a constitutional question comes up, the chief justice appoints a three-judge panel to hear the case.

The jurisdiction of the CIT is far broader than that of the old Customs Court. The court is not only granted influence over trade matters previously handled by other federal courts but also has a jurisdiction and standards for judicial review akin to those of other federal courts. As before, determinations by the Commerce Department and the International Trade Commission (ITC) are presumed to be correct, but the CIT, unlike the Custom Court, tries cases de novo. The standard of review in preliminary AD and CVD cases is whether or not the original determination was "arbitrary, capricious, (an) abuse of discretion or otherwise not in accordance with law."

A final determination gets a more restricted review based on the administrative record, which is presented to the court and then evaluated under a "substantial evidence" standard. Since 1980, the court's power to grant "equitable relief" has increased. The pre-1979 Customs Court had no such power, which was unusual for an article 3 court. After 1979, the CIT could grant injunctions, and after 1980, the court was granted the right to make monetary rulings.[29]

From a legal perspective, the 1980 law was a halfway measure for dealing with the problems that arose in judicial review of trade cases, especially CD and CVD cases. As with the old Customs Court, the CIT is still subject to problems of jurisdiction: plaintiffs have successfully argued that federal district courts, not the CIT, have authority if a decision has any impact on domestic production. Still, traders can now get judicial review more easily and on a larger range of issues than at any time in the past. From a political perspective, the evolution of the court's powers reflects the tension between the executive and legislative branches over trade issues. In inception, the court was a congressional agent with no independence; if it strayed, Congress could appoint new justices. It was thus akin to any of the standing bureaucracies over which Congress has jurisdiction through its appointment and budget powers. In 1956, however, the court was granted independence. Justices had life tenure, allowing them to have preferences apart from those of Congress. Consistent with the expansion of the president's trade responsibilities, he was now granted his first explicit authority over the trade court, the power to appoint its justices.

The effect of the post-1956 reform of the court was to move the preferences of the court on tariffs closer to the bureaucracy's. The change in the court's standing made it less likely that the court would be "captured" by interest groups. Still, the court's opinions stayed close to those of the bureaucracy, especially after the 1979 Trade Act, when Congress expanded the rights of producers to secure trade relief. Since 1980, the American bureaucracy has strayed from the president's position and has routinely granted trade protection to industries under unfair-trade laws. One-third of these investigations eventually go to the CIT. In the majority of these appealed cases, the judiciary endorses the decisions of the bureaucracy.[30]

How significantly did judicial intervention change American trade policy? Of the cases brought by American industry, the court ruled in favor of the plaintiff relatively seldom — only about 12 percent of the time. The great majority of cases affirmed the judgment of the bureaucracy on the duties it assessed and denied plaintiffs any additional relief. The court directly overturned the bureaucracy's decision to grant an extra duty in less than one-quarter of the cases. Given the rise in bureaucratic support for producer claims of unfair trade, from a 15 percent acceptance rate for AD cases filed under the 1974 Trade Act to almost 40 percent after 1979, this judicial acquiescence constituted a problem for presidents committed to free trade.[31] Instead of supporting the president's trade policy agenda, the court's decisions reinforced the autonomy of the bureaucracy. And to the extent that the bureaucracies making these decisions had been "captured" by pro-protection groups, the courts were likewise.

Apart from either remanding or overturning a decision, the CIT conducts oversight through its power to grant injunctions. The request for a preliminary injunction may be made for a variety of reasons, such as to prevent disclosure of documents or data to other parties, to keep the Commerce Department from initiating a review of a dumping order, or to "stay" or enjoin liquidation of merchandise by the Customs Bureau. The latter kind of request is the most significant, since it prevents the Customs Bureau from assessing duties on the merchandise in question until the appeal is concluded or the injunction is lifted. For a domestic producer, a stay can be used as a way to harass foreign producers; it creates uncertainty over how much of a duty will be assessed and thus on the correct price to charge a customer. This uncertainty will last until the case is resolved, which can take years. Such legal harassment by a domestic industry is not uncommon and occurs at all levels of the trade process. By filing multiple unfair-trade cases, for example, or making informational and other demands upon importers, an American industry can significantly increase the cost of doing business in the United States.

Foreign producers use the injunction powers of the court for a different purpose. They will ask for a stay if they feel that the original duty will be either overturned or at least reduced. For them the risk is minimal: the duty will not go any higher upon reconsideration. Further, the fear of a high duty in the future may actually increase demand, if buyers are hedging against possible price hikes. The court has granted over half of the requests for a "stay" that have been submitted to it. The rate of request by domestic and foreign petitioners was almost equal. Foreign petitioners were granted the injunctions they requested 54 percent of the time, domestic petitioners, 47 percent.

This rise of judicial activism in the 1980s was part of a more general increase in both the interest in, and ability of, groups to gain government aid against import pressures. This move toward trade closure more closely mirrored changes in the preferences of Congress than of the president. With these shifting preferences, presidents became increasingly constrained. This was particularly evident in "unfair trade" cases, as noted above. Unfair-trade laws written prior to 1934 have an administrative structure that forecloses direct presidential intervention. While, for example, the president can veto a decision by the International Trade Commission on international copyright violations, he has no direct authority to stop a pro-protection finding in either a dumping or countervailing-duty case. The reaction of presidents is consistent with their overall commitment to free trade. Presidents have attempted to circumvent these laws, using side payments, voluntary export agreements, and any other means available to them.

A president can attempt to sway the courts through his appointments. This strategy works to the extent that the president can predict an appointee's behavior in the future. Even given powers of appointment, presidents frequently find themselves constrained in their autonomy by court decisions. One of the more innovative examples of a successful circumvention of the court's authority was seen in the late 1980s. Using his right to negotiate international trade agreements under fast-track authority, the president found an international solution to the problem of judicial independence. This solution involved creating a higher-order court whose membership was binational, undermining the bias toward American producers that characterized CIT decisions.

Specifically, in chapter 19 of the United States–Canada Free Trade Agreement (FTA) and subsequently under NAFTA, either side could request the creation of a binational panel to review the decisions of the administrative agencies on either antidumping or countervailing duty cases. The panels replaced national judicial review, hence circumvented, direct appeals to the Court of International Trade (CIT). Under procedures specified in the FTA, either government had discretion to ask for review upon its own initiative but was required to ask for review at the request of a private party (who was entitled to seek domestic judicial review of a final determination by an administrative body). Decisions made by the binational panel were binding upon both governments. In addition, the agreement provided that "[n]either Party shall provide in its domestic legislation for an appeal from a panel decision to its domestic courts."

In making its decision, the binational panel was to be guided by the general legal principle that a "court of the importing Party otherwise would apply to a review of a determination of the competent investigating authority." The panel was given the right either to uphold a final determination by an administrative body or to remand it back to the administrative authority for "action not inconsistent with the panel's decision." Panels were composed of five members, two appointed by each government, the fifth agreed upon jointly. Governments could veto up to four candidates but there needed to be agreement on the fifth. Panelists were selected from rosters of eligible individuals, nominated in equal numbers by each side.

Even though the domestic judicial route was not foreclosed, the FTA created incentives for petitioners to turn to international arbitration. One's own nation would be represented among the arbiters, and, even more important, one was guaranteed a decision in less than half the time it took for domestic courts to adjudicate cases. Also, the costs of an appeal — the most expensive part of the unfair-trade process — were significantly reduced under FTA procedures.

This relatively small change in procedures led to a consequential change in American behavior.[32] With passage of the treaty, binational judicial review replaced domestic courts as the "veto player," or the last mover, in the administration of unfair-trade law in US-Canada-Mexico cases. Because of their cross-national makeup, the panels inclined more toward free trade than the courts did, and the outcomes of petitions for protection moved accordingly in the free trade direction. The panels altered American policy through their power to remand and by instructing agencies on the adjudication procedures that the judicial boards would and would not accept.[33]

Why would the president thus give away power to another country, undermining the authority of domestic institutions? Tracing the logic of such a move returns us to the initial premise of this chapter. Among the three institutions making trade policy — the president, Congress, and the courts — the president has the greatest interest in maintaining open trade. His interest derives from the size of his constituency. American presidents, however, have found their powers to make trade agreements limited, requiring the institutional fixes we have examined here. Presidents are not only thwarted by Congress but also by the courts and the bureaucracy. Because international courts counter this constraint on the president's ability to set trade policy, there emerged an international solution to a domestic problem of governance. The president was able to maintain openness, through the international regulation of his own bureaucracy and courts.

Conclusions

From the cases reviewed here, we can draw several conclusions, both about trade-policy making in the United States and the general issue of international influences on domestic politics. First, this essay suggests that U.S. trade policy has varied over time, but that the variation cannot be explained by changing international interests alone. Logically, the United States should have opened its borders to trade as early as the 1870s, that is, once the completion of the transnational railroad made American agriculture competitive on foreign markets. Certainly, after 1890, when the United States surpassed Britain in manufacturing output, or at the close of World War I, when the United States was the world's creditor nation, expanded trade would seem to have been the rational choice. Still, policy change was stalled until the Great Depression. This lack of earlier reform suggests that U.S. domestic institutions are quite insular.

Noting the insularity of American institutions is not to argue that increasing involvement in world affairs had no effect. The examples above suggest strongly that international market forces were an important factor in explaining both the incentive for, and the form of, institutional change. As the United States became increasingly involved in world trade in the nineteenth century, both exporters and producers using imported products were disadvantaged by American trade policy. With industrialization, an increasing number of groups articulated an interest in trade reform and by the mid-1890s, members of both political parties sought to reform U.S. trade institutions in order to increase America's share of world trade.[34] This pressure to become what Richard Rosecrance calls a "trading state" meant that some method had to be devised to quell the power of pro-protection interest groups. In particular, the nations that want to engage in trade must be in a position to commit itself credibly to agreements of reciprocal openness with other nations, even in the face of domestic resistance.

The degree to which such international forces require particular policies and governing forms has been a question of significant and long-standing research.[35] For some countries, international forces significantly influence institutional design, as suggested by Katzenstein in his study of small European states. Other studies, however, suggest that even small nations can resist international forces over significant periods of time, even given increasing economic interdependence.[36] Analysts can read the history of American trade policy in either of two ways. In the long term, the United States did respond to the need for international cooperation, broadly construed. Institutions were created that allowed reciprocal play; the government devised a means to make credible commitments. However, these institutional fixes were overlaid on a government that remains biased toward pro-protection groups. The "fixes" worked not only because they changed the way group interests were aggregated but because they facilitated a change in the underlying preferences of the electorate and their representatives. Although institutions aggregate preferences differently today than they did a hundred years ago, the U.S. government will promote free trade only if a majority favors it.

America's efforts at institutional redesign reflect this vulnerability to shifting preferences. Elected officials crafting a trade agreement must consider the possibility not only of ex post opportunism on the part of trading partners but of their own reneging in the face of social resistance. The solutions detailed above are all institutional fixes that addresses this pro-protection bias in trade-policy making. International courts control bureaucracies that may be captured by pro-protection groups; agenda control, multilateral agreements, trade agreements that do not have treaty status, and fast track — all aggregate preferences in ways that maintain majority support.

This institutional history suggests two general mechanisms by which international forces influence American politics. First, involvement in world affairs changes the interests of domestic actors. Second, international politics alters the "tool kit" of options available to leaders for making policy. In the case of trade policy, international agreements that lowered trade barriers served to reenforce an open trade policy: once FDR took the first steps to open up the American economy, liberalization itself increased the political, as well as economic, costs of a return to high barriers. The American economy adjusted to the changed prices of goods and services. Some import-competing producers were wiped out; jobs moved to sectors either unaffected by world trade or benefiting from continued openness. To keep prices down, more producers relied upon cheap imports of intermediate products.

This change in economic activity had political implications. Within the United States, more groups emerged that were ready to organize on behalf of open access to the world market and against those who would benefit from protection. The mounting number of multilateral treaties meant that the probability of any one agreement unraveling declined. Free trade policy became increasingly more stable as policymakers had a growing pool of groups among which to make trade-offs in support of new accords. Once an accord was signed, the threat of a retaliatory closure of a foreign market provided decision makers with political support to counter the potential reaction of protectionist groups.

International influences are also important because they enlarge the feasible policy set for elected officials. In making trade policy, the dilemma facing leaders today is the same one facing those at the start of the twentieth century: American governing institutions are poorly suited for a liberal trade policy. The key problem posed by institutional design is the electorate's organization into small districts that give considerable voice to import-competing groups. To sustain an open trade policy, America must have both a majority that stands to gain from it and institutional "fixes" that circumscribe the potential veto power of protectionist forces. Too often, the international system is viewed as a "constraint." But international agreements also can expand the set of policy options available for central decision makers. This essay demonstrates this "reverse" logic of international politics. By making use of international agreements, U.S. policymakers have been able to expand America's free trade coalition. Policymakers did not wait for a free trade ground swell before they entered into trade agreements but, rather, used the agreements to create support for openness. Trade agreements brought exporters into the coalition, increased the number of possible trade-offs for congressional representatives, undercut the agenda power of the legislature, and constrained interest group activity in the bureaucracy.[37]

Notes

1. Trade liberalization deviates from the PD metaphor in a number of ways, however. Perhaps most importantly, economic theory suggests that unilateral free trade is better than protection; that is, each country should have a dominant strategy to cooperate and lower barriers, even if the others do not.

2. See Keohane 1984.

3. On trade and interest groups, see Destler 1995 and Lohmann and O'Halloran 1994.

4. Numerous empirical studies document the importance of interest groups in setting trade policy. See, for example, Verdier 1994 for a cross-national, cross-sectional examination of interest-groups involvement.

5. The textbook example of this is the 1929–30 Smoot-Hawley Tariff (see Schattschneider 1935). No representative sought a huge tariff hike, but each representative wanted something for his constituents.

6. In the early years of the GATT regime, it is difficult to determine whether it was a shift in the balance of group interests or a shift in trade policy that allowed governments to lower barriers to trade. Certainly, in the United States interest-group activity was muted, because the costs of organizing increased as the president gained more control of trade policy. Still, the shift toward openness would not have occurred without sustained social support. See Bailey, Goldstein, and Weingast 1997 for an analysis of the relationship between institutional change and underlying social variables.

7. Consistent with section 317 of the previous tariff act (the Fordney-McCumber Act of 1922), agreements were to be generalized to all other nations receiving most-favored-nation status.

8. Cited in Goldstein 1993, 143.

9. See Tarillo 1986.

10. Bauer, Pool, and Dexter 1972; Destler 1995, 14; Schattschneider wrote of the "truly Sisyphean labor" to which the legislation condemned Congress: eleven thousand pages of testimony and briefs in forty-three days and five nights of hearings (1935, 29, 36).

11. Destler 1995, 14.

12. Goldstein 1993; Haggard 1988;

13. For a more complete review of congressional policy, see Pastor 1980; Preeg 1973; Evans 1971 and Goldstein 1993.

14. Chu 1957, 311; Bauer, Pool, and Dexter 1972, 33; Pastor 1980, 101.

15. Haggard 1988, 106–7. As well as Roosevelt, others in the "brain trust," such as Rexford Tugwell, Raymond Moley, and Adolf Berle, were inclined to use tariffs to deal with domestic problems. For example, the National Industrial Recovery Act (NIRA) and the Agriculture Assistance Act (AAA) allowed the government to limit imports that interfered with the operation of these programs (Goldstein 1993). Rank-and-file members of the party also were not united in favor of lower tariffs. The increased influence of blue-collar and immigrant labor on the party proved a counterweight to southern preferences for lower tariffs. Led by 1928 presidential nominee and 1932 candidate Al Smith, a major wing of the party supported high tariffs. In fact, by the time the Smoot-Hawley Tariff came up for debate, most Democrats had tempered their opposition to high tariffs (Fetter 1933, 416).

16. See Bailey, Goldstein, and Weingast 1997 for a more detailed explanation.

17. Goldstein 1993, 142; Schatz 1965, 51.

18. Woytinsky and Woytinsky 1955, 48; Pastor 1980, 332.

19. See Bailey, Goldstein, and Weingast 1997.

20. See Brady, Goldstein, and Kessler 2000.

21. Ibid.

22. Destler 1995, 72.

23. Ibid., 73.

24. Cohen, 1981, 277.

25. The Customs Court never heard cases brought by parties other than the direct producers of goods. For example, consumers, even if hurt by a classification error, were not regarded as an interest that deserved a hearing.

26. See Cohen 1981, 280.

27. The law also specified procedures by which interested parties could request access to confidential information and then provided for judicial review if such disclosure was not forthcoming.

28. For a term to end upon mandatory retirement at age sixty-five.

29. There are two exceptions, both having to do with adjustment assistance cases.

30. Between 1980 and 1990, the CIT collectively wrote 1,462 slip opinions. Of these, 597, or 41 percent, were written for AD or CVD cases. Twenty-nine percent of AD and CVD opinions were either dismissals or conclusions of cases; thirty-seven percent of the AD/CVD opinions settled procedural questions, such as the need for data disclosure, a motion for intervention by an interested party, or a request for a time extension. Of the 597 decisions on unfair-trade cases, 47 percent related to petitions from American producers who had failed to get the desired degree of protection. The remainder of the opinions pertained to a case brought by foreign exporters, represented either by the American importer or by the foreign producer. In this period, the court remanded about 22 percent of AD and CVD cases to the trade bureaucracy. (Remands are decisions that send a case back to the bureaucracy to be "redone," because the court finds some error in the original proceedings.) Fifty-one percent of all remands were responses to final determinations by the bureaucracy of a dumping and countervailing duty; 49 percent were because the bureaucracy had not, in the court's opinion, adequately considered a duty request by an American producer. There is some variation over agency and time. Of the two agencies involved in unfair-trade case determinations, the court was slightly more critical of Commerce than the ITC. Between 1986 and March 1993, the court upheld Commerce in about 54 percent of their determinations, ITC in over 60 percent. See Goldstein 1997. On the differences between judicial review of the bureaucracy see Ondeck and Lawrence 1993, 28.

31. Goldstein 1993, 217.

32. For a further exposition of this case, see Goldstein 1997.

33. This theoretical prediction was borne out by a change in American behavior. As expected, the panels found fault with the American bureaucracy at a rate higher than the CIT had. Where the CIT overturned decisions about 22 percent of the time, the panels ruled against the United States three-quarters of the time. The probability of getting a dumping finding against Canada was over .6 before the FTA, that number declined to .3 after the agreement went into effect. Similarly, CVD findings declined from over .6 to .25. See Goldstein 1997.

34. Goldstein 1993, 127–36.

35. Gourevitch 1977, 1978, 1985; Katzenstein 1984; Keohane and Milner 1996.

36. See, for example, Haggard and Maxfield 1996.

37. See Goldstein and Martin 2000 for the effects of international legalization on domestic trade policy.

Bibliography

Axelrod, Robert. 1981. The Emergence of Cooperation among Egoists. *American Political Science Review*, December.

Bailey, Michael, Judith Goldstein, and Barry Weingast. 1997. The Institutional Roots of American Trade Policy: Politics, Coalitions and International Trade. *World Politics*, April.

Baldwin, Robert. 1985. *The Political Economy of U.S. Import Policy*. Cambridge: MIT Press.

Bauer, Raymond, Ithiel de Sola Pool, and Lewis Dexter. 1972. *American Business and Public Policy*. 2d ed. Chicago: Aldine-Atherton.

Brady, David, Judith Goldstein, and Daniel Kessler. 2000. Does Party Matter? An Historical Test Using Tariff Votes over Three Institutional Periods. MS. Stanford University.

Chu, Power Yung-Chao. 1957. A History of the Hull Trade Program, 1934–1939. Ph.D. diss., Columbia University.

Cohen, Richard. 1981. The New United States International Court of International Trade. *Columbia Journal of Transnational Law* 20: 277.

Cox, Gary, and Mathew McCubbins. 1991. *Legislative Leviathan: Party Government in the House*. Berkeley: University of California Press.

Destler, I. M. 1995. *American Trade Politics*. 2d ed. Washington, D.C.: Institute for International Economics.

Evans, John. 1971. *The Kennedy Round in American Trade Policy*. Cambridge: Harvard University Press.

Ferguson, Thomas. 1984. From Normalcy to New Deal: Industrial Structure, Party Competition, and American Public Policy in the Great Depression. *International Organization* 38 (Winter): 41–94.

Fetter, Frank. 1933. Congressional Tariff Policy. *American Economic Review* 23: 413–27.

Goldstein, Judith. 1993. *Ideas, Interests, and American Trade Policy*. Ithaca: Cornell University Press.

———. 1997. International Law and Domestic Institutions. *International Organization* 50 (Autumn): 541–64.

———. 1998. International Institutions and Domestic Politics: GATT, WTO and the Liberalization of International Trade. In *The WTO as an International Organization*, ed. Ann Kruegar Chicago: University of Chicago Press.

Goldstein, Judith and Lisa Martin. 2000. Legalization, Trade Liberalization and Domestic Politics: A Cautionary Note. *International Organization* 54, no. 3:603–632.

Gourevitch, Peter A. 1977. International Trade, Domestic Coalitions, and Liberty: Comparative Responses to the Crisis of 1873–1896." *Journal of Interdisciplinary History* 8:281–313.

———. 1978. The Second Image Reversed: The International Sources of Domestic Politics. *International Organization* 32: 881–912.

———. 1986. *Politics in Hard Times: Comparative Responses to International Economic Crises*. Ithaca: Cornell University Press.

Haggard, Stephan. 1988. The Institutional Foundations of Hegemony: Explaining the Reciprocal Trade Agreements Act of 1934. In *The State and American Foreign Economic Policy*, ed. G. John Ikenberry, David Lake, and Michael Mastanduno. Ithaca: Cornell University Press.

Haggard, Stephan, and Sylvia Maxfield. 1996. The Political Economy of Financial Internationalization in the Developing World. In *Internationalization and Domestic Politics*, ed. Robert O. Keohane and Helen Milner. New York: Cambridge University Press.

Hinich, Melvin, and Michael Munger. 1994. *Ideology and the Theory of Political Choice*. Ann Arbor: University of Michigan Press.

Hull, Cordell. 1948. *Memoirs*. New York: Macmillan.

Katzenstein, Peter. 1985. *Small States in World Markets: Industrial Policy in Europe*. Ithaca: Cornell University Press.

Keohane, Robert O. 1984. *After Hegemony*. Princeton: Princeton University Press.

Keohane, Robert O., and Helen Milner. 1996. *Internationalization and Domestic Politics*. New York: Cambridge University Press.

Krehbiel, Keith. 1991. *Information and Legislative Organization*. Ann Arbor: University of Michigan Press.

Lohmann, Susanne, and Sharyn O'Halloran. 1994. Divided Government and U.S. Trade Policy: Theory and Evidence. *International Organization* 48, no. 4:595–632.

Nelson, Douglas. 1986. Domestic Political Preconditions of U.S. Trade Policy: Liberal Structure and Protectionist Dynamics. *Journal of Public Policy* 9: 83–108.

O'Halloran, Sharyn. 1994. *Politics, Process, and American Trade Policy*. Ann Arbor: University of Michigan Press.

Ondeck, Thomas, and Michael Lawrence. 1993. Court of International Trade Deference to International Trade Commission in International Trade Administration Anti-Dumping Determinations: An Empirical Look. *Law and Policy in International Business* 25, no. 1:28.

Pastor, Robert. 1980. *Congress and the Politics of U.S. Foreign Economic Policy*. Berkeley: University of California Press.

Poole, Keith, and Howard Rosenthal. 1991. Patterns of Congressional Voting. *American Journal of Political Science* 35: 228–78.

Preeg, Ernest. 1973. *Traders and Diplomats*. Washington, D.C.: Brookings Institution.

Schattschneider, E. E. 1935. *Politics, Pressure and the Tariff: A Study of Free Private Enterprise in Pressure Politics as Shown in the 1929–1930 Revision of the Tariff*. Hamden, Conn.: Archon Books.

Schatz, Arthur. 1965. Cordell Hull and the Struggle for the Reciprocal Trade Agreements Program, 1932–1940. Ph.D. diss., University of Oregon.

Schnietz, Karen. 1994. To Delegate or Not to Delegate: Congressional Institutional Choices in the Regulation of Foreign Trade, 1916–1934. Ph.D. diss., University of California.

Tarullo, Daniel. 1986. Law and Politics in Twentieth Century Tariff History. *UCLA Law Review* 34 (December):252–95.

Tasca, Henry. 1938. *The Reciprocal Trade Policy of the United States*. Philadelphia: University of Pennsylvania Press.

Verdier, Daniel. 1994. *Democracy and International Trade: Britain, France, and the United States, 1960–1999*. Princeton: Princeton University Press.

Weingast, Barry, and William Marshall. 1988. The Industrial Organization of Congress. *Journal of Economic Policy* 96: 132–63.

Weingast, Barry, Kenneth Shepsle, and Christopher Johnsen. 1981. The Political Economy of Benefits and Costs: A Neoclassical Approach to Distributive Politics. *Journal of Political Economy* 89: 642–64.

Woytinsky, E. S., and W. S. Woytinsky. 1955. *World Commerce and Governments: Trends and Outlooks*. New York: Twentieth Century Fund.

Part IV

AMERICA SINCE 1940

Nine

American Antistatism and the Founding of the Cold War State

AARON L. FRIEDBERG

THE PURPOSE of this chapter is to consider how the onset of the Cold War influenced the relationship between the American state[1] and the nation's economy and society. I will be concerned here not so much with changes in the shape, size, and internal workings of the federal government (with state building per se) as with the construction of a cluster of intermediary mechanisms, a parallel set of *power-creating institutions* that linked state and society, and through which the state transformed societal resources into the implements of military power. These institutions were the primary internal manifestations of America's external, strategic competition with the Soviet Union. If we want to understand the effects of the Cold War on the politics, society, and economy of the United States, we need to begin by asking why they took the form that they did.

The argument that I will advance here can be briefly summarized: in the United States at the middle of the twentieth century, as in other countries earlier in the history of the modern era, war and the continuing threat of war produced pressures for the construction of a powerful central state. For the United States, these pressures came comparatively late in the process of political development; they were new and largely unfamiliar, and they were met and, to a degree, counterbalanced, by strong antistatist impulses that were deeply rooted in the circumstances of the nation's founding. The power-creating institutions put into place during the first fifteen years of the Cold War can best be understood as the product of a collision between these two sets of conflicting forces. It is impossible to explain the impact of the Cold War on the United States — indeed, it is not possible adequately to explain the overall course of the nation's political evolution — without reference to the persistent presence of forces tending to oppose expansions in state power.

Sources and Effects of American Antistatism

The Founders of the American republic created a regime in which the powers of the central government were sharply limited and in which it would be difficult, though not impossible, to expand them over time. To borrow a metaphor from modern science, the Founders succeeded, in effect, in encoding a strong strain of antistatism into the new nation's political DNA, one that would reproduce itself and continue to fulfill its protective function in future generations. They did this in two ways. First, and most obviously, the architects of the American Constitution designed a set of institutions in which authority and decision-making power were widely dispersed: among the three branches of the federal government, between the federal government and the states, and, in a sense, between the people (as the ultimate locus of sovereignty) and government at all levels. These institutional arrangements were intended to make it very difficult for one group or one branch of government to increase its power at the expense of the others, or for the federal government as a whole to exercise its authority over the people, without a significant measure of consensus and consent. This system of dispersed power and multiple checks and balances was, in the words of one scholar, "as much an antistate as a state."[2] As the essays by Ira Katznelson and Aristide Zolberg in this volume suggest, the early American state was neither as inconsequential nor as ineffectual as it has sometimes been made to seem in retrospect. Still, there can be no question that, by European standards, the organs of central government were small, weak, and, when viewed from afar, difficult even to locate reliably.[3]

In addition to designing a unique set of institutions, the Founders also promulgated an ideology, a set of beliefs that emphasized above all the virtues of individual liberty and the dangers of excessive concentrations of governmental power. Power and liberty were, by their nature, fundamentally opposed. Power, in the view of the revolutionary theorists, was "endlessly propulsive," expansionary and aggressive; "its natural prey, its necessary victim, was liberty, or law, or right."[4] Although the Revolution replaced monarchical rule with popular government, "opposition to power, and suspicion of government as the most dangerous embodiment of power" remained, according to Samuel Huntington, "the central themes of American political thought."[5] Having struggled against "a centralized monarchical state, the founding fathers distrusted unified government" and they passed on to their successors a "chronic antagonism to the state."[6] Albeit with some modest variations, this general attitude was widely shared. Writing at the turn of the twentieth century, H. G. Wells concluded that "from the English point of view" all Americans were adherents of some form of eighteenth-century liberalism, an ideology which was, in its essence, "anti-State."[7]

Over the course of the past two hundred years, American ideology and the structure of American institutions have combined to give significant advantages to those intent on limiting the powers of the executive agencies of the federal government, while imposing substantial burdens on those who have sought to expand them. Because of the way decision-making authority is dispersed in the American political system, the advocates of a stronger central state have generally had to win support (or at least acquiescence) in all three branches of the federal government; their opponents have often been able to block them by exerting a decisive influence in only one. In national debate, the advocates of a stronger state have been vulnerable to the charge that their proposals are unsound and even "un-American." Their opponents, meanwhile, have had ready access to evocative slogans and potent symbols that ease the task of rallying public support. This tilting of the political playing field has not prevented increases in the size and capacities of the American state, but it has constrained its growth, rendering it episodic and subject to periodic reversals, and shaping the directions, the extent, and the forms in which it has gone forward over time.

Embedded antistatism may help to explain why the great episodes of American state building have followed a similar pattern: events originating either inside the United States or beyond its boundaries, are interpreted by some Americans as requiring a strengthening of the federal government in response. *Dramatic* events, wars and economic or social crises, are especially important, because, at least for a time, they can have the effect of galvanizing opinion and temporarily suppressing resistance to expansions in state power. But proposals for movement in this direction inevitably provoke a counterreaction from those who are opposed in principle to state expansion or because they fear that a stronger state will be able to act in ways that are contrary to their individual or group interests. Or, as is often the case, they are motivated by some inextricable blend of abstract belief and material self-interest. A period of political struggle ensues, in which the opponents of a stronger state use their institutional and ideological advantages to block some of the initiatives of their opponents, and, in some cases, to advance alternative solutions to the problems at hand that they regard as less offensive to their beliefs and less threatening to their interests. What emerges ultimately is a package of new policies and institutional innovations that is the product of many conflicting influences, but which bears the strong and readily recognizable imprint of the antistatist inclinations that have been present since the creation of the American republic. This dynamic is visible in the turn-of-the-century debate over how best to deal with the rise of large-scale industrialism, in the American mobilization for the First and Second World Wars, in the nation's response to the Great Depression, and, as I will demonstrate, in its reaction to the onset of what would turn out to be a half-century-long strategic competition with the Soviet Union.[8]

One aspect of the distinctive American pattern of state building deserves particular attention. Students of the growth of the modern state have pointed to the existence of a war-related "ratchet effect." Once undertaken, they note, emergency increases in the size of central government bureaucracies, the bulk of the revenues they extract, and the range of activities they seek to control are rarely completely reversed.[9] In the United States, however, this tendency has been offset by what might be termed a "rollback effect." The centrifugal tendencies that are built into the American constitutional design tend to reassert themselves when the galvanizing energy of a crisis begins to subside. Congress and the courts may fall into alignment with the executive while a war is under way, but once peace has been restored, the three branches are more likely to pull in different directions, the states are less likely to accept federal dictates, and citizens are less inclined to defer to government at any level. Typically, the very act of strengthening the state also produces an intellectual backlash. What was tolerable in an emergency becomes repellent in its wake, as assorted critics, commentators, and prophets attack the deviations of the recent past and call the American people back to their fundamental faith in liberty. The "rollback effect" evident in postwar periods is, in short, a product of the same antistatist institutional and ideological forces at work during intervals of state building; its presence can help to account for the relatively weak pattern of path dependence described in other essays in this volume.

The Problem of Power Creation

States create military power by extracting societal resources (principally money and manpower) and by directing their flow toward activities intended to enhance immediate and long-term military capabilities (the manufacture of armaments, the production of materials essential to arms making, and the conduct of strategically significant scientific research). Historically, war has (in Charles Tilly's pithy phrase) "made" states by encouraging them to increase their capacity to perform these various functions. Thus, in Europe, from the fourteenth century onward, war and military rivalry stimulated the development of tax and conscription systems (and the bureaucracies and police forces necessary to administer and enforce them) and the establishment either of state-owned and -operated facilities for the development and production of arms or the creation, support, and direction, through state subsidies, of their quasi-private functional equivalents. By the second half of the nineteenth century, at the latest, all of the major European states were "strong" in the sense that they had evolved into highly capable power creators.[10]

The American republic was born while this larger historical process was already well under way, and, indeed, it was founded in part in reaction against the trend toward ever greater concentrations of state power (and ever expanding state capacities for military power creation) taking place on the other side of the Atlantic.[11] As the preceding discussion makes clear, power creation involves extensive interventions and intrusions by the state into society and the economy. Extraction, in particular, leads very directly to abridgements of personal liberty, as when the state taxes its citizen's wealth or income to pay for its armed forces, or when it compels them to give up their livelihoods (and often their lives) to military service. It was precisely because they were intent on limiting the capacity of government to impose such burdens that the Founders created a system in which, by European standards, the state and the institutions of power creation were greatly underdeveloped.

If not for its geopolitical good fortune, the United States might well have undergone an early, traumatic transformation or, perhaps more likely, simply ceased to exist. Instead, the comparative absence of immediate military threats permitted the new republic to survive and thrive during the first century and a half of its existence without developing a central state that was "strong" in the traditional ways. By the early part of the nineteenth century, the United States was no longer faced with any substantial possibility of attack over land. The French and Spanish had been bought out or expelled from their holdings in North America; the British had accommodated themselves to the loss of their former colonies and had withdrawn to Canada; and the Native American tribes with whom the colonists had long engaged in bloody skirmishes had been pacified, decimated, or driven to the West. With Britain firmly in command of the seas, no other European power could use its fleet to strike at America's shores. Attack through the air was not only impossible but unimaginable.[12]

From the end of the eighteenth century to the the middle of the twentieth, American military expenditures and overall tax burdens were generally quite low, and conscription was applied sparingly and for brief intervals. The military's peacetime needs for weapons were supplied, for the most part, by a small network of federal arsenals and shipyards. Although the government did take periodic, modest steps to promote the development of science and technology, these were usually motivated more by a concern for national economic welfare than by any anxiety over national military security. Episodes of domestic and international warfare that *did* lead to temporary increases in the power-creating activities of the central state were quickly followed by "rollback" or retrenchment, and by reversion to more typical peacetime patterns. Thus, after both the Civil War and the First World War, military expenditures were cut drastically, conscription was halted, federal arsenals and laboratories were constricted, and the industries that had expanded to meet the government's needs for arms, materials, and supplies were left to fend for themselves as best they could.[13]

The Cold War "Founding"

Changed Strategic Circumstances

Although it was foreshadowed to some extent by the events of the first four decades of the twentieth century, the emergence of the United States as one of two global superpowers and the onset of the Cold War competition with the Soviet Union created a unique external situation and a unique set of internal tensions. For a combination of geopolitical and technological reasons, the United States found itself after 1945 possessed of far-flung alliances, interests, and commitments, and, at the same time, potentially vulnerable to direct and devastating attack on its own territory.

As early as 1917 some Americans had begun to recognize that a hostile power or coalition, if it were permitted to gain preponderance in Eurasia, would be able to pose a direct threat to U.S. security. During the opening stages of the First and Second World Wars, however, the United States had been able to rely on the other democracies to fend off the initial assaults of expansionist authoritarian regimes. From 1914 to 1917 and, again, from 1939 to 1941, the United States had time to put into place the power-creating mechanisms and the armed forces necessary for the defense of its territory and its interests. After 1945, with the other democracies devastated or exhausted, there was no assurance of a similar breathing space between the onset of war and the beginning of American involvement.

Technological change aggravated this uncomfortable situation. At the outset of the Second World War, as for most of the preceding century and a half, America's enemies had no means of striking at it directly and with great force. As shocking as it was, even the Japanese attack on Pearl Harbor was essentially an unrepeatable stunt, carried out with great exertion against an American outpost that was extended, exposed, and inadequately prepared. During the war, however, the United States took the lead in developing several of the technologies that would soon combine to erode its own sense of security. With the appearance of long-range bombers, ballistic missiles, and atomic bombs it seemed obvious that, as President Truman told Congress in October 1945, "our geographical security is now gone. . . . Never again can we count on the luxury of time with which to arm ourselves. In any future war, the heart of the United States would be the enemy's first target."[14]

Resurgent Antistatism

As the Second World War ended and the Cold War got under way, the defense of American interests, and of the United States itself, seemed to demand the maintenance, on a continuing peacetime basis, of substantial military capabilities. The generation of those capabilities, in turn, appeared to require the establishment of new, permanent power-creating institutions. In effect, in 1945 the United States found itself in a strategic position more like that of a continental European country than the one to which it had been accustomed for most of its previous history. But, despite all the changes associated with the Great Depression and the world war, it confronted these changed external circumstances with a basic institutional structure, and a set of prevailing beliefs, inherited from an earlier and less threatening era.

Postwar American politics were also characterized by an upsurge in antistatist sentiment. This tendency fed from a variety of sources. Having tolerated a sustained expansion in the size and authority of the executive, many members of Congress on both sides of the aisle were eager to see the legislative branch reassert itself and to right what they regarded as a dangerous shift in the balance of intragovernmental power. The coalition of Republicans and conservative southern Democrats that had come together in the late 1930s to oppose key aspects of the New Deal had continued to function during the war. "The cement that held the coalition together," according to historian Richard Polenberg, "was provided not only by a mutual desire to protect states' rights, regulate labor unions and curb welfare spending, but also by a shared resentment over the mammoth wartime expansion of executive authority and the corresponding erosion of legislative influence." Even before the war had ended, members of both parties in Congress were looking for "ways to reassert their prerogatives," to rein in and roll back the powers of the executive branch.[15]

This dynamic, rooted in the institutional structure of the American regime, gathered strength as the war drew to a close and was further reinforced by partisan political calculations. In 1944 the Republicans lost their fourth straight presidential election. At the same time, although they remained in the minority in both the House and the Senate, the Republicans had managed to regain considerable strength in the congressional elections of 1938, 1940, and 1942. With the war over and the overwhelmingly popular Franklin Roosevelt finally gone from the scene, Republican strategists hoped to benefit from public exhaustion after more than a decade of crisis and mobilization and from evident public hostility to a greatly expanded and increasingly intrusive federal government. Republicans wanted to cut taxes, end economic controls, and prevent any further expansion in social-welfare spending, both because they regarded these measures as harmful to the nation's future, and because they believed that, by resisting them, they would improve their chances of recapturing the White House and Congress.

The limits of popular enthusiasm for what were perceived to be "statist" solutions to the nation's problems, and for accompanying increases in state power, were already much in evidence before the war began. What has been called the "thermidor" of the New Deal came after the 1936 elections, when, the Democrats, convinced that they had won a mandate for such changes, brought forward sweeping proposals for a reorganization of the federal government and took steps designed to increase the power of the executive branch in relation both to Congress and to the courts.[16] These efforts, as Alan Brinkley observes, "encountered unexpectedly intense opposition," not only in Washington, but in the country as a whole. As events would prove, "support for Franklin Roosevelt was not the same, either within Congress or among the public, as support for a liberal vision of a powerful state."[17]

Experience with higher taxes and wartime wage and price controls served only to increase popular distaste for anything that smacked of excessive state intervention in everyday life. Brinkley notes, for example, that the Office of Price Administration was perhaps "the most intrusive federal bureaucracy ever created in America" and that, unsurprisingly, it became "a target for all the frustrations and disappointments of people unaccustomed to regimentation and control."[18] By the war's end such sentiments had reached a fever pitch, a trend reflected in the striking success of the Republican Party's blunt 1946 campaign theme: "Had Enough?"

As eager as ordinary citizens may have been to get the government off their backs and out of their pockets, businessmen were even more so. Although the war brought increased profits for many, most farmers, manufacturers, and distributors objected to the higher taxes and the wage, price, and material controls that came with them. In addition to throwing off wartime restraints, the leaders of many individual manufacturing firms, and of peak associations like the National Association of Manufacturers and the U.S. Chamber of Commerce, also had a larger agenda in mind. "Despite real differences in interest and ideology," writes historian Robert Griffith, "most business leaders shared a body of broad common assumptions and . . . they also shared a commitment to arresting the disorderly momentum of New Deal liberalism."[19] With this end in view, business groups united to oppose specific policies (such as increased federal housing construction or the introduction of national health insurance) and proposed institutional innovations (such as a National Resources Planning Board or a powerful new economic agency charged with ensuring "full employment") that they believed would increase unduly the federal government's ability to intervene in society and the economy. Business groups also invested heavily in public relations efforts to promote the virtues of the "American enterprise system." By the early 1950s, Griffith reports, "American businesses were spending more than $100 million annually for such campaigns, littering the cultural landscape with books, articles, and pamphlets; billboards and posters; radio and television spots; ads on buses, trains, and trolleys; even comic books and matchbook covers."[20]

Expressions of hostility toward planning, "statism," and socialism, and outpourings of enthusiasm for limited government and "free markets," were not confined to pro-business propaganda, nor can they be understood simply as an expression of the material interests of a particular group or class. The confrontation with fascism, and the increasingly widespread recognition of the true nature of the Soviet regime, had a profound intellectual impact. On both sides of the American political spectrum, the experiences of the thirties and forties were widely interpreted as demonstrating both the ultimate superiority of liberal democracy and the dangers posed by unchecked expansions in the powers of the state. As Friedrich Hayek warned in his 1944 book *The Road to Serfdom*, statism, whether of the left- or the right-wing variety, could lead all too easily to totalitarianism.[21]

Reflecting the tone of the times, Hayek's book went on to become a bestseller and, the crowning symbol of mass-market appeal, a Book-of-the-Month Club selection. As Alan Brinkley observes, authors like Hayek and James Burnham, who advanced similar ideas, were influential, not because they were especially original, but because "they had articulated concerns that were already familiar, and deeply rooted in American history."

> For all the efforts of the New Dealers in the 1930s to celebrate and legitimize the new functions they were creating for the state, a broad suspicion of centralized bureaucratic power — rooted in traditions of republicanism and populism stretching back to the earliest years of the American polity — remained a staple of popular discourse and a constant impediment to many liberal aims.

Hayek, Brinkley concludes, was giving voice to "a powerful strain of Jeffersonian anti-statism in American political culture that a decade of the New Deal had done relatively little to eliminate."[22]

Anxiety over "statism" was fed by the collapse of the wartime alliance with the Soviet Union and the dawning of the Cold War. Having dispatched one totalitarian menace, the United States now found itself confronted by another. Almost as troubling as the threat of devastation or conquest was the prospect that, if it tried indefinitely to sustain a high level of military preparedness, the United States might find itself transformed into the likeness of its enemies. This concern was reflected in the frequent invocation of the term "garrison state," a concept first introduced in 1941 by Yale political scientist Harold Lasswell. Under conditions of perpetual crisis and constant mobilization, Lasswell warned, every aspect of life in modern societies would eventually fall under the control of the "specialists on violence." Populations would be conscripted, economies controlled, and dissent suppressed. Even a country like the United States, which started with "a minimum of state-ism," might soon find itself swept up in a general movement "towards a world of 'garrison states.'"[23]

Lasswell's phrase, and the fear that lay behind it, were constant features of the postwar debate over defense policy. The question, as one observer put it in 1947, was how the United States could prepare itself to confront, contain, and, if necessary, defeat the Soviet Union "without becoming a 'garrison state' and destroying the very qualities and virtues and principles we originally set about to save? This . . . is the grand dilemma . . . of our age."[24]

The American Strategic Synthesis

Taken as a whole, the period from the end of the Second World War to the early 1960s can best be understood as an interval of "founding" (or, "punctuation") followed by thirty years of rough equilibrium.[25] Out of this period of instability and struggle there emerged a "strategic synthesis," an outward-directed military strategy and a complementary set of domestic mechanisms for the creation of military power.[26] The two halves of this synthesis were mutually determinative; the power-creating mechanisms put in place during the opening years of the Cold War were a reflection of American military strategy and of the external environment to which it was designed to respond. But that strategy, in turn, was also shaped by the character of the American domestic regime and, in particular, by the constraints that it imposed on the institutions of power creation.

A close examination of this period reveals that this particular equilibrium point was not the only one conceivable. In fact, given the anxieties and uncertainties of the early Cold War period there were considerable pressures for the United States to adopt a more ambitious military strategy, along with a set of domestic mechanisms broader in scope and capable of deeper penetration into society and the economy than those that eventually emerged. The fact that this did not happen owes a great deal to the constraints on power creation that have already been mentioned. In any case, the strategic synthesis that had taken shape by the beginning of the 1960s would prove over time to be quite stable. Both halves persisted, with relatively minor modifications, down to the end of the Cold War.

Strategy

By the early 1960s the United States had settled on what came in the Kennedy administration to be referred to as a strategy of "flexible response." In order to discourage an attack on itself or its allies, the United States maintained substantial, technologically sophisticated forces-in-being. These, it was assumed, would be large and diverse enough to strike back with devastating power in response to enemy nuclear attack, to deal with certain kinds of limited conflicts against lesser opponents, and to hold their own in at least the opening stages of a nonnuclear war with the Soviet Union and its allies.[27]

Although it has sometimes been pictured so in retrospect, this posture was not the only one conceivable under the circumstances, and its adoption cannot be explained merely as an inescapable response to objective, material conditions. The sheer destructiveness of nuclear weapons did not dictate a single, rational strategic response. The United States *could* have chosen to prepare itself far more extensively for the conduct of a full-scale war against the Soviet Union, one fought with both conventional and nuclear weapons or perhaps, if the nuclear arsenals of the two superpowers effectively canceled one another out, with conventional weapons alone. Especially during the first decade of the Cold War, when the arsenals of the two superpowers were still relatively small, even a war fought with atomic weapons could have dragged on for some time and involved the extensive use of conventional forces.[28] As the stockpiles on both sides grew and diversified, the possibility of an all-out conventional war, in which nuclear weapons were held in reserve, seemed to many observers to grow in plausibility.[29]

Neither of these two strategies was so obviously unreasonable as to be entirely outside the realm of serious consideration. Indeed, from the 1950s to the 1970s, *Soviet* military preparations were driven by the first of these alternative visions of a future war between the superpowers; but from the 1970s to at least the mid-1980s, more and more by the second.[30] Both notions had their supporters in the United States as well, but by the late-1950s, both had been effectively abandoned.[31] The rejection of these two alternatives by the United States had more to do with their likely internal implications than with their perceived strategic plausibility. Actively pursued, either approach would have required much larger forces-in-being and far more extensive preparations for the rapid and sustained mobilization of manpower and industrial production than the strategy of flexible response did. The power-creating mechanisms necessary to support sustained conventional or nuclear combat would have involved a much more extensive and intrusive role for the state, and it was largely for this reason that, by the end of the 1950s, these possibilities had been eliminated from serious consideration in the United States. Free of similar constraints on their domestic powers, the leaders of the Soviet state were able to pursue military strategies that were more ambitious, more costly, and ultimately more damaging to the society and economy over which they ruled.

Power Creation

EXTRACTION

Money

The single most important reason for the movement toward a strategy of flexible response was the fact that either of the two most obvious alternatives to it would have cost a good deal more money. A bigger defense program could have been financed either by raising taxes or by deliberately permitting federal revenues to exceed expenditures and accepting the resulting deficits. Except during the opening stages of the Korean War (and the exception is only a partial one), neither approach was politically acceptable. Thus, throughout the 1940s and 1950s, there was strong downward pressure on defense expenditures. While military spending rose considerably during this period, it did not do so by nearly as much as most military planners believed desirable.

The federal tax system had been greatly expanded in scope and yield during the Second World War, but it was precisely for this reason that anti-tax sentiment was so strong in the immediate postwar period. Between 1945 and 1950, motivated by a mix of ideology and an instinct for electoral self-preservation, a coalition of congressional Republicans and some Democrats forced President Truman to make faster, deeper reductions in wartime taxes than he considered desirable. In 1948 Congress passed a tax cut over the president's veto, and in 1949 and the first half of 1950, it refused to raise rates again to make up for lost revenues. In the inital heat of the Korean emergency, Congress did agree to temporary tax hikes, but after 1951 it refused to accede to any further increases and, even before the conflict had officially ended, began to press for immediate elimination of all wartime taxes. Although he had been elected, in part, on a tax-cutting platform, President Eisenhower concluded that some of these emergency measures would have to be retained, at least for a while. In 1954 most, but not all, of the wartime increases were rolled back, and for the next eight years the structure of the nation's tax system remained essentially unchanged. Popular hostility and congressional resistance meant that, as one observer has described it, there was "a continuous force operating like gravity to push tax legislation in the direction of tax reduction, a force that [could] . . . really be overcome only by the abnormal revenue demands of severe national crisis."[32]

Instead of higher taxes, bigger defense budgets could have been financed through deficit spending. At the end of the Second World War the more liberal American interpreters of John Maynard Keynes had argued, in fact, that the federal government should be prepared to run sustained deficits in order to raise the level of aggregate demand and stimulate higher rates of economic growth. Faster growth would mean more jobs, a bigger economy, and, even if tax rates remained fixed, more revenues to fund federal programs of every variety, including defense. This approach, which the liberal Keynesians sought to have enshrined in the Full Employment Act of 1945, was subjected to withering attack by business groups and congressional conservatives. The bill's opponents argued that it would lead to inflation, an endless expansion in public works and social-welfare spending, and a dangerous increase in the federal government's ability to control the national economy. The choice, according to a 1946 report by the majority of the House Expenditures Committee, was "either private enterprise or statism."[33]

What emerged from the early postwar struggle over fiscal policy was a compromise, but one clearly weighted toward the "right wing of the Keynesian spectrum."[34] Recognition of the federal government's role in minimizing economic fluctuations increased and rigid insistence on balanced annual budgets faded. Still, during the late 1940s and the 1950s, deficit spending was generally considered to be acceptable only during periods of recession. Substantial, sustained deficits were simply out of the question in peacetime, even for purposes of funding a larger defense program.[35]

Albeit for somewhat different reasons, Presidents Truman and Eisenhower remained strongly committed to the goal of budgets balanced, if not each year, then at least over the course of the business cycle. Both feared that excessive deficits would lead to the politically damaging possibilities of inflation or, even worse, wage and price controls. Eisenhower also feared that controls, like ever higher taxes, would pose a positive threat to American liberty. Excessive government intervention in the economy, he believed, would "lead to statism and, therefore, slavery."[36]

It was these convictions that underlay Eisenhower's determination, manifest throughout his two terms in office, to prevent still greater increases in defense expenditures. Thus, when confronted in 1954 by arguments from the army that an emerging thermonuclear stalemate required a massive buildup in conventional forces (accompanied by higher taxes and, in all likelihood, economic controls), the president responded that, if such measures were truly necessary, "we might just as well stop any further talk about preserving a sound U.S. economy and proceed to transform ourselves forthwith into a garrison state."[37]

Manpower

In the early years of the Cold War the American state might well have armed itself with powers of compulsion far more extensive than those that it was eventually able to obtain. Indeed, if matters had rested entirely in the hands of the highest-ranking government officials, there can be little doubt that this is precisely what would have occurred. Between 1945 and 1952, the president, backed by his top military and civilian advisers, made repeated attempts (in 1945, 1947, 1948, and 1951) to gain acceptance for what was, in effect, a form of universal peacetime conscription. Each of the plans put forward from 1945 onward would have required that, upon reaching a specified age, all young men who satisfied minimal physical and intellectual requirements be required to undergo a period of basic military training, followed by a number of years of reserve duty. Such a system would have touched the life of virtually every male citizen, extracting from the general population anywhere from 750,000 to nearly 1 million new trainees annually.[38]

The advocates of univeral military training (UMT) argued that it was essential to preserving the nation's security. In contrast to their rejection of similar proposals after World War I, the willingness of the American people to submit in peacetime to compulsory military training would, it was argued, give clear evidence of their determination to resist future aggression.[39] If deterrence failed, the availability of a vast supply of ready reservists would permit the United States to multiply its fighting power virtually overnight, rather than after months or even years of painstaking mobilization and training. In the event of a surprise attack on the United States, especially one involving the use of atomic weapons, Secretary of War Robert Patterson advised Congress that UMT would "insure, as no other method would, that trained men would be near at hand to alleviate the effects of the initial attack . . . [W]ithout such preparedness annihilation may be our lot."[40]

Despite the urgency of these appeals, and the status and authority of those making them, the United States never adopted UMT. The defeat of universal conscription was the result, first of all, of strong, vocal resistance from an assortment of labor, education, farm, church, left-wing, and pacifist groups. The members of these organizations were motivated by a mix of self-interest and deeply held conviction. While they were themselves comparatively small (and, in some cases, espoused other views that put them on the fringes of American politics) these groups deployed arguments that resonated with a broad consensus about the appropriate limits of state power, and they were able, therefore, to exert an influence out of proportion to their numbers. Widespread compulsion, in the absence of a clear and present danger to the nation's survival, would, they argued, represent an excessive imposition on the liberties of a free people. Universal peacetime conscription (even if only for the purposes of military training) was dangerous, evil, and "un-American."[41]

If not for the fact that Congress, rather than the president, had the constitutionally mandated authority to "raise and support Armies," these arguments might have had little effect. But all proposals for adoption of conscription had first to be approved by the legislative branch, and it was here that universal training ran aground. Public opposition to UMT helped to bolster the resolve of those in Congress who were already inclined, for a variety of reasons, to vote against it. To Republican conservatives (especially those from the agricultural, and previously isolationist, midwestern states), universal conscription in peacetime was, as Senator Robert Taft of Ohio put it, "contrary to the whole concept of American liberty." "It is hard to think of any more drastic limitation of personal freedom," Taft declared, "than to permit the state to take boys from their homes, their education, or their chosen occupations and subject them for a year to the arbitrary direction of some military officer, and indoctrination courses prepared by some ideological bureau of the War Department."[42] Despite their general enthusiasm for military preparedness, many in the solidly Democratic South feared that a truly universal training program would promote "race mixing" and undermine segregation.[43] On the issue of mandatory military training, therefore, pacifists, socialists, and labor leaders made common cause with racists and antistatist conservatives.

Organized opposition helped to increase uncertainty about the political advisability of adopting universal military training among those in Congress who lacked either strong philosophical or clear-cut electoral reasons for voting against it. Despite opinion polls showing that a majority of the public would support such a measure, many members of Congress (including a majority of Republicans and a substantial number of Democrats) were deeply ambivalent about how to proceed. The outpouring of opposition that accompanied each effort to pass UMT suggested that the nationwide polls could be wrong (as they had been in the presidential election of 1948) or, at the very least, that they might not accurately reflect the climate of opinion in particular states and districts. Many in Congress seemed also to sense that support for UMT in answering a pollster's question would not necessarily translate into "support for the program when it involved sending relatives and friends to a year of military training."[44] The net effect of the various pressures for and against UMT is manifest in the pattern of congressional behavior. Rather than reject administration proposals openly, Congress repeatedly sought opportunities to avoid making a decision and, by so doing, succeeded eventually in killing universal training.

Were it not for two crises, by the early 1950s the United States would probably have placed its armed forces on an all-volunteer basis. In 1948, in response to a sharp deterioration in U.S.-Soviet relations, Congress approved a temporary, two-year reimposition of the draft to satisfy the military's immediate demands for manpower. Two years later Congress was set either to deny a presidential request for extended draft authority or to grant it only under conditions that would have given the legislative branch an effective veto over its future use. If the Korean War had not broken out (one day after the old law lapsed, without having been renewed), limited conscription would likely have died in June 1950. Instead "selective service" was hastily reinstated.[45]

Although it would remain in place for twenty-three years, the limited peacetime draft enjoyed only a decade of largely unquestioned acceptance. Conscription was tolerable during the 1950s in large part because it was used so sparingly, but its limited use also served over time to undermine its legitimacy. Over the course of the decade the numbers of men drafted, and the portion of those eligible who were actually compelled to serve, fell sharply.[46] By the beginning of the 1960s there was growing discomfort with the mounting inequities of limited conscription.[47] The Vietnam War intensified these concerns and reopened old questions about the acceptability of compulsion in anything short of a war for national survival. In 1973 the draft was abolished, and the United States reverted to its more traditional, voluntary means of obtaining men and women for military service.

DIRECTION

Supporting Industries

As the Cold War got under way, many observers believed that the federal government would have to take on a permanent, direct, and far-reaching role in planning and shaping the structure, and even the geographical distribution, of American industry. If, as was widely anticipated, the next world war began suddenly, and especially if it opened with atomic air attacks on the continental United States, advanced preparation for industrial mobilization might make the difference between defeat and victory. Estimating the emergency demand for critical products and materials (such as machine tools and steel) and, where necessary, expanding productive capacity in advance would speed the transition from peace to war. Taking steps to disperse factories and facilities would reduce the vulnerability of the nation's industrial base and improve the chances that war production could continue, even after an initial aerial assault. In the next war, wrote one pair of authors in the *Harvard Business Review*, "victory will be achieved by the nation that can best protect its industrial potential at the outset of hostilities and strike back speedily and vigorously with an expanding volume of planes and air missiles. . . . American industry must be able to discount the effects of an initial attack and still be in position to accelerate output to required peak levels immediately after the onset of hostilities."[48]

Despite the apparent importance of these goals, very little was actually done to achieve them. The National Security Act of 1947 called into existence a National Security Resources Board (NSRB) charged with coordinating military and industrial mobilization planning, but the Board was denied the authority necessary to carry out its mission. Many members of Congress were allergic to anything that smacked of New Deal–style economic planning, and, despite urgent appeals from the advocates of "preparedness" in his own administration, President Truman was careful to do nothing that might arouse congressional wrath. The NSRB survived for a time, because it did little and kept a low profile. Indeed, as historian Robert Cuff notes, "given the fierce hostility to 'planning' and 'big government' evident in postwar political debate, it is remarkable that the agency survived at all."[49]

Prior to the outbreak of the Korean War, government mobilization planners had few instruments with which to compel industry to follow their wishes. Efforts to win compliance through warnings and patriotic appeals accomplished very little. In the late 1940s NSRB studies identified a number of potentially crippling production "bottlenecks," areas in which emergency demand for basic metals, minerals, fuel, and electric power were virtually certain to exceed supply. Having gone this far, however, the board could do little more than exhort businessmen to invest in expanded productive capacity — capacity that might prove useless and costly if a national emergency failed to arise. Industry responded with a mix of indifference, suspicion, and outright hostility.

Government planners encountered similar obstacles when they set out to increase the geographical dispersal of the nation's industrial base and thus to minimize its vulnerability to atomic air attack. "Ours being a democratic Nation dedicated to the principles of free enterprise," noted one official document rather ruefully, "the Government can neither dictate nor finance . . . a large-scale change in the industrial pattern."[50] Instead, in the late 1940s, federal bureaucrats encouraged businessmen to locate new plants outside of existing industrial concentrations by pointing out (none too subtly) that both the factories and their owners would have a better chance of surviving a war if they did so. Even these rather mild suggestions aroused considerable controversy. The mere hint that the federal government might prefer plants to be built in certain areas of the country provoked howls of protest from those who feared that their cities and states would be slighted. In response to inquiries and complaints from governors, business groups, and members of Congress, the NSRB was forced to issue statements explaining that it was concerned only with dispersal of plants and facilities *within* regions rather than between them.[51] Efforts to promote dispersal through exhortation, like those intended to promote expansions in industrial capacity, had virtually no effect.

The Korean War led to a limited, and temporary, increase in the federal government's directive powers. Between 1950 and 1953 Congress agreed to grant executive-branch planners the authority to prepare numerical targets for output in over two hundred industries and to offer tax incentives to those who expanded capacity accordingly and agreed to locate new facilities outside already crowded urban areas. Presidential requests for authority to use federal dollars to build industrial facilities, on the other hand, were flatly denied.[52] The use of indirect financial inducements to private industry was, as one contemporary observer pointed out, a "typically American" approach to the problems of national industrial planning.[53] The goal was "to get expansion of productive capacity, to get it quickly . . . and to get it by encouraging business to take the initiative with a minimum of Government intervention and assistance."[54]

The Truman administration apparently intended to continue an active program of defense industrial planning indefinitely after the war had ended. What was envisioned was "not a one shot program . . . but one which must be pursued slowly and steadily over a long period of time" so as to mold the national economy into "an organized machinery for production which . . . can be marshalled for action in an orderly and disciplined way," and at a moment's notice.[55]

Not surprisingly, given his concerns about "statism," Dwight Eisenhower had very different ideas. Shortly after taking office, Eisenhower dissolved the NSRB and cut the staff and budget of the Office of Defense Mobilization, the Korean War industrial-planning agency. Work on new and more powerful planning techniques (most notably input-output models of the national economy that would have permitted more accurate estimates of wartime needs and peacetime production targets) was curtailed.[56] Responding to arguments that wartime practices involved "granting favors to a selected group of taxpayers, [thereby] unfairly discriminating against the remainder," the administration moved quickly to constrict the use of tax incentives for planning purposes. The applications of such instruments was "dangerous," warned Treasury Secretary George Humphrey, because "artificial stimulants [could] well become artificial controls." Government efforts to shape the evolution of the nation's economy were not "the American way."[57] As fewer applicants received tax breaks, complaints that the government was discriminating between industries and, within industries, between firms, grew in intensity. By the end of the 1950s, urged on by Congress, the executive branch had all but abandoned its efforts at industrial planning.

The reasons for this shift cannot be explained purely in terms of strategic logic. Over the course of the 1950s, as both Soviet and American nuclear capabilities grew, U.S. military planners began to raise their estimates of the destructiveness of a future war and to lower their estimates of its duration. In a short war, forces-in-being would be decisive, and resources expended on prewar mobilization planning would most likely turn out to have been wasted. As the United States moved away from preparations for protracted combat and toward a strategy of deterrence, the importance of industrial mobilization planning (and preparations for the mass mobilization of manpower) appeared to dwindle. As with UMT, however, the rejection of the necessary power-creating mechanisms *preceded*, and helped to promote, the evolution of strategy and was not simply its result. Ideological, institutional, and interest-based constraints tended to limit the directive powers of the American state, just as they had served to constrict its capacity for extraction.

Arms and Research

Prior to the Second World War (as prior to the First), the federal government relied heavily on its own laboratories and arsenals for the development and production of weapons and other military systems.[58] As American entry into the conflict began to seem more likely, some in the Roosevelt administration urged that existing federal facilities be expanded, new ones built, and privately owned factories and research centers requisitioned and placed under direct state control. These proposals met with predictable objections from industry representatives, who warned that the deepening world crisis might give the New Dealers "a golden opportunity to do away with the profit system and the Constitution at one fell swoop."[59]

The idea of a vastly extended system of government-owned and -operated facilities for the design and production of weapons was quickly abandoned. Instead, although it did finance a good portion of the necessary expansion in capacity, the government left most of the management of production, and much of the conduct of research, in private hands. Rather than being drafted, industrialists, workers, and scientists were hired by the state and paid for their efforts. The advice of Secretary of War Henry Stimson was amply heeded: "If you are going to try to go to war, or to prepare for war, in a capitalist country, you have got to let business make money out of the process or business won't work."[60]

In all, as Alan Brinkley notes, the United States "approached the task of organizing the economy for war in a way that suggested a degree of antistatism."[61] In addition to placing heavy reliance on private institutions for the design and manufacture of arms, the federal government was slow to develop the administrative capacity to manage the production effort and control the nation's economy. Even after December 1941 there was considerable resistance to building a single, central mobilization agency, endowed with the necessary directive powers. Both as a matter of necessity, and to assuage the anxieties of the business community, the most important wartime agencies also tended to be staffed by "dollar-a-year men," executives on loan from industry and "implacably hostile to anything that smacked of centralized planning and considered it their mission not only to expedite war mobilization but to resist any attempt to make the war the occasion for the permanent expansion of the state."[62]

The same considerations that combined to create the wartime contract system tended to promote its persistence once the hot war had ended and the Cold War began. In 1940, with war fast approaching, mobilizing science and industry "in place" had seemed the most efficient means of redirecting the nation's resources toward the creation of military power. After 1945 (and especially after 1950), with an indefinite period of partial mobilization lying ahead, contracts still offered considerable advantages to all parties. Rather than trying to build and manage its own facilities and to recruit the best available personnel to work in them, government could tap the expertise of industrialists and civilian scientists, shifting resources among them as the circumstances of the evolving competition with the Soviet Union appeared to demand. And, instead of being compelled to submit to the rigors and restrictions of government service, private citizens could do well by doing good, contributing to the nation's defense while at the same time pursuing their own research agendas or earning handsome profits. Reliance on contracts was, in the words of one contemporary enthusiast, "pleasing both [to] those who want a small government and those who want big new governmental programs . . . [G]iven the demand for services and for the continuation of a 'free enterprise' system [it is] probably essential."[63]

Any attempt, after the Second World War, to shift back to a more heavily state-owned and -managed system for the development and production of arms would have met with strong opposition from both industry and academe. In the early years of the Cold War, Congress kept a watchful and disapproving eye out for indications that the executive branch was expanding federal facilities at the expense of private entities. But there was very little inclination, in any quarter, to do anything of the kind. In the public mind, as well as in the minds of those government officials who managed and participated in it, the wartime mobilization of civilian scientists and private industry was almost universally regarded as an outstanding success. After all, it was this unique, quasi-private system that had mass-produced the weapons, and made the critical technological breakthroughs, that together had helped to defeat the Axis powers. With the United States now confronting a new threat to its security, there seemed little reason to depart from a winning formula.[64]

In addition to its presumed benefits for the nation as a whole (and its undeniable benefits for certain groups), the contract system enjoyed one final, intangible advantage. Arrangements under which the government paid private entities to do its research and build its weapons "resonated symbolically to the culture of the marketplace"; they were compatible with prevailing beliefs about the appropriate economic role of the state in a way that no other means of mobilizing the nation's scientific and industrial resources could possibly have been.[65] Symbolically as well as in practice, and in the Cold War as in World War II, the use of contracts was America's answer to the more centralized, "top-down," and overtly statist power-creating programs of its totalitarian rivals. Whatever its dangers, deficiencies, and disadvantages, most Americans preferred a "contract state" to a garrison state.[66]

Impact and Aftermath

The onset of the Cold War could easily have led to the creation of a sizeable state sector for the development and production of arms, to a centrally directed defense industrial policy aimed at shaping the composition and geographical distribution of the nation's industrial base, and to much higher levels of extraction of both money and manpower. That none of these emerged has more to do with the character of the American domestic regime than with the nature of the international environment. The advent of the superpower rivalry and the invention of nuclear weapons created pressures for a considerable expansion in the peacetime powers of the American state. During the formative, opening stages of the Cold War, however, these pressures were met by countervailing, antistatist influences. The power-creating institutions put into place in the 1940s and 1950s can best be understood as the product of a collision between these two sets of forces. Let me close with some brief, speculative comments on the impact of these institutions, both on the United States and on the outcome of the Cold War.

A power-creating program that constrained extraction, constricted the scope of the state's directive activities, and relied heavily on private institutions for the performance of key functions proved to be quite sustainable. Persistent efforts to extract even more money and manpower, or to impose a higher degree of centralized control over the American economy, would have stimulated greater domestic political resistance and might, in the long run, have undermined public support for containment. On the other hand, the widespread use of contracts helped to create groups in American society with a strong interest in "staying the course," and, of course, in the continuation of the substantial expenditures necessary to do so.

The program of power creation necessary to support a military strategy of flexible response probably also had fewer distorting internal effects than the most likely alternatives. Although it is impossible to say with certainty, it seems plausible that even bigger budgets, and the stronger central planning effort necessary to prepare the United States for all-out conventional or nuclear war, would have had a greater and more damaging impact on the American economy. The implications for the nation's political life of a state endowed with far greater directive and extractive powers are uncertain, but potentially troubling. Some of the advocates of universal military training clearly hoped that a year of mandatory "political education" would help to inculcate patriotism and obedience to authority, and to inoculate American youth against dangerous ideas and subversive ideologies. Whether such training would have led to "regimentation" (as the opponents of UMT feared) or to cynicism and rebellion cannot be known.

As regards external effects: contrary to the warnings of those who favored the more ambitious alternatives, American strategy and the force posture that accompanied it proved sufficient to deter a war with the Soviet Union. Over time, the superior performance of a decentralized, contract-based mechanism for developing new military technologies appears also to have placed a significant strain on the Soviet Union. In trying to keep pace with the more flexible and innovative American system, Soviet planners distorted and overburdened their economy, thereby contributing to its eventual collapse.[67] In the long run, the "weak" American state proved to be more than a match for its "strong" Soviet counterpart.

Ironically, the same antistatist influences that helped to shape and constrain America's power-creating institutions at the outset of the Cold War may be contributing to their longevity now that the Soviet Union is gone and the Cold War is over. However large and wasteful they may seem to their critics, the mechanisms put into place half a century ago do not appear to weigh very heavily on American society or on the American economy. A state that extracted more money and manpower, and which involved itself more directly in production and industrial planning, would probably find itself subject to much stronger pressures for contraction and retrenchment.

Notes

1. Throughout this paper I will use the term "American state" to refer to the various agencies and organizations included within, or under the direct control of, the executive branch of the federal government.

2. Daniel Deudney, "The Philadelphian System: Sovereignty, Arms Control, and Balance of Power in the American-States Union, circa 1787–1861," *International Organization* 49, no. 2 (1995): 207.

3. Regarding the bemused reactions of European observers to American political arrangements, see Stephen Skowronek, *Building a New American State: The Expansion of National Administrative Capacities, 1877–1920* (New York: Cambridge University Press, 1982), 5–8. See also the discussion in J. P. Nettl, "The State as a Conceptual Variable," *World Politics* 20, no. 4 (1968): 559–92. On the movement from confederation to federal republic and the struggle over how best both to expand and to contain the powers of the central state, see Gordon S. Wood, *The Creation of the American Republic, 1776–1787* (New York: W. W. Norton, 1969), especially 469–564; Forrest McDonald, *Novus Ordo Seclorum: The Intellectual Origins of the Constitution* (Lawrence: University of Kansas Press, 1985); Bernard Bailyn, *The Ideological Origins of the American Revolution* (Cambridge: Harvard University Press, 1992), 321–79; Herbert J. Storing, *What the Anti-Federalists Were For: The Political Thought of the Opponents of the Constitution* (Chicago: University of Chicago Press, 1981).

4. Bailyn, *Ideological Origins*, 58–59.

5. See the discussion in Samuel P. Huntington, *American Politics: The Promise of Disharmony* (Cambridge: Harvard University Press, 1981), 33 and 39.

6. Seymour Martin Lipset, *American Exceptionalism: A Double-Edged Sword* (New York: W. W. Norton, 1996), 39.

7. Quoted in *ibid.*, 32. The uniformity of American liberalism is the theme of Louis Hartz, *The Liberal Tradition in America* (New York: Harcourt, Brace, 1955).

8. The persistent American suspicion of, and resistance to, a strong central gov-

ernment in the twentieth century is the theme of Barry D. Karl, *The Uneasy State: The United States from 1915 to 1945* (Chicago: University of Chicago Press, 1983). Regarding the response to industrialism, see, in addition to Skowronek, *New American State*; Martin J. Sklar, *The Corporate Reconstruction of American Capitalism, 1890–1916* (New York: Cambridge University Press, 1988). Sklar concludes that the emergence of "regulatory corporate liberalism" (as compared to a system of more extensive and intrusive government economic management) was due primarily to the "prevalent antistatism of all major classes and strata" in American society. *Ibid.*, 438. See also Gary G. Hamilton and John R. Sutton, "The Problem of Control in the Weak State: Domination in the United States, 1880–1920," *Theory and Society* 18 (1989): 1–46. On the role of American institutions and political culture in shaping the mobilization for both world wars, see Robert Cuff, "American Mobilization for Total War, 1917–45: Political Culture vs. Bureaucratic Administration," in *Mobilization for Total War: The Canadian, American and British Experience*, ed. N. F. Dreisziger (Waterloo, Canada: Wilfrid Laurier University Press, 1981), 73–86. For more on the First World War, see Cuff, "Herbert Hoover, The Ideology of Voluntarism and War Organization during the Great War," *Journal of American History* 64, no. 2 (1977): 358–72; and *The War Industries Board: Business-Government Relations during World War I* (Baltimore: Johns Hopkins University Press, 1973). On the "failed search" undertaken in the period from 1917 to 1933 to find a way of "meeting the needs for coordination and control without creating a welfare, regulatory, or military state," see Ellis W. Hawley, *The Great War and the Search for a Modern Order* (New York: St. Martin's Press, 1979); quote from page 227. On the role of antistatism in checking and shaping the New Deal, see Alan Brinkley, *The End of Reform: New Deal Liberalism in Recession and War* (New York: Knopf, 1995); also James Holt, "The New Deal and the American Anti-Statist Tradition," in *The New Deal: The National Level*, ed. John Braeman (Columbus: Ohio State University Press, 1975), 27–49. On the role of American institutions and ideology in shaping the mobilization for the Second World War, see John Morton Blum, *V Was for Victory: Politics and American Culture during World War II* (New York: Harcourt Brace Jovanovich, 1976); Robert O'Neill, *A Democracy at War* (New York: Free Press, 1995). Similar dynamics are evident in more recent times as well. On the role of the American "anti-statist tradition" in blocking implementation of a national industrial policy in the 1970s and 1980s, see William S. Dietrich, *In the Shadow of the Rising Sun: The Political Roots of American Economic Decline* (University Park: Pennsylvania State University Press, 1991), especially 146–243. Similarly, Otis L. Graham Jr. blames what he calls "an excess of Madisonian balance" for American inaction in this regard. See Graham, *Losing Time: The Industrial Policy Debate* (Cambridge: Harvard University Press, 1992); quote from p. 2. On the role of antistatist rhetoric (and the separation of powers) in defeating recent efforts to create a national health insurance system, see Theda Skocpol, *Boomerang: Clinton's Health Security Effort and the Turn against Government in U.S. Politics* (New York: W. W. Norton, 1996), especially 133–72.

9. See Alan T. Peacock and Jack Wiseman, *The Growth of Public Expenditure in the United Kingdom* (Princeton: Princeton University Press, 1961); Bruce D. Porter, *War and the Rise of the State: The Military Foundations of Modern Politics* (New York: Free Press, 1994).

10. For a useful overview of these developments, see Porter, *War*, 1–147.

11. Skowronek, *New American State*, 20. See also the discussion in Samuel P. Huntington, *Political Order in Changing Societies* (New Haven: Yale University Press, 1968), 93–139.

12. Regarding the implications for the early republic of a benign external environment, see Aristide Zolberg, "International Engagement and American Democracy: A Comparative Perspective," in this volume.

13. On the effects and aftermath of the Civil War, see Richard Franklin Bensel, *Yankee Leviathan: The Origins of Central State Authority in America, 1859–1877* (New York: Cambridge University Press, 1990). Regarding the First World War, see, in addition to the works by Cuff and Karl, David Kennedy, *Over Here: The First World War and American Society* (New York: Oxford University Press, 1980).

14. Harry S. Truman, "Address before a Joint Session of the Congress on Universal Military Training, October 23, 1945," in *Public Papers of the Presidents of the United States (1945)* (Washington: U.S. Government Printing Office, 1961), 405. The emergence of these anxieties is a central theme in Michael Sherry, *Preparing for the Next War: American Plans for Postwar Defense, 1941–1945* (New Haven: Yale University Press, 1977).

15. Richard Pollenberg, *War and Society: The United States 1941–1945* (New York: Lippincott, 1972), 193.

16. Karl, *Uneasy State*, 155–81.

17. Brinkley, *End of Reform*, 17.

18. *Ibid.*, 147. On the public's eagerness to shed controls, see Jack Stokes Ballard, *The Shock of Peace: Military and Economic Demobilization after World War II* (Washington: University Press of America, 1983), 155–92.

19. Robert Griffith, "Forging America's Postwar Order: Domestic Politics and Political Economy in the Age of Truman," in *The Truman Presidency*, ed. Michael J. Lacey (New York: Cambridge University Press, 1989), 67.

20. *Ibid.*, 85. For a discussion of postwar business attitudes on fiscal policy and economic planning, see Robert M. Collins, *The Business Response to Keynes, 1929–1964* (New York: Columbia University Press, 1981), 77–112. See also Ira Katznelson and Bruce Pietrykowski, "Rebuilding the American State: Evidence from the 1940s," *Studies in American Political Development* 5 (Fall 1991): 301–39. Regarding the demise of postwar proposals for greatly expanded social programs, see Edwin Amenta and Theda Skocpol, "Redefining the New Deal: World War II and the Development of Social Provision in the United States," in *The Politics of Social Policy in the United States*, ed. Margaret Weir, Ann Shola Orloff, and Theda Skocpol (Princeton: Princeton University Press, 1988), 81–122.

21. See Theodore Rosenof, "Freedom, Planning, and Totalitarianism: The Reception of F. A. Hayek's *Road to Serfdom*," *Canadian Review of American Studies* 5, no. 2 (1974): 149–65.

22. Brinkley, *End of Reform*, 160. For an excellent overview of these intellectual trends, see *ibid.*, 137–74.

23. Harold Lasswell, "The Universal Peril: Perpetual Crisis and the Garrison-Prison State," in *Perspectives on a Troubled Decade: Science, Philosophy, and Religion, 1939–1949*, ed. Lyman Bryson, Louis Finkelstein, and R. M. MacIver (New York: Harper, 1950), 325.

24. Hanson Baldwin, *The Price of Power* (New York: Harper, 1947), 18–20.

25. On "punctuated equilibrium" as a metaphor for institutional evolution, see Stephen D. Krasner, "Approaches to the State: Alternative Conceptions and Historical Dynamics," *Comparative Politics* 16, no. 2 (1984): 223–46.

26. Although he uses it in a somewhat different way, I have borrowed this phrase from Alan S. Milward, *War, Economy and Society, 1939–1945* (Berkeley: University of California Press, 1979), 19–23.

27. For all that has been written about its various elements and stages, there is as yet no definitive account of the evolution of American military strategy over the course of the Cold War. For useful general introductions, see Russell F. Weigley, *The American Way of War* (Bloomington: Indiana University Press, 1973), 363–477; Allan R. Millett and Peter Maslowski, *For the Common Defense* (New York: Free Press, 1994), 494–646. Although it covers a broad span of time, as its title suggests, Lawrence Freedman, *The Evolution of Nuclear Strategy* (London: St. Martin's Press, 1981) deals primarily with nuclear issues and is mainly a work of intellectual history rather than a study of actual war plans. Fred Kaplan, *The Wizards of Armageddon* (New York: Touchstone, 1983) has similar limitations. For an authoritative discussion of the early stages in the development of U.S. nuclear strategy see Samuel R. Williamson Jr., and Steven L. Rearden, *The Origins of U.S. Nuclear Strategy, 1945– 1953* (New York: St. Martin's Press, 1993). Samuel Huntington, *The Common Defense* (New York: Columbia University Press, 1961), 25–112, contains what is still among the best overviews of the evolution of U.S. military strategy during the period 1945–60. Regarding the emergence of "flexible response," see John Lewis Gaddis, *Strategies of Containment* (New York: Oxford University Press, 1982), 198–236. See also Jane E. Stromseth, *The Origins of Flexible Response* (London: Macmillan, 1988).

28. For a discussion of this possibility, which was taken quite seriously at the time, see Marc Trachtenberg's essay, "'A Wasting Asset': American Strategy and the Shifting Nuclear Balance, 1949–1954," in Trachtenberg, *History and Strategy* (Princeton: Princeton University Press, 1991), 100–52.

29. On the possible implications of a "nuclear stalemate," see, for example, Hanson Baldwin, "Strategy for Two Atomic Worlds," *Foreign Affairs* 28, no. 3 (1950): 386–97.

30. For early Soviet thinking on the conduct of nuclear war, see Herbert S. Dinerstein, *War and the Soviet Union* (New York: Praeger, 1958); Raymond L. Garthoff, *Soviet Strategy in the Nuclear Age* (New York: Praeger, 1958). Regarding the possibility of a nonnuclear superpower war, see Dale R. Herspring, *The Soviet High Command, 1967–1989* (Princeton: Princeton University Press, 1990), 119–78.

31. Over the course of the 1950s, U.S. strategists came increasingly to focus on *deterring* an all-out nuclear war, rather than preparing to fight and win one. Not surprisingly, in the 1950s it was the army, along with the industrial mobilization planners, that had the greatest interest in preparing for a protracted, conventional superpower war. Both of these notions had a brief revival in the early 1980s but were rejected for the same reasons that made them unacceptable in the 1950s.

32. John F. Witte, *The Politics and Development of the Federal Income Tax* (Madison: University of Wisconsin Press, 1985), 175. For useful treatments of the postwar period, see, in addition, A. E. Holmans, *United States Fiscal Policy, 1945–1959* (Ox-

ford: Oxford University Press, 1961); W. Elliot Brownlee, ed., *Funding the Modern American State, 1941–1995* (New York: Cambridge University Press, 1996); Ronald F. King, *Money, Time, and Politics* (New Haven: Yale University Press, 1993).

33. Quoted in Stephen K. Bailey, *Congress Makes a Law: The Story behind the Employment Act of 1946* (New York: Columbia University Press, 1950), 171.

34. Collins, *Business Response*, 16.

35. Regarding the emergence of what has been called "commercial Keynesianism," see, in addition to Collins, Herbert Stein, *The Fiscal Revolution in America* (Washington: American Enterprise Institute, 1990). Also Margaret Weir, "Ideas and Politics: The Acceptance of Keynesianism in Britain and the United States," in *The Political Power of Economic Ideas: Keynesianism across Nations*, ed. Peter A. Hall (Princeton: Princeton University Press, 1989), 53–86.

36. See the entry for January 14, 1949, in Robert H. Ferrell, ed., *The Eisenhower Diaries* (New York: W. W. Norton, 1981), 153.

37. Minutes of 204th National Security Council Meeting, June 24, 1954, in *Foreign Relations of the United States, 1952–1954*, vol. 2 (Washington: U.S. Government Printing Office, 1984), 689. Eisenhower's refusal to raise defense spending by 50 percent, as many experts demanded after the 1957 Sputnik crisis, was rooted in similar concerns. See the discussion in Minutes of the 343d Meeting of the National Security Council, November 7, 1957, and Minutes of the 346th Meeting of the National Security Council, November 22, 1957, in *Foreign Relations of the United States, 1955–1957*, vol. 19 (Washington: U.S. Government Printing Office, 1990), 632 and 693–694.

38. See President's Advisory Commission on Universal Training, *A Program for National Security* (Washington: U.S. Government Printing Office, 1947), 52–53.

39. "The basic purpose of universal military training," according to War Department planners, was to "encourage the other world powers to believe that the United States is not only desirous but is prepared to enforce its determination to outlaw aggression. War Department, "Notes on Universal Military Training," n.d. (September 1945), Harry S. Truman Library, President's Secretary's Files, Box 146, Subject File: Agencies, Military Training.

40. See statement of Secretary of War Robert P. Patterson in *Universal Military Training: Hearings before the House Committee on Military Affairs*, 79th Congr., 1st sess., 1945, 5.

41. The material interests of professional educators, farmers, and unionists are easiest to discern. Colleges and universities relied on a steady stream of high school graduates, a stream that would be interrupted, and perhaps thinned, by an intervening period of mandatory military training. Farmers depended on the labor of their sons. Having just come through a war in which the federal government had contemplated drafting workers and assigning them to work in particular industries, union leaders were understandably leery of any kind of universal obligation to the state. Church leaders feared for the souls of the young. Pacifists worried about militarism at home and war abroad. The left objected to any measures that might bring the United States closer to confrontation with the Soviet Union. For a concise summary of the views of these groups, see John M. Swomley Jr., "A Study of the Universal Military Training Campaign, 1944–1952" (Ph.D. diss., University of Colorado, 1959), 254–85.

42. Quoted in Lynn Eden, "Capitalist Conflict and the State: The Making of United States Military Policy in 1948," in *Statemaking and Social Movements: Essays in History and Theory*, ed. Charles Bright and Susan Harding (Ann Arbor: University of Michigan Press, 1984), 245.

43. Robert David Ward, "The Movement for Universal Military Training in the United States, 1942–1952," (Ph.D. diss., University of North Carolina, 1957), 461.

44. Perry McCoy Smith, *The Air Force Plans for Peace, 1943–45* (Baltimore: Johns Hopkins University Press, 1970), 96.

45. On these events see James M. Gerhardt, *The Draft and Public Policy: Issues in Military Manpower Procurement, 1945–1970* (Columbus: Ohio State University Press, 1971), 118–21; George Q. Flynn, *The Draft, 1940–1973* (Lawrence: University of Kansas Press, 1993), 107–13.

46. By the early 1960s less than 10 percent of active-duty military personnel were draftees, and less than one-half of 1 percent of all men between the ages of eighteen and twenty-six were being drafted. See *Review of the Administration and Operation of the Selective Service System: Hearings before the House Armed Services Committee*, 89th Congr., 2nd sess., 1966, 10001.

47. "Had it not been for the Vietnam War," writes sociologist David Segal, "conscription might have been phased out in the United States a decade earlier than it was." *Recruiting for Uncle Sam: Citizenship and Military Manpower Policy* (Lawrence: University Press of Kansas, 1989), 34.

48. See, for example, Sidney M. Robbins and Thomas E. Murphy, "Industrial Preparedness," *Harvard Business Review* 26, no. 3 (1948): 329–53. Thomas J. Hargrave, "A Blueprint for Industrial Mobilization," *Dun's Review*, June 1948, 11–14, 64, 68–74, 80. William S. Friedman, "Industrial Planning: A MUST for Security," *Air Force*, October 1949, 24–27, 47.

49. Robert Cuff, "From the Controlled Materials Plan to the Defense Materials System, 1942–1953," *Military Affairs* 51, no. 1 (1987): 3. For more on the origins and fate of the NSRB, see Louis C. Hunter, *Economic Mobilization Planning and National Security (1947–1953)* (Washington: Industrial College of the Armed Forces, 1954); Harry Yoshpe, *The National Security Resources Board 1947–53: A Case Study in Peacetime Mobilization Planning* (Washington: Executive Office of the President, 1953); Robert Cuff, "Ferdinand Eberstadt, the National Security Resources Board, and the Search for Integrated Mobilization Planning, 1947–1948," *Public Historian* 7, no. 4 (1985): 37–52.

50. National Security Resources Board, *National Security Factors in Industrial Location* (Washington: NSRB, 1948), 12.

51. Thus, as President Truman explained, "Our program . . . does not tell any industry or individual where to locate. . . . It merely encourages the spacing of *new* defense and defense-supporting industries *a few miles apart*. . . . This is a commonsense program which serves the national security in the atomic age and is consistent with the American system of competitive free enterprise." See "The President's News Conference, August 23, 1951," in *Public Papers of the Presidents: Harry S. Truman (1951)* (Washington: U.S. Government Printing Office, 1965), 484.

52. See "Proposed Amendments to the Defense Production Act," November 14, 1951, RG 304, entry 31, box 79, file C3-5. National Archives.

53. See Lt. Commander Joseph Z. Redya, "Industrial Mobilization in the U.S.," *U.S. Naval Institute Proceedings*, October 1953, 1065–75.

54. W. H. Harrison (Defense Production Administrator) to Stuart Symington (Director, NSRB), March 5, 1951, RG 304, entry 31, box 113, file 20-8.

55. Bureau of the Budget, "Organization for 'Mobilization Base' Activities," n.d. (Fall 1952?), RG 51, entry 51.26, box 25, file 96, National Archives, pp. 1–2.

56. See Sterling Green, "Here's Where War Mobilization Stands," *Nation's Business*, May 1954, 48–54; Cuff, 5.

57. Secretary of the Treasury George Humphrey, Statement before the Subcommittee on Legal and Monetary Affairs of the House Government Operations Committee, July 18, 1955, In RG 51, entry 51.26, box 23, file 88, National Archives, pp. 1–2.

58. For useful overviews of pre–World War II procurement patterns and practices, see the essays in Benjamin Franklin Cooling, ed., *War, Business, and American Society* (Port Washington, N.Y.: Kennikat Press, 1977); also, Michael Anton Evanchik, "A Transaction Cost Analysis of Defense Contracting" (Ph.D. diss., University of Washington, 1989).

59. Editorial in the April 22, 1939, edition of *Iron Age* (the journal of the iron and steel industry). Quoted in Roland N. Stromberg, "American Business and the Approach of War, 1935–1941," *Journal of Economic History* 13, no. 1 (1953): 69.

60. Entry in Stimson's diary dated August 26, 1940. Quoted in Paul A. C. Koistinen, *The Hammer and the Sword: Labor, the Military and Industrial Mobilization, 1920–1945* (New York: Arno Press, 1979), 580. Regarding the wartime mobilization, see Gregory Hooks, *Forging the Military-Industrial Complex: World War II's Battle of the Potomac* (Urbana: University of Illinois Press, 1991). See also Bartholomew H. Sparrow, *From the Outside In: World War II and the American State* (Princeton: Princeton University Press, 1996), especially 161–257. On the financing of industrial expansion, see George Vincent Sweeting, "Building the Arsenal of Democracy: The Government's Role in Expansion of Industrial Capacity, 1940 to 1945" (Ph.D diss., Columbia University, 1994).

61. Alan Brinkley, "The New Deal and the Idea of the State," in *The Rise and Fall of the New Deal Order, 1930–1980*, ed. Steve Fraser and Gary Gerstel (Princeton: Princeton University Press, 1989), 102.

62. *Ibid.*, 103.

63. Victor K. Heyman, "Government by Contract: Boon or Boner?" *Public Administration Review* 21, no. 2 (1961): 61.

64. On the transition from "hot" to "cold" war procurement, see Clarence H. Danhof, *Government Contracting and Technological Change* (Washington: Brookings Institution, 1968). Also Allen Kaufman, "In the Procurement Officer We Trust: Constitutional Norms, Air Force Procurement and Industrial Organization, 1938–1948," (Defense and Arms Control Studies Program, working paper, Massachusetts Institute of Technology, 1996).

65. Larry Owens, "The Struggle to Manage Science in the Second World War: Vannevar Bush and the Office of Scientific Research and Development" (University of Massachusetts, Amherst, October 12, 1993, mimeographed), 5.

66. On the "contract state," see H. L. Nieburg, *In the Name of Science* (Chicago: Quadrangle Paperback, 1970), 184–99.

67. See Aaron L. Friedberg, "Science, the Cold War, and the American State," *Diplomatic History* 20, no. 1 (1996): 107–18.

Ten

Limited Wars and the Attenuation of the State: Soldiers, Money, and Political Communication in World War II, Korea, and Vietnam

BARTHOLOMEW H. SPARROW

IN THE FALL of 1997, the U.S. Navy canceled plans to build a remote-operated "arsenal ship" designed to be stationed off the shore of any conflict area and capable of holding and firing some five hundred missiles. Despite the cancellation, the very concept of the arsenal ship illustrates two important developments evident since the Second World War: the emergence of American hegemony and the declining reliance of the American military on personnel for the conduct of warfare.

Not only does the United States after the Cold War have virtually complete command of the oceans, but its capacity to project force extends beyond the blue water to the brown water of littoral regions. As the lone superpower, little happens any place in the world where the U.S. government cannot project force, should it so wish. But wars of attrition have become increasingly less palatable. The military plans and participates in conflicts that involve minimal American casualties (e.g., the invasion of Panama, the invasion of Somalia, the police action in Kosovo), and it is able to do so because of the technological sophistication and training possessed by, and affordable to, the U.S. armed forces. It may well be that for the United States, wars of attrition, not to mention total wars, have become things of the past.

Both the United States' emergence as sole superpower and its reluctance to incur war casualties are legacies of changes that took place between the early 1940s and early 1970s. After World War II, the United States sought to have a "preponderance of power," the ability to get its way "eighty-five percent of the time," as President Harry Truman put it.[1] The Second World War and the onset of the Cold War demanded that the United States become a full-time military power. Policymakers invested heavily in the armed forces, and the United States has been (and remains) distinguished among its OECD counterparts for both its absolute and relative levels of defense spending.[2] The Soviet Union was outmatched, ultimately unable to compete with the United States.

Yet even amid the global struggle against Marxism-Leninism, the U.S. government avoided direct confrontations with the Soviet Union and the People's Republic of China, in view of the formidable nuclear and conventional arsenals available on each side. Wars were restricted with respect to means (waged without nuclear weapons and without a complete commitment of armed forces), geographic scope (not waged on superpowers' homelands), and extent to which individuals and organizations had to be mobilized.[3] The Cold War, despite the rhetoric of a twilight struggle for survival, manifested military constraint. In its aftermath, the United States has similarly refrained from engaging in wars of attrition (e.g., the Persian Gulf War, the intervention in the Balkans). In short, the United States' position as a global hegemon since the Second World War—first in a bipolar world and now in a unipolar world—has resulted in the U.S. government conducting limited wars in lieu of total (or absolute) wars requiring extensive personal and material sacrifices.

The reality of fighting limited wars set two mutually reinforcing dynamics into play, however, dynamics with implications for the legitimacy of and public trust in the U.S. government. One is that policymakers, for fear of political repercussions, have been reluctant to ask much of the public when America goes to war. This has been the case since immediately after World War II, when the Truman administration was faced with widespread outcry over the delay in bringing U.S. personnel home. The troops could not be brought back fast enough, even if the quick demobilization compromised the United States' postwar strategic position.[4] In Korea and Vietnam, too, it could be argued that domestic political constraints limited the United States' strategic options.

The other dynamic is that Americans, not being called upon to fight and not being asked to sacrifice their standards of living for wars of ambiguous purpose and ambiguous morality, have become more and more estranged from their national government. Between World War II and the end of the Vietnam War there was been a marked decline in Americans' approval of their government. As survey data indicate, and as the evidence below suggests, the public has become increasingly distrustful of politicians, the national government, and the political process.[5]

These two mutually reinforcing trends, both of which derive from the United States' pursuit of limited warfare, have resulted in *an attenuation of the state*. State power does not derive simply from coercive force, as students of international relations recognize, but also and ultimately from economic strength, governmental competence, and political stability.[6] Democratic government fundamentally depends on the consent of the governed; popular consent to military action and service in the military—where individual lives are at stake—is not a given. As Robert Osgood observes, "A nation's ability to sustain a defense program is not only a matter of the gross national product, per capita income, and the other objective criteria of economic strength but, just as much, *a reflection of what the citizenry, its political representatives, and government officials are willing to sacrifice in terms of competing values* for the sake of a particular national strategy."[7]

For it is the participation of societal actors in governmental activity that gives U.S. public policy and government its robustness, even as the fact of such formal or informal participation by private actors in government operations may obscure the "stateness" of the American political system. This political authority, which may be exercised by governmental and societal actors operating in tandem, involves not only (the tangible) relations of material resources but also (and intangibly) citizens' affect for and expectations of their government.[8]

Over the course of the postwar era, the voluntary ties between the American public and the U.S. government reveal a loss of the willingness of citizens to sacrifice, a deterioration of popular consent, and growing doubts with respect to governmental competence and political stability. As the unpopularity of U.S. military action in Korea, and then Vietnam, grew, the commitment of Americans to their government decreased. Such decay in the public's affect for the U.S. government, if genuine, suggests a profound weakness on the part of the postwar American state: a breakdown of the consent of the governed — of the sinews connecting the electorate with the government — and an undermining of the potential capacity of the government itself.[9]

Remarkably, however, leading students of U.S. civil-military relations, such as Morris Janowitz, Samuel Huntington, Robert Osgood, and Hans Morgenthau, did not and do not look at the linkage between the United States' conduct of limited warfare and the declining legitimacy of the American state. These analysts write about the theory of limited war, the need for domestic support and coalition building, and the protests against the involvement in Korea and Vietnam, but omit a discussion of the possible relationship between the waning popular support for the U.S. government and the fact that the United States has had to fight limited wars for the last several decades.[10]

One reason why international relations scholars (with the exception of Stephen Peter Rosen) overlook how the conduct of limited war breeds a mistrust of and distancing from government could be the difficulty of assessing and appraising "consent" or "legitimacy." There may be great difference between the *consent* of citizens, just short of the level of actual endorsement or voluntary activity, and actual *hostility*, just below the threshold of active protest, for instance, even though they may appear indistinguishable to the outside observer. There may also be many reasons for apparent consent and compliance besides actual agreement with or endorsement of governmental policies or politicians' behavior.[11] Political scientists and public opinion polls have not been very successful at grappling with the notion of legitimacy, as the sudden, unexpected collapse of Eastern Europe and the Soviet Union made apparent.

Nor does more recent work by Joseph Nye, Philip Zalikow, and David King on Americans' waning trust in government connect limited wars with the indications of the public's rising mistrust of the federal government since the Second World War.[12] Nye and his colleagues do make the argument that World War II "was a success story for government," but that the "wartime success of government led to too much confidence in government, overexpectations, and misapplication of the war analogy to other issues," which in turn led to a steady decline of legitimacy. Yet the authors in *Why People Don't Trust Government* do not develop the World War II hypothesis any further than that.[13]

This chapter explore's how the attachment of Americans to their government weakened, paradoxically, as the government grew from 1940 through 1974. The state became materially stronger even while it became more removed from the people on whom it ultimately depended and depends. I first look at the federal government's chronic deemphases of the importance of the American strategic position at the end of World War II, the significance of the Korean conflict, and the stakes of the Vietnam War. I then consider three instances of the growing detachment of the American public from the government: the reluctance of youth to serve in the military; the declining willingness of the public to invest in government bonds; and the increasingly dissenting reportage of the nation's wars. Last, I compare the limited-war explanation offered here with alternative explanations of the declining trust in the U.S. government.

Limited War

"Never before had so many troops been moved so far and so fast," write historians of the U.S. Army Transportation Corps on the demobilization of the armed forces after World War II. In response to the "mutinies" of American troops stationed at Yokohama, at Manila, "at Frankfurt, at Paris, at Hickam Field, Hawaii; at Seoul; at Calcutta; at London," and at other bases both overseas and within the United States, and in reaction to the political pressure of GIs, parents, reporters, and members of Congress — "near-hysteria," as General Eisenhower called it — the Truman administration reduced the armed forces from a wartime strength of more than 12 million persons in 1945 to just over 3 million one year later. The armed forces shrank to their postwar nadir of 1.5 million persons in the summer of 1948.[14]

The withdrawal of troops came at a price. The United States weakened the base from which it could negotiate with Joseph Stalin and the Soviet

Union. Secretary of State Robert Byrnes, Secretary of War Robert Patterson, Admiral Chester Nimitz, and members of the States-War-Navy Committee (the predecessor to the National Security Council) all worried that the United States was imprudently weakening itself. President Truman wrote to one member of Congress, "At the rate we are demobilizing troops, in a very short time we will have no means with which to enforce our demands — a just and fair peace — and unless we have that means we are headed directly for a third world war." The historian Davis Ross finds that Congress, the press, the political left, and the public itself were all to blame for the United States' failure "to meet the responsibilities of world power."[15]

The precedent set by the massive military demobilization following VJ Day — that the government did not sufficiently inform or otherwise persuade the press and public of the sacrifices needed for the new postwar world — was followed in the Korean conflict: President Truman never sought a declaration of war from Congress, despite the overwhelming opinion in favor of stopping the invasion of South Korea once it occurred. "We are not at war," he declared. UN forces were "going to the relief of the Korean Republic to suppress a bandit raid on the Republic of Korea." Even with the intervention of the Chinese and the threat of disaster for the UN forces, the Korean War never became a total war for the United States. Through the end of the 1940s and throughout the 1950s (and 1960s and 1970s), Europe remained the chief concern of U.S. foreign-policy makers.[16]

For most Americans, Korea illustrated the perplexing quality of limited war: there would be no invasion of China, no bombing of the Chinese homeland, no blockade of Chinese ports, and no use of nuclear weapons, despite the grim weeks of late 1950 and early 1951. There could be no war with China at all, not with the Soviet Union in the background and the possibility of another global conflagration. Nor, after the dismissal of General MacArthur, was Truman able to mobilize public opinion behind him. The Truman administration was unable to strike a balance between persuading the American public of Korea's strategic importance and avoiding potentially dangerous war hysteria. In October 1951, 56 percent of the respondents to a Gallup Poll agreed with the proposition that Korea was a "useless war"; in March 1952, 51 percent of respondents said that American involvement in the Korean war was a "mistake."[17]

Still, Korea had only "a limited impact on the daily lives and consciousness of many Americans," the historian Michael Sherry remarks. "With important exceptions — those drafted or called back into military service, those scrutinized for disloyalty — they rarely felt the heavy hand of a government at war, or of war itself." It was an "anomalous war" that "fit no script left behind" by World War II; "nobody liked it." "It," of course, was the United States' long, bloody fight for a stalemate, a return to the status quo ante.[18]

The U.S. government deliberately underplayed the importance of the

Vietnam War as well. The Kennedy administration "did everything in its power to ensure that the existence of a real war in Vietnam was kept from the American people." President Kennedy's assistant secretary of state admitted to the "long-standing desire of the United States government to see the American involvement minimized, even represented as something less in reality than it is." The Kennedy administration hid its involvement in the overthrow and assassination of Diem, too — even though President Kennedy himself disapproved of the coup — and downplayed the increase of U.S. troops in Vietnam to sixteen thousand in number.[19]

President Johnson was likewise unwilling to confront the public and Congress with the facts of the Vietnam War. George Herring comments that it is "striking . . . how little the administration did in the first years of the war to mobilize public support." Contrary to the advice given the President in 1965 by Secretary of Defense Robert McNamara and political adviser Horace Busby, Johnson rejected calling up reserves, declaring a national emergency, or creating a "blue-ribbon task force to explain the war and generate public support." The President deliberately understated U.S. involvement, did little to monitor, much less nurture, public opinion, and released news about U.S. troop increases in a low-key manner, if at all.

In the words of Secretary of State Dean Rusk, "we deliberately refrained from creating a war psychology in the United States. We did not try to stir up the anger of the American people in Vietnam and we did not have military troops parading through our cities or put on big war bond drives. Neither did we send movie actors across the country whipping up enthusiasm for the war [as the government did in World War II] . . . we tried to wage this war as calmly as possible, treating it as police action rather than as a full scale war."[20]

Johnson did not want to jeopardize Great Society legislation, "set loose pressures for escalation and victory that might provoke the larger war with the Soviet Union and China," much less risk nuclear war.[21]

The Johnson administration's public relations efforts were sporadic, defensive, and studiedly inattentive to the peace movement. Drawing up the 1966 budget, the Council of Economic Advisers felt that "such a small war . . . could be managed with ease, as if it were a part-time, moonlighting job," writes Samuel Lubell.[22] Even in the face of growing antiwar sentiment in 1966 and 1967, the Johnson administration essentially kept to its low-key approach. One way that the President minimized the impact of the war was to avoid making troop and budget projections. By mid- 1967, however, Johnson had begun to mount "a large-scale, multi-faceted public relations campaign to rally support for the war," taking influential people to Vietnam to see matters at first hand, and bringing General Westmoreland back from Vietnam to explain the war. President Johnson used the facts at hand and the testimony of others to support his claim that the war was not a stalemate. But the Tet offensive in early 1968 gave the lie to the President's claims of progress.[23]

President Nixon continued this dual strategy of embarking on selective public relations and obscuring the extent of U.S. involvement in Vietnam. Richard Nixon campaigned on the promise that he would bring the troops home and usher in peace in Vietnam; he also publicized the fact that he had a hidden timetable for the withdrawal of all U.S. troops. At the same time, the Nixon administration "wanted to encourage public apathy about the war by keeping as secret as possible the escalation of the bombing."[24] But subsequent news about U.S. military actions in Cambodia and Laos undermined the goodwill accrued from Nixon's plans to withdraw troops, end the draft, negotiate with Hanoi, and uphold American honor.[25] Following the bombing of North Vietnam in late 1972, the U.S. government and North Vietnam did come to an agreement on ending the war — essentially an agreement on the terms of the U.S. withdrawal from Vietnam.

Vietnam was a "limited war," not unlike the one in Korean. "Most Americans lacked a realistic way to categorize the war, much less grasp the issues behind it," Sherry remarks. "Never had an American war been so hard to conceptualize."[26] Stephen Peter Rosen and George Herring call it a "strange war": neither side declared war on the other; the U.S. government downplayed the extent of its involvement; and U.S. involvement escalated only gradually — starting with money, then adding hardware, then advisers, and then, following the Gulf of Tonkin Resolution, troops.[27]

There are some key differences between the Korean and Vietnam Wars and World War II and its immediate aftermath, to be sure. Whereas the dimensions of the Cold War were still being established in the mid- and late 1940s, it was the war in Korea that did much to frame the Cold War international system and by the mid-1950s the political and military doctrines of the Cold War were in place.[28] Whereas the Korean War evidenced clear military strategy, the military was never given clear strategic objectives in Vietnam, as Rosen and Herring point out. President Johnson "refused to make the hard decisions." But neither did other national leaders, from either political party or from the preceding or succeeding presidential administrations, manage to "persuasively define the American interests or ideals at stake in the Vietnam War."[29] Nor did it help that both Johnson and Nixon were particularly ineffective at reaching out to their domestic political opponents, often personally vindictive.

Moreover, World War II and the Korean War were waged during periods of a slack national economy; both wars consequently reaped economic benefits. The Vietnam War, in contrast, coincided with the expansionist public policies of the 1960s and early 1970s, the U.S. economy was already doing well. But neither Johnson, nor Nixon, nor Congress wanted to abandon the government's Great Society programs or raise taxes sufficiently to dampen inflationary pressures.[30] The war, therefore, made tax policy controversial (since higher taxes could be viewed as the cost of waging the war). President Nixon did freeze wages and prices in 1971, but with the Federal Reserve's inflationary monetary policy under the chairmanship of Arthur Burns, such controls were ineffective and merely postponed the economic reckoning.

In sum, the record from the end of World War II through the Vietnam War reveals a pattern of American presidents and their advisers who either refrained from asking much of the public or hid the extent of the government's foreign military operations. At the same time that the government began to disclose less to and demand less of the American public, however, the same public was coming to view its government less and less benignly — balking more and more at what *was* being asked of it and liking less and less what it *did* find out.

The Attenuation of the State

The growing reluctance of Americans to participate in or assist their government is reflected in the rising incidence of conscientious objection and the decreasing presence of women volunteers in the armed forces; in the declining investment by individual citizens in their government (as indicated by purchases of savings bonds and the payment of income taxes); and in the deteriorating relationship between journalists and government officials. These are, to be sure, imperfect indicators of the erosion of the voluntary relations between Americans and their government. Still, the study of these three dimensions of citizens' affect for the state suggests that even as the U.S. government relied less on the American public in the years between World War II and the end of the Vietnam War, fewer citizens sought to cooperate with the national government.

It became harder for federal officials to recruit soldiers, raise money, and disseminate official versions of U.S. foreign wars over the course of the postwar era — and there are arguably no more important spheres of state activity than national defense, revenue collection, and the management of political information. A perverse effect of the United States' new hegemonic status was, thus, the erosion of the legitimacy of its government — even as the state, by some measures, grew stronger.

Military Service: Conscientious Objectors and Women in the Armed Forces

The number of U.S. military personnel surged over the course of World War II, the Korean War, and the Vietnam War, while after each war the number of U.S. forces remained at higher-than-pre-war levels. Troop levels (active duty) rose from 3.9 million persons in 1942 to 12.1 million persons in 1945, while the number of American troops rose from well under a million persons in the late 1930s (and 450,000 in 1940) to about 1.5 million persons in the postwar years of 1947 to 1950. During the Korean War, the number of military personnel (active duty) rose to 3.2 million in 1951, and to 3.6 million in both 1952 and 1953. After the Korean War, between the years 1958 and 1965, the American armed forces reached a plateau of about 2.6 million active-duty personnel. In the late 1960s, the Vietnam War caused yet another increase in the size of the armed forces, from 3.1 million persons in 1966 to 3.4 million in 1967 and 3.5 million in 1969.

Yet this record of ratcheted personnel growth obscured the fact of a less involved citizenry: the young men of America were increasingly unwilling to go to war, and the military was less and less integrated by sex, as fewer and fewer women volunteered for the military.[31]

CONSCIENTIOUS OBJECTORS

About thirty-five million persons registered for the draft over the course of the Second World War (just over one-third of the 14 million who served were volunteers), and 72,354 of them — less than two-tenths of 1 percent — requested conscientious objector (CO) status. Of this number, 25,000 COs served in military support roles, and 12,000 were assigned to civilian work camps. Another 20,000 of those registering as COs did not receive official CO status, and about 6,000 were imprisoned — as felons (4,400 of the 6,200 were Jehovah's Witnesses). Those who claimed CO status on political and philosophical grounds numbered only 255.[32]

The proportion of CO applications to draft inductees rose to 1.64 percent during the Korean War (1952), more than ten times the corresponding figure for the Second World War (0.15 percent). This percentage dropped to 1.3 percent in 1953 and then shot up to 3.6 percent by 1954. Even so, "Draft protest from 1940 to 1960 was no more than a minor nuisance in the execution of the [Selective Service] mission," as one historian remarks.[33]

Young men avoided military service to a greater extent in the 1960s and early 1970s. By 1966, the ratio of CO exemptions to military inductions came to 6.1 per one hundred; by 1967, this ratio stood at 8.1; by 1968, 8.5; by 1969, 13.5; by 1970, 25; by 1971, 43; by 1972, 130; and by 1973, 73. In other words, in 1972 30 percent more men received CO status than were inducted into the military. Overall, 17,900 men registered as COs in 1964, whereas 61,000 persons claimed CO status in 1971. Of the 22,467 young men who were indicted for violating the draft law between the years 1965 and 1975, 8,756 were convicted and 4,001 were actually imprisoned. President Richard Nixon proceeded to end the draft in December 1972, and the All Volunteer Force (AVF) was introduced in 1973.[34]

A number of students of the draft and of draft resistance conclude that these percentage increases are explained by a lack of patriotism, the counterculture, and the widespread presence of civil disobedience, encouraged perhaps by the civil rights movement. (Jean Bethke Elshtain, who had a brother in the military, speaks of being "ashamed" of being an American: "I cannot believe my country had come to this.") Certainly there was more organized support for conscientious objection by the 1960s: organizations helping COs included the War Resisters League, the Student Peace Union, the American Friends Service Committee, the National Interreligious Board for Conscientious Objectors, the Central Committee for Conscientious Objectors, and other church-related groups. More important, it became easier to attain the CO exemption. The Supreme Court ruled that conscientious objector status no longer required a belief in a supreme being (*United States v. Seeger* [1965], upheld in *Welsh v. United States* [1970]), and local Muslim Sunnīdraft boards moderated their criteria for the CO status as the war progressed.[35]

Nonetheless, an increasing percentage of American males were resisting being drafted into the armed forces. Kenneth Boulding notes that "The [Vietnam military] draft may well be regarded as a symbol of a slow decline in the legitimacy of the national state." As early in the war as May 1964, twelve men burned their draft cards at a rally in New York City, as did four others in Berkeley, California. After the student deaths on the Kent State and Florida State campuses in 1970, more than 25,000 draft cards were returned to the government by November.[36]

Consistent with this growing lack of enthusiasm for mandatory military service, public opinion polls conducted at the end of World War II found that 79 percent of Americans held the local draft boards to be "fair"; by 1953, at the end of the Korean War, only 60 percent of respondents felt the same way; and by August 1966, only 49 percent of the public felt that the draft system was fair.[37]

WOMEN IN THE ARMED FORCES

Nor did the wars of the mid- and late twentieth century require American women to become more involved in the nation's defense. On the contrary, women participated only modestly in World War II and to an even lesser degree in the wars in Korea and Vietnam.[38]

Women made up about 3 percent of the U.S. armed forces during World War II, or about 350,000 service personnel in all (including 150,000 in the army, 100,000 in the navy, and 22,000 in the marines); they served in the WACs, WAVES, WASPs (aviators), and SPARS (Coast Guard).[39] Although the numbers of women in the military came to no more than about 266,000 of U.S. military personnel at any one time (2.3 percent), women nonetheless played a significant part in the war and facilitated the eventual Allied victory.[40] Their presence allowed more men to serve in front-line combat positions — men, to be sure, who did not always appreciate being "freed" for direct action — and "Eisenhower relied heavily on WACs as staff personnel in planning and communications." Some eight thousand WACs were in Europe when Germany surrendered.[41]

But U.S. policymakers and military planners virtually ignored women in the later Korean and Vietnam conflicts, despite legislation in 1947 that authorized the army and navy to integrate nursing and medical staff into the services proper, and new legislation in 1948 that permitted women veterans to rejoin the reserves (thereby creating a permanent place for women in the military). Only 47,800 women served during the Korean War — less than 1 percent of total U.S. forces, and under half the proportion of the World War II forces that were women — notwithstanding an active public relations campaign established in the early 1950s by the Defense Advisory Committee on Women in the Services (a committee of prominent civilian women), which called on American women to join the military in order to alleviate fears of a personnel shortage. But the publicity campaign, effected through radio, television, magazines, newspapers, and billboard advertisements, succeeded in recruiting only 6,000 women — or one-twelfth of the 72,000 recruits expected. By 1955 the number of women in the armed forces dropped to 35,000. The proportion of woman in the military services fell far short of the 2 percent authorized by law.[42]

The figures for the Vietnam War were worse yet. Only about 7,500 women actually served in Vietnam and southeast Asia between December 1961 and the pullout in 1973, and about five to six thousand of these women were nurses and medical specialists (4,500 served in the Army Medical Corps alone). By 1967, the peak year of American engagement in Vietnam, fewer than 1 percent of the 463,000 personnel on duty were women — an even lower proportion than during the Korean conflict, fifteen years before. About 70 percent of the women who served in the military during the Vietnam War era performed administrative and clerical work, moreover, whereas only half the women serving in World War II had administrative and clerical jobs.[43]

The remaining portion of women volunteers during the period of the Vietnam War typically worked as protocol officers and administrative assistants who served at the request of top army, air force, and (to a lesser extent) navy officials. Women were valued as attractive attendants, rather than as soldiers or the providers of other essential wartime functions. According to one historian, "The services began requiring full-length photographs of potential women recruits, taking only the best-looking among them. Recruits

were not instructed in marksmanship or combat survival, but they did learn
how to properly apply make-up and to conduct themselves as ladies. Their
physical training was intended to maintain trim figures, not to increase
strength, endurance, or coordination."[44] Similarly, a WAVES director re-
minded her charges that "Waves are ladies first and always." Women were in
the military to serve and help in what was ultimately and undeniably a
man's war.[45]

The situation of women in the U.S. armed forces contracts starkly with a
civilian world that was, during the same period, becoming increasingly integrated. Among the most visible women of the period were Jane Fonda and
Angela Davis, in fact, anti-war activists both. But the feminist movement
proceeded by and large independently of the war (and of the antiwar movement, too, for that matter); (Fonda and Davis were exceptions). Women on
the home front were not called upon to sacrifice by rationing food or house-
hold products or by otherwise reducing consumption; they were not asked
to take war jobs; and they never had to conduct air raid precautions. No
notable leaders emerged to play the roles in the Korean and Vietnam Wars
that Oveta Culp Hobby and Eleanor Roosevelt had played during World
War II.[46]

Members of Congress and the armed forces shared the assumption, along
with much of the public, that war was men's business. The male-oriented
quality of the Vietnam War was underscored in a speech given by President
Ronald Reagan in the early 1980s: "several years ago we brought home a
group of American fighting *men* who had obeyed their country's call. . . .
There's been no thank you for their sacrifice. There's been no effort to
honor and, thus, give pride to the families of more than 57,000 young *men*
who gave their lives. . . . There's been little or no recognition of the grati-
tude we owe to the more than 300,000 *men* who suffered wounds in that
war."[47] Only with the repeal of the draft and the advent of the AVF were
women included as near equals and integrated with the regular (male)
forces. Even so, the WAVES were not disbanded until March 1973 and the
Women's Air Force lasted until June 1976. The Women's Army Corps did
not lose its last director until April 1978; it was disestablished in October of
that year.

In sum, the record of conscientious objectors and women in the military
from the Second World War through the Vietnam War reveals that larger
and larger proportions of young men were claiming and receiving CO exemption and that fewer and fewer women were voluntarily participating in
American wars (and contributing in less and less crucial ways).[48] At the same
time, however, CO status became easier to come by, and the military relied
less on women in the armed forces. Yet this weakening of government-
citizen ties coincided with the growth of the military, one which had more
personnel after the Korean war than in the late 1940s, and more personnel

serving in Vietnam than in Korea. Judged by the size of the military, the American state was getting stronger, but smaller and smaller proportions of the populace were willing to serve and die for it.

Money: Individual Income Taxation and U.S. Savings Bonds

Both U.S. government expenditures and individual income tax revenues soared during World War II and the early postwar years. Total government expenditures rose from $9.1 billion in 1940 to a post–World War II plateau of about $40 billion in the late 1940s, then jumped to a over $65 billion after the Korean War (1954–57), and continued to increase over the course of the 1960s and early 1970s. Meanwhile, the individual income tax emerged as the foremost source of federal revenues. Revenues from income taxation soared during World War II, rose moderately between 1950 and 1953, and then climbed steeply once again in the late 1960s and early 1970s. Table 10.1 shows the rapid rise of both the total amount of income tax revenues and the proportion of government expenditures composed of individual income tax receipts.

Yet the increase in government expenditures and income tax revenues over the course of the 1950s, 1960s, and 1970s coincided with a decline in the proportion of individual savings invested in U.S. government savings bonds. Savings bonds as a proportion of USG expenditures (the third column of table 10.1) plummeted by more than half between 1950 and 1953 — from about 14 percent of government spending in 1950 to 6 percent in 1952 and 1953. This proportion dropped again by half during the Vietnam years, from about one-twentieth of government expenditures in the early sixties to one-fortieth by the early 1970s. As the postwar years went on, government debt was being funded proportionally less through U.S. savings bonds and more through other bonds, treasury bills, treasury notes, and special issues. U.S. savings bonds took 22 percent of the total public debt in 1950, 21 percent in 1955, 17 percent in 1960, 16 percent in 1965, and 14 percent in 1970.[49]

The decreasing reliance on individual savings bonds investment is more marked if the net change in individual purchases of U.S. savings bonds (i.e., excluding other federal securities and state and local government securities) is compared to net individual income tax payments (not in table 10.1). In 1942 the U.S. government raised well over twice as much money from savings bonds ($7.98 billion) as from individual income taxation ($3.1 billion), and voluntary purchases of savings bonds accounted for almost a fifth of government expenditures. By the late 1940s, though, the government collected from savings bonds sales about one-tenth the amount it received from income taxes. The proportion of savings bonds

TABLE 10.1
U.S. Government Reliance on Savings Bonds

Fiscal Year	USG Exp. ($b)	IIT/ USG Exp.	USSB/ USG Exp.	USSB/ IS
1940	9.1	0.098	0.095	0.325
1941	12.8	0.102	0.215	0.881
1942	32.4	0.096	0.246	1.148
1943	78.2	0.085	0.142	0.931
1944	93.7	0.195	0.126	0.817
1945	100.4	0.189	0.068	0.388
1946	65	0.288	0.018	0.190
1947	42.5	0.461	0.049	0.618
1948	36.3	0.579	0.044	0.696
1949	40.1	0.446	0.037	0.577
1950	40.2	0.433	0.007	0.120
1951	44.6	0.525	−0.011	−0.111
1952	66.1	0.452	0.002	0.013
1953	74.3	0.441	0.003	0.024
1954	67.8	0.478	0.009	0.065
1955	64.6	0.491	0.005	0.034
1956	66.5	0.531	−0.002	−0.011
1957	69.4	0.562	−0.027	−0.157
1958	71.9	0.537	−0.007	−0.036
1959	80.3	0.457	−0.022	−0.158
1960	76.5	0.532	−0.004	−0.024
1961	81.5	0.507	0.010	0.047
1962	87.8	0.519	0.005	0.017
1963	92.7	0.513	0.013	0.052
1964	97.7	0.498	0.009	0.038
1965	96.5	0.506	0.006	0.023
1966	107	0.519	0.006	0.031
1967	153.3	0.401	0.007	0.030
1968	172.8	0.398	0.002	0.014
1969	183.1	0.476	−0.002	−0.030
1970	194.5	0.465	0.002	0.009
1971	211.4	0.408	0.011	0.034
1972	231.9	0.408	0.014	0.044
1973	246.5	0.419	0.011	0.040
1974	268.4	0.443	0.011	0.051

Note: USG = U.S. government. IIT = individual income tax. USSB = net sales of U.S. savings bonds. IS = individual savings. A minus sign indicates that the net sales of U.S. savings bonds declined (i.e., redemptions exceeded purchases).

Source: U.S. Department of Commerce, *Historical Statistics of the United States* (Washington, D.C.: U.S. Government Printing Office, 1975).

receipts to individual income tax receipts fell even further from 1950 through 1970.

Comparing the amount of individual investment in U.S. savings bonds with the amount of money Americans held in savings accounts (thus taking the absolute amount of savings into account) shows that the former was proportionally declining (the fourth column of table 10.1). ("Savings accounts" are defined as time deposits — not demand deposits — held by individuals in mutual savings banks, savings and loan associations, credit unions, the postal savings system, and commercial banks; insurance policies and pension plans are not included.) The net amount of money Americans invested in U.S. savings bonds essentially matched the net amount they had in savings accounts in the years 1941 through 1944, but the proportion of savings bonds investment to individual savings accounts declined thereafter in the postwar years (1947–1949) to about two-thirds of its former level, and then to negligible proportions in the 1950s and 1960s (as the last column of table 10.1 shows). It was not that Americans were no longer saving money in financial institutions, but rather that they were putting less and less in U.S. savings bonds.

The White House, Treasury Department, and Congress relied less and less on voluntary contributions for funding the Korean and Vietnam conflicts and more and more on coerced forms of revenue. The government was still borrowing money, and individual Americans still had savings to invest, but Congress and the Treasury chose not to make U.S. savings bonds the attractive and competitive option they had been in the 1940s. There were more effective ways for the government to raise money. In sum, just as fewer young men and women wanted to serve in the military over the course of the postwar years, so did fewer Americans want to buy U.S. government securities. Nor in either case, did the government work hard to persuade them otherwise.

Political Communication: The Government and the Media

The postwar years brought about a stronger state with respect to political communication in two ways. First, the introduction of television in the late 1940s and early 1950s allowed U.S. presidents to reach individual Americans both directly and intimately. Given that television (and radio) broadcasters were subject to the federal regulation of scarce airwaves, presidents could address a national audience by preempting other programming. More, the technology of television caused the U. S. government to become increasingly identified with the person of the president; television thus had the potential to unify the nation politically.[50] Second, the stakes were higher. The salience and omnipresence of the Cold War meant that American journalists had to exercise responsible judgment — be willing to alter, delay, or omit the publication of politically sensitive news if national security so warranted — in the face of what seemed to be a global communist threat.

Despite the power of television and the major media's cooperation with the U.S. government, the record of media-government cooperation with respect to news about World War II, the Korean War, and the Vietnam War reveals a pattern of diminishing government control. News coverage became ever more critical of incumbent presidential administrations and U.S. policies, and journalists paid less and less deference to political and military leaders. Over the course of the postwar years, it became even easier for the government to communicate with the public, but at the same time, ironically, it became ever more difficult for the government to dictate what information be disseminated.

WORLD WAR II

Through both formal and informal means, the U.S. government effectively monopolized news coverage of the Second World War. The government had the explicit power to censor the news and also made use of advertising and public relations campaigns and the cooperation and goodwill of American journalists reporting on the war.[51]

Confronted with the severity and scale of World War II, the Roosevelt administration created the Office of Censorship on December 16, 1941, for the purpose of managing political communication (although such an office had been in the planning phase since the late 1930s). The Office of Censorship, headed by the Associated Press's executive news director, succeeded in hiding the damage done by the Japanese at the Pearl Harbor naval base, for instance, and kept the bad news of early 1942 (e.g., U.S. merchant ships burning off the East Coast, the sinking of U.S. naval vessels) out of the newspapers and off the radio. The President himself helped manage political communication by holding news conferences infrequently and be ensuring that there was little to report in those that were held. He referred often to the Office of Censorship in his press conferences, pretending that he was powerless when it came to the release of much newsworthy information. The office quickly affected government-press relations, its budget growing from $7 million in its first year to $29.7 million by 1945.[52]

Meanwhile, the Navy Department monitored cable traffic, the War Department checked the mail, and the Federal Bureau of Investigation wiretapped journalists and denied others access to war information. In addition, the Justice Department investigated and threatened the *Chicago Tribune* (historically hostile to FDR), for its profascist positions; Roosevelt succeeded in closing down Father Coughlin's *Social Justice* in May 1942 for publishing charges that Jews and communists had tricked the United States into entering the war (FDR's postmaster general threatened to use the still-in-effect powers of the 1917 Espionage Act); other newspapers and magazines were suppressed; and still other publications were indicted for disloyalty.[53] News about transportation schedules, industrial production, and government budgets was routinely kept secret as well.

The U.S. government also produced its own news through the Office of War Information, established in June 1942 (replacing the Office of Facts and Figures). The OWI was led by Elmer Davis, a former journalist, and it collaborated with advertisers on campaigns to recruit military personnel, sell war bonds and war savings stamps, salvage and recycle needed materials, stop rumors, etcetera. But the OWI was circumscribed in its authority, caught as it was between the War and Navy Departments (which determined what news would be released), the President (who had his own considerable public relations skills as a politician and former editor of the Harvard *Crimson*, and who typically deferred to the military in determining what could or could not be made public), the Office of Strategic Services, and the precedent set by the Creel Committee of World War I. Davis was often prevented from releasing information he thought the public should have.[54] After the war the OWI was replaced by U.S. Information Service, which administers the Voice of America.

Explicit controls over newspaper correspondence were rarely needed, however, as U.S. journalists themselves enforced the censorship codes. American reporters and editors, who were overwhelmingly pro-British, thereby provided their readers with a distorted view of the war that bolstered national confidence. The attack on Pearl Harbor, while clearly bad news, was portrayed as far less serious a blow to the American navy than in fact it was. When CBS reporter Edward Murrow interviewed Roosevelt about the damage at Pearl Harbor, for instance, Murrow kept the scoop to himself, although Roosevelt said nothing about the interview being off the record. (The full extent of the damage from the Japanese attack on Pearl Harbor would not be widely known until after the war.)

From the eastern front of the war in Europe, there was virtually no reportage of the 800,000 Soviet citizens who fought for Germany, of the Battle of Kursk — arguably the turning point of the war — or of the Katyn Forest massacre. Neither was there coverage of the most decisive battle in the Pacific, the Battle of Midway. Nor was there accurate coverage of Chinese politics under the Chiang Kai-shek regime of the early 1940s; readers received instead only glowing accounts of China and of the heroism of the Chinese people.[55] Meanwhile, journalists kept to themselves wartime news of poor living conditions, military defeats, homosexuality, and other unpalarable subjects.

At other times, American journalists went along with the public relations efforts of the U.S. military, especially those of the most image-conscious generals: Mack Clark, Dwight Eisenhower, Douglas MacArthur, and George Patton.[56] Indeed, the biggest stories of the war were all ones favorable to the United States: the invasion of North Africa, the landing in Normandy, VE Day, the bombing of Hiroshima and Nagasaki, and VJ Day.

With President Roosevelt allowing the army and navy to decide what had to be kept secret, journalists had little choice but to do the same, given the combined power of the president, the attorney general, the military, and the FBI. As a result, the Roosevelt administration received perhaps more favorable coverage and freedom of movement and activity during the Second World War than the news media have accorded any president since. Americans received "a cleaned up, cosmetically-enhanced version of reality." Military censors "succeeded in putting over the legend that the war was won without a single mistake by a command consisting exclusively of geniuses."[57] In short, news coverage of World War II was not good journalism but, as one wartime correspondent put it, "crap." Reporters willingly censored themselves and this because, as Phillip Knightley writes, a "propaganda arm" of government, "cheerleaders" for the war effort.[58]

KOREA

The U.S. government also censored news about the Korean War, but the censorship was exercised by the military itself rather than by domestic agencies. The Eighth Army in Korea was authorized to check, clear, and oversee the transmission of stories, to ensure that information not be supplied to the enemy and that news not injure the morale of U.S. or allied forces, or embarrass the United States, its UN allies, or neutral nations. Military personnel who gave or released to reporters news of enemy action that would "cause despondency in our own forces or people" were subject to court martial. News accounts were suppressed because they breached "security," could impair morale or trigger "unwarranted criticism," or were just "lousy stories" — especially during the disastrous retreat of July 1950. The journalist who was the first to break the story of the Inchon landing was removed from the front, for instance, and two wire service writers were sent back to Tokyo for "reorientation."[59]

The U.S. media were extremely supportive of the military intervention at first, and war reporters and editors largely censored themselves throughout most of the war, just as they had during World War II.[60] General MacArthur subsequently praised American journalists for their unparalleled and unprecedented ability to walk the fine line between the provision of public information and the protection of military security.

But the picture included more than official and self-imposed censorship. There was considerable bad press about the war, too, at first in the British and French papers, and eventually in the American as well. No one could miss the severe setbacks occurring early on in the war, the unpopularity of "Truman's war," the dismissal of General MacArthur (who had Republican support on Capitol Hill and who used Republican House Minority Leader Joe Martin to release his own news about the Korean command), and the controversial Steel Seizure of April 1952. Meanwhile, the Soviet Union — the real enemy, as most Americans saw it — appeared to be left unaffected U.S. actions.[61] The media were not the simple instrument of the Truman administration or the military: they also covered stories unfavorable to the U.S. government or the Truman White House.

The unfavorable publicity reflected the difficult reality of covering a war whose mission few understood and where the press was positioned between the Truman administration on the one hand and the domestic critics of the war on the other. Neither the military nor the Truman and Eisenhower administrations were very successful at selling the war to American citizens, nor did it help matters that Truman — and not Roosevelt — was now commander in chief. But the difficult political communication of the Korean War also reflected the larger divisions within Washington, American society, and the military over American involvement in East Asia, the military strategy in Korea, and Truman's leadership.

VIETNAM

Vietnam was the first war in which American correspondents were not censored, and throughout much of the war censorship was not needed. A deep consensus prevailed among journalists, public officials, and most Americans on the Cold War and its implications for world order, a consensus that included even a David Halberstam or a Neil Sheehan. Members of the news media, like most other Americans, were convinced of the necessity of the Cold War and accepted the government's view. Meanwhile, the military and the Kennedy, Johnson, and Nixon administrations used the press to pass along their versions of events. The press amounted to a fourth branch of government, as Daniel Hallin notes, practicing "responsible journalism" supportive of the government. Both the New York Times and the Washington Post endorsed the war.[62]

As the war went on, however, the political consensus among the major media and the government dissolved. Journalists found out that the Kennedy administration, the Johnson administration, and the succeeding Nixon administration were all misleading them, even lying to them, about the war. Walter Lippmann came out against the Vietnam War early on, followed by Halberstam, Sheehan, and Walter Cronkite, among others.[63] The publication of the Pentagon Papers in 1971 epitomized the division between the media and the government: the New York Times and the Washington Post were both willing to take positions on Vietnam independent of those of the

Nixon administration and the Joint Chiefs of Staff. Yet this division between journalists and government officials was itself reflective of the growing divisions within the White House, Congress, the military, and the American public. Americans saw pictures of Buddhist monks immolating themselves, U.S. Marines using cigarette lighters to set thatched huts on fire, a naked girl running screaming down a road, fleeing napalm, and a man being summarily executed with a bullet to the head by a South Vietnamese official. Then there was the publicity given of the My Lai massacre and, of course, the Pentagon Papers.

Much of the news of Vietnam was not only outside governmental control but shocking to the American public. To be sure, reporters scarcely commented on racism in the military, the mutilation of Vietminh and Vietnamese civilian bodies by American servicemen, the degree of heroin and marijuana usage by U.S. forces, the often indiscriminate killing of Vietminh (or Vietnamese civilians, whether or not they could be linked with the North Vietnamese government), or the bombing of North Vietnam and Laos and the invasion of Cambodia during the de-escalation phase of 1969 to 1973. Still, Vietnam "was better reported" than its predecessors—even if "this is not saying a lot," as one correspondent concedes.[64]

In sum, the history of the reporting of World War II, the Korean War, and the Vietnam War evidences eroding consensus both among and between journalists and government officials and, after World War II, a decline of journalists' trust in the quality of the government's information. An increasingly interpretive and critical news media emerged in both of the later wars (press reporters becoming more negative over the course of each conflict) and across all three wars (with the almost wholly favorable reporting of World War II, the moderately negative reporting of the Korean War, and, by the late 1960s and early 1970s, the markedly negative reporting of the Vietnam War).[65] For journalists to adhere to the norms of objective journalism—that is, to report on the government's actions without comment—was to invite further betrayals of confidence by politicians, top political advisers, and military leaders; they were no longer going to be taken in by public officials.

Over time, then, we see the government removing itself from the media by lessening its explicit controls: the tight censorship during World War II yielded to the milder monitoring of information during the Korean War, and finally to the removal of formal limitations on coverage of the Vietnam War. At the same time, journalists' self-censorship and voluntary cooperation with the U.S. government gradually eroded, as the press became increasingly independent and critical. These two developments jointly brought about an attenuation of the state, notwithstanding the the government's enhanced ability to disseminate information.

Conclusions

World War II and its Cold War offspring, the Korean and Vietnam Wars, exerted Janus-like effects on the American state. The cumulative record from the 1940s to the mid-1970s points to a deterioration of the state: the government distanced itself from its citizens by not adequately explaining the stakes of the postwar era, by avoiding the imposition of personal and financial burdens — arguably, to the detriment of the United States' strategic position and economic health — and by hiding the full extent of the U.S. government's foreign military (and intelligence) actions.

The Korean and Vietnam Wars were not regarded as national emergencies. An increasing percentage of draftees were granted CO status, and women, except for a few secretaries, assistants, and nurses, were scarcely needed by the military at all. The U.S. government did not have to rely on the voluntary efforts of civilians to finance these war and relaxed its controls over the press, thereby allowing journalists more room to dispute official claims. The attenuation of the state, other words, was partly by design, given that the government chose to ease CO criteria, not to call on women to sacrifice home comforts for military ends, not to make government securities financially competitive, and not to impose press censorship.

At the same time, the histories of these conflicts reveal that the national government acquired greater capability to mobilize and employ personnel, fund the military, and harness and disseminate information helpful to the conduct of war. The state was stronger in terms of the number of citizens serving in the military, the amount of money being raised, and the ease by which the government could reach out to a mass audience. The Cold War contributed to the growth of the U.S. federal government, as measured by employees, absolute expenditures, and share of GDP — a growth that was particularly evident during the Korean and Vietnam conflicts.

But this growth happened to come at a price. The government gradually became more detached from Americans, less trusted by the public. An ever larger percentage of men sought to escape military service, and one-half of young adult Americans — the women — participated proportionally less in the nation's defense. Fewer and fewer individuals voluntarily invested in the U.S. government, moreover, while the government relied more and more on the involuntary income tax for its funding. And journalists were less and less willing to cooperate with the U.S. government when reporting on the nation at war. Then, with the introduction of the volunteer army — in contrast to the European and Soviet-bloc nations, among others, which continued to rely on obligatory military service — the Nixon administration and Congress put the American public at a yet further remove from the military and the national government.

These two trends — the government distancing itself from public attention, and the public distancing itself from the government — reinforced each
other over the course of the postwar years, which suggests a logic of path
dependence. As the government asked less of, and explained less to, the
American people, so did Americans, faced with the horror of wars whose
significance they could not fully grasp and learning of public officials' dis-
sembling, want less and less to do with the national government. It is tempting to blame it all on Vietnam. Indeed, Vietnam (and the Johnson and
Nixon administrations) figure prominently in explanations of the erosion of
confidence in the national government, whether these explanations target
poor leadership, corruption and dishonesty, the changing role of the news
media in American political life, inadequate governmental performance,
the onset of political realignment and division among elites, or the impact
of specific events.[66]

But those who focus on the Vietnam War often miss the continuity between that conflict and the earlier one in Korea: each was a complex and
ambiguous "limited war" in which the presidential administration understated the threat to, and stakes of, the United States in fighting it; each
caused a decline in presidential popularity as military costs rose, along with
injuries and fatalities. Moving from World War II to the Korean War and
then to the Vietnam War, one sees proportionally more conscientious objectors and proportionally fewer women were serving in the military, less public investment in U.S. savings bonds, and more dissension expressed in the
news media.

Although survey data certainly show a marked decline in the public's
confidence in government institutions between the mid-1960s and the
mid-1970s, the weakening of government-citizen ties *predates* the polling
data, according to the findings above on attitudes toward military service,
savings-bond ownership, and media-government relationships.[67] While most
of the polling data do not begin until 1958, neither do the analysts of these
data question whether confidence in American government might have begun to wane prior to the 1960s — that is, during and immediately following
the Korean war.[68] Rather than seeing 1966 as the high point of trust in
government, as Nye and others do (although they admit that in light of the
World War II hypothesis, level of trust during the 1950s "seems abnormally
high"), public opinion of the late 1960s and 1970s may be viewed as a
repetition of the public attitudes of the early 1950s — Vietnam being a more
controversial, more devastating Korea.

It is because of the question of timing that I reject the alternative politi-
cal-realignment hypotheses that Nye and Zelikow offer for the decline in
trust in government.[69] The *political realignment* hypothesis (no. 7 on Nye
and Zelikow's list of possibilities) begs the question of what underlies partisan transformation, and it cannot account for the stability of the New Deal

coalition up until the late 1960s, despite earlier evidence of rising mistrust. The hypothesis that it is the *effects of the media on party decline* and negative marketing that cause a lack of confidence in government (no. 8) omits the key policy changes of the McGovern-Fraser reforms and the Federal Election Campaign Act and its amendments.[70] Neither does this model address why the medium of television does not precipitate party decline in the 1950s, a decade when both parties still appeared in robust health. As for the notion that it is the *changed role of the media* in American society (and in other OECD nations) that causes mistrust in government (no. 9), this argument misses the earlier rise of the television news media and the complicity of politicians and government officials in the condition of political life (see the "Increased corruption/dishonesty" hypothesis, no. 10).

The "Third Industrial Revolution" hypothesis (no. 14), for its part, does not feature a causal mechanism to connect the advent of new technologies and new lifestyles with changing attitudes toward government. Nor does it account for the deterioration of voluntaristic ties between individuals and the government in the 1950s. The same criticism holds for the hypothesis that it is the "Authority patterns and postmaterialist values" of the 1960s and subsequent decades (no. 17) that explains the waning legitimacy of government: why did the government's authority, readily accepted during World War II and the early phase of the Korean and Vietnam Wars become suspect in the later phases of those conflicts and continue to be suspect thereafter?

This study underscores the fact that the Second World War stands as a remarkable episode in American history. Such a reality is consistent with a redefined World War II thesis that puts the fact of limited warfare at the *core* of what makes the post–war era distinctive. In fact, the declining intensity of the relationship between individual Americans and the national government from World War II onward suggests a return to earlier patterns of political behavior: the United States did not even have a peacetime draft prior to 1940; most Americans invested little in the federal government in the nineteenth and early twentieth centuries; and government-press relations with respect to national security had been subject to great controversy at previous points in U.S. history, such as the the late Federalist period, the Civil War era, and the McKinley and Wilson administrations.[71] Although Americans may have become more distant from the U.S. government in the late twentieth century, they often defied or questioned it in the nineteenth — even to the extent that some refused to fight in the War of 1812, and many more engaged in a civil war. World War II, as a war of attrition and a total war — and a much larger version of World War I[72] — thus stands as a clear contrast to the Korean and Vietnam Wars and to most other foreign wars fought by the United States.

And it was soon after World War II that the attenuation of the state began. In this sense, President Truman, for all the credit he has received for establishing the political institutions of the Cold War and making the tough decision to drop the atomic bomb and to cede Eastern Europe to the Soviet Union, bears some responsibility. His administration was willing to bend to domestic political pressures, as the three above case studies indicate. His handling of the demobilization after VJ Day and the Korean crisis — not to mention the license he granted to the intelligence community and his non-response to the overtures of Ho Chi Minh after the declaration of an independent Vietnam[73] — started a pattern of deemphasizing the United States' stakes in waging limited war fare, of obscuring the degree of American military involvement abroad, and of failing to adequately explain why Americans needed to cooperate with their government.

Political and military experts often make the claim that Americans are unwilling to fight wars of attrition, and the military has accepted this premise, steadily replacing personnel (labor) with technology (capital).[74] Yet large proportions of young Americans were willing to fight in the Second World War, the First World War, and the Spanish-American War. The unwillingness of Americans to sacrifice their own lives or that of a loved one in combat has hardly been a constant in American history. Nor is it a necessary component of democratic government. The argument that Americans cannot tolerate significant war casualties is at once "presentist" — applying the standards and norms of the present to the past — and very possibly the artifact of the kind of wars that have been fought in the last five-plus decades.

What, then, are the general implications of this discussion for our understanding of international influences on the American state?

First, my study shows that the postwar world order affected the United States in contradictory ways. A larger and more powerful national government emerged, one that was able to extract and dedicate tremendous domestic resources for military ends, but at the very same time the relational state deteriorated, in terms of citizens' voluntary ties of to the national government. There was thus statebuilding over the course of the mid- to late twentieth century with respect to the size and scale of the U.S. government, its greater role in international affairs, and the growth in power and independence of government organizations such as the Department of Defense, the State Department, the Treasury, and intelligence agencies, not to mention the rise of the "imperial presidency." At the same time there was an erosion of the state as measured by the voluntary attachments individuals had to their government, erosion that makes national government more costly to administer and arguably threatens its stability.

This research further suggests that the nation of the state as an *autonomous sector of authority* (Nettl's second definition of the state) stands in opposition to his later claim that the United States does not *have* a state in sociocultural terms (the state as a sociocultural phenomenon being his fourth definition). How could the American state (one increasingly visible as the United States assumed the status of hegemon) be viewed separately from society—as began to happen in the 1960s and 1970s—if the United States were "relatively stateless"?[75] The fact that the U.S. government (in the sense of "regime" or "political system" rather than a particular administration) was becoming increasingly unpopular and untrustworthy at the same time that it was surviving military threats and economic crises may have led to the greater prominence of the "state" as a construct. I suggest it is no coincidence that social scientists did not start to return to the state as a concept of political analysis until the late 1960s and 1970s. Nor was it to the state as a legal system, contra Nettl, that these scholars turned.[76]

Third, the trajectory of political development of the postwar years has extended into the 1980s, the 1990s, and the new millennium. In today's world of limited warfare and a volunteer military, the U.S. government appears to have adopted a two-pronged strategy to reduce the influence of foreign military engagements on American morale and public confidence. First, policymakers continue to make few demands on the public's consent. The ongoing reliance on the all-volunteer army—that is, a professional army made up of Americans of both sexes who receive technical and organizational training, scholarships, a small salary, and other benefits in return for military service—is a case in point. Troops are no longer drafted, but attracted to and contracted into military service; Americans now only go to war if they have agreed to do so (although it is debatable how informed their consent is, since military marketing deemphasizes risk of death).

Policymakers and military planners have finessed the need for public cooperation and popular consent by returning to a model of news censorship and control, as was evident during the invasions of Granada (1983) and Panama (1989), the Persian Gulf War (1991), and the intervention in Kosovo (1999). To this end, the government has imposed harsher penalties on active or former government employees who release information pertaining to national security without official permission (e.g., President Reagan's Executive Order 12356). Significantly, conflicts which have exposed U.S. troops to active duty in the years since Vietnam have been of short duration. The Vietnam war stands as an example of what *not* to do, and politicians have not allowed wars to drag on.[77]

The second prong of the government's strategy has been to magnify threats to the American public through the conduct of orchestrated public-relations efforts. Presidents, their advisers, military personnel, and other politicians and officials have learned to use public diplomacy to persuade Americans that they are or may be materially affected by a particular adversary.[78] The personalization of international relations through the demonization of foreign leaders such as Muammar Qaddafi, Manuel Noriega, Saddam Hussein, Slobodan Milosevic, and others is a case in point. Government officials (over)emphasize the seriousness of the threats posed by other states. Most recently, the government has mobilized public opinion by focusing on the possibility of biological agents, chemical weapons, conventional explosives, or other instruments of terrorism being used against the American people.

It may be tempting to argue that after the Reagan years and the Persian Gulf War, the consensus-breaking legacy of Korea and especially Vietnam is a thing of the past, but it is not.[79] The Cold War has ended, but the U.S. government still fights wars limited with respect to weaponry, objective, and degree of mobilization. If anything, wars are being fought under even more restrictive conditions than the Korean and Vietnam Wars given their expected brevity and the greater role played by multilateral coalitions. But it is not clear what can be done to arrest the decay of the affect individual citizens feel for their national government, despite the government's efforts to mitigate the adverse effects of limited wars. As Robert McNamara observed in the early 1960s, before the rise of the anitwar movement, wars like Vietnam, fought "without arousing the public ire," were precisely the kind of wars the United States would "likely be facing for the next fifty years."[80]

Notes

I would like to thank the editors of this volume, Ira Katznelson and Martin Shefter, my fellow contributors, my colleagues in the Department of Government at the University of Texas, and Gary Freeman, in particular, for their comments on earlier versions of this chapter.

1. Harry S. Truman, *Memoirs*, vol. 1, *Year of Decisions* (Garden City, N.J.: Doubleday, 1955), 71; Melvyn P. Leffler, *A Preponderance of Power: National Security, the Truman Administration, and the Cold War* (Stanford: Stanford University Press, 1994), 15; Alonzo Hamby, *Man of the People: A Life of Harry S. Truman* (New York: Oxford University Press, 1995), 316.

2. See Richard Rose, "Is American Public Policy Exceptional?" in *Is America Different?*, ed. Byron E. Shafer (Oxford: Clarendon Press, 1991).

3. Hans Morgenthau defines total war in four ways: "(1) with respect to the fraction of the population engaged in activities essential for the conduct of the war, (2) with regard to the fraction of the population affected by the conduct of the war, (3) with respect to the fraction of the population completely identified in its convictions and emotions with the conduct of the war, and (4) with respect to the objective of the war" (*Politics among Nations*, 3d ed. [New York: Knopf, 1960], 242, 365). U.S. military engagements since World War II have been limited in all of these ways.

4. Davis B. Ross, *Preparing for Ulysses: Politics and Veterans during World War II* (New York: Columbia University Press, 1969); David McCullough, *Truman* (New York: Simon and Schuster, 1992), 468–69; Leffler, *A Preponderance of Power*, 97–98.

5. See Joseph S. Nye Jr., Philip D. Zelikow, and David C. King, eds., *Why People Don't Trust Government* (Cambridge: Harvard University Press, 1997); Marc Hetherington, "The Effect of Political Trust on Presidential Vote, 1968–96," *American Political Science Review* 93, no. 2 (1999): 311–26.

6. Robert Gilpin, *U.S. Power and the Multinational Corporation* (New York: Basic Books, 1975), 24–25; Kenneth Waltz, *Theory of International Politics* (New York: Random House, 1979), 131; Paul Kennedy, *The Rise and Fall of Great Powers* (New York: Random House, 1987). Seymour Martin Lipset and William Schneider explore the legitimacy issue explicitly in the final chapter of *The Confidence Gap: Business, Labor, and Government in the Public Mind* (New York: Free Press, 1983). They determine that the "confidence gap" is largely event-driven, although they also take note of other more systematic causes, including economics and television viewership.

7. Robert Osgood, *Limited War: The Challenge to American Strategy* (Chicago: University of Chicago Press, 1957), 275, emphasis added. But Stephen Peter Rosen ("Vietnam and the American Theory of Limited War," *International Security* 7, no. 2 (1983): 83–113) points out that Osgood generally overlooks domestic politics (as opposed to the international realpolitik) and focuses on the use of limited wars for diplomatic signaling, neglecting the role of military strategy.

8. See Bartholomew H. Sparrow, *From the Outside In: World War II and the American State* (Princeton: Princeton University Press, 1996), 13–16; Michael Mann, "The Autonomous Power of the State: Its Origins, Mechanisms and Results," *Archives Européennes de sociologie* 25 (1984): 185–213; Alfred Stepan, *The State and Society: Peru in Comparative Perspective* (Princeton: Princeton University Press, 1978). Nettl recognizes an admixture of public and private authority—what he identifies as a loss of state autonomy—but only, apparently, in the case of the U.S. Congress (569). In fact, Nettl holds that the notion of the "state," if it "is to be at all meaningful . . . must be divorced from and even *opposed* to personal power—not in the legal but in the political sense." J. P. Nettl, "The State as a Conceptual Variable," *World Politics* 20, no. 4 (1968): 563.

9. Paul R. Abramson, *Political Attitudes in America: Formulation and Change* (San Francisco: W.H. Freeman, 1983); Norman H. Nie, Sidney Verba, and John R. Petrocik, *The Changing American Voter* (Cambridge: Harvard University Press, 1975); Lipset and Schneider, *The Confidence Gap*; Richard G. Niemi, John Mueller, and Tom W. Smith, *Trends in Public Opinion* (Westport, Conn.: Greenwood Press, 1989). Niemi, Mueller, and Smith point out that measures of confidence in the institutions of government "are middle-range indicators of support. They do not tap underlying confidence in the sociopolitical system, such as our democratic form of government or our free enterprise system; nor do they focus on the day-to-day job performance of specific incumbents as presidential popularity measures do." *Trends in Public Opinion*, 93. Also see Margaret Levi, *Consent, Dissent, and Patriotism* (New York: Cambridge University Press, 1997); and Michael Walzer, "Political Alienation and Military Service," in *The Military Draft*, ed. Martin Anderson (Stanford, Calif.: Hoover Institution Press, 1982), 153–70.

10. See Morris Janowitz, *The Professional Soldier: A Social and Political Portrait* (New York: Macmillan, 1971); Samuel Huntington, *The Common Defense* (New York: Columbia University Press, 1961); Huntington, *The Soldier and the State: The*

Theory and Politics of Civil-Military Relations (Cambridge: Belknap Press of Harvard University Press, 1975 [1964]); Thomas C. Schelling, *Strategy of Conflict* (Cambridge: Harvard University Press, 1960); Bernard Brodie, *War & Politics* (New York: Macmillan, 1973); Osgood, *Limited War*; Morgenthau, *Politics among Nations*. Nor does Levi make the more general connection between consent and limited warfare in her studies of conscientious objection across nations. *Consent, Dissent, and Patriotism*; Margaret Levi and Stephen DeTray, "A Weapon against War: Conscientious Objection in the United States, Australia, and France," *Politics & Society*, 21 no. 4 (1993): 425–64.

11. Rosen, "Vietnam"; Levi, *Consent, Dissent, and Patriotism*, 17–30.

12. Richard E. Neustadt, "The Politics of Mistrust," in *Why People Don't Trust Government*, ed. Nye et al. 192–96; and, in the same ovlume, Nye, introduction, 15, and Nye and Zelikow, "Conclusion: Reflections, Conjectures, and Puzzles," 264–65, 270. Korea gets some attention in the volume, and Vietnam a little more, but only in connection with other theories of declining trust.

13. Nye, introduction, *Why People Don't Trust Government*, 16; Nye and Zelikow, "Reflections, Conjectures and Puzzles,"

14. Joseph Bykofsky and Harold Larson, *The History of the United States Army in World War II*, vol. 9, *The Technical Services; The Transportation Corps: Operations Overseas* (Washington, D.C.: Office of the Chief of Military History, Department of the Army, 1957), cited in Ross, *Preparing for Ulysses*, 185.

15. Ross, *Preparing for Ulysses*, 185, 182, 186, 188–89. President Truman to Representative John M. Folger (D-N.C.), November 16, 1945, cited in Ross, *Preparing for Ulysses*, 187.

16. Robert H. Ferrell, *Harry S. Truman: A Life* (Columbia: University of Missouri Press, 1995), 324–25; Leffler, *A Preponderance of Power*, 379, 383–90, 406–18; McCullough, *Truman*, 789–90; Maeva Marcus, *Truman and the Steel Seizure Case: The Limits of Presidential Power* (Durham, N.C.: Duke University Press, 1994 [1971], 2–3). The Truman administration also misread the relationship between the North Koreans and the Chinese, and that between the Soviet Union and China, as was evident when the president gave General MacArthur license to cross the 38th parallel.

17. Hamby, *Man of the People*, 564; McCullough, *Truman*, 817–18, 835–36, 855; Marcus, *Truman and the Steel Seizure Case*, 33–34. The Truman administration did take a few extraordinary measures to ensure its ability to support the war in Korea. It received supplemental appropriations for the defense budget, made requests for higher taxes, imposed credit restrictions, and in September 1950 received authority to allocate scarce materials and impose wage/price controls through the passage of the Defense Production Act. On December 15, 1950, the President established the Office of Defense Mobilization, and on December 16 proclaimed a "limited" national emergency. Hamby, *Man of the People*, 549–50; Leffler, *A Preponderance of Power*, 403; Marcus, *Truman and the Steel Seizure Case*, 3.

18. Michael S. Sherry, *In the Shadow of War* (New Haven: Yale University Press, 1995), 186–87; McCullough, *Truman*, 847.

19. Quoted in Knightley, *The First Casualty*, 376; Sherry, *In the Shadow of War*, 250; Rust, *Kennedy in Vietnam*.

20. Quoted in Miles Hudson and John Stanier, *War and the Media* (Phoenix Mill, U.K.: Sutton Publishing, 1997), 108.

21. George C. Herring, "'Cold Blood': LBJ's Conduct of Limited War in Vietnam," *Harmon Memorial Lectures in Military History*, no. 33, (Colorado: U.S. Air Force Academy, 1990), 15–16.

22. Samuel Lubell, *The Hidden Crisis in American Politics* (New York: Norton, 1971), 263.

23. Herring, "'Cold Blood,'" 16–18, 21–22; Lubell, *Hidden Crisis in American Politics*, 264; see also George C. Herring, "Johnson as Commander in Chief," in *Shadow on the White House: Presidents and the Vietnam War, 1945–1975*, ed. David L. Anderson (Lawrence: University Press of Kansas, 1993); Louis Harris, *The Anguish of Change* (New York: Norton, 1973), 53–65.

24. Knightley, *First Casualty*, 420–21.

25. Harris, *Anguish of Change*, 69–71.

26. Sherry, *In the Shadow of War*, 287.

27. Herring, "'Cold Blood'"; Rosen, "Vietnam."

28. William J. Rust, *Kennedy in Vietnam* (New York: Charles Scribner's Sons, 1985), 51; David L. Anderson, "Dwight D. Eisenhower and Wholehearted Support of Ngo Dinh Diem," in *Shadow on the White House: Presidents and the Vietnam War, 1945–1975*, ed. David L. Anderson (Lawrence: University Press of Kansas, 1993), 43.

29. Herring, "'Cold Blood,'" 20–21; Sherry, *In the Shadow of War*, 274; Rosen, "Vietnam."

30. Cathie J. Martin, *Shifting the Burden: The Struggle over Growth and Corporate Taxation* (Chicago: University of Chicago Press, 1991), 23, 81, 85, 87, 99, 101.

31. Obligatory military service may be problematic for democratic societies, especially ones with strong rights-based political traditions, as Margaret Levi points out in *Consent, Dissent, and Patriotism*.

32. Stephen M. Kohn, *Jailed for Peace: The History of American Draft Law Violators, 1658–1985* (Westport, Conn.: Greenwood Press, 1987), 46–47. It took a postwar Supreme Court decision for COs to lose the felon label and to get their civil rights back. Michael C. C. Adams, *The Best War Ever* (Baltimore: Johns Hopkins University Press, 1994), 78. With the end of the federal government's powers to enlist military personnel at the close of the Second World War, Congress passed the Selective Service Act in 1948 as the basis for future military mobilization. The 1948 law allowed for the drafts of American servicemen for the Korean and Vietnam conflicts. It was under the provisions of the 1948 law that Jimmy Carter in 1980 revived the requirement that young men register with the selective service system. See Kohn, *Jailed for Peace*, 28–29; Levi, *Consent, Dissent, and Patriotism*, 170–71.

33. George Q. Flynn, *The Draft, 1940–1973* (Lawrence: University Press of Kansas, 1993), 174; Levi, *Consent, Dissent, and Patriotism*, 172.

34. Kohn, *Jailed for Peace*, 92; Flynn, *The Draft*, 179–81; Jean Bethke Elshtain, *Women and War* (New York: Basic Books, 1987), 203–4; Levi, *Consent, Dissent, and Patriotism*, 171–77. The AVF eliminated the tension between the selectivity of the draft and the political goal of equality of sacrifice, to be replaced by a market logic: the military now selected those fit to serve from among those willing to serve (with compensation). The AVF also standardized procedures across the highly uneven selective service system. In addition, the AVF undercut the rationale for the protest against the draft and the war in Vietnam. Flynn, *The Draft*, 166–68; James W. Davis

and Kenneth M. Dolbeare, *Little Groups of Neighbors: The Selective Service System* (Chicago: University of Chicago Press, 1968).

35. Levi, *Consent, Dissent, and Patriotism*, 173–77; Davis and Dolbeare, *Little Groups of Neighbors*, 89, 93, 108–10; Elshtain, *Women and War*, 37. Indicatively, the proportion of indicted COs who were convicted declined from 75 percent in 1967 to about one-half that level in the early 1970s, and those imprisoned for draft law violations received shorter sentences. Kohn, *Jailed for Peace*, 90–91. The relaxing of qualifying conditions for CO status paralleled the passage of the Twenty-sixth Amendment to the U.S. Constitution, which lowered the voting age to eighteen. See Benjamin Ginsberg, *The Consequences of Consent: Elections, Citizen Control and Popular Acquiescence* (Reading, Mass.: Addison-Wesley, 1982).

36. Boulding, quoted in Kohn, *Jailed for Peace*, 127; Flynn, *The Draft*, 175; Levi, *Consent, Dissent, and Patriotism*, 172.

37. Flynn, *The Draft*, 219.

38. American women have never been drafted into the armed services. Nor are they required to register with the Selective Service. Britain did conscript women during the Second World War, beginning in 1942 (and female officers could command men). Israel routinely drafts women into its defense force.

39. The WAACs became the WACs in 1943. Women volunteered in the First World War, too, but sought the establishment of formal military services for the recognition and compensation that they could provide. Leisa Meyer, *Creating GI Jane: Sexuality and Power in the Women's Army Corps during World War II* (New York: Columbia University Press, 1996), 11, 13–14).

40. Brian Mitchell, *Weak Link: The Feminization of the American Military* (Washington, D.C.: Regnery Gateway Press, 1989), 14; Elshtain, *Women and War*, 189. Elshtain notes that the behavior of American women during wartime was consistent with and antecedent to a "cultural ideal of postwar domesticity": most had clerical or custodial positions. Nor could they issue orders to male personnel. Married women were not welcome in the armed forces, and pregnant women were discharged. Women were expected to remain "women" and serve as full-time homemakers. As Elshtain writes, "women were not crudely coerced *en masse* to 'return' to the home: most of them had never left it to begin with, and those who had shared the domestic dreams of those who had not." *Women and War*, 7, 189–91; see also Adams, *The Best War Ever*, 85, 134, 144).

41. Adams, *The Best War Ever*, 85. Historians note that sexism was rampant in the U.S. military. It was widely believed that women in the military were "loose" and housed in brothels for the pleasure of officers. Indeed, for women from small towns and with little worldly experience, the military did afford an unprecedented opportunity for sexual expression, whether heterosexual or homosexual. But the pregnancy rate for women in the military — only 48 per 1,000, as compared to 117 per 1,000 for civilian women — hardly suggests rampant sexual activity, assuming that women in the military had access to birth control and engaged in homosexual relations in the same proportion as the general population (Meyer, *Creating GI Jane*, 108. Other evidence indicates, rather, that the change in women's role posed a threat to men and to traditional conceptions of womanhood. Most women found military service unappealing, and women who entered the military did not usually stay long. The discrepancy between the proportion of women who served in the military in all

(3 percent) and those serving at any one time (2.3 percent) reveals the high turnover rate for women in the military, given their minuscule casualty rates. Meyer, *Creating GI Jane*, 73, 147–78; D'Ann Campbell, *Women at War with America: Private Lives in a Patriotic Era* (Cambridge: Harvard University Press, 1984); Adams, *The Best War Ever*, 86; Campbell, Elshtain, *Women at War*; Mitchell, *Weak Link* (re: high turnover rate for women, see 14, 17–18).

42. Mitchell, *Weak Link*, 19; Jeanne Holm, *Women in the Military* (Novato, Calif.: Presidio Press), 159–60. As Mitchell points out, the use by the government of slogans such as "America's Finest Women Stand beside Her Finest Men" in public-relations campaigns to recruit female volunteers may well have been counterproductive (19).

43. Sherry, *In the Shadow of War*, 301; Mitchell, *Weak Link*, 20–21.

44. Mitchell, *Weak Link*, 20.

45. Elshtain, *Women and War*, 185; Mitchell, *Weak Link*, 20.

46. Sherry, *In the Shadow of War*, 300–301.

47. Quoted in Holm, *Women in the Military*, 242, emphasis added. The issue of the role of women in the military is not a simple one. It might be argued that women should be allowed to serve in combat if they wish to: if they might be raped or otherwise sexually abused by the enemy, how is that different from the threat a man faces of being sodomized or tortured? But there is, of course, a profound biological reason to keep women away from prolonged combat roles: whereas men are almost wholly expendable in sustaining national populations, women, as the bearers and nursers of children, are not. Women could also be captured by enemy troops and become pregnant with their children, thereby sustaining the enemy population.

48. It should be noted that the military's employment of women during World War II is subject to important qualifications: there was considerable discrimination against black women as well as against much smaller populations of Hispanic and Jewish women serving in the military; there was a marked class bias in the recruitment, assignment, and promotion of women by the military; and there was considerable discrimination against lesbians. Meyer, *Creating GI Jane*, 66–67, 90–99, 147–78. Nor did these problems go away in the 1950s and 1960s.

49. U.S. Bureau of the Census, *Public Debt of the Federal Government: 1791 to 1970*, Series Y 493–504 (Washington, D.C.: U.S. GPO, 1975), 1117.

50. Roderick P. Hart, *The Sound of Leadership* (Chicago: University of Chicago Press, 1984); Joshua Meyrowitz, *No Sense of Place* (New York: Oxford University Press, 1986).

51. There were about 300 American newspaper correspondents covering World War II within a year of the attack on Pearl Harbor and 435 correspondents by early 1943. The number of correspondents never exceeded 500 persons at any one time, and the military accredited about 1,600 journalists in all. Frank Luther Mott, *American Journalism*, 3d ed. (New York: Macmillan, 1962), 742.

52. Betty Houchin Winfield, *FDR and the News Media* (New York: Columbia University Press, 1994), 176.

53. Mott, *American Journalism*, 764; Winfield, *FDR and the News Media*, 180. The Roosevelt administration also used its censorship powers to keep the President's visits to munitions plants in the West out of the news, blacked out information on

FDR's overseas trips, and covered up the President's trips to Lucy Mercer Ruther-
ford's estate in New Jersey. Winfield, FDR and the News Media, 181–82.

54. Davis was thus unable to live up to his word that a steady flow of truth, and
nothing but, would issue from his office.

55. Phillip Knightley, The First Casualty (New York: Harcourt Brace Jovanovich,
1975), 135, 244, 262, 264, 274–79, 283–85.

56. Adams, The Best War Ever, 10; Knightley, The First Casualty, 280.

57. Adams, The Best War Ever, 9; Knightley, The First Casualty, 296.

58. Knightley, The First Casualty, 333.

59. Mott, American Journalism, 852; Knightley, The First Casualty, 345–46.

60. About 600 journalists visited the war area; 175–250 of these were on the UN
command roster. They were divided into front-line reporters and those who stayed at
headquarters (the large majority). Hudson and Stanier, War and the Media, 90.

61. Knightley, The First Casualty, 347–49; Hudson and Stanier, War and the
Media, 96, 97–98; McCullough, Truman, 790–808, 819, 843–47; Marcus, Truman
and the Steel Seizure Case.

62. See James Reston, The Artillery of the Press (New York: Harper and Row,
1966); Tom Wicker, On Press (New York: Viking, 1975); Daniel Hallin, The "Uncensored War" (New York: Oxford University Press, 1986); Thomas Patterson, Out of
Order (New York: Knopf, 1993); Herring, "'Cold Blood.'"

63. Ronald Steel, Walter Lippmann and the American Century (Boston: Little,
Brown, 1992); Hallin, The "Uncensored War"; Herring, "Johnson as Commander in
Chief"; Melvin Small, "Nixon and the War at Home," in Shadow on the White
House, ed. Anderson, 130–51; Jeffrey P. Kimball, "Nixon and the Diplomacy of
Threat and Symbolism," in Shadow on the White House, ed. Anderson, 152–83. The
military also became increasingly divided over the Vietnam War, as did President
Johnson's cabinet and the American public, and the press on Vietnam reflected this
political and societal split.

64. Knightley, The First Casualty, 386–88, 423. Television also plays a big role in
the evolution of criteria for reporting the news. Television, with its massive audience
and short news hole, favors interpretive, thematic news stories. There were 100 million television sets in the United States by 1967, as compared to just 10 million in
1952. In response to the pervasiveness of television coverage, newspaper coverage has
also become more interpretive over the course of the 1960s and 1970s — especially
since television may have already broken a story the day before. See Patterson, Out
of Order.

65. See Patterson, Out of Order, on the increase in reportage that is briefer, more
critical, less descriptive, more interpretive, and oriented more to political controversy
than to substantive issues.

66. Nye, introduction to Why People Don't Trust Government, 15–17; Nye and
Zelikow, "Reflections, Conjectures, and Puzzles," 269–70; Lipset and Schneider,
Confidence Gap, 382, 399–401.

67. Nie et al., Changing American Voter, 277–280; Lipset and Schneider, The
Confidence Gap, 7, 33, 50, 54; Abramson, Political Attitudes in America, 12–13,
228–38.

68. One possible reason for this lack of inquiry is that survey data on trust of
government between 1958 and 1968 shows either no change or an increase, depend-

ing on the indicator of "trust." Nie et al., *The Changing American Voter*, 276–79; Lipset and Schneider, *Confidence Gap*, 17, 33; Abramson, *Political Attitudes in America*, 12; Robert Z. Lawrence, "Is It Really the Economy, Stupid?" in *Why People Don't Trust Government*, ed. Nye and Zelikow, 129. Nie et al. include data from 1952 through 1958 that show a marked *drop* in political involvement across all education levels and consistent with the findings here, but the authors do not attempt to explain these data. *The Changing American Voter*, 276. Nye et al. use data on governmental trust dating from 1958 onward, as well as other data (not directly on governmental trust) that range both well before and well after the late 1950s. Nye and Zelikow, *Why People Don't Trust Government*, 129. Patterson's data in *Out of Order* do not go back before 1960, and Hetherington begins his study in 1964. "Effect of Political Trust," 313.

69. Nye and Zelikow, "Reflections, Conjectures, and Puzzles," 269–76.

70. See Patterson, *Out of Order*, 31–32, 212–15; Bartholomew H. Sparrow, *Uncertain Guardians: The News Media as a Political Institution* (Baltimore: Johns Hopkins University Press, 1999), 28–29, 51.

71. On the impact of the Second World War on American government and society, see Sherry, *In The Shadow of War*; Sparrow, *From the Outside In*; John Morton Blum, *V Was for Victory: Politics and American Culture during World War II* (New York: Harcourt Brace Jovanovich, 1973); Doris Kearns Goodwin, *No Ordinary Time: Franklin and Eleanor Roosevelt: The Home Front in World War II* (New York: Simon and Schuster, 1994); Geoffrey Perrett, *Days of Sadness, Years of Triumph* (New York: Coward, McCann, and Geoghegan, 1973); Adams, *The Best War Ever*; Harold G. Vatter, *The U.S. Economy in World War II* (New York: Columbia University Press, 1985); Alan Brinkley, *The End of Reform: New Deal Liberalism in Recession and War* (New York: Knopf, 1995).

72. For a comparison between World War I and World War II, see Sporrow, *From the Outside In*, 286–306.

73. Robert J. McMahon, "Truman and the Roots of U.S. Involvement," in *Shadow on the White House*, ed. Anderson, 25–26. It is frequently pointed out that President Eisenhower was prescient and cautious enough to avoid sending American troops into Vietnam (e.g., Anderson, "Dwight D. Eisenhower," 43–62). Yet Eisenhower did continue to use the rhetoric of the Cold War and to build up the military (especially with respect to nuclear weapons and aeronautics), and he supported Diem with money, equipment, and personnel. More importantly, he nowhere provided the strategic rationale for *refusing* assistance to the titular rulers of South Vietnam.

74. A recent U.S. Navy white paper "Forward . . . From the Sea" takes as its premise that U.S. forces are not prepared to fight wars of attrition.

75. Nettl, "The State as a Conceptual Variable," 561, 562–63, 565–66, 573–74, 586.

76. See Samuel Huntington, *Political Order In Changing Societies* (New Haven: Yale University Press, 1968); James O'Connor, *The Fiscal Crisis of the State* (New York: St. Martin's, 1973); Charles Tilly, ed., *The Formation of National States in Western Europe* (Princeton: Princeton University Press, 1975); Stephen D. Krasner, *Defending the National Interest: Raw Materials Investment and U.S. Foreign Policy* (Princeton: Princeton University Press, 1978); Peter Katzenstein, ed., *Between Power*

and Plenty: Foreign Economic Policies of Advanced Industrial States (Madison: University of Wisconsin Press, 1978); Theda Skocpol, States and Social Revolutions (Cambridge: Cambridge University Press, 1979).

77. See Hudson and Stanier, War and the Media; Ted Galen Carpenter, The Captive Press: Foreign Policy Crises and the First Amendment (Washington, D.C.: Cato Institute, 1995); Sparrow, Uncertain Guardians.

78. See the second and third points of Morgenthau's definition of total war (note 3 above).

79. David L. Anderson, "Presidential Leadership and U.S. Intervention," in Shadow on the White House, ed. Anderson, 15.

80. McNamara, cited in Herring, "'Cold Blood,'" 16.

Eleven

Reinventing the American State: Political Dynamics in the Post–Cold War Era

PETER A. GOUREVITCH

THE END OF the Cold War brings before the American polity another round of familiar questions about its institutions and politics: What public policies should be adopted to position the United States effectively in the world arena? What changes, if any, in the nation's institutions would this require? There is a long-standing disagreement on the proper answers to these questions. One side sees institutional insufficiency and weakness in the present American system: it does not and cannot sustain the policies required for an effective projection of power in the international arena. The other side sees great capacity: The American system can be very effective when it wishes to be. Each side stresses a different aspect of American reality. The insufficiency school focuses on the fragmentation of power that lies in the system of check and balances. The capacity school focuses on how a democracy enables its leaders with ample power when they are able to work through the exigencies of the system. The debate between these two poles is not restricted to the interaction of international and domestic politics, but it has particular resonance there because of the presumed distinctive features of foreign policy in national political life.

From the colonial period to the present, American institutions and politics have been strongly influenced by interaction with forces outside U.S. borders. International factors have had an important bearing on American security needs, economic policies, political institutions, partisan political cleavages, culture, and, through migration, the very composition of the nation's population, and membership in the American polity. The international arena shapes definitions of American identity, of American interests, and of the identity and interests of component pieces of the American polity.

Political scientists who specialize in the United States have not particularly appreciated the significance of international factors. Specialists in international relations and comparative politics who analyze the linkage between international and domestic politics have drawn largely on European experience, drawing comparisons to Asia and Latin America. They have explored the way war and trade have shaped the growth of state institutions and the struggles between democratic and authoritarian political forms.[1] Specialists in U.S. political life have been less interested in these influences, but that form of isolationism seems to be eroding.[2]

As the United States has come to play a substantial role in world affairs, students of American political development have debated the connection between U.S. institutions and its international activities. Huntington has seen American institutions as flawed.[3] He characterized the United States as having a "Tudor Polity," designed for a bygone era of few foreign enemies and unable to deal with the demands on the executive posed by present-day foreign policy. In contrast, theorists of democracy and the democratic peace argue that the very features which Huntington saw as weakness — checks and balances, restrictions on executive authority — should be seen as a source of strength, a set of democratic checks that encourage greater mobilization of social support around foreign policy and stronger commitments in the world arena, a means of preventing a "democratic deficit" that would, in the long run, enfeeble the executive.

This old debate is renewed in the United States with the sharp change in the global environment brought about by the end of the Cold War. American politics and institutions were profoundly affected by a sequence of international pressures which began in 1929: economic depression, world war, the Cold War, substantial expansion of international trade, of economic competition and of human migration. The United States developed a pattern of institutions and policy that can be labeled the "Cold War state." International factors played a major role in shaping this pattern. Global conflict, especially with the USSR, influenced considerably the political alignments that shaped public policy in many domestic fields (e.g., labor, income, economic policy, race, health, and cities) in addition to obvious international policy arenas concerning the deployment of military force and international alliances.

With the end of the Cold War, the international factor in those alignments has changed considerably. The American polity now confronts substantial disagreements about the proper purpose of government action, at home and abroad. As a result, political forces in the United States have been reevaluating their views of the goals of government and the institutions that these goals require. Fragmented about the ends of government, American politics struggles over its political institutions as well. Ends and means — objectives and institutions — bear some significant relation to each other. The institutional apparatus designed to deal with the depression, World War II, postwar Reconstruction, and the Cold War no longer fits the goals of political actors experiencing intense international economic competition, structural readjustment of the American economy, extensive social and economic change, and a multipolar security environment. Under the new conditions of the post–Cold War era, we are reliving an episode in an old story: the reworking of the institutions of government to fit new purposes and politics.

The Interaction of Domestic and International Politics

The relationship between international influences and American institutions raises some interesting analytic issues. Through what mechanisms do international factors influence domestic political development and institutions? This question is the subject of extensive arguments in the field of international relations. Here I shall focus on a particular answer, one that stresses the logic of domestic politics in shaping responses to foreign influences: international factors affect national behavior if those influences impact the preferences of domestic actors. Short of an outright invasion — when Hitler invaded Denmark, the preferences of Danish domestic actors were irrelevant: he wanted to control Denmark and conquered it in one day — it is domestic actors who decide how to interpret a foreign influence. If India sets off a bomb, actors in Pakistan decide how to respond. If the United States presses Japan on trade barriers, it is actors in Japan who decide whether to accede or resist. Thus, I reject a purely realist line of reasoning which treats the state as a unitary actor in which there are no internal considerations shaping response to external forces.

International forces appear through the behaviors of domestic political actors in two noticeable ways. First, international forces shape cleavages on policy actions. International pressures — trade issues, security, culture, migration — require a policy response. Actors line up for or against a particular policy: higher or lower tariffs, more or less military spending, open or closed migration policies. In so doing, external forces shape conflict around alternative policies having to do with foreign policy, and thus shape party structures and electoral alignments. For much of the nineteenth century, the tariff divided Republicans from Democrats; in the late twentieth century, trade issues cut through each party. Military spending divided Republicans and Democrats in the late 1990s, while migration issues continue to cut across both parties in complex ways.

By influencing cleavages and alliances, international forces influence policy outputs in areas that may have nothing to do with foreign policy. If Americans vote for the Republicans because they want higher defense spending to deal with foreign threats, the effect of a Republican majority is likely also to produce limits on abortion and initiatives to introduce prayer into public schools, as groups supporting these policies are part of the Republican coalition. Similarly, those who want limits on abortion may get more defense spending, whether they want it or not.

A second impact of international forces is on institutional development. Each policy response requires institutions to implement it. In the early modern period, the European powers involved in continental power struggles saw rapid growth of bureaucratic structures to sustain armed forces and the taxes these required. A similar process has been at work in the United States. The National Security Council, the Pentagon, the U.S. Trade Office, the Central Intelligence Agency all reflect the demands of policy choices dealing with international affairs. As capacity and institutions grow, they have their own impact on policy debates.

These two forces, cleavages around policy preferences and institutional development, take place within each country, but in interaction with similar forces within others. Tariffs in one country provoke tariffs in another. Arms buildups in one country provoke arms buildups in others. Coalitions within one country interact with developments in another. Domestic political responses to international pressures are thus an example of strategic interaction.[4]

International pressures operate on a country's policies through their impact on the policy preferences of domestic actors as refracted by institutions. Governments respond to constituency demands. In a democracy the electorate is broad; in an authoritarian regime, the selectorate[5] may be narrow, but in both systems, governments have constituents to worry about. How demands turn into policy depends on the mechanism by which preferences are aggregate, the institutions. To understand what politicians do, we need to know something about how institutions combine preferences through procedures that force results to emerge.

The distinct role of preferences and institutions fuels the disagreement on the American polity's ability to sustain new challenges in the world arena. Those who stress demand pressures fear that American institutions fail to provide leaders with sufficient latitude to define and promote a coherent national interest. Conversely, those who stress democratic capacity believe that institutional process strengthens leaders, by producing consensus in support of decisions made.

Huntington's discussion of the United States as a "Tudor polity" is the best-known statement of the "insufficiency position": the institutions of the United States hinder its ability to deal with the world. While Huntington applies the phrase "Tudor polity" specifically to the United States, his argument is part of a broader concern about democracy and foreign policy more generally: too many popular demands on the executive limit its ability to take actions vital to the national interest.

The American "Tudor polity" was framed by Lockean liberals in the eighteenth century to deal with a frontier society remote from the struggles of the great powers. It was designed to limit government, to constrain the executive. This, Huntington worried, is a handicap for international relations. A strong executive, the ability to act decisively and with determination, is required for effective foreign policy. Legislatures cannot respond to the character of international issues. Huntington is also worried about the effect of democracy itself: the public's priorities and time horizons are myopic and short-term. Effective foreign policy requires some distance from public pressures, the capacity to make unpopular decisions. Kissinger and De Gaulle have written in a similar vein.

A very different position has been taken by several theorists of democratic institutions. These writers stress "democratic capacity"; they think that democratic institutions are flexible, that they can be adapted to fit the demands made of them, and that democracy per se confers strengths which authoritarian institutions lack. Where Huntington sees democracy and separation of powers as the hallmarks of a weak state, these authors see in democracy considerable strength. Lack of autonomy by the executive, substantial democratic pressure, a bureaucracy subordinated to popular will and legislative supervision—these are seen by the democracy/credibility school as advantages. What makes a government strong is not the will of a unitary sovereign, but rather the capacity to mobilize resources and deploy them for specific purposes. That capacity arises from a committed population, a public that supports the actions of government and is willing to give it money and authority. Democracy does better than oligarchy or autocracy because democratic governments have to mobilize a broader social consensus.[6]

Precisely because consensus has to be won, democratic governments are more credible in the commitments they make. Their processes are transparent. Because decisions require many approval steps, working through veto gates, decisions, once made, are likely to stick. By contrast, the powerful executive, for which Huntington yearns, is capricious. He can change his mind, while the president of a democracy has a harder time changing hers. Democracies are thus able to make agreements, with their own citizens and with others, to make alliances, to form institutions, to make commitments.

This "democratic capacity" position turns on its head a set of arguments about state power. Comparisons of political systems often classified states into "strong" and "weak," based on the degree of autonomy from social pressures and the extent of highly articulated bureaucratic structures with which to implement policy. Britain and the United States, were often classified as weak states because their bureaucracy was less fully developed and the executive subject to parliamentary supervision.[7]

The democratic-capacity approach leads to a quite different analysis. Britain is seen as a strong state, able to project power in international relations: to engage in extensive colonization and successful war, through alliances, with continental rivals.[8] Parliamentary oversight of the Crown is not a weakness but a strength, for Parliament provides taxes and other forms of support for executive action. The transparency of parliamentary process and the constraints on the executive made British policy more reliable and predictable. One example of the benefit this provided was the ability of the British crown to borrow money at a lower rate; creditors judged the British monarchy more likely to repay than those who did not have to face parliaments. By contrast, the absolutist states of the Continent were weakened by their bureaucratic capacity, because it came at the expense of less engagement by the population, who had not been consulted on the policies they were asked to support, and less credibility for the word of the monarchy. Thus, the supposedly weaker English state proved more effective in mobilizing resources for international engagement than its "strong" absolutist rivals.

These two approaches — institutional insufficiency and democratic capacity — can be applied to the analytic issues of the relationship of foreign policy to the evolution of U.S. institutions. Huntington stresses the constraints of America's formal institutions: they limit the executive in ways that hinder effective response to international developments, and without changing the Constitution, these constraints cannot be overcome. The democratic capacity approach sees greater possibility within the frame of the formal institutions. Whatever the polity wants, it can do. If there is a strong desire for some kind of action, public authorities can create the institutions needed to do it. Congress and the president are able to create structures to implement policy. Reciprocal trade and fast-track authorization are good examples in the field of trade policy. Foreign governments are reluctant to engage in trade negotiations with the United States because they know that whatever the president negotiates Congress can amend — a point on Huntington's side of the debate. But knowing this, Congress authorizes fast-track negotiations: it binds itself to voting for or against a treaty submitted by the president, without possibility of amendments. If a majority desires free trade, it can create an institutional process that favors it — a point on the side of the democratic capacity school.[9]

These conflicting approaches help us to understand the impact of new developments in the international arena upon American politics, policies, and institutions in the post–Cold War era. The demand/capacity approach calls our attention to the way international developments influenced policy preferences inside the United States. The institutional approach calls our attention to the way existing structures in the United States influenced the policy debates and to how institutions were adjusted in response to policy developments.

The first step in the analysis below will be to examine the origins of the Cold War state in the United States, a process that began in 1929 and continued till the 1980s. While that period can be defined, the next phase is still in process and cannot yet be confidently characterized. It is too soon to see how the sharp changes in America's political environment will work itself out through institutional change. The struggle takes place before our eyes. We are little more than a decade away from 1989. A decade after 1929, the transformation in the American state was just beginning. Yet it is an interesting and important exercise to explore what caused the creation of the modern American state in midcentury, to examine what causes the persistence of its characteristic forms long after the forces that molded them have ceased to exist, and to ask what political combinations might lead to various changes in the future.

The Origins of the Cold War State

The political system in place when the Berlin Wall fell in 1989 had emerged rapidly during the years following 1929. The American state was by no means weak before then. It had, after all, conquered a continent, kept out foreign powers, defeated the Native American populations, fought and resolved a civil war, supported the growth of what became the world's largest economy, ended formal slavery, built elements of an empire in Asia and the Western Hemisphere and helped defeat the Entente in World War I.

After 1929, though, the American political system and its institutional apparatus changed substantially. Its ability to do so marks the importance of the demand school of analysis. The basic arrangements of the Constitution were not altered, yet the institutions of the U.S. government were modified quite extensively. The transformations that took place were thus done within the framework of the original constitution and its institutions.

This underscores the importance of demands. We can see three major pressures leading to demands that influenced political and institutional development. Each type of pressure is analytically and politically autonomous. None occurs without the other; the political game lies in their interaction. These demands are (1) the social desire for economic security and equality, leading to the "welfare state"; (2) the economic interest in orderly markets, leading to the "regulatory state"; and (3) the foreign policy interest of confronting first the Axis Powers, then the USSR, leading to the "security state." These forces have long influenced the character of U.S. political institutions:

Social stability and redistribution. States have intervened to preserve social stability, respond to the pressure of interest groups, and sometimes to promote demands for equality. Social insurance, child labor laws, health and factory inspection are but some of the many examples of social programs which involve expanding state capacity.

Economic development. To promote economic wealth, states developed legal systems, courts, taxation, education, and physical infrastructure. Effective states encouraged growth, and growth helped sustain effective states.[11]

Political-military. In an anarchic world of military conflict, states were constructed by rulers who could mobilize the resources necessary to sustain armies capable of extending and maintaining frontiers, in processes familiar to us from the writings of Hintze, Tilly, et al. Bureaucracies and institutions grew up to maintain the states so created.[10]

These three processes interact. War requires economic resources; economic development makes war making possible; war may mobilize populations into demanding a greater voice and share of resources; political and social breakthroughs may enhance war-making capacity. While all of these processes are at work in all "modern" countries, they differ in the blend of the three elements.

The American Version of the Midcentury "Historical Compromise": The Depression, the War and the New Deal

All of these processes may be observed in the midcentury explosion of the American state. Economic, social, and military demands converged to drive forward dramatic expansion of the state apparatus and the projection of American power into domestic society and the world outside. The American constitution did not prevent this expansion or paralyze the government; political support enabled a substantial reframing of the American state. State expansion happened in other industrial countries as well, regardless of their institutional structure. Where institutions did matter was on some of the specific features of each country's policies; the expansion of the American welfare state, for example, was limited compared to its European counterparts.

In the 1930s, it was economic weakness that drove expansion of the American state, not political-military considerations — in contrast to Europe, where rearmament rose substantially from the midthirties onward. After World War I, the United States shrank back from international military entanglements and kept its armed forces quite small. Social security, labor relations systems, agricultural assistance, and regulation of securities, banking, oil, interstate transport, and airline industries — the legislation of the New Deal is quite familiar to the readers of this volume.[12]

These measures cannot be understood solely as expressing democratic populist demands for equality and security. They reflect as well a drive for economic efficiency and rationality. There has always been a vigorous debate within capitalist economies over their management: how much mercantilism or regulation, how much untrammeled competition? The New Deal represented a substantial victory for American mercantilism, a tradition dating back to Hamilton. The twentieth-century Hamiltonians held that efficient markets required some degree of regulation. Banking reform would encourage investment and productivity by making markets more orderly, stable, and honest. Agricultural price supports and marketing boards would rationalize long-term investment in agriculture by stabilizing prices. Highly capital-intensive industries saw that regulation would encourage investment by stabilizing markets—hence the enthusiasm of oil and airlines for this approach. Social security would prevent poverty among the aged; it would also help to stabilize demand, by providing a countercyclical force to flatten the business fluctuations. Labor legislation would empower unions to demand more wages and better working conditions; it would also institutionalize and regularize labor markets.

Thus, in the thirties, government expansion into the economy marked the interaction of welfare/equality goals with notions of efficiency and long-term growth, as well as the simple economic self-defense of interest groups. The combination of these incentives is what gets things done in American politics: it is not clear that any one of them gets very far when it acts alone; each requires the others as allies. These programs did lead to massive expansion of government activity and bureaucratic structure and to the physical growth of the city of Washington.

While the Roosevelt administration became increasingly engaged with international issues during the thirties, international factors were not at first substantial drivers of the expansion of state capacity. Reciprocal trade legislation was a substantial policy step toward international involvement, but it did not generate a big bureaucratic apparatus with reinforcing interest groups.

The war, of course, changed quite profoundly the role of international factors in American politics and the institutions of the American state. War provided powerful new allies to the expansion of government. In 1941 the United States had one of the smallest military establishments of all the major powers; just four years later, it had one of the greatest. The professional structure for war making exploded. The number of people in the armed forces shot into the millions. America's wartime production sustained not only its own war effort but that of its allies as well.

The war shifted FDR's priorities and political alliances within the New Deal. Winning the war took precedence over other objectives. FDR compromised New Deal reform to win over corporate support for his foreign policy and to expand the production needed for full mobilization. Cost-plus contracting, production quotas, production boards, and many other measures substantially extended the corporatist, regulatory economy, based on business-government partnership, that had begun during the peacetime New Deal. The push for extending social reform (national health, civil rights) receded.

Military needs added strong allies to demands for active state involvement in education and research. Since the nineteenth century, agriculture and the high-tech industries of the day (chemistry, electrical equipment) had supported the growth of higher education and government support for research. Now military objectives sustained research in a wide array of fields, from atomic weapons to medicines, jets and radar to foods and clothing.

World War II created a coalition around a pattern of policy that was sustained by the Cold War and its hot spots (Korea, Vietnam). This had happened before. Crises such as the Civil War and World War I had expanded the state, but it was cut back when peace came.[13] After 1945, there were certainly pressures for a similar retrenchment, and with the end of actual fighting, extensive demobilization took place.[14] But this time, the historical pattern did not repeat itself: the Cold War halted military retrenchment and solidified the patterns that had emerged from 1933 to 1945. There was, to be sure, considerable conflict over U.S. policy. Unilateralist and isolationist sentiment certainly came forward in opposition to treaties that engaged the United States in world affairs. The definition of U.S. interests and commitments was hotly debated. But the outcome, reached in a few years by the late 1940s, marked a strong victory for the activist internationalists, against the unilateralists and isolationists, against forces on the left that wanted accommodation with the USSR, and against forces on the right that wanted to stay out of foreign engagement altogether.

International issues profoundly altered the character of domestic political conflicts in the United States. It altered the New Deal coalition, creating Cold War liberalism. It strengthened some areas of reform and weakened others. It preserved the expanded state and fended off some attacks on the New Deal. It did so in ways which linked New Deal policies to foreign policy activism, defined as a fight against the USSR and world communism.

International security, equality and social welfare, and economic efficiency — these concerns interacted in interesting and important ways, sometimes driving wedges between groups and sometimes uniting them. On the right, isolationists were also against New Deal welfare, labor, and regulatory policies, and those who opposed these policies were often also isolationists. Eisenhower's defeat of Taft broke the isolationist's grip on the Republican Party, and also set back efforts to unravel the New Deal. Moderate and conservative internationalists were willing to work with New Deal reformers to sustain a coalition of support for the projection of American power, the preservation and extension of the military, the construction of alliances in Europe, extensive foreign aid such as the Marshall Plan, intervention in Korea, and so on.

On the left, many supporters of extending the social and economic goals of the New Deal were also against the Cold War. The defeat of the Wallace forces by Truman and Humphrey clipped the influence of left-wing isolationism and accommodation with the USSR. On the right, the McCarthyite terror weakened the institutional strength of forces that supported extension of New Deal welfare programs. Cold War liberals dominated the Democratic Party; Eisenhower internationalists, the Republican.

In foreign policy, this configuration led to a bipartisan consensus around international obligations, containment, and alliances, providing support for the Marshall Plan, NATO, GATT, the Korean War, and massive expansion of the armed forces and the CIA. The domestic correlates of this foreign-policy consensus were preservation of the New Deal reforms but, compared to Europe, little in the way of further advance of a social-democratic platform. Internationalist American business worked out a cross-party bargain with American labor, agriculture, and domestic industries: the American "historical compromise."

Counterparts of this postwar "pact" emerged in the advanced industrial countries of Asia and Europe as well, but the American version was distinctive in several ways important to the forces of state building. First, on the security dimension, U.S. international commitments were more extensive. The United States projected force around the world, with overseas troops and bases supporting international treaty commitments for security. By contrast, France and Britain retrenched and decolonized. Japan created only peacekeeping forces; and did not send any troops abroad. Neither did Germany, despite its gradual development of an army. Aside from the French colonial wars in Indochina and Algeria, only the United States fought extensive wars, in Korea and Vietnam.

Second, on the equality/social reform dimensions, the U.S. welfare state was substantially less generous than the European ones: no national health plans, shorter vacation days, less job security and unemployment compensation, less aid to families and children, no worker participation in industry. (Indeed, passage of the Taft-Hartley Act marked a partial roll-back of the American labor relations system.)

Third, in terms of economic policy and institutions, the United States did not develop the institutions of a mercantilist trading state. The U.S. economy dominated the world after 1945. It accounted for 50 percent of world GNP (an artifact of wartime destruction of the other economic powers: the United States' prewar share was about 22 percent, as it was again in the 1990s). With such vast superiority, the United States could, like Britain in its hegemonic heyday, take the free-trade approach to the international system. The American effort focused on creating the rules and institutions of universal rules of free trade—hence the support for GATT, Bretton Woods, the IMF, the World Bank, and larger regional agglomerations, like the European Economic Community, which would replace nationalist protectionism.[15]

With globally dominant firms, and no immediate challengers, the demand for a mercantilist approach to economic policy was muted. The thirties generated and left some elements of a regulatory state, such as agencies to manage airlines, interstate commerce, agriculture, oil, and a variety of other industries. But industries were not nationalized, as they so often were in Europe.

Some limited elements of an industrial policy were created. The military supported extensive research and investment and influenced economic development through procurement. This had a substantial effect on airplane manufacturing and helped generate the silicon revolution. High-technology industry supported research and educational training. Some machinery for export assistance developed, such as the OPIC and the Ex-Im Bank. But much of American economic policy and industrial strategy did not focus on the trade effects of specific industries. Until the 1980s, it was hard to persuade specialists on monetary policy, for example, that trade might be a variable to consider in shaping monetary policy. The United States had DARPA and the NSF, but no MITI, no "Tresor," no "main banks," and little in the way of corporatist arrangements to promote and develop company interests in trade. Presidents and cabinet members did not noticeably travel to sell business contracts. The contrast with France, Japan, Germany is apparent.[16]

Two decades into the Cold War, the American state had changed dramatically from what it was before 1929, yet still differed from its counterparts elsewhere. Most notably, it had a permanent military establishment of substantial size, unprecedented for the United States, at a time when Germany and Japan had reduced the role of the military, historically prominent in both countries. The United States had created something of a welfare state, with social security, unemployment compensation, Medicare and Medicaid, and welfare, but compared to Europe it was not universal and the benefits were more limited. The United States had created a regulatory system for elements of the economy, but compared to Germany, Japan, and France, it lacked key elements of a "trading state" apparatus.[17]

Politically, the three elements of this system reinforced each other. The system was part of a vast log roll, a coalition of trade-offs, where groups paid costs in one arena to get benefits in another. Cold War liberalism was a glue that held these elements together across partisan lines. The system lasted quite a long time, some elements surviving through the 1990s. From the late sixties onward, as we shall explore below, intense political conflict generated "wedges" which broke the bonds of the glue.

What lessons can we draw from the development of the Cold War state that have bearing on the debate between demand and institutions, between insufficiency and democratic capacity, and between domestic and international politics?

On the side of democratic capacity, we see vast transformation within the boundaries of the formal constitutional system. Congress authorized the formation of a great bureaucracy, with many new agencies and institutions.

The Constitution did not prevent this. Indeed, if anything, it made sure this expansion of state apparatus, if it happened, would have democratic support. The party system evolved and changed to fit new politics and demands. The Republicans abandoned isolationism; the Democrats accepted Cold War institutions.

At the same time, institutions did influence the outcome. This is most notable when we compare the United States to Europe. The expansion of the welfare state was more limited than in Europe (no universal health care), and certain key features of the American market system remained quite distinct, such as less nationalization of industry and autonomy of managerial control (no "mitbestimmung"). Is this because American politics did not "demand" these changes? In that regard, the Cold War played a role in "weakening" demand, because it weakened the bonds among progressive forces, the social-democratic coalition that would have spearheaded such reforms. Or did these efforts falter because of American institutions which weakened the reform coalition by fragmenting power and by giving strength to its opponents through overrepresentation of farmers and rural forces?[18]

But in foreign policy terms, the striking feature of these years is the ability of the American system to generate a wide range of institutional arrangements and to mobilize political support for a great deployment of force and authority around the world. International relations and the Cold War played an important role in shaping these outcomes.

Change: Unraveling the Cold War Compromise

The demise of the Cold War loosened the demand side of the forces that had built the American state and helped dissolve the bonds among the coalitions contending with each other over public policy. Other forces were at work, some dating back to well before the fall of the Berlin Wall in 1989. International influences interacted with domestic ones. Foreign policy was not the determining cleavage line of politics but a key ingredient, one which often served as glue to bind contradictory elements, inherent in all coalitions, together. Foreign policy issues no longer play the role that they did during the Cold War and have become instead a cleavage element within each party and coalition. The linkages formed during the Cold War years have decoupled, precipitating out into components which can be moved around and recombined into shifting coalitions. Thus, autonomous but interactive processes have been at work. Policy conflict on foreign policy eroded the cold War consensus on international relations. Changing views on equality/welfare and on economic policy played an important role as well.

Security

On the security side, the war in Vietnam sharply challenged the consensus on international activism, producing significant cleavages within each of the governing parties. Among the Democrats, an isolationist current revived ("Bring our boys home," "Stop foreign entanglements") and conflicted with the multilateralism of the internationalist left, which favored getting other countries to share costs and working cooperatively with them. On the right, the Vietnam experience contributed initially to the mobilization of strong anticommunist arguments by the Reagan administration, which increased military spending while pressing against the social and regulatory side of government activism. Then, when the USSR crumbled, the glue holding together diverse viewpoints on foreign policy dissolved, releasing three distinct strands of thought on the American right: (a) neo-isolationism, in both left and right versions; (b) unilateral internationalism (the United States should be involved in the world but act on its own, not sharing command or being impeded by alliances with others); (c) and some degree of multilateralism (some commitment to international institutions is needed for the benefit of trade and security).

Both parties have fragmented on foreign policy, weakening bipartisanship in foreign policy and making policy less a product of either party than of transitory coalitions that form around specific issues. In recent years, these splits revealed themselves in several conflicts. Without a mobilized USSR, the military budget has become an object of controversy. The Democratic coalition wants to cut defense spending, while the Republicans want to expand them; but there are complex swirls of opinion that cut across party lines.

On trade and economic issues, we see growing conflict on trade agreements and international financial institutions. Several important policy issues reveal erosion of internationalist positions in both parties and growing opposition to the United States as "final payer," the hegemon that underwrites the costs of providing collective goods to the system as whole. In the past few years Congress has dealt with the Mexican loan bailout, ratification of NAFTA, ratification of the WTO agreement, and expanding loan commitments to the International Monetary Fund to deal with the Asian financial crisis (AFC).

Ratification of NAFTA and the WTO required a Democratic president to offend a core constituency (unions) and join with Republicans to defend a national posture of internationalism. By the time GATT came up for passage, Republican support for paying these costs of these treaties was eroding; Dole had to work hard to overcome the hostility of Helms and other unilateralists. Erosion of internationalism went even further with the Mexican crisis. Republican leaders told the Clinton White House they would support a bailout, but when this became public, popular hostility burst out so strongly that the Republicans backed away and the president had to act unilaterally. The new Republican majority in Congress after 1994 failed to pass a renewal of fast-track authority for trade negotiations. After the AFC in 1997, Congress showed considerable hostility on both sides of the aisle toward adding American funds to the IMF. In late 1999, the Senate defeated the Nuclear Test Ban Treaty, which sought to limit the proliferation of nuclear weapons. Many observers saw this as marking an important step in the erosion of internationalism among Republicans and the intensity of partisanship in foreign policy. At the same time the Clinton administration seemed willing to compromise on abortion funding in international institutions in order to procure congressional approval of dues payments to the United Nations.

Thus, we see lack of consensus on internationalist values in several areas of foreign policy. Some dissenters remain quite committed to the international arena but stress unilateral projection of American power, in contrast to multilateralists. Other dissenters are more clearly isolationist in their views. The distinction has important implications for the American state. The unilateralists require a strong state, especially in security terms. The isolationists do not.

Economic Efficiency

In domestic economic policy, key elements of the New Deal–Cold War compromise have come unraveled in ways which alter the interaction of demand for state action with the evolution of state institutions. The New Deal developed new regulatory institutions, social welfare programs, demand stimulus approaches to full employment, and commitment to free trade. Party alliances played a big role in the coalitions which enacted the legislation to sustain these policies. Now, significant divisions cleave through the parties in some respects, and the parties have shifted positions in others. In some areas, the regulatory structures of the New Deal have been cut back. In others, there is more government activity than ever.

DOMESTIC REGULATION

The most striking changes in policy lie in regulation. Starting in the 1970s, already in the Carter administration, bipartisan support for a regulatory system began to shift toward market efficiency through competition, and several industries (airlines, interstate shipping, telecommunications) were gradually deregulated. By the 1990s, this process had extended even to agriculture, where elements of core New Deal programs were repealed, and in the summer of 1996, substantial portions of family assistance programs were revised. After the air controllers' strike early in the Reagan administration, it became clear that the executive would not use the labor relations system to defend unions.

Welfare was altered substantially by the Republican majority of 1994. In late 1999, after many years of discussion without action, regulation on banking and finance was approved, modifying the Glass Steagall Act passed under the New Deal. Social security so far has remained inviolate, though there has been talk of partial privatization (along with additional funding).

In fiscal policy, the disruption of traditional positions by the parties has been dramatic. The Democrats had championed Keynesian deficit spending against the withering scorn of Republican fiscal probity. Then, supply-side doctrines split the Republican Party. Reagan slashed taxes dramatically without a corresponding cut in spending; indeed, defense spending rose. The effect was a massive budget deficit (the largest ever in peacetime), immense trade deficits (the largest in U.S. history), and a gigantic expansion of the national debt (again the largest in peacetime). For the first time since the nineteenth century, the United States became a net debtor on capital account.

By the 1990s, it was the Democrats who turned to arguments about fiscal responsibility, balancing the budget, increasing savings, encouraging long-run investment, and other traditional conservative themes. Both parties have split deeply on this issue: the Republicans are torn between fiscal conservatism and supply-side "dynamic accounting" that waves off deficits; the Democrats, between budget balancing as a way of lowering interest rates to promote growth (and justify the taxes needed to sustain social welfare spending) and traditional (for them) demand-stimulus arguments about full employment. In 1992, Perot's minority candidacy pushed the deficit agenda forward, while in 1996, Dole's desperation to challenge Clinton induced him to abandon decades of fiscal conservatism for the supply-side line of Kemp. In 2001, Bush successfully pushed through a substantial tax cut, which the Democrats called "irresponsible." Here again debate within the parties is as strong as between them and creates complex lines of potential cleavage, as well as confusion for the electorate.

The conflict over fiscal policy appears more broadly in debates about growth and productivity. U.S. productivity growth has been low for two decades, compared to the high rates of the immediate postwar years. American politics remains deeply divided on the causes and solutions of this slowdown, and thus on the role of the state in counteracting it. The supply-side school stresses incentives to investors: cut taxes, especially capital gains, eliminate regulations, and reduce mandated payroll taxes for social services — an approach which in principle means a substantially smaller state.

Technology and knowledge-based industries worry more about research and development, as well as a range of regulatory issues involving standard setting, intellectual property, and foreign trade issues — concerns that makes them more favorable to state intervention. The political sociology of these positions needs further exploration. Most analyses of it see a split between "Main Street" (small businesses in medium and smallish towns) and "Wall Street" (large, multinational businesses and those related to them).[19] Low versus high technology is another frequently noted cleavage line.

The Democrats have their own cleavages. One wing of the party stresses prudent fiscal management and balancing the budget (the Tsongas campaign of 1992). Another group advocates spending more on education, training, and research. Yet another advocates more stimulus on fiscal policy to promote full employment, while others want more aggressive trade policy both to keep out cheap foreign goods and to push for open foreign markets. Trade issues divide the Democrats profoundly and show signs of doing the same to Republicans. Labor unions have shifted from a decades-old position of free trade toward protectionism — as Rogowski would predict, given that they are no longer an abundant factor of production.[20] Labor has found allies — namely, environmentalists and human rights advocates — who are disproportionately represented among the Democrats. Both groups fear that developing countries can subvert U.S. regulations concerning health, pollution, civil rights, child and female labor, and working conditions.

TRADE POLICY

Trade policy has also changed greatly since the New Deal. The two major parties have switched positions: the Republicans have gone from protectionism to free trade, while the Democrats, although splitting sharply on this issue, concentrate more protectionist sentiment than the GOP. Disagreement on trade (the demand side of policy) correlates with disagreement on what is needed from the American state (the institutional side of policy).

The new terms of debate reflect the growth of international competition and globalization of the American and world economies.[21] An open stance to world trade causes import penetration into the United States, with consequent loss of jobs and capital in these affected sectors. Greater exports reward the competitive sectors, resulting in a growth of jobs and capital.[22] This helps explain party realignments: as labor and labor unions have lost ground, they have become protectionist and pushed the Democratic Party in this direction; as capital has gained ground, it embraced free trade and pushed the Republicans in that direction.

These disagreements link to debates over institutions, at home and abroad. We may classify the various stances on international trade according to the role of the state as envisioned by each other. The continuum would stretch from "ardent free traders" at one end to "protectionists" at the other, with "rules interventionists," "trade promoters," and "mercantilists" in the middle.

The ardent free traders believe that little needs to be done in the way of public policy, because exchange rate adjustments balance out all restrictions. If the Japanese flood our markets by dumping, they favor our consumers at the expense of theirs (thereby subsidizing purchases useful to our own productivity) and create mechanisms that are offset by adjustments in the exchange rate. According to free traders, the U.S. government need do little. The protectionism of other countries is self-defeating and rebounds to our benefit.

The rules interventionists believe that the American economy is affected by the behavior of other countries and by the rules which govern world trade. They advocate a generalized set of rules which stress free flow of goods and uniform regulatory practices accepted by all nations with whom we trade. To achieve this, the rules interventionists say, we need an active state, a government that does more than just sit. They advocate mobilization of state power to put pressure on Japan, China, and other countries to open their markets and deregulate, so that their economies and institutional practices will resemble more closely those of the United States. They desire the U.S. government to be active in international negotiations about the rules of trade—the WTO discussions in particular, but regional arrangements as well, such as NAFTA, EC, APEC, and ASEAN—promoting generalized rules of conduct to which all countries and all firms would agree. This is particularly important for intellectual property and services, sectors in which the U.S. firms are particularly strong and where foreign incursions are costly.

American firms active in world markets focus on the value of contractual rules and free-floating, rapidly evolving, open markets because, as Peter Cowhey notes, this is what they themselves are good at.[23] They do not like the closed, highly corporatist, densely networked, particularistic system found in Japan and other parts of East Asia because they are excluded from these. They support the use of American power to alter these systems by direct country-to-country or multilateral negotiations.

Rules interventionists thus need the state to be active in world affairs, but they don't need a very well-developed state. The kinds of institutions that would further the goals of global "rule making" rely on rather small bureaucracies or agencies whose powers are quite restricted. Congress has been willing to delegate significant authority to the executive in order to promote free trade negotiations—a striking example of the flexibility of the U.S. Constitution where there is strong support for a policy measure. Fast-track authority allows the executive to negotiate an agreement which Congress then approves or rejects without amendment. The free trade majority accepts this "self-denying" ordinance because its members know that if amendments are allowed, they will be unable to resist the temptation to service the particular interests of their districts. A single comprehensive vote, on the other hand, allows a different coalition to form: the logroll for free trade. The failure of fast-track renewal in 1994–95 may be taken as an indication of waning support for that policy. Thus the institution of fast track reflects a specific purpose and does not function independently of policy objectives.[24]

While the authorization of fast track is a significant delegation by Congress to an executive agency, it is nonetheless a clearly bounded one. The USTR and the president must submit agreements, such as NAFTA and WTO, to Congress for approval. The agency may negotiate, but it has a very restricted organizational capacity to work autonomously from the private interests of the country and their allies in the political process. The USTR knows about companies only what they tell it. It does not have a substantial bureaucracy with its own sources of information — unlike, for example, MITI and JETRO in Japan. The USTR has developed a very extensive consulting network with the private sector, forming committees on various product groups. This is a corporatist model: delegation by public authorities to private groups of important information-gathering and reporting tasks. It reflects a desire by the private sector, expressed via its representatives in Congress, to limit government power, to deny it the bureaucratic capacity to escape dependence on the private sector.

The third policy approach to trade, the trade promoters, have not attracted substantial political support in the United States. Trade promoters see the state as a major player in making deals for specific industries and firms, as are MITI and JETRO in Japan and various ministries in France and other countries. These deals are often contracts for projects where the exporting state is a major owner (subways and railroads, energy, telecommunications, airplanes) and the purchaser is itself an agency of the importing state. A system of that kind requires well-developed state institutions.

The United States has not assumed this deal-making role — with some notable exceptions in fields such as armaments and oil. In the early years of the Clinton administration, it appeared that Secretary of Commerce Ron Brown was experimenting with this approach. Brown, with a strong base in the American left, built ties to corporate leaders, successfully persuading many of them that traveling around the world with him was a way of using the authority of the state to promote their own business in specific countries. Flying on Brown's plane was an opportunity they could not miss (although it cost some of them their lives when the plane crashed in 1996). So effective was Brown in building this coalition that he was able to fend off Republican efforts to close his department. Nevertheless, it appears that his approach has been abandoned by his successors. It may be a difficult one to pursue under a divided government (one party in the White House, the other dominating Congress), because the promotional measures required are vulnerable to charges of favoritism and fund-raising.

Mercantilism, or "industrial policy," has similarly not gotten very far in the United States, despite some talk of it in the early years of the Clinton administration. Japan in particular is associated with this policy approach, but it is tried in other countries as well. It consists of active government support of key industries, who receive subsidies, tax breaks, and regulatory assistance to promote their growth. In contrast to European and Asian countries, the concept of industrial policy remains highly controversial and politically weak in the United States. The Clinton administration made some stabs at it, for example, by promoting American capacity in flat panel displays. But the Republicans were ferociously opposed; they shut off the funding for that project and closed ARPA/DARPA in their budget-cutting drive. Industrial policy requires a substantial investment in public institutions. The lack of political support for it in the United States removes an important source for development of the U.S. state. As Japan and Europe faltered economically in the 1990s, the intellectual and political support for industrial policy in those countries also began to erode.

Defense and research are two arenas where the United States has had something of an industrial policy. The U.S. military budget has for decades been a motor to industrial development. This is most evident in the linkage between military and civilian airplane manufacturing. American dominance in the latter is related to its dominance in the former. Any substantial cuts in defense spending would have spillover effects on the civilian economy. For the present, defense spending remains high and provides a major support for a substantial state establishment.

The U.S. government also spends lavishly on research. Research and technology are major drivers of the American economy and receive very substantial assistance from the NSF, the Institutes of Health, and other federal institutions. Political debates have in recent years put pressure on public expenditures for research, while economic competition has put pressure on private spending. A major challenge to the U.S. economy for the future lies in rethinking the relationship among basic research, applied and process technology, and the public purse. As U.S. firms face vigorous competitive pressures, they have cut back substantially on basic research; note the reduction of Bell Labs, Xerox Park, and other famous private-sector laboratories. These firms have shifted research funds to process and engineering uses; this may be a gain to the economy, a proper response to the criticism that American firms neglected manufacturing, technology transfer, and process innovations. Changing the composition of research from basic to applied may serve firms well, but it does raise the issue of how basic research will be funded in the future. As firms find it harder to privatize the results of basic research, it is certainly market-rational for them to abandon it. From a macro point of view, basic research is a public good, the seed corn of future technology transfer and human resource training, and only government funding can adequately promote it. But to what extent the government should supply this public good remains a contentious issue, the outcome of which will influence demand for state action and strong institutions.

The fifth type of response to world trade issues, protectionism, means refusing to accept trade-opening treaties and accepting various barriers to imports. Sentiment for this rises and falls inversely with the U.S. economy. The boom of the 1990s muted the calls for protection heard at the beginning of the decade, but they would surely resound again with a rise in unemployment. Protectionist sentiment would provide substantial demand for a stronger state.

In sum, U.S. policy toward the international economy opens a major arena for conflict over public purpose and thus over institutions. How to promote productivity, open foreign markets, make contracts, increase investments, develop basic research, educate and train personnel, reduce unemployment, facilitate equality of opportunity, and establish a minimum floor on income—on all of these questions the U.S. polity is quite divided. The various policy positions have quite different implications for institutional design and lead to state institutions that vary greatly in their size, authority, and character.

The deep structure of American institutions—the features embedded in the Constitution—have not prevented substantial growth and adaptation of state institutions for public purposes. Where demand has been strong, creation and innovation have answered it. Where institutional development has not occurred, it is because the demand for it was weak.

A strong counterargument could be made by stressing the role of institutions in influencing the politics of demand and demand aggregation. The American system allows divided government, for the executive and the legislature to be in the hands of different parties. This creates rivalry between the two branches. For interest groups, this means they cannot be sure that political authority will be consistent in its policy leanings. In Japan conservative business groups have been able to count on LDP dominance, if not outright control, of the diet and cabinet; this makes them more comfortable about legislative delegation to the cabinet and ministries, as bureaucratic compliance with business interests is more easily monitored and assured than is the case in the United States, where either the executive or the legislature frequently passes into the hands of groups in conflict with business definitions. The much-noted hostility of American business to government may thus reflect less about culture than the fluidity of American politics as expressed through American institutions.

A demand-centered response to this counterargument would be that the key feature in divided government is that the electorate chooses to divide it. The electorate could eliminate this rivalry by electing a Congress and a president of the same coloration. That it does not do so expresses something about political disagreement. Policy is thus the result of practical demands, not formal institutions.

The American polity resists mercantilism and strong protectionism. As a result, American trade policy is likely to continue to demand "rules intervention" and "trade promotion," vigorous action on trade disputes, representation in international agencies, strong behavior in trade discussions such as airlines (open skies)[25] and telecommunications.[26] This will mean a moderate state role and partial, incremental growth of state institutions.

Social Services

Quarrels over the state's role in security and in economic efficiency take place in a context of struggles over the state's role in social services, welfare, and equality. In the United States, debates over the welfare state have historically been seen as quite separate from those about international relations and foreign policy. This view is inaccurate. Foreign trade, arms spending, military service, all impact society greatly and in ways that influence the demand for the welfare state and the politics of getting it. In this regard, social services are a key ingredient in the issue of state structure and international relations.

The linkages among these dimensions have been clearest for the smaller trading states, such as Belgium, the Netherlands, Denmark, Sweden, and Norway. As those states sought to earn a living in trade, they learned that domestic social conflict sharply hindered their ability to do so: domestic economies were not large enough to absorb production, and exports could not stand the shock of strikes, labor unrest, or other forms of social struggle. Preservation of domestic order was vital to a coherent national economic strategy of engagement in international trade. To promote internal peace, these countries developed extensive social welfare networks, job guarantees, and retraining systems in order to support a de facto policy of accord with labor. Katzenstein's interpretation of the small democracies stresses the "social contract."[27] Rogowski notes the institutional changes which helped bring this contract about and consolidate it; he sees the adoption of proportional representation as a means of giving voice to all significant players, so that accommodation takes place in the political process, not the workplace or the street.[28]

The middle powers — Germany, France, Britain, and Japan — also created extensive social service systems. They were designed mainly to prevent a repeat of the political disasters of the interwar years, but had important implications for trade as well. Germany institutionalized power sharing with trade unions, while Japan moved toward "company unions." Japan has the least well-developed social service system among these countries, but the lowest unemployment and strongest job security, and that in the context of the weakest unions.

All the advanced industrial countries face some kind of crisis over social services: grave fiscal pressures threaten the level of social services for health, retirement, unemployment compensation, and cradle to grave benefits. Critics increasingly argue that job guarantees inhibit employment, leading to the very high unemployment rates that Western Europe has experienced year after year.

Yet even those European countries that have pruned the welfare state most radically remain far ahead of the United States in comprehensiveness of social services. In the 1990s the United States failed again to create a national health system, although it spends a larger percentage of GNP on health than any other country and has a very widely skewed distribution of health benefits.[29] Welfare has been quite seriously reduced: recent legislation cuts off benefits after five years, regardless of circumstances. While it remains to be seen how this will all be implemented, what (if anything) will be restored to protect children, and what will be aimed at immigrants, this is certainly a more drastic reduction in social welfare than any other advanced mixed economy has seen fit to make.

Social security remains, so far, beyond the reach of the congressional knife, but the attempt is certainly under way. Fiscal conservatives of all political colorations argue that the system will not be able to pay for itself when the baby boomers retire and that some kind of change must occur. It is likely to require a bipartisan compromise, but of what nature remains unclear.

The differences between the United States and other countries in social services, equality, and welfare have surely something to do with ethnicity and race. The New Deal was relatively silent on race; it helped minorities through generic policies that helped all the poor. The war economy and postwar industrial expansion drew millions from the South into cities, integrated the armed forces, and started a process to end American apartheid. The Democrats led efforts to promote civil rights, thereby undermining their own coalition in the South and among whites in the big cities. Political and legal apartheid was ended, but immigration from Asia and Latin America, along with affirmative action and the problems of the inner cities, have created opportunities for "wedge issue politics" and have fueled white backlash, most frequently used by the Republicans. The women's movement has intensified backlash sentiments among white men; women responded in recent presidential elections with the largest gender gap in American history.

One effect of these resentments has been to identify many social programs with support of minorities. Social services are seen as particularistic not universal. This provides populist support for traditional conservative efforts to reduce social spending. Hostilities toward specific minorities and immigrant groups undermine general concerns for children and the poor. This weakens as well the "social investment" and countercyclical economic objectives that provided a rationale for welfare programs when they were developed.

A cause and symptom of these developments is the weakening of unions. As their numbers and political strength have fallen, unions are unable to put forward and defend broader social programs. Where once groups fought as part of a coalition, each has in recent years fought battles on its own — low-skilled labor, women, ethnic groups, immigrants. Alone, they are far weaker.

Arguments over social services have important implications for state development. Provision of social services marked a substantial increase in state institutions and state size. It is possible to limit state size through obligatory but privatized systems (privatized social security, for example), but even so, social services mean a larger state, in the United States, as elsewhere. As American society has internationalized (trade, foreign policy), welfare state issues have become increasingly important ingredients in the battle over state institutions.

New Directions for the State

The "New Deal/Cold War" policy system has broken into its component pieces, each floating autonomously, like electrons in a chemical soup. The bonding around traditional nuclei has weakened, leaving the electrons available for new forms of linkage and the formation of new compounds. Uncertainties about international and economic trends make the situation even more fluid.

Along each cleavage line there are contrasting positions, and each position has profound implications for the American state. On the *security* dimension, some want fewer obligations, fulfilled more cheaply, with a reduced security mission, while other political actors want to sustain an actively engaged United States, fully involved in world affairs, playing a leadership role, able and willing to deploy military forces abroad. On the *economy* dimension, some want to cut regulations, shrink state activities in many economic domains at home, and use government to promote rules of free trade internationally, while others want to restructure the state for the new conditions of the global economy, invest heavily in research and education, and use the state aggressively to promote trade, products, industries. On the *social* dimension, some wish to cut social services in order to reduce taxes, while others wish to extend the social safety net to balance the effects of increased trade competition.

Much is missing from these simplified and stylized description of the cleavage lines. Where, for example, to locate the cultural conflicts around abortion, family values, and the like? These resonate with certain positions on security, the economy, and welfare, but there are cross-cutting cleavages as well. Taken together, these preference clusters constitute the raw ingredients of the demand side for the politics of the future. Out of these, politicians will forge coalitions around policy clusters.

Each of these cleavage lines have implications for the size, character, and structure of American institutions.

American Politics at the Turn of the Century

These substantive issues about the goals of government are being processed by political institutions in the United States that have themselves changed substantially since the Cold War compromise was forged. The most striking changes have to do with the role of direct primaries in altering the forces that work upon elected politicians and the growth of safe seats in congressional elections. Before the 1960s, presidential and other candidates were chosen by party machines of varying kinds, with very limited input of the electorate. While the mass public was thus excluded from candidate selection, party bosses had a strong incentive to push the party toward the middle in order to carry the entire ticket into office.

In recent years, most notably following the McGovern reforms of the Democratic Party in the 1970s, primaries have greatly undermined the party hierarchy. The effect of giving the public a greater direct voice has been to polarize electoral choices in ways that make the electorate unhappy. Direct primaries reward party activists, who are far more likely to vote than the general electorate, single-interest groups, and money; they make candidates and issues heavily dependent on media, sound bites, and mass communications methods. The net effect is to favor less centrist candidates, and this, in turn, leads to the polarization of politics, greater swings in policy, and gridlock. Some developments suggest that congressional elections may become nationalized as a result of these changes: the "Contract with America" organized by Gingrich broke through American localism to bring in a new majority, and once in office, Gingrich went further in nationalizing policy by weakening the seniority system in his assignment of committee positions and committee powers. But the realities of running for office drove the Republicans back to particularism, so it is not clear that these nationalizing tendencies will persist. Nonetheless, the American party system is evolving in ways which may indeed make policy alternatives clearer. As conservatives leave the Democratic Party in the South and moderate progressives leave the Republicans elsewhere, the parties may present somewhat more distinct options. This will force them to develop institutional mechanisms for moving the party as a whole toward the center, where the swing voters are.

Coherent national parties presenting clear alternatives and having the discipline to enforce them — that would indeed be a revolution in American political life. Congressional experts do find that American parties are far more important in shaping policy than many observers have traditionally thought.[30] Nonetheless, the centripetal tendencies of American society and institutions remain a powerful influence on parties and the way they process issues. Federalism and separation of powers magnify the impact of tremendous social, ethnic, regional, and economic diversity. Together these forces undermine efforts to centralize power in parties. Within the framework of the Constitution, Congress could not nationalize politics fully without changing its rules of procedure quite drastically, and it is only likely to do so if very strong interests in the American polity find such a revision useful. In the highly decentralized system of elections that continues to prevail here, the floating issue spaces noted above will continue to agitate in an unstable manner, forming majorities around specific policy battles, falling apart to form a different majority for the next fight.

Conclusion

The present character of the American state expresses policy choices made in fifteen crucial years, from 1933 to 1948. The system adopted then, and the political coalition that sustained it, transformed the American state. The coalition and the system lasted for several decades. Some elements of the system had unraveled, however, by the 1970s and 1980s: agreements about economic regulation and social services were already crumbling, and the Vietnam War cracked the agreement on foreign policy. The Reagan years marked a return to military Keynesianism, a revival of Cold War arrangements. The collapse of the USSR undermined that foreign policy leg of the support tripod. Each leg has now broken into several component pieces, more autonomous than ever. They can be recombined into various shapes and sizes, expressing the interaction of preferences, rules/institutions, and political entrepreneurship. Each combination leads the American state down a different path.

Can these components be welded together into coherent and stable majorities? Is there so much fragmentation of the issue space that majorities will have trouble cohering? How much do institutional innovations allow political entrepreneurs to overcome the fractionating features of the American constitutional system?

The restructuring of the American state will turn pivotally on how much American political actors need that state, and to what degree entrepreneurs can forge coalitions that make them crucial in providing state services. The capitalist economy of the United States once had features that in many ways resembled those of its European and Japanese counterparts: a main bank system; interlocking directorates and trusts; government involvement in research and development, as well as trade. Political choices, such as Populism, Progressivism, and the antitrust movement, altered these institutions, and the American economic system changed, in ways which make it look quite different now from the Japanese or German models.[31] American business at times wants the state to help it; at other times, it finds the state in the hands of political opponents who want things they don't like, such as environmental and labor regulation, or more welfare spending. Lacking a reliably pro-business political majority, business goes into an antagonistic stance toward state involvement. When circumstances allow it, and state aid is needed, these business elements become potential allies for new coalitions. Their allies, in turn, are often fragmented by ethnicity, gender, culture, and other issues. Foreign policy has at times been the glue that held these elements together, but in the uncertain and fluid conditions of the world arena, it probably cannot play that role again. Foreign policy is likely to be another line of conflict, splitting existing cleavage lines yet further. The issue space will be quite fractionated. Institutions are likely to have a very tough time forcing the formation of stable majorities.

The international dimensions of the American state's development will turn on the interaction of economic, social and security issues. In economic terms, state development will turn on whether American businesses ever decide they need the institutions of a trading state.[32] On the security side, state development will turn on the directions of burden sharing and unilateral actions on the part of other major and minor powers. The social services side interacts with these, in that decisions on these two cleavages have implications for the others: mercantilist policies have implications for labor, education, and other social investments quite different from the laissez-faire approach. A United States mobilized for activist foreign policy will relate quite differently to social issues than a more isolationist one.

Conflicts over policy will continue to shape the evolution of American political institutions. International influences are internalized into domestic politics through their impact on the preferences of political actors in American society. These political forces push for or against various policy responses to external pressures or incentives. The interaction of these political factors, the aggregation of these demands, is certainly influenced by existing political institutions and formal structures, which thus affect policy outputs in significant ways. But where demands for policy are strong, the institutional system can be adapted to produce the desired results. The capacity of

Congress to delegate — for Congress and the president to work out structures, bureaucracies, rules and procedures for action — is quite high. Existing ideas and interests certainly root themselves in the political system. Yet, the record of U.S. institutions since 1929 shows an extraordinary capacity for institutional development and design. It is important not to confuse institutional limits with a dislike of preferences and policy outputs. Policies fail to happen not because the formal institutions prevent them but because they are not able to mobilize sufficient public support.

Notes

1. Otto Hintze, *The Historical Essays of Otto Hintze*, ed. Felix Gilbert (New York: Oxford University Press, 1975); Charles Tilly, ed., *The Formation of National States in Western Europe* (Princeton: Princeton University Press, 1975); Charles Tilly, *Coercion, Capital, and European States, A.D. 990–1992* (Cambridge, Mass.: Blackwell, 1992).

2. Peter A. Gourevitch, "The Second Image Reversed: The International Sources of Domestic Politics," *International Organization* 32 (Fall 1978), 881–911; Robert D. Putnam, "Diplomacy and Domestic Politics: The Logic of Two Level Games," *International Organization* 42 (Summer 1988): 427–60.

3. Samuel P. Huntington, *Political Order in Changing Societies* (New Haven: Yale University Press, 1968).

4. David Lake and Robert Powell, eds., *Strategic Interaction* (Princeton: Princeton University Press, 1999).

5. Philip G. Roeder, *Red Sunset: The Failure of Soviet Politics* (Princeton: Princeton University Press, 1993); Susan L. Shirk, *The Political Logic of Economic Reform in China* (Berkeley: University of California Press, 1993).

6. Michael Doyle, "Liberalism and World Politics," *American Political Science Review* 80 (1986):1151–69; David Lake, "Powerful Pacifists: Democratic States and War," *American Political Science Review* 86 (March 1992): 24–37; Bruce Russett, *Controlling the Sword: The Democratic Governance of International Security* (Cambridge: Harvard University Press, 1990).

7. Stephen Krasner, *Defending the National Interest* (Princeton: Princeton University Press, 1978); Peter J. Katzenstein, ed., *Between Power and Plenty* (Madison: University of Wisconsin Press, 1978).

8. John Brewer, *The Sinews of Power: War, Money, and the English State, 1688–1783* (New York: Knopf, 1989).

9. Susanne Lohmann and Sharon O'Halloran, "Divided Government and U.S. Trade Policy," *International Organization* 48 (Fall 1994):595–632.

10. Thomas Ertman, *Birth of the Leviathan: Building States and Regimes in Medieval and Early Modern Europe* (New York: Cambridge University Press, 1997); Brian Downing, *The Military Revolution and Political Change: Origins of Democracy and Autocracy in Early Modern Europe* (Princeton: Princeton University Press, 1992); Theda Skocpol, *States and Social Revolutions: A Comparative Analysis of France, Russia, and China* (Cambridge: Cambridge University Press, 1979).

11. Douglas North and Barry Weingast, "Constitutions and Commitment: The Evolution of Institutions Governing Public Choice in 17th Century England," *Journal of Economic History* 49 (December 1989):803–32.

12. The literature on the New Deal is, of course, vast and cannot be listed here. In addition to the studies of Ira Katznelson and Martin Shefter, I note two recent books that examine the impact of war on the New Deal: Alan Brinkley, *The End of Reform: New Deal Liberalism in Recession and War* (New York: Knopf, 1995); Doris Kearns Goodwin, *No Ordinary Time: Franklin and Eleanor Roosevelt: The Home Front in World War II* (New York: Simon and Schuster, 1994); Peter Alexis Gourevitch, *Politics in Hard Times: Comparative Responses to International Economic Crises* (Ithaca: Cornell University Press, 1986).

13. Theda Skocpol, *Protecting Soldiers and Mothers: The Political Origins of Social Policy in the United States* (Cambridge: Belknap Press of Harvard University Press, 1992).

14. Like the veterans of previous wars, those of World War II demanded university education, medical care, and housing. See Skocpol, *Protecting Soldiers and Mothers*.

15. Richard N. Rosecrance, *The Rise of the Trading State: Commerce and Conquest in the Modern World* (New York: Basic Books, 1986); Stephan Haggard, *Pathways from the Periphery: The Politics of Growth in the Newly Industrializing Countries* (Ithaca: Cornell University Press, 1990); Robert Wade, *Governing the Market: Economic Theory and the Role of Government in East Asian Industrialization* (Princeton: Princeton University Press,1990); Chalmers A. Johnson, *MITI and the Japanese Miracle: The Growth of Industrial Policy, 1925–1975* (Stanford: Stanford University Press, 1982).

16. Michel Albert, *Capitalism vs. Capitalism*, trans. Paul Haviland (New York: Four Walls Eight Windows, 1993); Peter A. Gourevitch, "The Macro-Politics of Micro-Institutional Differences in the Analysis of Comparative Capitalism," in *National Diversity and Global Capitalism*, ed. Suzanne Berger and Ronald Dore (Ithaca: Cornell University Press, 1996).

17. Rosecrance, *Rise of the Trading State*.

18. There are other arguments that lie outside the framework posed here—for example, the absence of a feudal experience in the United States.

19. Helen V. Milner, *Interests, Institutions, and Information: Domestic Politics and International Relations* (Princeton: Princeton University Press, 1997); David B. Yoffie, *Power and Protectionism: Strategies of the Newly Industrializing Countries* (New York: Columbia University Press, 1983); Jeffry A. Frieden, *Debt, Development, and Democracy: Modern Political Economy and Latin America, 1969–1985* (Princeton: Princeton University Press, 1991).

20. Ronald Rogowski, *Commerce and Coalitions: How Trade Affects Domestic Political Realignments* (Princeton: Princeton University Press, 1989).

21. Michael Hiscox, "The Magic Bullet? The RTAA, Institutional Reform, and Trade Liberalization," *International Organization* 53 (Fall 1999): 669–98; "Class versus Industry Cleavages: Inter-Industry Factor Mobility and the Politics of Trade," *International Organization* (forthcoming); and "Technological Change and Inter-Industry Factor Mobility: U.S. Wage and Profit Data from 1800 to 1990," *Journal of Economic History* (forthcoming).

22. Dani Rodrik, *Has Globalization Gone Too Far?* (Washington, D.C.: Institute

for International Economics, 1997); Peter Gourevitch, Roger Bohn, and David McKendrick, "Globalization of Production: Insights from the Hard Disk Drive Industry," *World Development* 28, no. 3 (2000): 301–17.

23. Thanks to Stephan Haggard for suggestions on this point. Peter Cowhey, "Telecommunications: Market Access Regimes in Services and Equipment," in *New Challenges to International Cooperation: Adjustment of Firms, Policies and Organizations to Global Competition*, ed. Peter Gourevitch and Paolo Guerrieri (La Jolla: University of California, San Diego, Graduate School of International Relations and Pacific Studies, 1993); Peter F. Cowhey and Mathew D. McCubbins, *Structure and Policy in Japan and the United States* (Cambridge: Cambridge University Press, 1995); Peter Gourevitch, "Domestic Politics in International Cooperation," in *A Vision of a New Liberalism: Critical Essays on Murakami's Anti-Classical Analysis*, ed. Kozo Yamamura (Stanford: Stanford University Press, 1997), 63–81.

24. Susanne Lohmann and Sharyn O'Halloran, "Divided Government and U.S. Trade Policy," *International Organization* 48 (Fall 1994): 595–632; Peter Gourevitch, "The Governance Problem in International Relations," in David Lake and Robert Powell, eds., *Strategic Interaction* (Princeton: Princeton University Press, 1999).

25. John Richards, "The Domestic Politics of International Institutions: The Regulatory Institutions for Trade in Aviation Services" (Ph.D. diss., University of California at San Diego, 1997).

26. Thanks to Peter Cowhey for conversations which explain these issues and their applications in U.S. negotiations over telecommunications.

27. Peter J. Katzenstein, *Small States in World Markets: Industrial Policy in Europe* (Ithaca: Cornell University Press, 1985).

28. Ronald Rogowski, "Political Cleavages and Changing Exposures to Trade," *American Political Science Review* 81 (1987):1121–37.

29. Theda Skocpol, *Boomerang: Clinton's Health Security Effort and the Turn against Government in U.S. Politics* (New York: Norton, 1996).

30. Mathew McCubbins, Roger Noll, and Barry Weingast, "Structure and Process, Politics and Policy: Administrative Arrangements and Political Control of Agencies," *Virginia Law Review*, March 1989, 431–82.

31. Gourevitch, "Macro Politics."

32. On the interconnectedness of domestic and international political action, see Gourevitch, "Second Image Reversed"; Putnam, "Diplomacy and Domestic Politics."

Part V

CONCLUSION

Twelve

International Influences on American Political Development

MARTIN SHEFTER

SINCE THE EARLIEST days of America's European settlement, international forces have profoundly influenced the character of the nation's governing institutions, the policies these institutions have pursued, and the conduct of American politics. The essays in this volume have analyzed how changes in the world economy and international political order, and in America's relations with these international systems, have affected the structure and conduct of U.S. government and politics over the course of the nation's history.

This chapter draws upon these contributions to review some major ways that international trade and warfare have made and remade politics and government in America since its initial settlement by Europeans in the seventeenth century. It focuses upon the interaction of international and domestic politics during the late eighteenth and late twentieth centuries. The final quarter of the eighteenth century witnessed the emergence of the United States as an independent country and the creation of a national state whose institutions, in broad outline, continue to govern the nation down to the present day. The last half of the twentieth century saw the United States develop what Peter Gourevitch terms a "welfare state," a "regulatory state," and a "national security state." This chapter will focus on the role that international conflicts played in these transformations.

Warfare almost surely is the most important of the international forces that historically has shaped government and politics. There is considerable truth in the familiar observation "War is the mother of states." The global wars of the sixteenth and seventeenth centuries gave rise to the modern system of sovereign states. Indeed, the very concept of sovereignty — the notion of a regime exercising ultimate authority over all the people within a geographically bounded territory — arose from the wars that swept the European world during the early modern era.[1] States were constructed to acquire the manpower and financial resources needed to fight those wars.[2]

The movement of commercial goods across national borders, that is, foreign trade, also greatly influences the behavior of governments at home and the conduct of domestic politics. Governments often seek to shield domestic producers from foreign competition and to help them acquire abroad raw materials, capital, and labor that may be unavailable (or more costly) at home. Regimes also support the efforts of domestic firms to secure customers abroad and attempt to ensure that their citizens engaged in commercial activities overseas are protected from physical attack and able to collect the money, goods, or services they are owed by foreigners.

To be sure, American political development has been greatly affected by the movement of people across its borders in various nonmilitary capacities (notably, as immigrants) and by the international flow of various non-economic goods (e.g., the flow of ideas).[3] But of all these international influences, war and trade exerted the most immediate impact upon the structure of U.S. governing institutions and the conduct of American politics.

The relationship between international forces and national politics is by no means simple or unidirectional. A change in the international arena often has a different impact on one domestic interest than it has on another. Political forces within a nation will seek to have the government promote those international developments from which they (or their political allies) expect to benefit and resist those trends abroad that they find disadvantageous. Thus, international developments can foster domestic political conflicts, and the outcome of these conflicts very much shapes how nations behave in the international arena. Finally, the policies that national governments pursue abroad (often in response to domestic considerations) produce international outcomes that benefit some domestic interests more than others, precipitating yet another phase of the cycle.[4]

A Country Made by War

The United States is very much "a country made by war," to borrow a phrase from Geoffrey Perret.[5] The settlement of North America by Europeans was closely associated with the global wars of the early modern era, for the settlers who first colonized North America in the seventeenth century were opponents of the states that European monarchs constructed to fight those wars. These settlers eventually gained their independence and established the United States of America through a war of their own, the American Revolution.

Both the outbreak and the outcome of this rebellion were greatly influenced by military conflicts between the two most powerful regimes of the eighteenth century, England and France.[6] England had levied taxes on its colonies to finance the "French and Indian Wars," as its Seven Years' War with France was known in the American theater. These imposts led many Americans to rally under the cry of "No taxation without representation," and to declare their independence. Then, the military intervention of

France — which was seeking to weaken its English rival — helped the Americans win their revolutionary war.

The United States won its independence in 1783. Within only a few years, the thirteen former colonies undertook to establish an overarching national government, in order to be better equipped to deal with various international problems.[7] In particular, the fundamental institutional structure of the American national state was shaped by military conflicts (actual and anticipated) with other regimes. Most immediately, as Robert Keohane and Aristide Zolberg note, the framers of the U.S. Constitution sought to construct a national government strong enough to implement the treaty that had concluded America's War of Independence. In the 1783 Treaty of Paris, England had agreed to withdraw its military forces and outposts from the newly independent United States. In return, the United States had promised that its citizens would pay whatever debts they owed to British creditors.

But under the Articles of Confederation, the national "government" of the United States was not able to enforce these commitments. It became evident that England would not voluntarily withdraw its forces, but the Congress of the United States, its sole national governmental institution, did not command an army capable of driving British troops from American territory. There were, moreover, no U.S. courts to determine how much individual American citizens owed to British creditors and require them to discharge these obligations, and, under the Articles of Confederation, state courts could interpret as they chose (or simply ignore) treaties the United States had made with other nations. If it could not make credible commitments, the United States would find it difficult to secure, in return, concessions from other regimes that would benefit the new nation and its citizens.

The Constitution drafted in 1787 established a set of national institutions designed to handle these problems. For example, a bicameral national legislature was created and granted the power "to raise and support Armies." And the Constitution created the office of U.S. president, who would serve as commander in chief of the armed forces. The president also was authorized to negotiate treaties, which would take effect if ratified by the chamber of the U.S. Congress that represented the states, and to appoint executive officials to administer the laws that Congress enacted. The third national institution established by the Constitution was a federal judiciary, which would try and punish American citizens who failed to heed the laws and treaties of the United States. Finally, the Constitution declared that the laws and treaties fashioned and interpreted by these various national officials "shall be the Supreme Law of the Land; and the judges in every state shall be bound thereby."

Alexander Hamilton, John Jay, and James Madison drafted the *Federalist Papers* to persuade Americans to support this new regime. As Zolberg notes, almost half of the first thirty papers discussed how a nation united by a strong central government would be better able than a loose confederation of thirteen petty states to avoid war and to successfully command, finance, and mobilize military forces when war could not be avoided.

As the international situation of the United States changed over the following centuries, the understanding of the document's clauses conferring power on the new national government changed accordingly. What kinds of military force could the national government deploy when it undertook "to raise and support Armies"? International developments shaped answers to this question that influential Americans regarded as reasonable. For example, as Peter Gourevitch, Bartholomew Sparrow, and Aaron Friedberg all argue, the expansionism of the Axis powers and the USSR encouraged the United States to construct an enormously powerful national security state in the 1940s. The challenges that these totalitarian regimes posed to the United States were not merely imagined by self-serving domestic interests, whatever may have been said at the time by isolationist forces on the right or by Communists and "fellow travelers" on the left.

But did not the regimes that governed the Axis powers and the Soviet bloc challenge the views, and threaten the interests, of some Americans more than others? Were policies that ostensibly had been fashioned to protect the security of the *entire* nation—policies purporting to serve the *national* interest—advocated by public officials or social forces seeking to advance their *particular* political or economic interests?

In other words, conditions originating abroad did not fully determine America's relations with the rest of the world. As Zolberg argues, the views of influential Americans—whether they regarded developments abroad as presenting them with opportunities or dangers—shaped how top U.S. officials perceived international developments, and the precise ways in which they responded to those they regarded as challenges. These perceptions and policy responses had important implications for the basic structure of the American national state.

During the early decades of the new republic, the sovereignty of its national government was not fully respected by the major European powers. As mentioned previously, despite commitments she had made in the 1783 Treaty of Paris, Great Britain stationed troops and occupied forts within the territory of the United States; and, during the wars of the French Revolution, both England and France attacked and seized U.S. merchantmen in an effort to impede the flow of supplies to the enemy. The British also boarded U.S. vessels in an effort to capture deserters and to impress seamen (including American citizens) into the Royal Navy. To protect American ships, Congress and the president established the U.S. Navy in 1798, the first of more than a dozen new cabinet departments they created after the initial four.

The activities of "Citizen" Genêt, revolutionary France's minister to the

United States in the 1790s, were another source of tension between the United States and a major European power. Defying American law, Genêt arranged to outfit privateers — vessels that would prey primarily on British shipping — in U.S. ports. As Robert Keohane notes, this activity directly challenged U.S. sovereignty, that is, the ability of the U.S. government to control military attacks launched from its territory.

Another way in which European powers failed to fully acknowledge U.S. sovereignty was by providing residents of the western territories with incentives to detach their settlements from the United States and place them under a European power. In particular, Spain sought to restrict use of the port of New Orleans to farmers and merchants who had sworn allegiance to the Spanish king, and thus gain control of the vast territory served by the Mississippi River system.

Finally, there were persistent conflicts between Indians and white settlers.[8] The great majority of U.S. citizens and voters rallied behind political and military leaders who proposed to drive America's indigenous peoples further west — and ultimately onto lands set aside as Indian "reservations." European powers with designs on North America — notably, Britain and Spain — forged alliances with Indians who sought to keep white settlers off their lands.

During the first half of the nineteenth century, a number of American political and military leaders who sought to extend the territory controlled by the United States rose to the very top of American politics. The most noteworthy of these figures was General Andrew Jackson, who during the War of 1812 had crushed the Creeks (loosely allied with Britain and Spain) in territory that was to be absorbed by the United States as the state of Alabama and in the last battle of the war defeated the British at New Orleans. Andrew Jackson, America's leading proponent and practitioner of "Indian removal," was the founding father of the party system that remade American politics during the second quarter of the nineteenth century. William Henry Harrison and Zachary Taylor were also presidents elected under the "second American party system."[9] As governor of the Indiana territory, Harrison had been the hero of Tippecanoe, a battle of the War of 1812 in which the United States defeated a confederation of Indians allied with Britain. Taylor was a leading general in the Mexican War, which increased the territory of the United States by more than 30 percent.

Indeed, through the balance of the nineteenth century, a central focus of American politics and a central policy of the U.S. national state was extending the nation's borders and the territory settled by its citizens. This territorial expansion of the United States was very much an *international* question: it involved relations between the United States and other nations, namely, the European colonial powers, the nations of European settlement on America's borders (Canada and Mexico), and various Indian nations.

But at the same time, throughout the nineteenth century, territorial expansion was America's most important *national* question. It was the key issue for constructing national majorities, that is, coalitions of voters that cut across America's deepest sectional cleavages and drew from all regions. Such coalitions were organized by leading politicians seeking to overcome divisions over the extension of slavery and the legitimacy of nullification, secession, and Reconstruction. These sectionally divisive issues dominated the attention of U.S. politicians and the activities of the U.S. national government during the third quarter of the nineteenth century, 1850–76. But, both before and after this quarter-century, top U.S. political leaders managed to overcome sectional divisions, and to mobilize national majorities, by undertaking to extend the territory of the United States. In this sense, territorial expansion was the central "national question" in U.S. politics.

Securing this territorial expansion did not, however, require or foster the development of a centralized U.S. national state akin to the expansionist regimes of Europe. Throughout European history, there has been a close relationship between warmaking and statemaking.[10] To defeat their foes, monarchs centralized and strengthened the institutions that provided money and manpower to their military machines. The locus classicus of the relationship between the foreign and domestic faces of sovereignty was, of course, continental Europe during the early modern era. Persistent warfare during the sixteenth and seventeenth centuries produced the world's first modern, sovereign states. This relationship between international warfare and the strengthening of national states endured into the nineteenth century and beyond. The most expansionist regimes on the European continent in the nineteenth century — Napoleonic France and Bismarck's Prussia — constructed centralized states to obtain the manpower and financial resources they needed to fuel their conquests.

From its early days, the American military has been enormously successful in extending the territory and influence of the United States.[11] The U.S. military was able to prevail over a succession of imperial powers: the British Empire, the Spanish Empire, Kaiser Wilhelm's Imperial Germany, Adolph Hitler's Third Reich, Imperial Japan, and the USSR. And in the United States, as in Europe, the character of the military has been closely related to the character of the regime it served.

The United States has enjoyed great military success without constructing a highly centralized, all-powerful national state akin to the regimes that have governed its most powerful military rivals. Several features of the U.S. military and of its relationship to the national government and to other political forces have contributed to its success.[12] First, from their early days, America's armed forces have been built around, and led by, an unusually talented professional core — officers drawn not from a narrow military caste but from a geographically extensive, socially heterogeneous base.[13] The leaders of the U.S. military—from Winfield Scott, through the great generals of the Civil War (Ulysses Grant, William Sherman, and Philip Sheridan), to such noteworthy successors as George Marshall to Colin Powell—have been extraordinarily able. One explanation for their considerable talent is that, prior to the middle of the twentieth century, the U.S. military academies were among the few American institutions of higher education open to young men of limited means. In addition, the U.S. military devotes enormous resources to education and training. The U.S. "military system" has thus embodied and drawn strength from the liberal character of the regime it serves.[14]

A second feature of America's armed forces that reflects the liberal character of the American regime and contributes to its remarkable success is the pluralistic structure of the U.S. military system. The U.S. military is anything but a highly centralized and insular institution. To the contrary, it is quite fragmented, and its components interact regularly with other institutions. The military services exert considerable influence over the institutions with which they interact and are themselves subject to the influence of those institutions.[15] Control over American military policy is *not* tightly centralized in the hands of top generals and admirals or of the president and his military secretaries. For example, interactions between congressional committees and the armed services have long influenced the location of military bases, the allocation of defense contracts, and the projects constructed by the U.S. Army Corps of Engineers.[16] And in the 1990s, interactions among feminists, the mass media, Congress, and the military services influenced the assignment, promotion, and disciplining of uniformed military personnel.[17] Finally, interactions between the U.S. military and the nation's industrial corporations have played a major role in the design and development of weapons and military equipment, with important consequences for the strategies that U.S. forces have been able to employ. For example, in the 1940s the design and development of the landing craft and amphibious vehicles so crucial to Allied victory in both Europe and the Pacific was an accomplishment of General Motors and the United Fruit Corporation as well as of the U.S. Army and Navy.[18]

American universities are another set of institutions with which the U.S. armed forces have collaborated since the 1940s.[19] This cooperation has taken a variety of forms and has increased the U.S. military's effectiveness in at least two important ways. First, the military services attract and reward soldiers by financing their higher education. Through the GI Bill, ROTC, and kindred programs, the U.S. armed forces have recruited unusually well-educated personnel. Secondly, over the past half-century, close ties between the U.S. military and American universities have fostered the development of the world's most advanced weaponry and military equipment. During World War II, the U.S. Office of Scientific Research and Development, led by Vannevar Bush of MIT and James B. Conant of Harvard, contracted with universities and research laboratories to produce the technological advances that contributed greatly to Allied victory, most notably, radar and the atomic bomb.[20]

How was the United States able to develop high-tech weaponry superior to that of its totalitarian opponents? The enormous wealth and productive capacity of the American economy was certainly an important factor. For example, the Manhattan Project, which developed the atomic bomb, spent more than $2 billion in less than three years — at a time when a billion dollars was truly an enormous sum of money! But just as important to the success of the Manhattan Project were certain liberal features of the American regime and the American military system.

The Manhattan Project was a subunit of the U.S. Army Corps of Engineers, but in order to attract the necessary scientific talent, control over the project was largely delegated to the scientists affiliated with it. To secure the unstinting cooperation of these scientists, the military director, General Leslie Groves, permitted laboratory director Robert Oppenheimer and his fellow "long hairs" to retain their civilian status, avoid military discipline, and live and work with little supervision and few restrictions at Los Alamos. To ensure that it could draw upon the talents of the world's most distinguished scientists and mathematicians, the Manhattan Project employed many refugees from fascist Europe, regardless of their status as enemy aliens. The dedication of the project's scientific staff goes a long way toward explaining how the United States developed nuclear weapons before Germany, which had been the world's premier center for advanced physics prior to the 1940s and was where the majority of the senior Manhattan Project scientists had completed their educations.

The U.S. military system has reflected and been strengthened by the democratic, as well as the liberal, features of the American regime.[21] *The central U.S. military doctrine has long been that American forces should meet their opponents with overwhelming firepower.*[22] This doctrine has political, as well as military, roots. American officers cannot expect to overwhelm the enemy by using massed troops as cannon fodder. Rather, they are expected to be concerned with the well-being of the "American boys" in their charge. Overwhelming firepower enables U.S. commanders to defeat the enemy at a low cost in American lives, thereby helping to retain voter support.[23]

Similarly, to maximize combat effectiveness and minimize casualties, the U.S. military long has sought to make use of the most advanced technology of the day. The best-known example of this was just mentioned: the atomic bomb. But the U.S. military's commitment to using high technology goes back to its early days. U.S. soldiers were among the world's first to be equipped with breech-loaded, repeating rifles. These rifles provided the U.S.

Army with an enormous firepower advantage over its opponents: with their magazines of gunpowder-charged cartridges, they could fire four times as many bullets per minute as the muskets they replaced, and their rifled barrels could shoot accurately at a much greater range.[24]

Another democratic feature of the American military that has contributed to its success is the considerable popular support its activities have enjoyed. Peter Gourevitch notes that overcoming constitutional impediments to using the armed forces required the president and other top officials to mobilize widespread backing for the nation's military ventures. This constitutional requirement was, if anything, heightened by the liberal character of the American regime. As Theda Skocpol, Ziad Munson, Andrew Karch, and Bayless Camp argue, U.S. officials do not sit atop institutions that can be used to mobilize the nation for total war. Rather, they and their supporters have established, or worked through, an array of voluntary membership associations to raise and care for American troops, equip the nation's armies, and finance military operations through the sale of war bonds. Modern American society, as we know it, was largely fashioned by membership associations that, as the data presented by Skocpol and her colleagues indicate, grew out of the Civil War and World War I: the PTA, the "Y," the Boy Scouts, the Red Cross, the American Legion, the Knights of Columbus, and the AFL. With the popular support that these associations mustered, there was little that the U.S. military system could not do. This was demonstrated during World War II, when American military forces organized genuine advances in nuclear physics, interned U.S. citizens of Japanese descent, and smashed totalitarian regimes whose central mission — indeed, whose very raison d'être — was the pursuit of victory in war. On the other hand, as Aaron Friedberg argues, a major reason that the U.S. military failed so miserably in Vietnam was that the institutionalization of the Cold War state enabled Presidents Johnson and Nixon to deploy a half-million U.S. troops to Vietnam *without* such support.

In sum, the liberal and democratic character of the U.S. military system have contributed to the nation's ability to mobilize and use enormous military power. From the Revolution in the 1770s through the Cold War in the 1980s, America has been involved in a significant war every thirty (plus or minus ten) years, and in all of these wars, the United States defeated a leading world power or a nation that enjoyed great-power support. Finally, America's military triumphs have had major consequences: winning it independence in the eighteenth century; securing its sovereignty, expanding its domain, and preserving its unity in the nineteenth century; and enabling it to dominate international politics though most of the twentieth century and into the twenty-first.

The association of military strength with liberal democracy in North America has differed from the common pattern on the European continent, where absolutist, Bonapartist, fascist, and communist rulers enhanced their military power by centralizing and strengthening their regimes. But the situation in the United States has some parallels to that in Great Britain, where, as the historian John Brewer argues, the emergence of a powerful "fiscal-military state" in the eighteenth century was associated with the triumph of liberal opposition to royal absolutism in the English revolutions of the seventeenth century. In England, as Brewer observes, opposition to an all-powerful monarchy "made the fiscal-military state stronger rather than weaker. . . . Public scrutiny reduced peculation, parliamentary consent lent greater legitimacy to government action."[25]

Aaron Friedberg argues that the enormous strength of America's national security state during the Cold War can be explained in broadly similar terms.

There is yet another way in which the successful use of military power by the United States has been related to the structure of American politics. Historically, the United States has relied upon coercive force to deal with groups outside (or peripheral to) its political system: American Indians, African Americans, and Asian Americans. Regarding the first of these, throughout the nineteenth century, the United States used its military power to subdue America's indigenous peoples and expel them from their lands. It was possible to use the army for this purpose because there was widespread agreement among groups incorporated into the U.S. political system that Indians should be forcibly subdued and their lands be made available to white settlers.

During the early decades of the nineteenth century, the situation with respect to African Americans was broadly similar. As Ira Katznelson notes, prior to the Civil War, the U.S. military regularly took actions to maintain the system of slavery in the southern states. But during the nineteenth century's middle decades, disputes over slavery and related questions intensified, and the contending sides went to war in 1861. The military conflict that ensued was the bloodiest the Western world had seen since the Napoleonic Wars or would again see until World War I. After the Confederacy was defeated, the South no longer could expect the U.S. national government and the U.S. Army to maintain its racial system. Rather, southern whites relied upon the use of coercive force by state and local law enforcement officials (and, in extreme cases, lynch mobs) to control blacks who did not "know their place" in the racial order of the New South, or who in some way challenged that order.

Americans also used considerable coercive force in their dealings with people they referred to as "Orientals." But most anti-Asian violence was conducted apart from the formal institutions of government. During the last decades of the nineteenth century, rioting mobs killed dozens of Chinese residents in San Francisco, Los Angeles, Seattle, Denver, and elsewhere in the West. Such attacks were commonly linked to labor strife: white workers and union leaders and their political spokesmen undertook to drive away Asian laborers who had gotten jobs that, in their view, should have gone to whites. But such attacks generally were opposed by businessmen who employed Asian labor, as well as by members of the local middle class, who did not want workers to secure gains by "taking the law into their own hands."[26] Public officials who devised ways to discriminate against Asians through the law (rather than outside it) succeeded in winning support among a larger segment of the white population in the Pacific and mountain states than the "demagogues" who fomented riots. Thus, at the turn of the twentieth century, anti-Oriental laws were enacted in many western states, just as white southerners were uniting behind their own "Jim Crow" laws during these years.[27] During the ensuing half-century, the federal government countenanced discrimination by state and local governments against Orientals in the West and blacks in the South, and pursued similar, albeit less harsh, policies itself on the national level.[28]

But in contrast to their activities regarding American Indians throughout the nineteenth century and African Americans before the Civil War, U.S. military forces were not deployed to suppress Chinese Americans. Presidents feared that if U.S. authorities used violence against Chinese nationals, the emperor's officials would turn away American merchants and missionaries who sought to enter China. U.S. officials faced fewer international constraints upon their ability to use violence (or to tolerate its use) against Indians and blacks.

However, as Robert Keohane notes, the Chinese government was not in a position to insist that the United States honor its commitment to deal with immigrants from China as favorably as immigrants from other nations. Between 1882 and 1943, U.S. law excluded further immigration from China. But to the extent that excluding new immigrants was less brutal than forcibly expelling Chinese people already living in the United States, the government of China succeeded in obtaining a measure of protection for its nationals.[29]

By contrast, American Indians had no home country outside the United States to defend their interests. At various times during the first two decades of the nineteenth century, European colonial powers did ally themselves with various Indian nations and defend them, but these alliances did not survive the joint effort of the United States and Great Britain to exclude continental powers from the New World.[30] The European powers did not interfere with the Jacksonian removal of Indians from the eastern states, their forced relocation to a separate Indian Territory across the Mississippi, and their ultimate consignment to Indian reservations in the West.

Prior to the Cold War, African Americans also did not have home countries capable of defending the interests of their compatriots in the New

World.[31] But in the 1960s, independent states were created on the African continent. The United States wished to win the good will of these new regimes, which is one reason why all Cold War presidents expressed support for the African-American fight against racial discrimination in the Deep South.[32] But such foreign policy considerations were not the only concern shaping how U.S. officials dealt with racial issues. As Robert Keohane notes, upholding the rule of law was another important reason why American national institutions supported the demands of the southern civil-rights movement. The U.S. Supreme Court declared that laws mandating racial segregation deprived blacks of the "equal protection of the laws" guaranteed by the Constitution; and, in the name of upholding the rule of law, presidents from both parties ordered troops to put down mobs seeking to block the implementation of the desegregation orders issued by federal courts.

Commerce and Coalitions

International economic considerations, as well as military and political concerns, played an important role in the founding and subsequent development of the American national state.[33] The U.S. Constitution established a common market encompassing the economies of the component states. The economic powers of the governmental institutions created by the Constitution and the geographic sway of these institutions were broadly comparable to those of the European Union under the Single European Act and the Maastricht treaty.

Like those measures, the U.S. Constitution sought to foster the emergence of an integrated economy, spanning much of a continent, that would be linked to world markets on favorable terms. It sought to accomplish this, first, by keeping the component states from erecting barriers to interstate commerce and from enacting laws that released their citizens from contractual obligations to the citizens of other states. Second, the Constitution established national governmental institutions with authority to promote the emergence of a nationwide economy by issuing a national currency, creating a national bank, and regulating interstate commerce. Third, the Constitution granted the new national government authority to promote favorable ties between America and the world economy. The new government was given exclusive jurisdiction over foreign trade, and because the authority of U.S. officials would extend over an enormous market, they would be in a position to grant valuable benefits to foreign regimes that agreed to trade with the United States on favorable terms.

Mercantile interests in the great port cities running from Baltimore to Boston could expect to benefit the most from any expansion of foreign and interstate commerce, and hence they were the most enthusiastic supporters of measures intended to promote such trade. The key leader of these forces was Alexander Hamilton of New York, whom President Washington appointed to head the U.S. Treasury. Hamilton's allies predominated in the administrations of Presidents Washington and Adams, and because they sought to strengthen the federal government, they were known as "Federalists."

Many nonmercantile interests opposed measures designed to nationalize the economy and expand international trade, because they believed that such policies would impose considerable costs, and confer few benefits, on people like themselves. The opponents of the Federalists called themselves Democratic-Republicans. They gained control of the national government in the election of 1800, elevating their leader, Thomas Jefferson, to the presidency.

Throughout the nineteenth century, and the first third of the twentieth, the U.S. Constitution's "commerce clause" served as the most important source of authority for the national government to extend its activities and to expand its involvement in various aspects of American life. To a considerable degree, political conflict in the United States centered around the question of how far the legitimate authority of the national government extended. Could Congress enact laws excluding slavery from particular territories? Did the Constitution grant Congress the authority to limit the hours that workers were required to labor? The hours of female or child laborers? To be sure, the views that Americans held on questions of institutional authority were not unrelated to their opinions regarding the substantive content of the policies at issue. But the idea of states' rights carried weight with many Americans and was frequently determinative. Prior to the mid-1960s, as James Q. Wilson observes, "[The federal government] had an imperfect claim to wield legitimate authority over many aspects of our lives. There were spirited debates over whether Congress had the right to pass a civil rights law or authorize federal aid to education. . . . Against any proposed expansion of federal power there was raised the doctrine of states' rights; as often as not that objection was decisive."[34]

As Robert Keohane and others have argued, some of the most intense conflicts in American politics have been those between spokesmen for sectors of the U.S. economy able to operate successfully in international markets and spokesmen for sectors unable to withstand foreign competition.[35] Throughout the nineteenth century, the producers of cotton and other bulk agricultural commodities in the South were among the American interests best able to compete in world markets, and southern Democrats tended to staunchly advocate free trade. By contrast, during the first century of the Industrial Revolution, the United States lagged behind Great Britain in key manufacturing industries, and politicians representing the owners and employees of these industries sought tariff protection for them. Securing the enactment of protective tariffs was a central goal of Whig and Republican politicians.

As I note in my chapter on party politics, during the nineteenth-century "party period" of American political development, the Whigs and Republicans advocated strengthening the American national state in other ways as well. Tariffs generated enormous revenues and a politically embarrassing "Treasury surplus." To dispose of these funds, the Whigs advocated federal spending on "internal improvements," that is, federal support for the construction of canals, roads, and railways.[36] Also, many Republicans advocated a cultural program—for example, laws restricting the sale of liquor—that was intended to transform the lower orders of the American population into productive industrial workers. Republicans also celebrated social relations and traits of character (e.g., self-reliance, self-improvement, self-restraint) that, they argued, were the reverse of the traits fostered among both white and black southerners by the institution of slavery. White voters in the South, who were appalled by this Republican "fanaticism," found the Democratic Party's defense of limited government and "states' rights" more appealing. And the Democrats' ideology of "personal liberty" (at least for white men) appealed to those northerners who did not care to be transformed into a temperate, disciplined, and productive industrial working class.

After the Second World War, most sectors of the U.S. economy were able to thrive in open world markets. U.S. presidents undertook to establish a complex of programs and institutions (e.g., the GATT, the IMF, the World Bank, and the Marshall Plan) to strengthen and manage this international economy. These international economic institutions supplemented the military agencies and alliances (i.e., the Department of Defense, the National Security Council, and NATO) that Cold War presidents fashioned to defend regimes that shared America's economic institutions and political values, and upon whose cooperation the United States depended for its prosperity and security.

There was a close interaction between the agreements that the United States negotiated with other nations and the political successes (or failures) that top U.S. politicians and public officials enjoyed (or suffered) at home. In particular, as Judith Goldstein argues, the package of economic benefits that presidents assembled in trade negotiations with foreign regimes greatly influenced the composition of the coalitions in Congress that they were able to mobilize behind measures promoting foreign trade.

The U.S. government's activities abroad have had important implications not only for the fate of trade legislation but, more generally, for the support (or opposition) that public officials encounter in the American political arena and for the power of the government institutions that they lead. In particular, the international policies and institutions that the U.S. constructed following World War II greatly transformed American domestic politics. The billions of dollars the United States expended for its overseas operations and the trillions in capital and trade that flowed though channels that it supervised—these huge sums enabled the American president during the Cold War to exercise enormous power at home and to serve as "the Leader of the Free World" abroad, as Aristide Zolberg notes. But presidents who were committed to economic and military internationalism only gained such power after defeating opponents to both their right and left. As Peter Gourevitch observes, right-wing isolationists spoke for small businessmen in America's heartland, whose firms were not directly involved in buying or selling goods abroad. The chief concern of these "Main Street" Republicans was limiting the costs and the restrictions imposed on business by social programs and labor unions that the New Deal had established or strengthened. The influence of these political forces within the Republican Party was challenged by the GOP's "Wall Street" wing, which spoke for large financial, commercial, and industrial corporations, more concerned with expanding opportunities for American firms abroad than with limiting the costs that the New Deal imposed upon business at home. To secure the enactment of measures designed to expand American trade overseas and to defend America's trading partners, Wall Street Republicans were prepared to ally with elements of the New Deal coalition.

Just as sharp conflicts between isolationists and internationalists divided Republicans in the 1940s, deep divisions over international issues beset forces on the American Left after World War II. As Peter Gourevitch notes, these disputes involved struggles between "Cold War liberals" (led by Harry Truman and Hubert Humphrey), on the one side, and "Progressives," (led by the Progressive Party's 1948 presidential candidate, Henry Wallace), on the other. To be sure, almost all American liberals and leftists denounced isolationism, which they viewed as a form of bigotry, and professed a devotion to internationalism, which they equated with broadmindedness. But to different elements of the American Left, "internationalism" meant very different things. To Cold War liberals, it meant forging military alliances with America's trading partners to contain the influence of the Soviet Union. To the Progressives who endorsed Henry Wallace in 1948, "internationalism" meant American leftists joining with the Left in other industrial nations and reaching accommodations with the Soviet Union.

In the election of 1948, Harry Truman secured a second term in the White House, while Henry Wallace did not win a single electoral vote. But the triumph of Cold War liberalism and the defeat of forces deemed to be "soft on Communism" went beyond this single electoral victory. More broadly, a consensus emerged in American politics to support the international economic and military policies advocated by Cold War liberals and Wall Street Republicans. Politicians who did not share this outlook were said to be located beyond the boundaries of the acceptable political spectrum, on the left- or right-wing "fringe" of American politics.

Several considerations help to explain the triumph of this Cold War consensus. First, the arguments deployed by Cold War liberals and Wall Street Republicans did, to a great extent, accord with reality; hence it is not terribly surprising that they prevailed. Because nearly all sectors of the American economy were internationally competitive following World War II, the great majority of U.S. producers and consumers did, in fact, benefit from an open international trading system, and the benefits to them significantly exceeded the losses that free trade imposed on a much smaller number of Americans. Also, the regime led by Joseph Stalin was, in point of fact, horrendous and did indeed seek to conquer unwilling neighbors, as most American opinion leaders and ordinary voters believed at the time.

Moreover, the postwar presidents pursued policies that won extensive support for the regime they led. As Peter Gourevitch puts it, the American "welfare state," "regulatory state," and "national security state" were all created at roughly the same time. The policies of these regimes comprised a package — a "vast log roll," as he terms it — whose components together appealed to a wide array of interests, ranging from the very peak of American society to the base of the social structure. For example, the institutions of the postwar international order — NATO, GATT, the IMF — were fashioned by alumni of America's most prestigious schools, in particular, Groton, Yale College and the Harvard Law School.[37] At the same time, social programs that were legacies of the New Deal provided a measure of protection from the vagaries of an industrial society — such as unemployment and industrial accidents — to blue-collar workers further down the social scale.[38] As Gourevitch notes, the balance that emerged among these features of the postwar American state was not identical to the balance prevailing in the European social democracies. But the policies endorsed by Cold War liberals and Wall Street Republicans enabled Harry Truman to overwhelm Henry Wallace in 1948 and Dwight Eisenhower to defeat Robert Taft in 1952.

In explaining this success, it is important to note that, in contrast to the Republican presidents of the decade following World Wa I, Dwight Eisenhower and his most important supporters in the GOP, had international concerns that they wanted the U. S. government to advance, and they were willing to acquiesce to domestic policies favored by voters who could be persuaded to support these internationalist foreign policies. It would be too crude to say that Wall Street Republicans backed New Deal social programs because doing so enabled them to win liberal support for international policies that organized labor and Democratic politicians otherwise would have opposed.[39] But it is surely true that the officials who fashioned U.S. domestic and international policies following World War II recognized the political benefits of the package of policies they endorsed and the prospect of reaping these benefits encouraged them to pursue those policies.

Beginning in the 1960s, a number of "wedge issues," as Gourevitch terms them, came to divide the coalition that liberal Democrats and moderate Republicans had assembled in the 1940s and 1950s to support the regime they led. Conflicts over U.S. military intervention in Vietnam were especially bitter. As antiwar forces gained influence in the Democratic Party, it became increasingly possible for the GOP to appeal to members of the postwar coalition who remained convinced that the Soviet Union was, in Ronald Reagan's words, an "evil empire." The economic well-being of many of these "Reagan Democrats" was linked to military spending: many were employed in defense industries or were residents of communities (often in the South) adjacent to military facilities. Although they formerly had voted Democratic, they were attracted to the GOP by President Reagan's defense buildup.[40]

After Ronald Reagan entered the White House, cleavages emerged in American politics over international issues that were similar to the divisions of the 1940s, but with the two parties largely switching sides. In recent decades, the Republicans on the whole have been the more internationalist of the two parties in both the military and economic arenas. Regarding questions of national security, since the 1970s, Republican executive and legislative officials have been more willing than their Democratic counterparts to deploy military force in hostile situations to defend American security interests. And in the economic realm, most Republicans have advocated free trade, while organized labor and its allies within the Democratic Party have increasingly sought to limit foreign imports. Also, as Gourevitch and I note above, various elements of the liberal "public interest movement"—environmentalists and Naderites—have taken to complaining that foreign trade enables multinational corporations to escape measures that the U.S. government enacts at their behest to preserve the natural environment and protect consumers. Finally, human-rights advocates in the Democratic camp object to the U.S. trading with nations that mistreat their own citizens.

Despite these general tendencies, international economic issues in some measure *divide* both the Democratic and Republican parties nowadays, as Gourevitch notes. That is, there are influential Democrats who advocate free trade and prominent Republicans who oppose it. Among Democrats, President Clinton was quite committed to expanding international trade, asking Congress to back the North American Free Trade Agreement during his first year as president and to endorse permanent normal trade relations (PNTR) with China during his last. But to avoid battles with organized labor, Clinton never pressed Congress to renew "fast track" procedures for enacting trade agreements, and prior to the congressional elections of 1994, he did not ask Congress to approve U.S. participation in the World Trade

Organization. Finally, Clinton contributed to the collapse of the 1999–2000 round of WTO negotiations by taking up the demand of the AFL-CIO that labor issues be linked to trade talks. As for opposition to internationalism within the GOP, in the presidential elections of 1992, 1996, and 2000, Pat Buchanan criticized mainstream Republicans for being committed to trade measures that, he claimed, served the interests of wealthy elites at the expense of "the little guy." And conservative evangelicals in the Republican coalition opposed America's establishing normal trade relations with nations (such as China) that persecute Christians. Finally, many conservatives in the GOP object to the United States bearing the costs of the IMF or financing UN programs that they see as promoting abortion.

In his chapter, Ronald Rogowski suggests an important reason why opposition to free trade is gaining force in both U.S. parties: In political systems, such as America's, that grant representation to many relatively small geographic constituencies, the advocates of trade protectionism are most influential when industries are characterized by intermediate levels of geographic concentration.[41] And, as data presented in his chapter indicate, many U.S. industries that were once highly concentrated have in recent decades become more dispersed. This has increased in the number of congressional districts in which there are enough voters who have a stake in protectionism to capture the attention of their representative in Congress. As the size of the protectionist bloc in Congress has grown in recent years, the advocates of trade restrictions have seen their political influence increase accordingly.

Another contemporary economic development that has greatly influenced America's relations with the world economy is a considerable increase in cross-border economic transactions. International trade, population movements, and capital flows have risen greatly in recent decades. Relatedly, multinational corporations and other transnational institutions have become ever more important forces in the United States and elsewhere in the world. These developments have reduced the ability of the U.S. government to supervise international transactions, as Robert Keohane argues. But the very weakness of the U.S. national state relative to giant corporations works to the advantage of the American economy — or so many free-market economists assert. Opponents of "excessive" government regulation and "overly generous" social programs argue that because the restrictions and the costs that the government imposes on firms are less burdensome in the United States than in many industrial democracies, American corporations are often in a position to undersell foreign (especially, European) competitors.

If these aspects of the U.S. political economy help American multinationals compete successfully against rivals in Europe, some other features of the American system bolster U.S. firms relative to competitors in Asia. It has been argued that "crony capitalism" is a central feature of many Asian economies: banks and other enterprises profit through connections with government officials and with other "cronies" in the local economy. But the personal connections that contribute to success in the economy of their home country are of less use in foreign markets. Away from their home base, firms that rely on cronyism often are unable to compete with American entrepreneurs, who learn how to succeed in a system characterized by much greater "transparency."[42]

The collapse of the Russian economy in the 1990s demonstrated that a capitalist political economy will not automatically succeed just because property is privately owned and the government abstains from excessive intervention in market processes. Its survival and prosperity requires that the national state be strong enough to enforce the law, and that the government adhere to norms Marxists formerly derided as expressions of "bourgeois liberalism." Recent experience confirms that if a capitalist political economy is to function successfully, the rule of law must prevail, contractual commitments must be enforced, and a "sound currency" must be available for conducting economic transactions. Since its early days, the U.S. government has adhered to these norms, and this helps to explain why American firms and the U.S. economy have done so well relative to competitors abroad.

As Ira Katznelson observes above, Stephen Skowronek's influential volume *Building a New American State* presumes that the only effective way to organize a state in the modern era is on the European model, and hence that the United States was compelled to bureaucratize and centralize its nineteenth-century "state of courts and parties" in order to meet the imperatives of modernity.[43] It is, indeed, true that the twentieth-century American presidents who are widely considered to have accomplished the most are the ones who expanded the responsibilities of the executive branch, thereby centralizing the institutions of American government.[44] But these presidents did not secure the enactment of the public policies and the institutional reforms that they advocated by bludgeoning other political actors into submission. Rather, they often reached accommodations with their opponents. The White House especially accommodated political forces enjoying access to institutions it could not ignore (especially, Congress).[45] In this way, the character of the policies that were enacted, and the conduct of the executive agencies that implemented these policies, reflected the continuing power of such institutions and political forces as Congress, the federal judiciary, state governments, and important interest groups. And this "pluralist" order — by virtue both of its institutional decentralization and the extensive support it required public officials to mobilize — was able to deal effectively with the political and economic challenges that the United States faced both at home and abroad.[46] In this way, as the essays in this volume indicate, the extensive dispersion of authority in the United States has been an important source of the nation's success, as well as presenting it with major challenges.

Conclusion

In conclusion, it should be noted that the national government of the United States was created largely to manage America's dealings with other nations; and over the two centuries since its founding, as this book has argued, the structure and behavior of the U.S. national government has been profoundly shaped by the challenges posed, and the opportunities presented, by other nation-states and their citizens. The essays in this volume argue that international forces do not by themselves completely determine domestic outcomes. There often are sharp disputes among major domestic political actors over how the U.S. government should deal with problems originating overseas. And the policies that the United States ultimately chooses to pursue may greatly influence what happens abroad. To cite the recent past, tensions between the United States and the Soviet Union, and also conflicts between the United States and various Third World regimes (e.g., Iran, Libya, Iraq), played a large role in the domestic political triumphs of Ronald Reagan and George Bush in the 1980s. The forceful foreign policies and the major military buildup sponsored by Presidents Reagan and Bush contributed to the collapse of the Soviet Union and the termination of the Cold War.[47]

The end of the Cold War, in turn, helped candidates with little claim to foreign policy expertise — Governors Bill Clinton and George W. Bush — to prevail in the presidential elections of 1992 and 2000. Moreover, the declining threat of major war may well have contributed to the heightening of political conflict in the United States over the past decade.[48] At the height of the Cold War, U.S. politicians almost certainly would have hesitated to divide the nation by employing tactics akin to those of President Clinton's opponents and supporters in the 1990s.[49]

The differing responses of the major candidates to questionable vote counts in the extremely close elections of 1960 and 2000 may be explained by similar considerations. In 1960, Cold War tensions were very severe, and Richard Nixon evidently feared that if he openly sought to overturn the vote count in Illinois and Texas, he would be accused of dividing the nation and weakening its leadership in the face of its foreign foes, thereby threatening his own (and his party's) political prospects. By contrast, for several weeks following the election of 2000, candidates Gore and Bush wrangled over Florida's electoral votes, filing numerous court suits and calling upon legislators and executive officials belonging to their party for support. Partisans on each side broadly hinted that if the candidate they opposed were installed in office, the legitimacy of the president and his administration would be challenged. During the five weeks of this jockeying, neither Bush nor Gore suffered a single defection among the leading members of his party. Prominent Republicans and Democrats evidently did *not* fear that they and their allies would be seen as making the nation vulnerable to foreign adversaries or competitors by being overly divisive.

Thus we see that in the first years of the new millennium, the internal political life of the United States continues to be shaped by America's place in the international political and economic order. We may safely assume that in the centuries to come, as in the preceding ones, interactions between domestic and international considerations will continue to influence politics and government in the United States.

Notes

1. Thomas Ertman, *Birth of Leviathan: Building States and Regimes in Early Modern Europe* (Cambridge: Cambridge University Press, 1997).

2. On the relationship between military conflict and the emergence of the modern state, see, for example, Bruce Porter, *War and the Rise of the State* (New York: Free Press, 1994); Karen A. Rasler and William R. Thompson, *War and State Making* (Boston: Unwin, Hyman, 1989); and Charles Tilly, *Coercion, Capital, and European States* (Oxford: Basil Blackwell, 1990).

3. On the impact of immigration on American political development, see Daniel Tichenor, *Regulating Community: Immigration, Nationhood, and American Political Development* (Princeton: Princeton University Press, forthcoming). On the international flow of ideas, see Daniel T. Rodgers, *Atlantic Crossings: Social Politics in a Progressive Age* (Cambridge: Harvard University Press, 1998).

4. Cf. Robert Putnam, "The Logic of Two-Level Games," *International Organization* 42 (Spring 1988): 427–60.

5. Geoffrey Perret, *A Country Made by War* (New York: Random House, 1989).

6. Giovanni Arrighi and Beverly J. Silver, *Chaos and Governance in the Modern World System* (Minneapolis: University of Minnesota Press, 1999), 56.

7. Frederick W. Marks III, *Independence on Trial: Foreign Affairs and the Making of the Constitution*, 2d ed. (Wilmington, Del.: Scholarly Resources, 1986).

8. To avoid confusion, this chapter uses the terminology of the eighteenth and nineteenth centuries to distinguish between America's indigenous peoples and citizens of the United States.

9. Richard P. McCormick, ed., *The Second American Party System: Party Formation during the Jackson Era* (Chapel Hill: University of North Carolina Press, 1966).

10. Ertman, *Birth of Leviathan*.

11. But cf. Samuel P. Huntington, *American Military Strategy*, Policy Papers in International Affairs, no. 28 (Berkeley, Calif.: Institute for International Studies, 1986).

12. Cf. Perret, *A Country Made by War*, chaps. 6–7.

13. To be sure, the U.S. military draws its troops and officers more heavily from some social groups than others. But what it claims in its propaganda is, to a considerable extent, true: military careers are, indeed, open to all Americans. Of course, prior to 1948, the U.S. armed services were racially segregated. But over the past half-century, the military services have been the most significant American institutions in which racial minorities have risen to top positions in accord with the liberal ideal of "careers open to talents."

14. By the U.S. "military system," I mean not simply the uniformed services but also the institutions that control the military and provide it with resources: the Department of Defense, the presidency, and the military committees of Congress.

15. To be sure, relationships between the armed services and other political forces are not identical to relations between civilian government agencies and the interest groups in their constituencies. Compare Samuel P. Huntington, *Changing Patterns of Military Politics* (New York: Free Press, 1962), and Mark Petracca, *The Politics of Interests* (Boulder, Col.: Westview, 1992).

16. The political forces that shaped the peacetime activities of the Army Corps of Engineers provide a classic example of the exercise of influence through "iron triangles" of interest groups, congressional committees, and executive agencies. See Arthur Maas, *Muddy Waters* (Cambridge: Harvard University Press, 1951).

17. Martha Raddatz, "Uniform Complaint," *New Republic*, November 30, 1998, 16; but see Mary Katzenstein, *Faithful and Fearless* (Princeton: Princeton University Press, 1997).

18. Geoffrey Perret, *There's a War to Be Won* (New York: Random House, 1991), 110–12.

19. For a hostile account of this relationship, from 1945 to the 1990s, see Noam Chomsky, *The Cold War and the University: Toward an Intellectual History of the Postwar Years* (New York: New Press, 1997).

20. Robert Buderi, *The Invention That Changed the World* (New York: Simon & Schuster, 1997); Richard Rhodes, *The Making of the Atomic Bomb* (New York: Simon & Schuster, 1986).

21. I would not deny that the distribution of authority within the U.S. military is hierarchical. A military force is "liberal" insofar as it offers "careers open to talents," that is, opportunities for employment and promotion that are awarded on merit and open to all elements of society. Military institutions are "democratic" insofar as they are subject to popular influence.

22. Perret, *A Country Made by War*, 101. See, for example, David Kennedy, *Freedom from Fear: The American People in Depression and War, 1929–1945* (New York: Oxford University Press, 1999), chap. 18.

23. The other side of this concern (minimizing losses among its own servicemen) is the U.S. military system's willingness to take the lives of the enemy—civilians as well as soldiers. For example, FDR and his generals displayed few qualms about killing a half-million enemy civilians in ordering the "strategic bombing" of German and Japanese cities. See Eric Hobsbawm, *The Age of Extremes* (New York: Vintage Books, 1996), 27.

24. Perret, *A Country Made by War*, 254. Michael Bellesiles, *Arming America: The Origins of a National Gun Culture* (New York: Knopf, 2000), discusses how advanced weaponry (such as breech-loaded rifles with Minié bullets) has historically

been of greater importance to U.S. military sources than a supposedly "armed citizenry."

25. John Brewer, *The Sinews of Power: War, Money, and the English State, 1688–1783* (New York: Knopf, 1989), xix. See also David Mayhew, *America's Congress: Actions in the Public Sphere, James Madison through Newt Gingrich* (New Haven: Yale University Press, 2000).

26. For example, to protect their city's Chinese residents in the riots of 1886, some six hundred middle-class residents of Seattle "agreed to serve as deputies should the sheriff need help quelling mobs bent on evicting the Chinese." They were joined by students from the University of Washington, who were armed by the authorities. That is, to preserve law and order against working-class mobs, the powers-that-be in Seattle—the governor, mayor, and sheriff—armed and deployed the local middle class. See Clayton Laurie, "'The Chinese Must Go': The U.S. Army and the Anti-Chinese Riots in Washington Territory, 1885–86," *Pacific Northwest Quarterly*, January 1990, 24–27.

27. Cf. Alexander Saxton, *The Indispensable Enemy: Labor and the Anti-Chinese Movement in California* (Berkeley: University of California Press, 1971) and C. Vann Woodward, *The Strange Career of Jim Crow*, 3d ed. (New York: Oxford University Press, 1974).

28. Racial discrimination by the U.S. national government was rarely so harsh as that countenanced by officials in the southern states. The segregation of blacks in the military and in public accommodations in the District of Columbia, and the exclusion of new immigrants from China, did not involve the violence that pervaded race relations in the Deep South.

29. During World War II, Chinese immigrants were treated considerably less harshly than their counterparts from Japan. Chinese exclusion was repealed, whereas Japanese Americans living in the western states were interned. The lineup of countries in the war explains these changes: China was a U.S. ally in World War II, whereas Japan was an enemy.

30. As mentioned in chapter 5 above, the British navy, in effect, gave force to the Monroe Doctrine. Arrighi and his associates observe that after the Congress of Vienna, Britain sought to contain the other European powers "by asserting the principle of nonintervention . . . and inviting the United States to support the principle. What later became the Monroe Doctrine . . . was initially a British policy." Arrighi and Silver, *Chaos and Governance*, 59.

31. Liberia was not a colony, but it was scarcely in a position to defend African Americans. It did not command military forces capable of threatening U.S. interests, nor did it control major markets that American merchants sought to enter.

32. Doug McAdam, "On the International Origin of Domestic Political Opportunities," in *Social Movements and American Political Institutions*, ed. Anne Costain and Andrew McFarland (Lanham, Md.: Rowman & Littlefield, 1998), chap. 15; Mary Dudziak, *Cold War Civil Rights: Race and the Image of American Democracy* (Princeton: Princeton University Press, 2000).

33. The title of this section is borrowed from Ronald Rogowski, *Commerce and Coalitions: How Trade Affects Domestic Political Alignments* (Princeton: Princeton University Press, 1989).

34. James Q. Wilson, "New Politics, New Elites, Old Publics," in *The New Poli-*

tics of Public Policy, ed. Marc K. Landy and Martin Levin (Baltimore: Johns Hopkins University Press, 1995), 250.

35. Robert O. Keohane, "Associative American Development," in *The Antinomies of Interdependence*, ed. John G. Ruggie (New York: Columbia University Press, 1983). See also Richard Bensel, *Regionalism in American Politics* (Madison: University of Wisconsin Press, 1982).

36. After the Civil War, the Republicans also advocated providing veterans of the Union army and their widows with relatively generous pensions. See Theda Skocpol, *Protecting Soldiers and Mothers* (Cambridge: Harvard University Press, 1992), chap. 2.

37. Some of the "wise men" who shaped the postwar international order attended prep schools other than Groton and Ivy League colleges other than Yale. But few attended law schools other than Harvard's! See Walter Isaacson and Evan Thomas, *The Wise Men* (New York: Simon & Schuster, 1986), chaps. 1–2.

38. In the 1960s, liberals argued that in rural Appalachia and in urban slums, there were many people New Deal social programs had not lifted from poverty. See Michael Harrington, *The Other America* (Baltimore: Penguin Books, 1962). The 1960s Community Action Program dealt with these communities as if they were underrepresented interest groups. See Theodore Lowi, *The End of Liberalism* (New York: Norton, 1969).

39. This scenario is too crude: President Eisenhower did not await instructions from GOP contributors before setting domestic and foreign policies. His administration actually took the lead in fashioning policies and assembling political coalitions. Nor did George Meany and his allies back free trade and the Cold War simply to win business support for liberal domestic policies. See the forthcoming work of Ira Katznelson on the stance of the postwar labor movement on international issues.

40. Daniel Wirls, *The Politics of Defense in the Reagan Era* (Ithaca: Cornell University Press, 1992).

41. If an industry is too widely dispersed, it may not be in the interest of any locally elected representative to protect it from foreign competition. If, on the other hand, production is highly concentrated, a few locally elected representatives may have a strong incentive to provide that industry with tariff protection but will be outvoted by the great majority of legislators who have no significant ties to producers in that industry.

42. Another reason why American firms have done well away from home is that since the 1940s, the rules specifying how firms are to compete with one another throughout the world increasingly have come to resemble those prevailing in the United States. One reason why this has occurred is that the U.S. has been a dominant force in international economic institutions over the past half-century. When an agency, such as the IMF, undertakes to "reform" a nation's economic institutions and practices, it generally seeks to bring them into line with America's. Not coincidently, such reforms make trading with that nation more attractive to American executives.

43. Stephen Skowronek, *Building a New American State* (New York: Cambridge University Press, 1982).

44. Of course, judgments of presidential "greatness" vary with the observer's evaluation of the policies that presidents pursued. Efforts to rank presidents are therefore inherently political. Nonetheless, there is fairly widespread agreement that the great-

est twentieth-century president was Franklin Roosevelt, and that the next three positions are occupied, in whatever order, by Theodore Roosevelt, Woodrow Wilson, and Harry Truman. Because the policies of more recent presidents cannot but evoke greater controversy among contemporary observers, consensus declines as you approach the present. But it is noteworthy that the presidents who are widely considered to have accomplished the most are those who sought to increase the responsibilities of the national government and to strengthen the executive branch relative to other political institutions.

45. For example, to avoid alienating proponents of racial segregation, who dominated Congress, FDR scrupulously refused to "interfere" in the southern system of race relations.

46. Charles E. Lindblom, *The Intelligence of Democracy* (New York: Free Press, 1965). See also Bruce Russett, *Controlling the Sword: The Democratic Governance of International Security* (Cambridge: Harvard University Press, 1990).

47. Peter Schweizer, *Victory: The Reagan Administration's Secret Strategy That Hastened the Collapse of the Soviet Union* (New York: Atlantic Monthly Press, 1998). Of course, there is considerable controversy over the extent to which Reagan's policies were responsible for America's triumph in the Cold War.

48. Daniel Deudney and G. John Ikenberry, "After the Long War," *Foreign Policy*, no. 94 (Spring 1994): 21–35.

49. On the behavior of Clinton, his supporters, and various "Clinton-haters," see Richard Posner, *An Affair of State: The Investigation, Impeachment, and Trial of President Clinton* (Cambridge: Harvard University Press, 1999).

Index

PRINCETON STUDIES IN AMERICAN POLITICS:
HISTORICAL, INTERNATIONAL, AND COMPARATIVE PERSPECTIVES

372